T5-CGB-845

County Longford and its People

An Index to the 1901 Census for County Longford

by

David Leahy

First published 1990 by
FLYLEAF PRESS,
4 Spencer Villas, Glenageary,
Co. Dublin, Ireland

© Flyleaf Press 1990

BRITISH LIBRARY CATALOGUING IN PUBLICATION DATA
Leahy, David 1964 –
Longford and its People – An index to the 1901 Census of County Longford.
1. (County) Longford. Population. Census data, history.
I. Title
304.670941812

ISBN 0-9508466-2-7

All rights reserved. No part of this publication may be reproduced, stored in a retrieval
system, or transmitted, in any form or by any means, electronic, mechanical,
photocopying, recording or otherwise without the prior permission of the copyright
owner.

Cover design by Beth O'Halloran

Printed in Ireland

Dedication

To my mother Pearl, my father Maurice and all County
Longford people wherever they may be

Thanks are due to the many people who assisted in the production
of this book. In particular to David V. Craig and the staff of the
National Archives for access to the census returns and assistance in
their use; to Gerald Brady of Longford Historical Society for the use
of the District Electoral Divisions Map; to the Director of the
Ordnance Survey Office for permission to reprint the Townland
index map; and to Karen McGonigle for typing the original
manuscript.

David Leahy was born at Edgeworthstown, Co. Longford in 1964,
the youngest of 4 sons of Maurice and Pearl Leahy. He attended
Ballinalee, Abbeylara and St Michael's National Schools, and St
Mel's College in Longford, and is a graduate of University College
Galway. He is currently employed as an Engineer with Limerick
County Council.

Contents

Figures & Tables

Introduction

This index to the 1901 census returns for County Longford is the first of its kind to be produced for any Irish county and is a valuable new source for the family and local history of the county. Census returns are among the most useful sources for family research since they describe both personal details of the family members (age, education, occupation etc) and also the circumstances of the entire family (housing details, family size, address etc). Census information is, however, regrettably scarce for 19th century Ireland. The individual household returns for the years 1861 to 1891 were deliberately destroyed by government order (either to protect confidentiality or to make new paper during the shortage of the First World War), while those for the years from 1821 to 1851 perished in 1922 when fire destroyed the Public Record Office of Ireland during the Civil War. Remnants of the returns for the latter years were saved for some counties, but none for County Longford.

Longford is among the smallest of Irish counties, occupying almost 270,000 acres. At the date of the 1901 census there were 46,672 people in the county, occupying 9,799 houses. The significant towns in the county were Longford Town (population 3,747), Granard (1,622), Ballymahon (711) and Edgeworthstown (578). All other towns had a population of less than 350. The population was thus predominantly rural, and the major occupations associated with agriculture. The population was also predominantly Roman Catholic (91.5%) with 3,403 members of the Church of Ireland; 256 Presbyterians; 203 Methodists; and 68 members of other religions. The population was mainly composed of natives of the county. Of the total population, only 4,634 persons, or less than 10%, were born outside the county. Of these 2,357 were born in one of the counties bordering Longford and 574 of them were born outside Ireland. (Table 1).

The population of Longford, like that of many other midland and western counties, had seen a drastic reduction during the latter half of the 19th century. In 1841, before the Great Famine of 1845-47, it had reached a peak of 115,491. The deaths due to the famine devastated the county, and the subsequent chain of emigration began a steady reduction in the population of the county. This reduction has continued during the 20th century and the population in 1986 stood at 31,491.

The categories of information on individuals which are available are;
- Name and Surname
- Relationship to head of family
- Religious Profession
- Education (ie "Read & Write", "Read" or "Cannot Read")

- Age & Sex
- Rank, Profession or Occupation
- Marriage (ie whether "Married, Widower, Widow or Not Married")
- Where born (ie County/City in Ireland, Country if outside Ireland)
- Irish Language (ie speaks Irish only, Irish & English or English only
  - left blank in the latter case)
- Infirmities

A complete household return is shown in Fig 1. In addition to the data on the household return, there is also a "House and Building Return" which provides "particulars of the inhabited houses" for each area returned. The particulars include a classification of the structure of the walls and roof, and of the numbers of rooms and windows. Fig 3 shows an example of the House and Building Return for the Townland of Derryglash which includes a classification of the house occupied by the Rowan family described in Fig 1.

Despite the relatively late date of the census, the data it provides is very useful in researching ancestors dating back even to the early and mid-19th century. In attempting to trace the families of emigrants, for instance, a common problem is to find where in the county the family may have lived. The index provides the addresses for all households occupied by every family or individual in the county. Many of these houses will have been occupied by the same family for generations while even newer houses will generally be located in areas with which the family has been traditionally associated. The address (or even the house) may therefore be that from which an ancestor emigrated in the previous century. The information in the index may also be the vital link between the 19th century emigrant, and the current members of the family in Ireland.

Other information of value includes the ages of the members of the family, although it should be noted that ages as given in census returns should only be viewed as approximate. These will provide a basis for a search for birth (or baptismal) information for these persons in the 19th century. The occupations of the family members will also provide a further lead in family research.

In using the information it is useful to know the basis of its compilation. The returns were compiled on the night of 31st March 1901 by members of the police force, ie the Royal Irish Constabulary. Each household listed only those members of the household who were actually present in the house on that night. Those who were temporarily absent were not included. The data was collected within Unions (of which there are 3 in Co. Longford, see Fig 2. These are further divided into District Electoral Divisions (DED's) of which there are 55 in the county. (See Fig 2). Within each DED the returns are organised by townland (for rural areas) or village, street etc (for urban areas). The townland is the smallest division of land area in use in Ireland and is the usual "address" used by people in rural areas. There are 893 townlands in County Longford. A map of the County, showing Unions and District Electoral Divisions is in Fig 2. A map of the townlands in the county is appended. Full information on the location of a specific townland within Barony, Civil Parish etc, is available in *General Alphabetical Index to the Townlands and Towns, Parishes and Baronies of Ireland*. This was produced for every census. The 1851 version, which is also relevant to the 1901 census, has been republished by the Genealogical Publishing Co. Inc., Baltimore, 1984.

The index is based on the family names (or surnames) of householders, or of individuals within households whose family name is different to that of the householder. For each householder the index provides the personal name and the townland or street in which the household was situated. Thus *"MEEHAN, John at Bundoon"* signifies that a John Meehan was a householder in the townland of Bundoon. For individuals resident within households the name of whose head is different to theirs, the index provides the name of the householder in whose house they are resident, and also its location. For example, *"PETTIT, Bridget at Philip Brady's of Kiltycon"* shows that a Bridget Pettit was resident at Philip Brady's household in the townland of Kiltycon. The index therefore provides a complete picture of the location of persons of every family name found in the county.

Where two or more townlands of the same name occur the index differentiates between them by specifying the DED or other land division in which each is located. At the end of the names index (Page 201) there is an index of townlands and a reference to the position of each on the map appended to this book.

As an example, if the reader was searching for a family of the name **ROWAN**, the index would show that there are three entries for persons of this name in 1901. These are the households of **Daniel Rowan at Derryglash** townland, and of **Bridget Rowan at Derrynagowna** townland, while the third is a **Catherine Rowan resident at the O'Farrell household in Moor**(?). The "(?)" here indicates that there was some difficulty in deciphering the handwriting on the original returns. If the index for the O'Farrell household is referred to, it will be found that it is that of Rev. James O'Farrell at Moor.

If any of these are felt to be of interest, the original returns for the relevant households may be consulted. These original returns are kept at the National Archives in Dublin (formerly the Public Record Office of Ireland) where they can be directly accessed by visitors, or sometimes searched by the staff on behalf of enquirers. Postal enquiries, specifying the name of the householder and the street or townland (and other location details where necessary) should be directed to the National Archives, Four Courts, Dublin 7, Ireland. A minimum fee of IR£2 is payable for the search and for a copy of each household or buildings return. Two to four weeks should be allowed for delivery. An example of a copy of a return, such as can be obtained by a visit or a postal enquiry, is shown in Fig 1.

The index contains references to over 10,000 heads of households, and also to almost 7,000 servants, visitors, relatives and others who were residing at, or visiting, these Longford households on the night of the census. It is an exhaustive and comprehensive guide to the family names found in the county in 1901. These range from the most numerous (See Table 2) to the many rare names represented by single households eg Wixted, Sargaison, Spinks, Makim, Jobe, Giddings and many others.

The information in the index was abstracted from the individual returns in the course of over 50 visits by the author to the National Archives. The data was then indexed and rechecked. The result is a unique aid to the geography and history of Longford and its people, in which the author has an abiding interest. Enquiries from readers about Longford families and places, or further information about the families contained in the index, would be welcomed by the author.

Mr. David Leahy,
Glack, Park Road,
Longford,
Ireland.

Table 1　　　**Residents of Co. Longford in 1901 who were born outside Ireland indicating Place of Birth**

Place of Birth	Number
England	288
America/U.S./U.S.A.	121
Scotland	83
India	21
Australia	12
Canada	11
South America	11
France	4
Wales	4
Germany	2
Guernsey	2
Italy	2
Malta	2
Russia	2
Bermuda	1
East Indies	1
Honduras	1
Hong Kong	1
Isle of Man	1
Singapore	1
South Africa	1
St. Helena	1
Sweden	1
	Total　574

(This Table was compiled by D. Leahy during indexing and shows some discrepancies with the General Report on 1901 Census).

Table 2   **The 20 Most Numerous Householder names in the 1901 Longford Census**

	Names & Synonyms	No. Households
1.	Reilly, O'Reilly	374
2.	Farrell, O'Farrell, O'Ferrall	343
3.	Kiernan, McKiernan	175
4.	Brady	149
5.	Kelly	142
6.	Kenny	129
7.	Cormack, McCormack, McCormick	111
8.	Quinn	98
9.	Smyth, Smith	95
10.	Mulligan	90
11.	Murphy	84
12.	Casey	80
13.	Duffy	78
14.	Donohoe	76
15.	Hughes	69
16.	Murtagh	67
17.	Connor, O'Connor	65
18.	Skelly, Skally, Scally	64
19.	Maguire, McGuire	63
20.	Reynolds	62

Fig 1 A sample Household return from the 1901 Census of County Longford

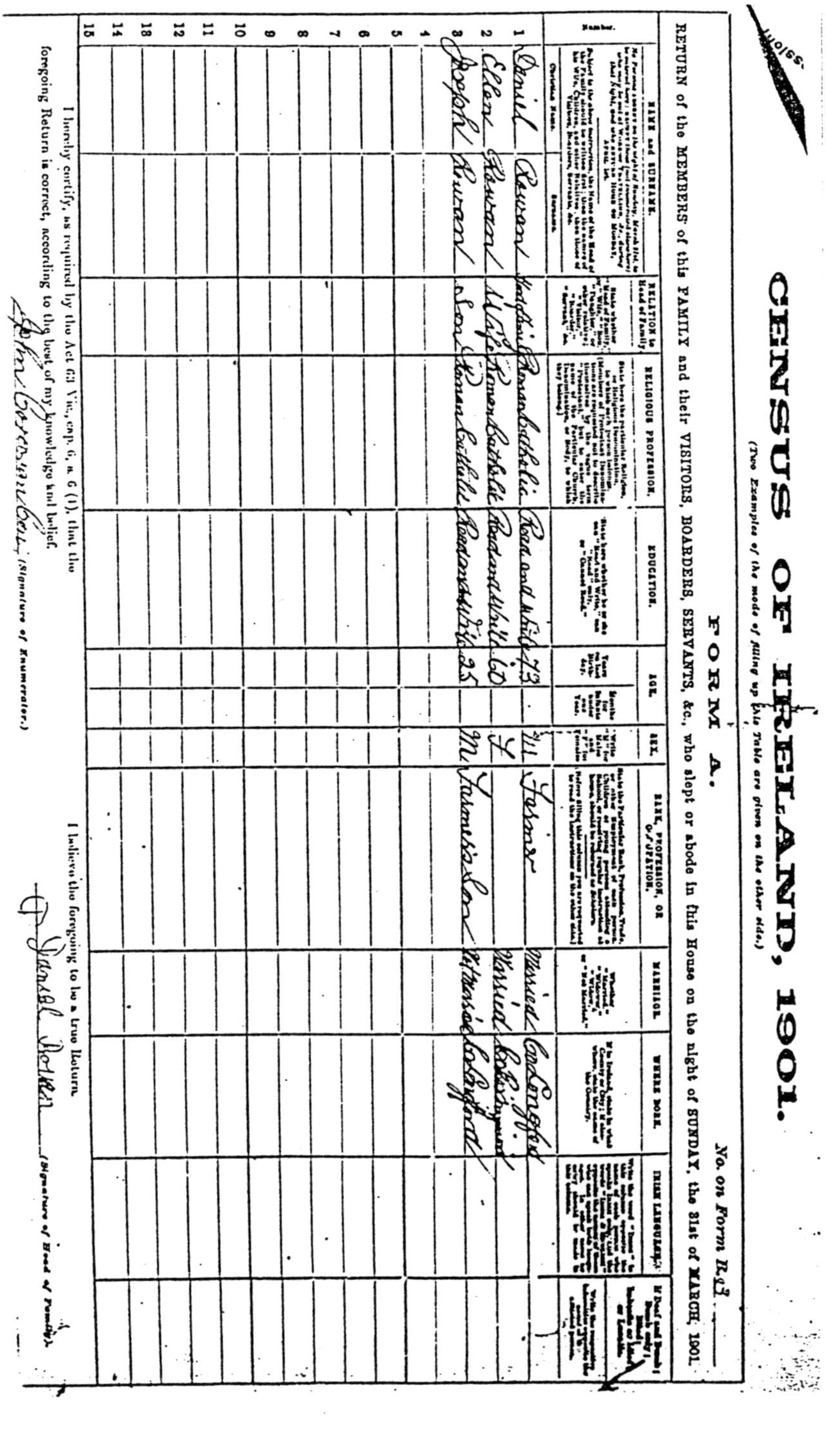

CENSUS OF IRELAND, 1901.

(Two Examples of the mode of filling up this Table are given on the other side.)

FORM A.

No. on Form B. 93

RETURN of the MEMBERS of this FAMILY and their VISITORS, BOARDERS, SERVANTS, &c., who slept or abode in this House on the night of SUNDAY, the 31st of MARCH, 1901.

Number	Christian Name	Surname	Relation to Head of Family	Religious Profession	Education	Age (Years)	Age (Months)	Sex	Rank, Profession, or Occupation	Marriage	Where Born	Irish Language	If Deaf and Dumb; Dumb only; Blind; Imbecile or Idiot; or Lunatic
1	Daniel	Rowan	Head of Family	Roman Catholic	Read and Write	73		M	Farmer	Married	Co Longford		
2	Ellen	Rowan	Wife	Roman Catholic	Read and Write	60		F		Married	Co Roscommon		
3	Joseph	Rowan	Son	Roman Catholic	Read and Write	25		M	Farmer's Son	Not Married	Co Longford		
4													
5													
6													
7													
8													
9													
10													
11													
12													
13													
14													
15													

I hereby certify, as required by the Act 63 Vic., cap. 6, s. 6 (1), that the foregoing Return is correct, according to the best of my knowledge and belief.

John Corcoran Con. (Signature of Enumerator.)

I believe the foregoing to be a true Return.

Daniel Rowan (Signature of Head of Family.)

Fig 2   **District Electoral Divisions of Co. Longford with (inset) the Poor Law) Unions**

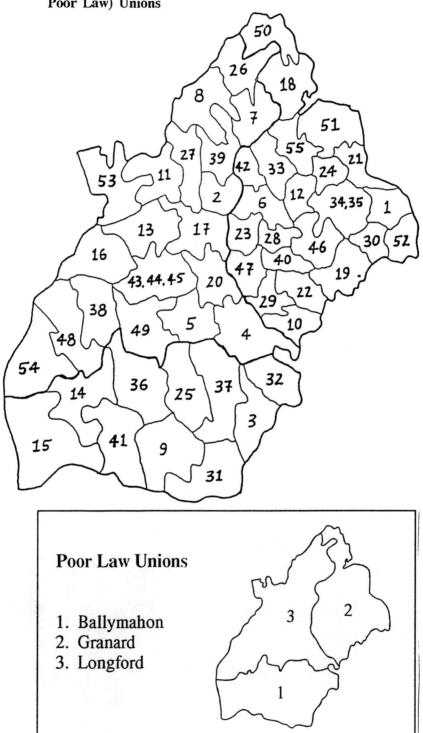

Poor Law Unions

1. Ballymahon
2. Granard
3. Longford

Index to Longford District Electoral Divisions Map (opposite)

Fig 3   **A sample House and Buildings return from the 1901 Census**
               of Co. Longford

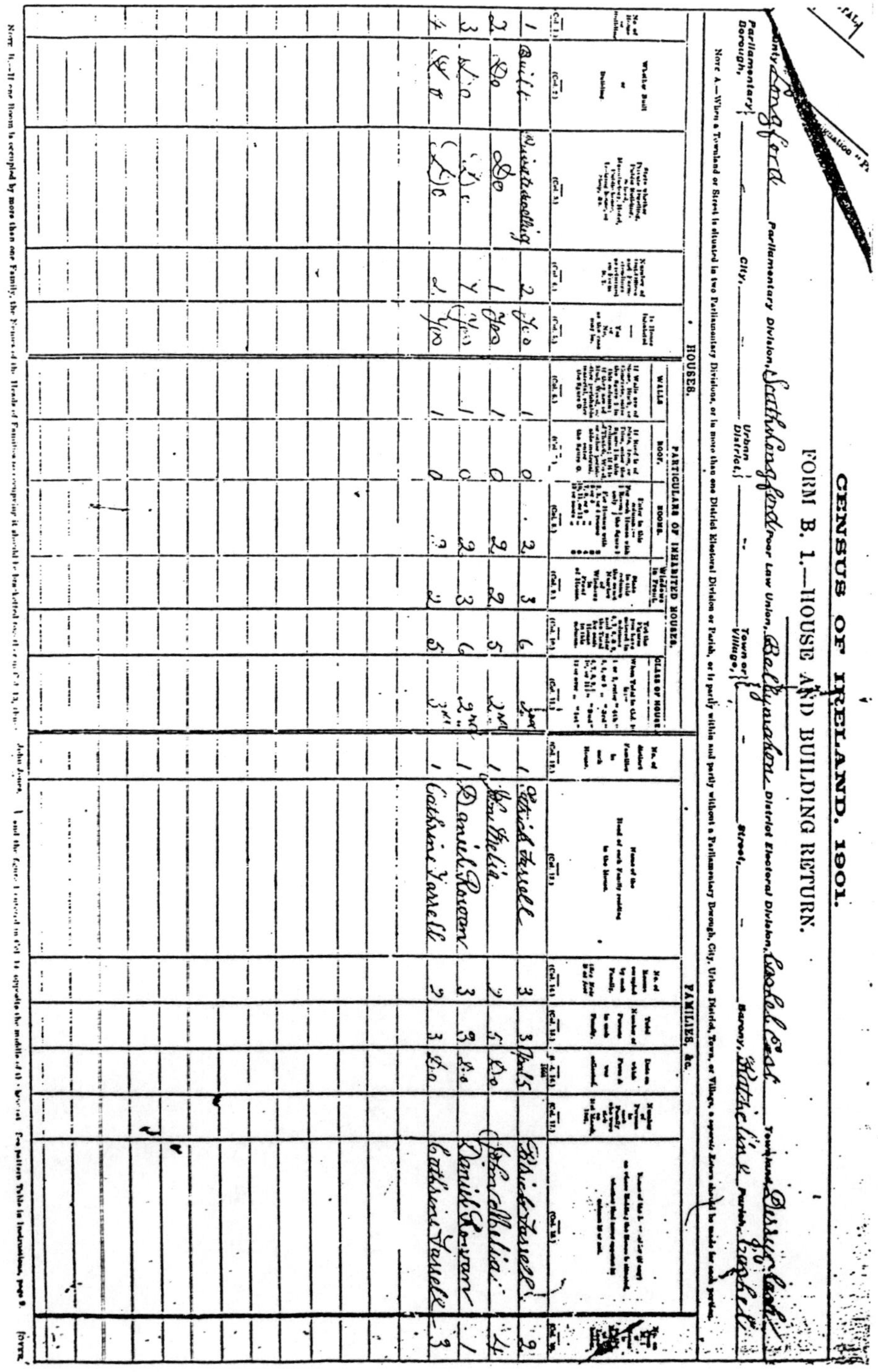

ABBOT: Thomas at Drummeel, John, George, George at Drumderg. Fanny at Glenmore (Ballinamuck East D.E.D.) John at Chapel Lane, Longford Town. Annie at Abbeycartron. *ALSO:* Kate at Wilson's of Currygrane. Robert and Margaret at Wahab's of Ferskill. Robert at Fee's of Church Street, Longford Town.

ACHESON: Robert at Derawley. Francis at Carrickglass Demesne (Templemichael Civil Ph.).

ACHMUTY: See Auchmuty.

ADAMS: Robert at Corry (Caldragh D.E.D.). Elizabeth, Richard at Lisnabo. Richard at Mullolagher. Ralph at Cloonmore. Randal at Craane. *ALSO:* Reginald V. at Brabazon's of Higginstown. Maggie at Fee's of Church Street, Longford Town.

ADDY: George at Richmond Street, Longford Town.

McADEN: Patrick at Edgeworthstown Town. (See Cadden).

ADLUM: Bridget at Cloghan (Forgney D.E.D.). Catherine at Tennalough. Charles at Derryglogher.

McAFEE: Mary at Musters' of Brianstown.

AHEARN: John at Martin's of Ballymahon Town.

AHMOOTY: See Auchmuty.

AIKENS: See Eakins.

AIRLIE: James at Main Street, Longford Town. Annie at St. Mel's Road, Longford Town. *ALSO:* Rosanna at Boyle's of Corglass. (See Early).

McALARNEY: See McLarney.

McALINEY: James at Cartrongolan. (See McEliney, McLiney).

ALLARD: Honoria at Kilnacarrow, (Kilglass D.E.D.).

ALLEN:(16): Joseph at Carn. Samuel at Corry (Kilglass D.E.D.). Michael at Polladooey. Edith at Drumnacooha. Bernard at Gaigue. Kate at Lismoy. Arthur at Breany. Ellen at Aghanageeragh. Charlotte at Treel (Corboy D.E.D.). George at Agharickard. John W. at Ballymacwilliam. John F. at Cartron Little. Edward G. at Cloonturk. James at Ardnacassagh. Lizzie at Little Water St. Longford Town. Rev. Samuel at Abbeycartron. *ALSO:*

George at King-Harman's of Newcastle. Mary at Brady's of Fostragh. Jane at Moffett's of Cloonfiugh. James at O'Donnell's of Dublin St., Longford Town. Kate and Bridget at Legge's of Main St. Longford Town.

ALLEY: Charles H. at Mullen's of Main Street, Granard Town.

McALLISTER, McALISTER: Randal at The Hill, Granard Town. *ALSO:* Mary at Monaghan's of Leitrim (Granard Rural D.E.D.).

AMOOTY: See Auchmuty.

AMPHLET, AMPHLETT: Anne J. and William J. at Carney's of Great Water Street, Longford Town.

AMROD: T. at Duncan McGregor's of Lisbrack (Longford Rural D.E.D.).

McANALLY: See McNally.

ANDERSON: Thomas, William, Thomas at Rathmore (Ballinamuck East D.E.D.). Patrick at Derryheelan. Mary at Conroy's Court, Longford Town. *ALSO:* Annie at King-Harman's of Newcastle. Patrick at Slacke's of Kiltycreevagh. John J. at Martin's of Moneylagan.

McANIFF: See McNiff.

McANN: See McCann.

ANTHONY: James at Thomas Halpin's of Richmond St., Longford Town.

ARCHBOLD: Francis at Gorteenrevagh. James at Soran.

McARDLE: Bridget at Keel (Forgney D.E.D.). Philip at Derrycolumb.

ARKINS: James at Grehan's of Main Street, Granard Town.

ARKINSON: Mary at Kilcurry.

ARMSTRONG:(19): James at Kildordan. Thomas at Garrycam. Matthew at Ballymahon Town. Bridget at Cloonard (Ballymahon D.E.D.). Alexander at Creevaghmore (Forgney Civil Ph.). John at Creevagh Beg, Ballymahon Town. Thomas N. at Glenmore (Kilcommock D.E.D.). Francis, Robert at Main Street, Keenagh Village. Patrick at Tober. Allen at Killeen (Bunlahy D.E.D.). Henry at Rathbrackan. George at Aghareagh (Coolamber D.E.D.). Alexander at Lisryan. Patrick at Drumlish Village. William at Ballydrum. Annie at Killeenatruan. John at Knockloughlin. Annie at Main Street, Longford Town. *ALSO:* Mary at John Farrell's of Mornin. Elizabeth at

Jessop's of Doory. Michael at William Seales' of Ballymahon Town. Andrew at Colo's of Creevagh Beg. Ballymahon Town. Ellen at Hayes's of Main Street, Keenagh Village. Samuel at McCormack's of Ledwithstown (Kilcommock Civil Ph.). James at Mansergh's of Ballinalee Village. Mary A. at Murphy's of Drumderg. George at Ballinamuck Barracks, Shanmullagh. Marian B. at Little's of Church Street, Longford Town.

ASHCROFT: Caroline at Carrickglass Demesne (Templemichael Civil Ph.).

ASHE: Henry at Drumlish Village. *ALSO:* Michael at Teresa Casey's of Dublin Street, Longford Town.

ASHWELL: James at Kate Brady's of Main Street, Longford Town.

McATEE: Mary at Cloghan (Forgney D.E.D.). John at Kilnacarrow (Kilglass D.E.D.). Mary at Barry (Ballymahon D.E.D.). *ALSO:* Anne at James Fox's of Ballymahon Town. Margaret at Robinson's of Lisglassock.

ATKINSON: Mary at Kilcurry (?). James at Toome (Ballymahon D.E.D.). Bridget at Main Street, Longford Town.

ATWELL: William J. at Abbeycartron.

AUCHMUTY, AMOOTY: Mathew at Cartronboy. James at Creevaghmore (Forgney Civil Ph.). John at Garrynagh. Charles at Carrickmoyragh. Joseph at Cloontagh. Anne, William at Briskil. (see Moughty).

McAULEY: See McCauley.

McAULIFFE: Thomas at Lanesborough Village. *ALSO:* James J. at Maria Farrell's (23) of Lanesborough Village (?).

AUSTIN: Robert at Drumanure.

McAVEY, McAVEIGH:(12): James, Michael at Cloontagh. John, Patrick at Bawn (Breakrisk D.E.D.). John at Kilnashee. Patrick, Bernard, Patrick, Patrick, Mary at Briskil. Thomas, John at Deerpark (Newtownforbes D.E.D.). *ALSO:* John at Michael Donohoe's of Carrickmaguirk. Anne at Clarke's of Kilnashee. Teresa at Bartley's of Aghareagh (Cloondara D.E.D.).

McAVOY: See McEvoy.

McAWEENY: See McWeeney.

AWLY: James at Michael Murphy's of Enybegs.

AYLETT: F. at Hewetson's of Church Street, Longford Town.

AYLING: A. at Hewetson's of Church Street, Longford Town.

BACON: Mary at Aghnavealoge. John at Clontymullan. William at Great Water Street, Longford Town.

BAILIE: Joseph at Patterson's of Church Street, Longford Town.

BAIRD,BEARD: Thomas at Tullybaun. William at Ballinalee Village. John at Aghaward.

BAKER: Ada at Farrington's of Newtownforbes Village. J.A. and G. at Hewetson's of Church Street, Longford Town.

BALFE: Edward at Ellen Larkin's of Dublin Street, Longford Town.

BALL: Mary at Caltragh Beg. Mary, Michael, Thomas at Derrygowna. *ALSO:* Bridget at Catherine Farrell's (5) of Carrowstrawly. Michael at McGrath's of Derrygeel. Teresa at Donnellan's of Tullyvrane. J.W. at Hewetson's of Church Street, Longford Town. (See Bawle).

BALLESTY, BALLASTY: Michael at Kilsallagh. Charles at Lisdreenagh. *ALSO:* Jane at James Dempsey's of Edgeworthstown Town.

BANKS: Patrick at Aghamore Upper. Philip at Mullinroe. Patrick, Philip, Julia at Ballinulty Lower. Francis, Thomas, Mary at Derrycassan. Sarah at Carrickmoyragh. *ALSO:* Matthew at Bridget Doyle's of Sonnagh.

BANNING: John at Church Street, Longford Town.

BANNON:(12): John at Ballintober (Bonny). Margaret, Anne at Lisnacreevy. Bridget at Ballynahinch. Thomas at Glebe (Cloondara D.E.D.). Peter, Patrick, Mary at Barney. Mary, Denis at Coolcaw. Thomas at Cross (Ardagh East D.E.D.). Annie M. at Fee's Terrace, Longford Town. *ALSO:* Patrick at Heffernan's of Abbeyshrule. James at Kearney's of Cornadowagh. Patrick at Daly's of Doonacurry (Kilcommock Civil Ph.) (?). Patrick at Philip Greene's of Edgeworthstown Town. Maggie at Egan's of Drumroe.

BARCLAY: Richard at Coolnahinch (Kilcommock D.E.D.).

BARDEN,BARDON: William at Main Street, Keenagh Village. Winifred at Kilmore Lower. Thomas at Kilmore Upper. Mary at Templeton Glebe.

Edward at Dunbeggan (Moydow D.E.D.). John, Mary at Feraghfad. *ALSO:* James at Dooner's of Dunbeggan (Moydow D.E.D.). William at Little's of Main Street, Longford Town.

BARLOW: Annie et al. at Fahey's of Chapel Lane, Longford Town.

BARNAN: Patrick at Daly's of Doonacurry (Kilcommock Civil Ph.).

BARRETT: Mary at Clooncullen.

BARRS, BARS: John at Lisbrack (Longford Rural D.E.D.).

BARRY: Mary at Larkin's of Corry (Kilglass D.E.D.). James at Thomas H. Murray's of Ballymahon Town. Sr. Mary J. at Sr. Green's of Convent Lane, Longford Town.

BARTLEY: John at Liscormick. Elizabeth at Abbeylara Village. John at Aghareagh (Cloondara D.E.D.). Hugh at Fee's Terrace, Longford Town. Thomas at Little Water Street, Longford Town. *ALSO:* Catherine and Catherine at Henry's of Bridge Street, Longford Town.

BARTON: William at Miller's of Kinard.

BATCHELOR: G.W. at Duncan McGregor's of Lisbrack (Longford Rural D.E.D.).

BATRIM, BATTRIM: Francis at Cloghchurnel.

BAWLE: Michael at Corrool (Brennan). John at Corrool (Kenny). James at Ledwithstown (Kilcommock Civil Ph.). (See Ball).

BAXTER: John at Drumderg. Patrick at Grillagh (Ardagh West D.E.D.). Elizabeth at Gorteenagloon. Christopher at Killinlastra. *ALSO:* Kath at McGiff's of Brickeens. Patrick at McNamara's of Main St., Longford Town.

BEADE: Gladys H. at Walsh's of Ballyclamay. (See Bede).

BEARD: See Baird.

BEATTIE, BEATTY: John at Main Street, Granard Town. Martha, William at Cleggill. William at Lamagh. James at Corlagan. *ALSO:* George at Armstrong's of Glenmore (Kilcommock D.E.D.). Mary and John at Dennehy's of Glenmore (Kilcommock D.E.D.).

BEAZOR: H. at Hewetson's of Church Street, Longford Town.

BEDE: B. at Hewetson's of Church Street, Longford Town. (See Beade).

BEGLAN, BEGLIN:(12): John at Gelshagh. James at Culray. Michael, Elizabeth at Aghabrack. John at Greville. Patrick at Tonywardan. William at Derrycassan. Michael at Lisryan. Edward at Caldraghmore. William, Peter at Cloonker. Owen at Ardnacassagh. *ALSO:* Ellen at Hargadon's of Culray. Mary A. at McNally's of Killasona. Anne at Travers' of Aghabrack. William at Mary Nannery's of Ballymore. John at Thomas Masterson's of Edgeworthstown Town.

BEGLEY: Thomas at Aghaboy (Aghaboy D.E.D.).

BEHAN: John at Abbeylara Village. John at Barrack St., Granard Town.

BEIRNE:(11): Patrick at Island. James at Balloo. John at Cloonellan. Francis at Cornacullew. Ellen at Drumlish Village. James at Kilmacannon. John at Clooncolligan. Catherine at Cartrons (Caldragh D.E.D.). Alexander at Ardnacassagh. Mary at Little Water Street, Longford Town. William at St. Michael's Road, Longford Town. *ALSO:* Mary J. at Senter's of Cartronawar (Kilcommock D.E.D.). Edward at Stephenson's of Ballinlough. Mary C. at Hagan's of Newtownforbes Village. Thomas and Patrick at Patrick Cox's of Cloonart N. John at Ross's of Main St., Longford Town. Patrick at Molloy's of Main St., Longford Town. (See Byrne, Burns).

O'BEIRNE: Patrick at Grassyard. John at Clooneen (Beirne). Mary at Dublin Street, Longford Town. *ALSO:* Francis at Hosey's of Edgeworthstown Town. Ellen and Ellie F. at Farrell's of Bunanass.

BELFORD: John at Clooniher. Ellen at Great Water St., Longford Town.

BELL: Florence M. at Burd's of Ballymahon Town.

BELLEW: Michael at Creevaghmore (Forgney Civil Ph.). Michael at Foygh. *ALSO:* Patrick at May's of Clooncallow.

BELTON: Joseph at Clontymullan. William, John, John, Thomas at Corlea. Hugh at Cartrons (Kilcommock D.E.D.). Richard at Rathcline. John at Ballymahon St., Longford Town. Henry at Noud's Yard, Longford Town. *ALSO:* George at James Casey's of Derraghan More. Thomas at Quinn's of Island. Robert at Peter Igoe's of Ballymahon St., Longford Town.

BENNER: Rebecca at Pollard's of Templeton Glebe. Marie at Adams's of Craane.

BENNETT: Alexander at Keel (Kilglass D.E.D.). William at Currygrane. Joseph H. at Drumderg. Robert at Leitrim (Granard Rural D.E.D.). Thomas at Lismoy. James at Cartron Little. Elizabeth at Glack (Longford Rural D.E.D.). *ALSO:* Agnes at King-Harman's of Newcastle. Kate of Wilson's of Currygrane. Annie at Fannin's of Mullaghavorneen.

BENSON: William at Lloyd's of Main Street, Longford Town.

BERESFORD: Jean at Thompson's of Glack (Longford Urban No. 1 D.E.D.).

BERGIN: Martin at Silver Street, Granard Town. Mary at Freaghmeen. *ALSO:* Lily at Bennett's of Currygrane.

BERMINGHAM: Mary, Elizabeth at Cloontirm. Thomas at Mullaghavorneen. *ALSO:* Bridget at Heavey's of Clooneeny.

BERNE: See Beirne.

BERNIE: See Birney.

BERRANE: Patrick at Carrickglass Demesne (Templemichael Civil Ph.).

BERRY: Joseph at Aghnacliff. Michael at Carrickadorrish. Michael, Bernard at Enaghan. Mary at Edenmore. James at Fostragh. Patrick at Glenmore (Ballinamuck East D.E.D.). *ALSO:* Francis and Margaret at Margaret Sullivan's of Aghakine. James at Mary Seery's of Edenmore. Mary at Jones's of Glenmore (Ballinamuck East D.E.D.).

BETTS: F. at Duncan McGregor's of Lisbrack (Longford Rural D.E.D.).

BIERNEY: See Birney.

BIGGINS: Mary at Farrington's of Newtownforbes Village.

BIRD: Liddie (?) at John McCormack's of Dublin Street, Longford Town. (See Burd).

BIRMINGHAM: See Bermingham.

BIRNEY, BIERNEY, BERNIE: Augusta S. at Aghafad. James at Great Water Street, Longford Town. *ALSO:* Catherine at Newman's of Knockawalky.

BLACK: Rose at Kinard. Thomas at Moor.

BLACKALL: D. at Hewetson's of Church Street, Longford Town.

BLAIR: F. at Dowler's of Edgeworthstown Town.

BLAKE: Mary at Cartron (Granard Urban D.E.D.). Patrick J. at St. Michael's Road, Longford Town. George at Church Street, Longford Town. *ALSO:* Margaret at McGoey's of Grillagh (Ardagh West D.E.D.). Mathew at McCullagh's of Killashee Street, Longford Town.

BLAKELEY: Anne E. et al. at Anne McCoy's of Smear.

BLANEY: John at Clooneen (Creevy D.E.D.). Bridget at Ball Alley Street Upper, Granard Town. Mary at Silver Street, Granard Town. Charles at Toome (Mullanalaghta D.E.D.). *ALSO:* Catherine at Thomas Kiernan's of Barrack Street, Granard Town. Mathew at Myles Reilly's of Barrack Street, Granard Town. Bridget at O'Connor's of New Road, Granard Town.

BLANFORD: Alfred E. at Clynan.

BLESSINGTON: Thomas, Owen at Aghakilmore. Thomas at Fihoragh. Anne at Cloondara. Michael at Templeton Glebe. *ALSO:* Eugene at Michael Duffy's of Aghagah. Mary at Nixon's of Ballyduffy.

BLIGH: John C. at Lismagoneen.

BLOOMER: Jane at Cam. Robert at Ballindagny and Cullyvore. Abraham at Bracklon.

BODELL: John W. at Culleenmore.

BOGAN: Alexander at Aghaboy (Milltown D.E.D.).

BOHAN: James at Esker North.

BOLAND: Patrick at Peter J. Joyce's of Main Street, Longford Town.

BOLE: Ambrose at Parkplace.

BOLES: Mary at Aghaboy (Aghaboy D.E.D.). *ALSO:* Benjamin at Wilson's of Ballymahon Road, Keenagh Village. Robert H. at Hanley's of Cooleeshil or Richfort.

BOLGER: Thomas, Patrick, John at Ballymahon Town. *ALSO:* Maggie M. at Catherine Mahon's of Ballymahon Town.

BOLLARD: John at Rose Coyne's of Ballymahon Town.

BOND: William at Newtownbond. Willoughby at Aghaboy (Aghaboy

D.E.D.). James W. at Farraghroe. Willoughby J. at Ballygarve. (See McGeough-Bond).

BONIFACE: Mary et al. at Ellen Quinn's of Little Water Street, Longford Town.

BORRIS: John at Killeenboy.

BOTHWELL: J. at Edgeworthstown Town.

BOUGHY: Mary at New Street, Longford Town.

BOURKE: See Burke.

BOWEN: William at Ballymahon Town.

BOYCE: Michael at Lissanure. Kate at Lisnageeragh. John at Coolcaw. Hugh at Lisduff (Montgomery). Michael, Thomas at Lissaghanedan. James at Cloonahard. *ALSO:* John at Flynn's of Drumanure.

BOYD, BOYDE: William at Newcastle. Letitia at Glebe (Kilglass D.E.D.). David at Kilmore Lower. Samuel at Main Street, Longford Town.

BOYERS: John (absent from No. 2), John at Main Street, Longford Town.

BOYHAN: James at Rincoolagh. John at Killashee Street, Longford Town.

BOYLAN:(10): Rose at Kilbride. Hugh at Ballymaurice (Granard Rural D.E.D.). James at Tromra (Granard Rural D.E.D.). Bridget at Ball Alley Street Upper, Granard Town. Edward at Barrack Street, Granard Town. Thomas at Silver Street, Granard Town. Mary at Tuite's Lane, Granard Town. James at Water Lane, Granard Town. Alice at Cleenrah. John at Leggagh. *ALSO:* Patrick at Mollaghan's of Aghamore (Ballinalee D.E.D.). Katie at Edward Donohoe's (8) of Drumard. Francis at McGovern's of Cloontirm. Mary at John McCormack's of Dublin Street, Longford Town.

BOYLE: Mary A. at Ballinrud Glebe. Daniel at Drumard. Bridget at Corglass. Patrick at Glen. Mary at Great Water Street, Longford Town. Catherine at St. Mel's Road, Longford Town. *ALSO:* Patrick at Kelly's of Moygh (Ballymahon D.E.D.). Christina at Curneen's of Tromra (Granard Rural D.E.D.). Bridget at Kerrigan's of Edgeworthstown Town. Mary A. at Skelly's of Edgeworthstown Town. Bridget and Kate at Kennedy's of Glen. Patrick at O'Connor's of Conroy's Court, Longford Town. Maria at McCann's of Abbeycartron.

BRABAZON: Kate at Higginstown.

BRACKEN: John at Cashel. James at Ballinalee Village. Anne at Breaghy. Peter at Ringowny. John at Kiltybegs. *ALSO:* Kate at Farrell's of Roos. Ellen at Burns' of Main Street, Longford Town.

BRADFORD: R.N. at Hewetson's of Church Street, Longford Town.

BRADLEY: William at Molly. Thomas at Prucklish. *ALSO:* Elizabeth at Thomas Reilly's of Aghagreagh. J. and W. at Hewetson's of Church Street, Longford Town.

BRADY:(149): Peter at Garrycam. John at Aghamore (Ballinalee D.E.D.). Edward at Aghnashannagh. James, John at Derryneel. James, Thomas at Prucklishtown. Bernard at Tullybaun. Catherine at Ballinalee Village. Francis at Castlebrock. Edward at Laughil (Edgeworth). William at Lisduff (Drummeel D.E.D.). Peter, John, Matthew, Patrick at Gelshagh. Michael, Bernard at Aghaward. Francis at Carrickateane. Patrick, Michael at Carrowlinan. James, Francis, Patrick at Kiltyclogh. Anne at Lislea (Lislea D.E.D.). James, Mary, Patrick at Ballinrooey. Michael at Cranally. Charles at Culray. Patrick, Michael, Patrick at Aghakeeran. John, James, Catherine, Thomas at Aghakine. Bernard at Tonymore North. Bridget, James at Cartronbore. Bernard at Cartronamarkey. Patrick, Patrick at Mullinroe. Francis at Clogh (Dalystown D.E.D.). Thomas at Rathbrackan. Terence at Ballinulty Upper. James at Ballyboy. Rose, James at Ballygilchrist. Patrick at Ballymore. Philip, Hugh at Leitrim (Granard Rural D.E.D.). Patrick at Grassyard. John L., Lizzie, Mary, Hugh at Main Street, Granard Town. Patrick (absent from home) at Barrack Street, Granard Town. Thomas at Lisraghtigan. Bryan at Cartroncar. James, Mary, Michael at Graffoge (Milltown D.E.D.). John at Cooldoney. Patrick at Derragh. John at Cornadrung. Anne at Polladooey. Bernard, Anne, Philip at Rosduff. Charles, Michael, John, Patrick at Smear. Thomas, Bernard at Enaghan. Charles, John at Lisraherty. Thomas, Mary, Francis at Ballyduffy. Thomas at Birrinagh. Nicholas at Drumard. John, Patrick at Cloonagh (Mullanalaghta D.E.D.). Michael, John at Corbaun or Leitrim. James, John at Kilmore. Patrick, John, Patrick, Patrick at Larkfield. Catherine, John, Charles at Cam. Francis at Lisnagrish. John at Cranalagh More. Hugh at Lisnageeragh. John at Edgeworthstown Town. Mary, Francis at Edenmore. Mary at Fostragh. John at Creelaghta. John, Peter, Ellen, Bridget at Crowdrumman. Patrick at Fardrumman. Patrick at Corglass. Mary, Francis, Philip, Matthew, Margaret at Kiltycon. Patrick at Leggagh. John, Thomas at Enybegs. Michael, Michael at Oghil. Patrick at Brocklagh. Patrick, Patrick, Philip, Mary, John at Gaigue. Philip, Patrick at Kilmahon. Thomas at Lettergonnell. James, Patrick at Cloonrallagh. Peter at Aghaboy (Aghaboy D.E.D.). Patrick at Clontumper. Michael, Patrick, Michael, Patrick, John at Esker South. Thomas at Soran. Bridget, Simon at Rhine. James at Cartronawar (Corboy D.E.D.). James at Lissardowlan. Mary at Creeve. Matthew at Farnagh. Elizabeth at Ballymahon Street, Longford Town. James, Kate S. at Main

Street, Longford Town. William at St. Mel's Road, Longford Town. *ALSO:* Bridget at McHugh's of Corryena. James and Margaret at Cannivan's of Gorteen. Kate at Margaret Treacy's of Aghakilmore. Michael at Thomas Doyle's of Molly. Ellen at McGivney's of Kiltyclogh. Mary J. at Dixon's of Bunlahy. John at Luke Higgins's of Killeen (Bunlahy D.E.D.). James at Clyne's of Clooneen (Creevy D.E.D.). Kate at Bridget Fitzsimons' of Culleenmore. Hugh at Fullam's of Creevy. John at Michael Kelly's of Main Street, Granard Town. Francis at Peter Kiernan's of Main Street, Granard Town. Patrick at Flood's of Main Street, Granard Town. Patrick at Laurence Ward's of Main Street, Granard Town. Patrick at James Smith's (62) of Main Street, Granard Town. Owen at Reilly's of New Road, Granard Town. Bridget at Michael Smyth's (13) of The Hill, Granard Town. Thomas and Mary at John Clarke's of Mollyglass. Felix at Campbell's of Rosduff. Patrick at Mary McKeon's of Smear. Thomas at Bridget Kiernan's of Smear. Kate at John Reilly's (34) of Drumhalry. Ellen at Curry's of Aghanoran. Ellen at Carty's of Larkfield. Kate at Thomas Masterson's of Edgeworthstown Town. Michael at Quinn's of Edgeworthstown Town. William at Devany's of Aghadowry. Sarah at Moorhead's of Creelaghta. Philip at Reilly's of Aghamore Lower. Patrick et al. at Pettit's of Annagh (Drumgort D.E.D.). Elizabeth at John Cooney's of Barragh Beg. Mary at McDonnell's of Drumlish. Patrick at Thompson's of Drumlish Village. Catherine at Connolly's of Brocklagh. Elizabeth at Farrington's of Newtownforbes Village. Joseph at Clarke's of Cloonrallagh. Mary at James Kenny's of Cloonrallagh. John at Hughes's of Clontumpher. Hugh at Maguire's of Esker South. Patrick at Cosgrove's of Soran. Hugh at Coyle's of Soran. Mathew at Peter Reynolds's of Soran. Thomas at Allen's of Ballymacwilliam. Michael at Clarke's of Ballymahon Street, Longford Town. Joseph at Hanley's of Dublin Street, Longford Town. Peter at Jones's of Dublin Street, Longford Town.

BRANDON: John at Caltragh Beg.

BRANNON: Catherine, James, John at Cooleeny. *ALSO:* James at McGovern's of Cooleeny. (See Brennan).

BRATTON: Mary, James at Kiltyreher (Killoe Civil Ph.).

BRAY: Bridget and Christina at Farrington's of Newtownforbes Village.

BREDIN, BREADEN: John at Currycreaghan. Andrew at Clooncallow. Thomas at Great Water Street, Longford Town.

BREE: John at Granard Barracks.

BREEN: Patrick at Corglass. *ALSO:* Anne at Lefroy's of Carrickglass Demesne (Templemichael Civil Ph.).

BRENNAN:(31): James at Daroge. Michael at Derraghan Beg. James at Claras. James at Cornadowagh. Mary at Drumnee. Patrick at Fortwilliam. Bridget at Clawinch Island. (Cashel West D.E.D.). Mary A. at Derrymacar. John at Drummeel. Thomas at Tennyphobble. Patrick, Thomas at Muckerstaff. Patrick at Barne. Bernard, Owen at Creelaghta. Timothy at Fardrumman. John at Currygranny. Catherine at Greagh. James at Cloonart South. Henry at Lisnabo. Kate at Aghnagore. Peter at Ballyclare (Moydow D.E.D.). Margaret at Newtown (Moydow D.E.D.). Thomas, Michael at Lismacmanus. Catherine, James, John at Cooleeny (?). John, Thomas at Coach Yard, Longford Town. Ellen at Hyde's Yard, Longford Town. *ALSO:* Kate at Richard Egan's of Mornin. James et al. at Mahedy's of Cornadowagh. James et al. at Greene's of Greenhall Lower. Ellen et al. at John Connaughton's of Cullentragh (Rathcline Civil Ph.). Elizabeth at Barden's of Main Street, Keenagh Village. Timothy at Patrick Brady's of Ballinrooey. James at McGovern's of Cooleeny (?). Patrick at Toole's of Dublin Street, Longford Town. John at Whelan's of Harbour Row, Longford Town. Patrick at King's of Main Street, Longford Town. (See Brannon).

BRESLIN: Edward at Shanmullagh. Joseph at Enybegs. John, Michael at Esker South. *ALSO:* Mary at Mernagh's of Shanmullagh.

BRETT: Michael at Tirlickeen. Patrick at Derryad (Mountdavis D.E.D.). *ALSO:* James at Mary Lenahan's of Castlerea Mountain. Patrick at McGaver's of Cloontamore.

BRIDE: Arthur S. at Heany's of Toome (Ballymahon D.E.D.).

McBRIDE: Peter at Fee's Terrace, Longford Town. *ALSO:* Catherine at Montgomery's of Glebe (Cloondara D.E.D.). Michael at Reilly's of Richmond Street, Longford Town.

BRIEN, BRYAN: J. at Dowler's of Edgeworthstown Town. Bridget at McCusker's of Harbour Row, Longford Town.

McBRIEN: Patrick, Hugh at Mullinroe. John, Patrick at Corglass.

O'BRIEN:(18): Anne at Tennalick. Edwin at Daroge. Barbara at Creevagh Beg, Ballymahon Town. Patrick at Aghnacranagh. Andrew at Aghnacliff. Anne at Cartronamarkey. William at Killeen (Bunlahy D.E.D.). John at Ballyboy. Bridget at Cloonaghmore. John at Rincoolagh. Patrick at Barrack Street, Granard Town. Bartholomew at Smear. Patrick at Clonca. Catherine at Drumlish Village. James at Ballagh (Newtownforbes D.E.D.). David at Cahanagh. Kate at Creenagh. Catherine at Esker South. *ALSO:* James at Julia Fox's of Aghakilmore. James at Lynch's of Ballinrooey. James at Kane's of Abbeylara Village. Annie at Stephenson's of Ballinlough. Patrick at Reilly's of New Road, Granard Town. John at McGovern's of Farmullagh. Catherine at Gilchriest's of Cranalagh More. Patrick at Creegan's of Leggagh. G.F. at Duncan McGregor's of Lisbrack (Longford Rural D.E.D.). Margaret M. at John McCormack's of Dublin Street, Longford Town. C. at Hewetson's of Church Street, Longford Town.

BRIODY:(15): John at Aghacordrinan (?). Hugh at Ballinrooey. James at Cartronbore. Patrick at Aghnagarron. Patrick at Rossan. Hugh, Patrick at Killasona. Mary, Peter at Corbaun or Leitrim. Anne, Alice, Peter at Toome (Mullanalaghta D.E.D.). Peter at Corrinagh. Thomas at Moyne. Thomas at Leggagh. *ALSO:* James at Gilsenan's of Kilbride. Mary at Caffrey's of Tober. Philip at Newman's of Cloghchurnel. Patrick at McGivney's of Kilmore. Fanny at Brady's of Fardrumman. Rosetta at Matthew Brady's of Kiltycon.

BRIORDY: John at Aghacordrinan.

BRISCOE: Edward at Moydow Glebe.

BROCK: Emily at Cartroncar.

BRODERICK: Mary at Corry (Kilglass D.E.D.). Patrick at Rathcline. *ALSO:* Edward at McCabe's of Edgeworthstown Town.

BROGAN: Thomas at Abbeylara Village. *ALSO:* William at Reilly's of New Road, Granard Town. Thomas at Coyle's of Camagh (Newgrove D.E.D.). Christopher at John W. Sheridan's of Camagh (Newgrove D.E.D.). Elizabeth at Fegan's of Ballaghgowla and Froghan. Edward at Maguire's of Ballymahon Street, Longford Town.

BROOKS: Fred at Sullivan's of Main Street, Granard Town. James at Muir's of Edgeworthstown Town.

BROWNE, BROWN:(16): Thomas at Kilcurry. John at Ballymahon Town. John at Streamstown (Cashel East D.E.D.). Rev. John at Glebe (Cashel West D.E.D.). Mary at Kilshruley. Rev. Charles at Vicarsfield Glebe. Robert at Kiltyclogh. Francis at Killeen (Bunlahy D.E.D.). Francis at Leitrim (Granard Rural D.E.D.). Patrick at Teemore. Luke at Aghaboy (Milltown D.E.D.). Lizzie at Cooldoney. Anne at Currygranny. Jane at Killashee Village. Christopher at Creeve. William at Templemichael Glebe. *ALSO:* Mary M. at Coffey's of Cloonard (Ballymahon D.E.D.). Mary at Anne Reilly's of Cartron (Granard Rural D.E.D.). Sr. Annie at Sr. Hoare's of Grassyard. James at Kiernan's of Cooldoney. Mary A. at Elliott's of Fihoragh. Catherine at Courtney's of Edgeworthstown Town. Anne at Farrington's of Newtownforbes Village. Martin at Neill's of Middleton. Arthur at Potterton's of Templemichael Glebe. Patrick at O'Connor's of

Conroy's Court, Longford Town. Elizabeth at McQuaid's of Great Water Street, Longford Town. Honor at Felix Larkin's of Main Street, Longford Town.

BRUEN: Ellen at Cloncowley.

BRUSH: Elizabeth at Strong's of Ballybrien.

BRYAN: See Brien.

BUCHAN: Christina at Cameron's of Main Street, Longford Town.

BUCHANAN: Margaret at Killashee and Aghakeeran.

BUCKLEY: Thomas at Cloontagh.

BULL: William at Newcastle.

BURBAGE, BURBIDGE: James at Barrack Street, Granard Town. Anne at New Road, Granard Town. Thomas at Tuite's Lane, Granard Town. Edward at Greagh. John J. at Drumlish Village. Margaret at Newtownforbes Village. Edward at Cloonageeher. Charles at Clooncolligan. David at Tully (Cloondara D.E.D.). *ALSO:* Bridget at John Murta's of Main Street, Granard Town. Kate at Conlon's of New Road, Granard Town. Michael at Farrell's of Aughine.

BURD: Henry S. at Ballymahon Town. (See Bird).

BOURKE: Mary at Cloondara. Samuel at Dublin Street, Longford Town.

BURKE:(24): John at Rathsallagh. Patrick at Doory. Thomas, Thomas at Ballymaclifford. Richard at Rockpeyton. Anne at Castlecore. Anne at Ballymahon Town. Edward at Toome (Ballymahon D.E.D.). Patrick at Lismacmurrogh. Patrick at Foygh. Thomas at Killeen (Bunlahy D.E.D.). Henry at Lissanure. James at Rinnenny. Francis at Edgeworthstown Town. Kate at Prucklish. Patrick at Caldragh. Henry at Fihoges. Elizabeth at Cloondara. Elizabeth at Glebe (Cloondara D.E.D.). Thomas at Slieve. Joseph at Aghnaskea. James at Killeter. Peter at Main Street, Longford Town. Peter at Townparks (Longford Urban No. 1 D.E.D.). *ALSO:* Ellen at Connell's of Killeen (Bunlahy D.E.D.). William at Reynolds's of Killasona. Anne at Peter J. Joyce's of Edgeworthstown Town. Srs. Bridget, Annie and Mary at Rev. Mother Farrington's of Newtownforbes Village. Gregory at Magan's of Killashee Village. Thomas at Michael Farrell's of Lanesborough Village. Christopher at Callahan's of Esker South. Fr. Michael at O'Farrell's of Moor. Bridget at Kilkelly's of Lisnamuck. John at Quinn's of Earl Street, Longford Town. Michael at Plunkett's of Main

Street, Longford Town. Patrick at Abbeycartron Barracks. Mary at O'Connell's of Demesne.

BURLEIGH, BURLEY: George T. at Lisbrack (Longford Rural D.E.D.).

BURNETT: Susan, John at Cornamucklagh. George, Samuel at Abbeyderg. John at Ballymahon Road, Keenagh Village. Andrew at Lisnageeragh. Andrew at Clontumpher. *ALSO:* Georgina at Sarah Corry's of Keel (Kilglass D.E.D.). Anne at Rhatigan's of Camlisk More. Maggie at Whyte's of Drumlish Village. Thomas at Fetherston's of Newtownforbes Village. Charles W. at Boyers' (2) of Main Street, Longford Town. Lizzie A. at Boyers' (4) of Main Street, Longford Town.

BURNS:(32): Patrick at Treel (Foxhall D.E.D.). John at Ballycloghan. Patrick at Ballyglassin. John, Thomas at Screeboge. Patrick at Daroge. Edward at Tirlickeen. John at Lislom. Patrick at Rathmore (Ballymahon D.E.D.). Edward, Patrick at Edera. Bernard at Glenoghil. Patrick at Glannagh. Anne, Ellen, Terence, Michael, Catherine, Mary at Druminacrehir. Bernard at Aghnagarron. Patrick at Rincoolagh. Bernard at Cartron (Granard Rural D.E.D.). James, John, Mary E., James W. at Main Street, Granard Town. Charles at the Hill, Granard Town. James at Water Lane, Granard Town. Joseph at Edgeworthstown Town. Rose at Newtownforbes Village. Edward at Lisduff (Ardagh East D.E.D.). Phoebe at Main Street, Longford Town. *ALSO:* John and Bridget at Peter Clyne's of Ballymahon Town. Mary at Patrick McGrath's of Edera. Michael at Donohoe's of Ball Alley Street Lower, Granard Town. Kate and Marsella at Toher's of Lackan. (See Beirne, Byrne).

BUSHELL: Michael at Campbell's Row, Longford Town. Sarah at Killashee Street, Longford Town.

BUTLER: Francis, Frederick at Ratharney. Richard at Kildordan. Stephen at Cartronageeragh. *ALSO:* Edward and Thomas at William Fitzmaurice's of Ballymahon Town. Patrick at Bridget Sweeney's of Derrygowna. Delia at Mary E. Burns' of Main Street, Granard Town. Mary at Farrington's of Newtownforbes Village. Patrick at O'Connor's of Main Street, Longford Town. Elizabeth at Hanratty's of St. Mel's Road, Longford Town.

BUTTIMORE: Elizabeth at James Farrell's of Glack (Longford Rural D.E.D.).

BYE: Hannah L. et al. at Forster's of Aghnashannagh.

BYRNE:(16): Elizabeth at Drumanure. Thomas at Keel (Forgney D.E.D.). John at Tennalick. Sarah at Ballybranigan. William at Creevagh Beg. William at Clogh (Kilcommock D.E.D.). William at Lislea (Lislea D.E.D.).

Catherine at Abbeylara Village. Catherine at Dring. Simon at Kilfintan. Michael at Shanmullagh. John at Derryheelan. Patrick, Bernard at Edercloon. Patrick at Kiltyreher (Templemichael Civil Ph.). Bernard at Great Water Street, Longford Town. *ALSO:* Anne at Fee's of Killinbore. Agnes at Ann Martin's of Ballymahon Town. Bridget at Rafferty's of Rathmore (Ballymahon D.E.D.). Philip at Briordy's of Aghacordrinan. Mary K. at Michael Kiernan's of Main Street, Granard Town. James at Mary Dennan's of Derrycassan. Mary at Michael Greene's of Lissanure. Andrew at Martin's of Edgeworthstown Town. James at Ward's of Edgeworthstown Town. Anne at Herson's of Lettergullion. Mary A., Elizabeth and Sarah, Mary A. and Anne at Farrington's of Newtownforbes Village. Mary and John at Sheridan's of Cloonbalt. Thomas at Moorcroft's of Kiltyreher (Templemichael Civil Ph.). Agnes A. at James Farrell's of Glack (Longford Rural D.E.D.). Margaret at Ussher-Roberts' of Knockahaw. Patrick J. at Robinson's of Earl Street, Longford Town. (See Beirne, Burns).

O'BYRNE: A. at Hewetson's of Church Street, Longford Town.

McCABE:(46): Hugh at Aghacordrinan. Bridget at Aghagreagh. Felix at Aghamore Upper. Edward, Peter, John at Derreenavoggy. Myles at Gelshagh. Anne, Owen at Aghakine. Mary, Mary at Aghnacliff. John at Sonnagh. Michael at Tober. Anne at Clooneen (Creevy D.E.D.). James at Culleenmore. Margaret at Aghnagarron. Catherine, John at Cloghchurnel. Charles at Carrickduff. Charles, Bridget at Dalystown. Patrick at Rathbrackan. Thomas, Patrick at Cartron (Granard Rural D.E.D.). Mary, Bridget at Bank Street, Granard Town. Thomas at Barrack Street, Granard Town. John at Drumhalry. Sarah, Patrick, Mary at Aghanoran. Patrick, Patrick at Derrycassan. Thomas, Patrick at Toome (Mullanalaghta D.E.D.). Felix at Lisnageeragh. Madge at Edgeworthstown Town. Mary at Cloonback. John at Cuingareen. Bernard at Corglass. Francis at Cornacullew. Mary at Garvary. Patrick at Cartrongolan. Patrick at Lismoy. John, Michael at Esker South. *ALSO:* Katie at John Connolly's of France. Patrick at William Denniston's (9) of Drummeel. Bernard and Kate at Owen Reilly's of Molly. Rose at Cox's of Cranally. Ellie at Maria Donohoe's of Springtown. Maggie at James Cooke's of Tober. Mary at Wrenn's of Coolcor. Mary at Clarke's of Druminacrehir. Mathew at Reynold's of Dalystown. Rose at Masterson's of Rinroe. Elizabeth at Monahan's of Balnagall (Granard Urban D.E.D.). Patrick at Hyland's of Barrack Street, Granard Town. Maggie at John Macken's of Muckerstaff. Bridget at Peter Masterson's of Enaghan. Mary at Dopping-Hepenstal's of Derrycassan. James et al. at Hugh Higgins's of Rathmore (Ballinamuck East D.E.D.). Mary at Mahon's of Aghamore Lower. Peter at Bridget Kelly's of Kilnacarrow (Aghaboy D.E.D.). Mathew at Donohoe's of Killoe Glebe. Elizabeth at Carney's of Great Water Street, Longford Town. Margaret at Kate Brady's of Main Street, Longford Town.

CADAM: Owen at Molly. *ALSO:* Luke at Charles Murphy's of Fostragh.

CADAMS: Silvester at Hosey's of Edgeworthstown Town.

CADDEN: Thomas at Moxham Street, Granard Town. (See McAden).

CADDOW: William at Lissanurlan. *ALSO:* Henry at Arthur Holmes's of Kilmore Lower.

CAFFREY: Denis, Patrick at Abbeylara Village. Edward at Tober. Patrick at Clooneen (Creevy D.E.D.). Bernard at Ballyboy. Patrick at Carragh (Granard Urban D.E.D.). Michael at Edgeworthstown Town. Patrick at Greagh. *ALSO:* Maggie at Ryan's of Drumnacor. John at Cosgrove's of Gelshagh. Elizabeth at Hugh Sullivan's of Aghakine. Denis at Noble's of Tonymore North. Mary at Hanlon's of Culleenmore. James at Flood's of Killasona. Lizzie at Jones's of Earl Street, Longford Town.

McCAFFREY: James at Gorteenclareen. John at Ball Alley Street Lower, Granard Town. *ALSO:* Helena at Clarke's of Lanesborough Village.

McCAGHAN: Mary A. at Hughes's of Carrowbeg (Drumlish D.E.D.).

CAHALAN: Patrick L. at Taghshinny.

CAHERLY: Patrick at Killeter. Owen at Mucknagh.

CAHILL:(24): John at Ardanragh. John at Liscormick. Michael at Sheeroe (Kilglass D.E.D.). Michael at Tennalick. Rev. Francis, Anne at Ballymahon Town. Thomas at Garvagh (Currygrane D.E.D.). Ellen, Patrick, at Aghagreagh. Patrick, Thomas at Lislea (Lislea D.E.D.). Anne at Killasona. Thomas at Aghamore (Coolamber D.E.D.). James at Lackan. Elizabeth at Edgeworthstown Town. Rev. Patrick at Leggagh. Patrick, John at Lismoy. Margaret at Ballinreaghan. James at Cornapark. William at Lisnamuck. Bridget at Great Water Street, Longford Town. James at Harbour Row, Longford Town. Annie at St. Michael's Road, Longford Town. *ALSO:* Patrick and Mary at Campbell's of Abbeyshrule. Margaret at John Burns' of Screeboge. Thomas at Catherine Moran's of Tennalick. Rose A. at Francis Flower's of Barry (Ballymahon D.E.D.). John and Mary at Reynolds's of Ballinalee Village. Thomas at O'Neill's of Lislea (Lislea D.E.D.). James at Dalton's of Aghnagarron. Eugene at Patrick Donohoe's of Drumard. Cornelius at Latimer's of Castlenugent. Julia at Dolan's of Bracklon. John and Margaret at McKenna's of Edgeworthstown Town. Mary at Langan's of Edgeworthstown Town. Rose at Casey's of Derryharrow. Mary at Gordon's of Demesne.

CAINEN: Michael at Cornollen.

CAIRNS: Jane at McKenzie's of Earl Street, Longford Town.

CALDWELL: Simon, Thomas at Glenoghil. Robert at Lissameen. James at Glannagh. William at Tennyphobble. Bernard at Granardkill (Granard Urban D.E.D.). Mary at Graffoge (Milltown D.E.D.). John at Cloonmacart. Rev. Samuel E. at Corboy. *ALSO:* Maggie at Kingstone's of Mosstown (Rathcline Barony). Mary at McCormack's of Tully (Cloondara D.E.D.). Ellen at O'Donnell's of Soran.

CALERY: See Collery.

CALLAGHAN, CALLAHAN: (14): Mary at Garvagh (Currygrane D.E.D.). Peter at Lissameen. Patrick at Lisnagerragh. Michael at Castleforbes Demesne. Joseph at Newtownforbes Village. Bernard at Esker South. Patrick at Coolcaw. William at Drumhaughly. Thomas at Coach Yard, Longford Town. Mary, Mary A. at Dublin Street, Longford Town. John at Main Street, Longford Town. Mathew at Richmond Street, Longford Town. John at St. Mel's Road, Longford Town. *ALSO:* Patrick at Conroy's of Prucklishtown. Bridget at Mahon's of Kilcourcey. Patrick at Denis Eivers' of Kilcourcey.

O'CALLAGHAN: Sophie at Ballyduffy.

CALLARAN: Patrick at Ballymahon Town.

CALLERY: See Collery.

McCALLEY: Margaret at Patrick Fennan's of Barrack Street, Granard Town.

CALLWELL, CALWELL: See Caldwell.

CALVERT: Margaret at Abbeycartron.

CAMERON: Donald at Main Street, Longford Town.

CAMP: Charlotte G. at Abbeycartron.

CAMPBELL:(36): Martin at Abbeyshrule. John at Lislom. Bernard at Lislea (Lislea D.E.D.). Anne at Aghnacliff. Ellen at Rathcronan. Patrick at Muckerstaff. John at Rosduff. John at Clonca. James at Keelogenasause. Peter, James at Fardrumman. Francis at Prucklish. Anne at Cloonagh (Breanrisk D.E.D.). John at Garvary. Mary at Barragh Beg. John J. at Bohernameeltoge. Bernard at Enybegs. James, Alexander at Oghil. James at Brocklagh. Elizabeth at Gaigue. James at Ballydrum. Thomas at Aghaboy (Aghaboy D.E.D.). Terence at Corneddan. Patrick at Lenaboy. Lizzie A. at

Corradooey. Thomas at Farraghroe. Peter at Killeter. Alicia at Killyfad. Mary at Farranyoogan. Ellen at Chapel Lane, Longford Town. Mary at Killashee Street, Longford Town. James, Patrick at Noud's Yard, Longford Town. Michael at Richmond Street, Longford Town. Joseph at St. Mel's Road, Longford Town. *ALSO:* Rose at O'Brien's of Tennalick. James at Alice O'Reilly's of Aghakine. Francis at Kate Mulligan's of Aghnacliff. Owen at John Macken's of Muckerstaff. John at Flaherty's of Glenmore (Ballinamuck East D.E.D.). Mary A. at Duignan's of Shanmullagh. Peter and Maria at Patrick McGarry's of Leitrim (Breanrisk D.E.D.). Bridget at James Sheridan's of Moyne. Anne at Brady's of Brocklagh. Mary A. at McWade's of Gaigue. John J. at Jane Shaw's of Cloonageeher. Sr. Mary A. at Sr. Green's of Convent Lane, Longford Town.

CANAVAN, CANNIVAN: James at Gorteen. Mary at Edgeworthstown Town. John, Patrick, Bernard at Cartrongolan. Rose A. at Farranyoogan. Winifred at Chapel Lane, Longford Town. *ALSO:* John at Winifred Reilly's of Castlenugent.

CANE: Mary A. at John L. Brady's of Main Street, Granard Town. Mary A. and Patrick at Confrey's of Enybegs. (See Kane).

McCANN:(33): Harry at Tirlickeen. Patrick at Cloontagh. Patrick at Leitrim (Breanrisk D.E.D.). Patrick, Richard, James at Aghnamaddoo. Catherine, James, Bridget at Ballincurry. Michael at Bawn (Breanrisk D.E.D.). Francis, Michael, Bernard, Mary, James, Bernard, Thomas at Cloonagh (Breanrisk D.E.D.). Elizabeth, Michael at Carrowbeg (Drumlish D.E.D.). Thomas at Enybegs. Mary at Ballagh (Achmuty). Bernard at Briskil. Owen at Treel (Newtownforbes D.E.D.). Michael at Newtownforbes Village. James at Creenagh. Catherine at Ballykenny. Nicholas at Toneen (Moydow D.E.D.). Patrick at Cloonee. Patrick, Michael at Ballymahon Street, Longford Town. Patrick at Dublin Street, Longford Town. Harry at Keon's Terrace, Longford Town. Edward at Abbeycartron. *ALSO:* Charles at Kate Whelan's of Ballymahon Town. Kate at McNally's of Cornadowagh. Mary A. at Lynch's of Polladooey. Patrick at Devine's of Bawn (Breanrisk D.E.D.). Mary A. at Green's of Convent Lane, Longford Town. Edward at James Joyce's of Main Street, Longford Town. James at Felix Larkin's of Main Street, Longford Town. (See McConn, McGann).

CANNING: James at Killeenboy. John at Smithfield. John at Cloncowley. Charles at Kilmacannon. James at Knockloughlin. *ALSO:* Mary at Thomas Duncan's of Ballymahon Town. Elizabeth at Thomas Duff's of Ballymahon Town.

CANNIVAN: See Canavan.

CANNON: Patrick at Mulligan's of Aghakilmore.

CARBERRY, CARBERY: Bridget, Peter at Derraghan More. John at Glebe (Cloondara D.E.D.). Francis at Knockagowny. *ALSO:* James et al. at Lawrence's of Laughil (Kilcommock D.E.D.). Rose and Maggie at Edward Mulligan's of Ballywillin. Maria and Elizabeth at Farrington's of Newtownforbes Village. Ellen at Patrick Feeney's of Cloondara. Edward and Kate at Fannin's of Cartronageeragh. William at John Mathews' of Main Street, Longford Town. Patrick at Cameron's of Main Street, Longford Town.

CAREY: Patrick at Cornahoo (?). Patrick, George at Monascallaghan. James at Church Street, Longford Town. *ALSO:* Patrick at Thompson's of Newcastle. Georgina at Patrick Doyle's of Ballymahon Town. Bernard at Michael Thompson's of Ballymahon Street, Longford Town. (See Keary).

CARLETON: William at Culloge.

CARLEY: Patrick, John, John at Portanure. Owen at Aghaboy (Aghaboy D.E.D.). *ALSO:* John at James Hughes's (18) of Soran.

CARLIN, CARLON: See Carolan.

CARLOS: James at Tennalick. John at Cloonbony. *ALSO:* Sarah et al. at Rafferty's of Deerpark (Newtownforbes D.E.D.). Mary K. at Burke's of Main Street, Longford Town.

CARMODY: Mary M. at Green's of Convent Lane, Longford Town.

CARNEY:(14): Thomas at Currycreaghan. James at Aghnavealoge. Michael at Lurgan. Bernard at Lisnacreevy. Catherine at Kilsallagh. James at Edgeworthstown Town. Mary at Kiltycreevagh. Michael at Lisrevagh. Mary, John at Cartronawar (Corboy D.E.D.). Francis at Cloontirm. Catherine at Cloonturk. Mary at Chapel Lane. Longford Town. John at Great Water Street, Longford Town. *ALSO:* Daniel at Skelly's of Corrool (Kenny). Rose at Fitzsimons' of Carrickateane. John at Pettit's of Main Street, Granard Town. Thomas at Knockloughlin Barracks. Kate at Flaherty's of Cloontirm. Farrell at Boyhan's of Killashee Street, Longford Town. Thomas at Abbeycartron Barracks (?). (See Kearney).

CAROLAN, CARLON:(16): Michael at Ballymahon Town. Bernard, Mary at Culray. John at Grassyard. Anne at Silver Street, Granard Town. Bridget at Farmullagh. Michael at Ballincurry. Mary at Cloonagh (Breanrisk D.E.D.). Bernard, John at Cloonmacart. John at Bohernameeltoge. John at Drumlish. James, Patrick at Oghil. Bernard at Drumlish Village. James at Minard. *ALSO:* James at Hargadon's of Culray. Catherine at Charles Connolly's of Aghakine. Mary E. at Bernard Reilly's of Killeen (Bunlahy D.E.D.). Mary at Burke's of Prucklish. Catherine at Rose Mimnagh's of

Kilnashee. Mary at Harte's of Ballymahon Street, Longford Town. John at Wynne's of Great Water Street, Longford Town. Lizzie at Cooney's of Main Street, Longford Town.

CAROTHERS: John F. at Abbeycartron. (See McCrothers).

CARR: John at Ball Alley Street Lower, Granard Town. James at Newtownforbes Village. Edward at Aghinaspick. *ALSO:* Catherine at Curley's of Drumnacross. Elizabeth at Michael Farrell's (4) of Cartron (Granard Rural D.E.D.). John at Donlon's of Abbeycartron. (See Corr, Kerr).

CARREY: Patrick at Cornahoo.

CARRIGY, CARRIAGY:(17): Michael at Castlerea Mountain. John at Curraghmore. Charles at Mornin. Bridget at Torboy. Mary at Ballymaclifford. Patrick at Aghnasillagh. Thomas, James at Ballycloghan. Michael at Knocknaskea. Richard at Glenoghil. Michael at Aghaward. Michael at Tonywardan. Bernard at Freaghmeen. Francis at Cloonevit. Matthew at Clooncoose (Cloonee D.E.D.). Patrick at Killeenatruan. Patrick at Killeter. *ALSO:* Mary at Farrell's of Aghnasillagh. Patrick at Bridget Dawson's of Leitrim (Granard Rural D.E.D.). Michael et al. at Gelshinan's of Robinstown. Bernard at Dawson's of Barrack Street, Granard Town. Matthew at Mahon's of Killeter.

CARROLL:(12): Margaret, John at Clontymullan. Patrick at Tennalick. Kate M. at Barrack Street, Granard Town. Rody at Aghaboy (Milltown D.E.D.). Edward at Tully (Cloondara D.E.D.). Michael at Rathcline. Anne at Cornapark. Francis at Meeltanagh (Ardagh East D.E.D.). John at Oldtown. John at St. Mel's Road, Longford Town. William at St. Michael's Road, Longford Town. *ALSO:* Thomas at Granard Barracks. Michael at Nangle's of Lanesborough Village. Charles at John Dooner's of Cartrongarrow. Mary at Thomas Dennigan's of Cartronageeragh. Elizabeth at James Farrell's of Glack (Longford Rural D.E.D.). Patrick at James Brady's of Main Street, Longford Town.

O'CARROLL: Albert H. at John Casey's of Lanesborough Village. Michael at O'Leary's of Dublin Street, Longford Town. James at Gilhooly's of Keon's Terrace, Longford Town.

CARSON: William at Island. Joseph at Aghaward. Joseph at Drumderg. John at Glenmore (Ballinamuck East D.E.D.).

McCARTAN, McCARTIN, McCARTON: Elizabeth at Newtownforbes Village. Elizabeth at Demesne. *ALSO:* Kate at Devine's of Kiltycreevagh. Kate at Peter Farrell's of Great Water Street, Longford Town.

CARTER, CARTERS: Michael at Ball Alley Street Upper, Granard Town. Sarah at Cleenrah. *ALSO:* Florence at Edward Reehil's of Carrickadorrish. Bessie at Boylan's of Ball Alley Street Upper, Granard Town. Mary at Macken's of Barrack Street, Granard Town. J.H. at Hewetson's of Church Street, Longford Town. (See Charters).

CARTHY: See Carty.

McCARTHY:(13): Hugh, Francis, Patrick at Aghagreagh. Robert at Leitrim (Granard Rural D.E.D.). John, Michael, Joseph, Patrick at Aghadowry. Thomas at Bawn (Breanrisk D.E.D.). Mary at Carrickglass Demesne (Killoe Civil Ph.). Patrick at Drumhaughly. John at Farraghroe. Margaret at Rhine. *ALSO:* James at Thomas Kiernan's of Barrack Street, Granard Town. Mary at Martin's of Edgeworthstown Town. John at Ward's of Edgeworthstown Town. James at Winifred McGuiness's of Aghaboy (Aghaboy D.E.D.). Elizabeth at Margaret Kenny's of Main Street, Longford Town. Mary A. et al. at Lyons's of Noud's Yard, Longford Town.

McCARTIN: See McCartan.

McCARTNEY: James at Barrack Street, Granard Town.

McCARTON: See McCartan

CARTWRIGHT: Julia at Julia Mulligan's of Culray. Mary K. at Gormley's of Birrinagh.

CARTY, CARTHY:(20): John at Kilglass and Cloonagh. John, Hugh at Aghagreagh. John at Castlebaun. Patrick at Lislea (Lislea D.E.D.). Ellen at Cartronbore. John at Enaghan. Bridget at Cloonagh (Mullanalaghta D.E.D.). Catherine at Larkfield. Patrick at Lisnageeragh. Edward at Longfield. Charles at Bracklon. Patrick at Cloncowley. John at Drumbad. Mary at Currygranny. Maria at Doonameran. Bridget, Catherine at Aghanahown. Patrick at Corboy. Michael at St. Michael's Road, Longford Town. *ALSO:* Thomas at Thomas Masterson's of Edgeworthstown Town. Rose at James Joyce's of Main Street, Longford Town. (See Garty).

CASEY:(80): Patrick at Lissawarriff. James at Forgney. John at Clooncullen. Patrick at Aghnavealoge. Bridget at Carrickedmond. Ellen at Tennalick. William at Cloonkeen (Ballymahon D.E.D.). Patrick at Tirlickeen. John, Patrick at Ballymahon Town. Thomas at Cloonard (Ballymahon D.E.D.). Edward at Creevagh Beg. Ballymahon Town. Peter at Barry (Ballymahon D.E.D.). Matthew at Derrynaskea. Bridget at Caltragh Beg. Michael at Cormaglava. Bernard, Thomas, James at Derraghan More. John at Forthill. Thomas at Ballagh (Cashel West D.E.D.). John, James, Elizabeth at Claras. Mary, Joseph, Thomas James at Cornadowagh. Bridget at Corrool (Brennan). Bridget at Aghaward. Patrick at Springtown. Patrick at Breanrisk. James at Oghil. Patrick, Elizabeth, William at Ballagh (Newtownforbes D.E.D.). Peter at Derryharrow. John at Tully (Cloondara D.E.D.). Anne, Kate at Glebe (Cloondara D.E.D.). Peter at Knappoge (Cloondara D.E.D.). John, Patrick at Corragarrow (Killashee D.E.D.). Mary at Killashee and Aghakeeran. Patrick, Thomas at Killeeny. Michael, Michael, Martin at Cloonbrock. Edward at Cloonkeel. Anne at Rappareehill. John, James at Cloonfore. Patrick, James, John at Derryloughbannow. Denis, Mary, John at Magheraveen. Patrick at Toneen (Moydow D.E.D.). James at Cashelbeg. John at Lisrevagh. John, Michael at Lanesborough Village. Thomas at Ballygar. William at Ballywalter. Catherine at Lyanmore. Mary at Breany. Patrick at Cloontirm. Patrick at Mullaghavorneen. Michael at Cooleeny. Teresa, Lizzie at Dublin Street, Longford Town. Annie, John at Great Water Street, Longford Town. Luke at Healy's Terrace, Longford Town. William at Killashee Street, Longford Town. Michael at St. Mel's Road, Longford Town. Bridget, Peter at St. Michael's Road, Longford Town. *ALSO:* Maggie M. at Keenan's of Cloonscott. Catherine at Mahon's of Clooncallow. Mary K. at John Nolan's of Ballygibbagh. Mary at Joseph Gannon's of Ballymahon Town. John at John Gill's of Ballymahon Town. Patrick at Skally's of Aghavadden. Bridget at Dunne's of Elfeet (Adamson). Patrick et al. at Michael Tiernan's of Greenhall Upper. Thomas at Connor's of Tipper (Cashel West D.E.D.). Mary at John Dillon's (1) of Ballyreaghan. Bernard at Finnan's of Liscahill. Edward at Keville's of Drumlish Village. Mary at McQuaid's of Drumlish Village. Catherine at Devany's of Treel (Newtownforbes D.E.D.). John at Patrick Farrell's of Aghnagore. Patrick at Joseph Gouldsbury's of Cloonbrock. Kate at Patrick Shanley's (2) of Derryad (Mountdavis D.E.D.). Mary at Murray's of Corralough. Thomas at Manning's of Cornapark. Elizabeth at Tiernan's of Clooneeny. John at O'Connor's of Conroy's Court, Longford Town. Winifred at Kiernan's of Little Water Street, Longford Town. Lizzie at Gallagher's of Main Street, Longford Town. Thomas at Abbeycartron Barracks (?).

CASH: Peter at Deerpark (Newtownforbes D.E.D.).

CASHIN: Patrick at Aghnamaddoo. (See Cassin).

McCASHIN: Joseph at Kate Brady's of Main Street, Longford Town.

CASSEDY: See Cassidy.

CASSELLS, CASSELL: Patrick at Forgney. John at Clooncullen. Andrew at Carrickedmond. Patrick at Cloonart North. *ALSO:* Thomas and Patrick at Lennon's of Torboy. Ellie et al. at Hannigan's of Main Street, Longford Town.

CASSERLY:(16): Mary at Ballagh (Cashel West D.E.D.). Bridget at Ballynahinch. James at Carrowrory. Patrick at Collum. William at Loughfarm. Michael at Glenmore (Kilcommock D.E.D.). Patrick at Kilcommock Glebe. Peter at Lislea (Lislea D.E.D.). Peter at Cloontagh. James at Drumlish Village. Mary at Ballagh (Newtownforbes D.E.D.). Thomas at Ballagh (Achmuty). John at Briskil. Thomas at Begnagh. Patrick at Cashelbeg. Patrick at Killyfad. *ALSO:* Michael at Reilly's of Forthill. Betsy at Patrick Hevehan's of Cloonmee. James at Feeney's of Barnacor (Rathcline D.E.D.). Susan at Dermody's of Creeve.

CASSIDY, CASSEDY:(22): James at Cloghan (Forgney D.E.D.). James at Ballymahon Town. Mary at Kilshruley. John at Mullinroe. John at Ball Alley Street Upper, Granard Town. William at Moxham Street, Granard Town. Michael at Camagh (Newgrove D.E.D.). Michael, Kate at Ballyduffy. John at Garryandrew. Francis, Mary, Thomas, Patrick, James, William, Thomas at Fardrumman. Patrick at Kiltycreevagh. Patrick at Shanmullagh. John, Patrick at Derryad (Mountdavis D.E.D.). Patrick at Chapel Lane, Longford Town. *ALSO:* Ann at Francis Cahill's of Ballymahon Town. Bridget at Lynch's of Polladooey. James at Sweeney's of Lisnageeragh. Michael at Larkin's of Drumlish Village. Mary and Anne at Farrington's of Newtownforbes Village. Honor at John Farrell's of Derryad (Mountdavis D.E.D.). Mary at Flynn's of Ballygarve. Nanny at Farrell's of Townparks (Longford Rural D.E.D.). Mary at McKenzie's of Earl Street, Longford Town. Lizzie at Maxwell's of Main Street, Longford Town.

CASSIN: Mathew at Knockloughlin Barracks. (See Cashin).

CASTLETON: James at Mitchell's of Curry (Kilcommock D.E.D.).

CATHCART: Peter at Ballyreaghan. Robert at Drumnacooha.

CAUGHLIN: See Coughlan.

McCAULEY, McAULEY: Kate M. at Abbeylara. James at Coolagherty. John at Sragarrow. Thomas at Cloonmore (?). John at Mountjessop. Henry at Mullaghavorneen. Thomas at St. Mel's Road, Longford Town. *ALSO:* Margaret at Kelly's of Kilcourcey. Margaret at Bond's of Newtownbond. Patrick at Carrigy's of Tonywardan. Joseph at Turner's of Ballaghgowla and Froghan. James at Michael Murphy's of Enybegs (?). Sarah at Atkinson's of Main Street, Longford Town. (See McCalley, Cawley).

CAULFIELD: Ellen at Clontymullan. Anna, Peter at Ballymahon Town. Ellen at Barnacor (Ledwithstown D.E.D.). Bernard at Aghakilmore. *ALSO:* James and Mary at James Ryan's of Ballymahon Town. John at Dunican's of Drumnacor.

CAULTEE: Lizzie B. et al. at William White's of Castleforbes Demesne.

CAVANAGH: Margaret at Drinan. Anne at Ballynascraw. Daniel at Ballyduffy. Alice at Cloontamore. (See Kavanagh).

CAWFIELD: See Caulfield.

CAWLEY: Minnie at Reardon's of Drumroe. (See McCauley).

CEARY: See Keary.

CHAPMAN: Patrick at Lisnacush. Patrick, Margaret at Lissawly or St. Albans. Margaret at Dublin Street, Longford Town. George J. at Keon's Terrace, Longford Town.

CHARTERS: Richard, David, Robert at Garvagh (Currygrane D.E.D.). James at The Hill, Granard Town. William at Lissavaddy. (See Carters).

CHEASTY: Catherine at Hassett's of Lissanisky (Ballymahon D.E.D.).

CHEEVERS, CHIEVERS: Anne at Farrelly's of Springtown.

CHRISTIE, CHRISTY: Mary, Anne at Drumlish Village. Patrick at Newtownforbes Village. Isabella at Gorteenorna. Bridget at Abbeycartron.

CHRYSTAL: William at Killashee Street, Longford Town.

CLABBY:(10): John at Drumlish. Ellen at Clogher and Rinn. John at Glebe (Cloondara D.E.D.). James at Aghnaskea. Patrick at Ballynakill. James at Aghintemple. Margaret, Anne at Feraghfad. Patrick at Cooleeny. Thomas at Great Water Street, Longford Town. *ALSO:* Catherine and Thomas at Patrick Farrell's of Aghnagore. Mary at Gouldsbury's of Glebe (Cloondara D.E.D.). Anne at Francis McCormack's of Cartronlebagh. Margaret at Corrigan's of Cooleeny. John at Molloy's of Ballymahon Street, Longford Town. James at Kelly's of Richmond Street, Longford Town.

CLAFFEY: Joseph at St. Mel's Road, Longford Town.

CLANCY: Francis at Drummeel. *ALSO:* Sr. Mary at Sr. Hoare's of Grassyard. Patrick at Edward Donohoe's (12) of Drumard. Thomas at Nevin's of Market Square, Longford Town. (See Glancy).

McCLANE: See McClean.

CLARE: Annie J. at Patrick Lee's (42) of Aghagreagh.

CLARKE:(57): Thomas at Abbeyshrule. Peter at Corrycorka. Mary at Mornin. Martin at Clooncullen. Patrick, Catherine at Clontymullan. James at Sleehaun (Sankey). Catherine at Tennalick. William at Ballymahon Town. Thomas, Patrick at Corrool (Fox). William at Portanure. John, Edward at Saints Island. Daniel at Aghakeel. Patrick at Cullentragh (Rathcline Civil Ph.). John H. at Kilshruley. George at Gorteenrevagh, Ballinalee Village. Francis at Breaghy. William at Roos. Patrick, Francis at Aghareagh. Rose at Carrickateane. William, Patrick at Tober. Thomas at Killeen (Bunlahy D.E.D.). Mary at Druminacrehir. Cornelius at Leitrim (Granard Rural D.E.D.). Thomas at Granard. Patrick at Grassyard. James at Coolagherty. Michael, John at Mollyglass. Rose at Ballindagny and Cullyvore. Michael at Cloonback. James at Derrynacrit. John at Kilnashee. John, Bernard at Corglass. Peter, Michael, Patrick at Garrowhill. Patrick at Enybegs. Charles, John, Thomas at Oghil. John at Sragarrow. John at Newtownforbes Village. Michael at Creenagh. John at Cloonrallagh. John at Cashelbeg. Peter at Lanesborough Village. John at Clontumpher. Patrick at Crossea North. James at Drumure. Thomas at Ballymahon Street, Longford Town. Thomas at Bog Lane, Longford Town. *ALSO:* Annie at Kilbride's of Tennalick. Joseph at Shanley's of Cornadowagh. Mary at John Sullivan's of Bunlahy. James and John at Hugh Brady's of Main Street, Granard Town. James at Glancy's of Ferskill. Patrick at John Sheridan's of Farmullagh. Anne et al. at Timothy Gorman's of Coolamber. Peter at Duffy's of Monadarragh. Francis of Gregory's of Carrickmoyragh. James at McKenna's of Bawn (Breanrisk D.E.D.). Teresa at Thomas Doherty's of Clontumpher. James et al. at Egan's of Coolcaw. Catherine at John Kennedy's of Crossea South. Mary at Lee's of Bog Lane, Longford Town. John at O'Beirne's of Dublin Street, Longford Town.

McCLAUGHRY: See McCloughry.

CLAVIN: Daniel at William Rickard's of Ballymahon Town.

McCLEAN, McCLANE: Alexander at Edgeworthstown Town. *ALSO:* John at Burns' of Edgeworthstown Town. James at Muir's of Edgeworthstown Town (?).

CLEARY: Thomas, Thomas at Keelbaun. *ALSO:* Patrick and Kate at Fegan's of Clooncullen. Patrick at Mulvihill's of Moygh (Ballymahon D.E.D.).

McCLELLAND: David at Shekelton's of Cloonshannagh or Coolamber Manor Demesne. Bridget at Farrington's of Newtownforbes Village.

CLEMENTS: Thomas at Farraghroe.

CLIFFORD: John T. at Margaret Mathews' of Main Street, Longford

Town.

CLINCH, CLYNCH: Bernard at Begnagh. Bridget at Cartronageeragh.

CLINE, CLINES: See Clyne.

McCLINOCK, McCLINTOCK (?): Samuel at Thomas Sutton's of Ballyclamay.

CLINTON: Bridget at Creevy. Thomas at Cloonagh (Mullanalaghta D.E.D.). Bridget at Clooncoose (Cloonee D.E.D.). Ellen at Chapel Lane, Longford Town. *ALSO:* Rose at Kiernan's of Ballyboy. Thomas et al. at Charters' of The Hill, Granard Town. Margaret at Kelly's of Earl Street, Longford Town.

CLOONAN: Elizabeth at Legan. Patrick at Collum. James at Pollagh. *ALSO:* James at Lyons's of Rockpeyton. Patrick et al. at Connor's of Derrydarragh.

McCLOSKEY: See McCluskey.

McCLOUGHRY, McCLAUGHRY, McLOUGHRY: William, Mary at Cleggill. *ALSO:* Patrick at George Carey's of Monascallaghan. Margaret at James Murray's of Great Water Street, Longford Town. (See Loughrey).

CLOYNE: See Clyne.

McCLUNE: James at Muir's of Edgeworthstown Town.

CLUSKEY: James at Ballymore. Laurence, Anne at Kilmore. *ALSO:* Mary at Whitney's of Freaghmeen.

McCLUSKEY, McCLOSKEY: James at Rathmore (Ballymahon D.E.D.). Henry at Aghabrack. John at Cooldoney. *ALSO:* John at Fagan's of Shrule. Mary at Edgeworth's of Kilshruley. Patrick at Flood's of Main Street, Granard Town.

CLYNCH: See Clinch.

CLYNE, CLYNES:(29): John at Listobit. Michael at Keel (Forgney D.E.D.). Michael, Patrick at Killeen (Foxhall D.E.D.). Peter at Newtown (Foxhall D.E.D.). Michael at Ballymulvey. Peter at Ballymahon Town. John at Caltragh Beg. Thomas, James, Michael at Derrygowna. Anne at Cornadowagh. William at Coolnahinch (Kilcommock D.E.D.). James at Snugborough. Michael at Firmount. Mary at Moatfarrell. Charles at Clooneen (Creevy D.E.D.). James at Ball Alley Street Lower, Granard

Town. Kate at Moxham Street, Granard Town. Owen at The Hill, Granard Town. Mary at Cleenrah. Bridget at Bracklon. Timothy at Cloonevit. John at Meeltanagh (Moydow D.E.D.). Peter at Aghamore (Rathcline D.E.D.). Teresa at Barnacor (Rathcline D.E.D.). Timothy at Breany. Michael at Fee's Terrace, Longford Town. Michael at Great Water Street, Longford Town. *ALSO:* Bernard at Keegan's of Deerpark (Kilglass D.E.D.). Ellen at Nolan's of Ballyglassin. John at John Brown's of Ballymahon Town. Charles at Fitzsimons' of Carrickateane. Joseph at Fagan's of Moatfarrell. Patrick at Keegan's of Clooneen (Creevy D.E.D.). Bridget at Edward Drake's of Ballinulty Upper. Elizabeth at James Hourican's of Dunbeggan (Columbkille D.E.D.). Bernard at Dennigan's of Tomisky. Julia at William Farrell's of Lehery. Frances at Catherine Farrell's of Lanesborough Village.

COATES, COATS: George E. at Abbeyshrule. Thomas at Cloghan (Forgney D.E.D.). Isabella at Mullawornia.

COBEY: Peter at Richmond Street, Longford Town.

COBURN: James at Bridge Street, Longford Town. *ALSO:* Patrick and Mary at Patrick Campbell's of Noud's Yard, Longford Town.

COCHRANE: Robert at Ballaghgowla and Froghan.

CODY: William at Drumanure. Charles at Killeenboy. Robert at Killinbore. Edward at Streamstown (Kilglass D.E.D.). Margaret at Knockmartin. Elizabeth at Ballinamore. Margaret at Church Street, Longford Town.

CODYRE: Emily at Moore's of Main Street, Granard Town.

COEN: James at Cloonagh (Mullanalaghta D.E.D.).

COFFEY:(13): Timothy at Castlewilder. Peter at Druming. John at Taghshinny. James at Cloonard (Ballymahon D.E.D.). Lawrence at Barry (Ballymahon D.E.D.). Kate at Edgeworthstown Town. Mary at Drumlougher. John at Laughil (Ardagh West D.E.D.). Thomas at Carrickglass Demesne (Templemichael Civil Ph.). Andrew at Creeve. Sarah, Patrick, Catherine at Chapel Lane, Longford Town. *ALSO:* Bridget at Anne McHugh's of Tennalick. Christopher at Charles Conroy's of Ballymahon Town. Margaret at Farrell's of Firmount. Winifred of Keegan's of Corboy. Kate at James Farrell's of Glack (Longford Rural D.E.D.).

COGAN: Rose at Dooner's of Templeton Glebe. (See Coogan).

COGHLAN: See Coughlan.

COLE: Patrick, John, Andrew at Gaigue. *ALSO:* John at Thomas

McCormack's of Great Water Street, Longford Town. Martha at Armstrong's of Main Street, Longford Town.

COLEMAN, COLMAN: Mary at Keel (Kilglass D.E.D.). Thomas at Portanure Bog. John at Coolamber. Mary at Edgeworthstown Town. Peter at Lanesborough Village. William at Derrymore. Patrick at Graffoge (Ardagh West D.E.D.). Michael, Catherine at Bawn Mountain. *ALSO:* James at Regan's of Smithfield. Margaret at James McCord's of Mullawornia. Sr. Julia at Sr. Hoare's of Grassyard. Esther B. at Green's of Convent Lane, Longford Town.

COLESTEN: See Colsten.

COLLENA: John at Patrick E. Fitzgerald's of Main Street, Longford Town.

COLLERY, COLLARY, CALERY: Bernard at Drumlish Village. *ALSO:* John at O'Ferrall's of Corbeagh. Anne at Donohoe's of Annagh (Drumgort D.E.D.).

COLLIGAN: James at Creevagh Beg, Ballymahon Town. Edward at Clogher and Rinn. (See Culligan).

COLLINS: Patrick, Mary at Ballymahon Town. Elizabeth at Tuite's Lane, Granard Town. Joseph at Cartronageeragh. Lawrence at Dublin Street, Longford Town. John at Dwyer's Yard, Longford Town. *ALSO:* Thomas et al. at Larkin's of Drumlish Village. Rebecka at Jackson's of Earl Street, Longford Town (?).

COLLUM, COLLUMB, COLUMB:(30): Daniel at Aghacordrinan. John at Aghamore Upper. Margaret at Aghakine. Denis at Carrickadorrish. Julia, Julia, Rose, Annie at Sonnagh. Peter at Silver Street, Granard Town. Bernard at Water Lane, Granard Town. Catherine at Corbaun or Leitrim. Bridget at Derrycassan. Patrick, Ellen at Larkfield. Patrick at Lettergeeragh. Mary, Bridget at Lettergullion. Peter, Patrick, Peter, Patrick, James, Patrick, John at Barragh More. Hugh at Drumlish Village. Hugh at Cornafunshin. James at Derryheelan. John, Patrick at Lettergonnell. Bridget at Aghadegnan (Longford Rural D.E.D.). *ALSO:* Kate at Rose Flood's of Ballinrooey. Susan at Hourican's of Sonnagh. Rose at Michael Ward's of Sonnagh. Margaret et al. at Cronogue's of Cartronamarkey. Patrick at Anne McGlade's of Smear. John at Gillespie's of Derrycassan. Anne at Catherine Smith's of Glenmore (Ballinamuck East D.E.D.). Maria at James Irwin's of Lettergullion. Bernard at Heaney's of Dublin Street, Longford Town. Caroline at Hughes's of Little Water Street, Longford Town.

COLMAN: See Coleman.

COLO, COLOE: Bridget at Keel (Forgney D.E.D.). James at Creevagh Beg, Ballymahon Town.

COLREAVY, CULREAVY: Michael at Farmullagh. Philip at Shanmullagh. Michael at Cloontagh. Patrick at Garvary. *ALSO:* Catherine at Banks' of Aghamore Upper. James at Lennon's of Barragh More.

COLSTEN: Henry at Ballaghgowla and Froghan.

COLUMB: See Collum.

COLVIN: Thomas at Larkfield.

COMISKEY, COMASKEY, CUMISKEY, CUMMISKEY:(18): James, Christopher, Patrick at Currycreaghan. Mathew at Lisnacreevy. Margaret at Kilbride. Thomas, Margaret at Cartron (Granard Rural D.E.D.). Owen at Ball Alley Street Upper, Granard Town. Peter at Ballynacross (Granard Urban D.E.D.). Cornelius at Granardkill (Granard Urban D.E.D.). Patrick at Lisraherty. John at Aghanoran. Peter, James, Charles at Cloonagh (Mullanalaghta D.E.D.). Bridget at Kilmore. John at Aghnagore. William at Cloonahard. *ALSO:* Patrick at Gaffney's of Cartron (Granard Rural D.E.D.). John at Connelly's of Aghanoran.

McCONAGHY, McCONOHY, McCONAHY: Thomas at Cornadrung. Patrick at Drumhalry. Thomas at Lanesborough Village. (See McConkey).

CONATY: Michael at Farrelly's of Springtown.

CONBOY: John at Ahanagh. Ellen at Clooneen (Shanly). Michael at Tomisky. *ALSO:* Michael at Patrick McCormack's of Great Water Street, Longford Town.

CONCANNON: Anne at Castlerea Mountain. Mary at Creevagh Beg. Patrick at Greenhall Lower. *ALSO:* Kate at Fox's of Corryena.

McCONCHY: See McConkey.

CONDRON: Thomas at Camagh (Newgrove D.E.D.). James at Edgeworthstown Town. *ALSO:* Gerald at Kelly's of Bracklon.

CONDULON: Bridget at Whitney's of Barragh More.

CONEFREY, CONEFRY, CONFREY: Michael at Camagh (Ballinamuck East D.E.D.). James at Corglass. Rev. Thomas at Enybegs. *ALSO:* John at Mahon's of St. Michael's Road, Longford Town.

McCONKEY, McCONCHY, McKONKEY: Kate at Drumhalry. Michael at Barne. Michael at Cornacullew. Bridget, Thomas at Leggagh. (See McConaghy).

CONLON:(22): James, Patrick, Michael at Forgney. William at Kildordan. John, James at Ballymahon Town. John at Rathmore (Ballymahon D.E.D.). James at Main Street, Keenagh Village. Thomas, Michael at Castlebaun. Patrick at Aghakeeran. John at New Road, Granard Town. Michael at Edenmore. Patrick at Breanriskcullew. Charles (?), Anne at Drumlish Village. Maria at Cornafunshin. Peter at Corneddan. Catherine at Soran. James H. at Main Street, Longford Town. Joseph at New Street, Longford Town. *ALSO:* Patrick at Francis Reilly's (16) of Gelshagh. Bridget at Whitney's of Barragh More (?). Patrick at Anne Davis's of Drumlish Village (?). Mary M. at Hanoria Farrell's of Tullvrane. (See Connellan).

CONMEE: Patrick at Killashee Village. John at Bridge Street, Longford Town.

McCONN: W. at Hewetson's of Church Street, Longford Town. (See McCann).

CONNAUGHTON, CONNAGHTON, CONNORTON:(23): Bridget at Cormaglava. Michael at Carrow More. James at Collum. John at Elfeet (Adamson). Michael at Fortwilliam. Luke at Glebe (Cashel West D.E.D.). Michael at Loughfarm. Anne at Pollagh. Thomas, John at Cullentragh (Rathcline Civil Ph.). Michael at Cartronbrack. Michael, Patrick at Derrynagalliagh. Elizabeth at Derryveagh. Michael at Mullolagher. Bridget, Catherine at Cloontamore. Ellen at Derryad (Mountdavis D.E.D.). Francis at Carrowroe. Patrick at Commons North. Patrick at Inchenagh Island. (Rathcline D.E.D.). James at Corradooey. Lawrence at Ballymahon Street, Longford Town. *ALSO:* James at Hugh Flood's of Ballymahon Town. Kate at Connor's of Carrowrory. John at John Mulvihill's of Cornadowagh. James et al. at Farrell's of Derrydarragh. Kate et al. at Catherine Dowd's of Kilmore Upper. Catherine and Patrick at Peter Corrigan's of Esker South. Edward at Peter J. Joyce's of Main Street, Longford Town. Michael at Lenehan's of New Street, Longford Town.

CONNELL:(24): Anne at Killeenboy. James at Rathsallagh. Edward at Carrow Beg (Cashel West D.E.D.). Anne at Ballinalee Village. Patrick at Springtown. Delia at Killeen (Bunlahy D.E.D.). James at Ballinulty Upper. Mary at Killasona. Margaret at Main Street, Granard Town. Patrick at Mollyglass. John at Smear. Patrick at Breanriskcullew. Francis, William, John, James at Fardrumman. Patrick at Castleforbes Demesne. William at Newtownforbes Village. John at Aghnagore. Patrick at Clogher and Rinn. Michael at Soran. James at Moor. Anne at Cloonee. Laurence at Great Water Street, Longford Town. *ALSO:* Sr. Stanislaus at Rev. Mother

Whelan's of Ballymahon Town. John at Andrew King's of Main Street, Keenagh Village. Rose M. at Regan's of Moxham Street, Granard Town. Patrick at Patrick Dooris's of Edgeworthstown Town. James and Elizabeth at Fealy's of Mucknagh. Anthony at James Brady's of Main Street, Longford Town.

McCONNELL: Andrew at Newtownforbes Village. Catherine at Healy's Terrace, Longford Town. *ALSO:* Thomas at Catherine Fitzsimons' of Kilsallagh. Anne at McElnea's of Main Street, Longford Town. John at Mayne's of Abbeycartron (?).

O'CONNELL: John at Lisnanagh. Mary J. at Commons North. Thomas J. at Dublin Street, Longford Town. Jeremiah A. at Demesne. *ALSO:* Patrick D. at Conlon's of New Road, Granard Town. Thomas at Noud's of Main Street, Longford Town.

CONNELLAN: Thomas at Drumnacross. (See Conlon).

CONNOLLY, CONNELLY:(37): Daniel, Daniel at Derrygowna. Michael, John at France. Anne, William at Lissameen. Michael at Molly. Charles, Patrick, Patrick at Aghakine. Hugh at Ballywillin. James at Creevy. James at Tromra (Granard urban D.E.D.). Catherine at Carrickmaguirk. John at Crott. John, Thomas at Ballyduffy. James at Drumhalry. Owen at Aghanoran. Patrick at Liscahill. Margaret at Garryandrew. John at Cornacullew. Mary, Anne, Alice at Derawley. James at Brocklagh. Michael at Glebe (Cloondara D.E.D.). Patrick at Begnagh. James at Turreen. Thomas, John at Cloonkeen (Ardagh West D.E.D.). Thomas at Cartronawar (Corboy D.E.D.). Patrick at Canal Harbour, Longford Town. Mary A., Bernard at Chapel Lane, Longford Town. Robert at Killashee Street, Longford Town. Edward at Little Water Street, Longford Town. *ALSO:* James at John Mulligan's of Gelshagh. Patrick and Catherine at Flynn's of Barrack Street, Granard Town. Fr. Eugene at Rev. James Smyth's (56) of Main Street, Granard Town. James at Edward Murphy's of New Road, Granard Town. Owen at Leavey's of Liscahill. Thomas at Greene's of Lisnagrish. Bridget at Edgeworth's of Edgeworthstown. Mary at Jones's of Cloonageeher. John at O'Brien's of Creenagh. Mary at O'Rourke's of Glebe (Cloondara D.E.D.). Lizzie at James McDermott's of Killashee Village. Patrick at Dowdall's of Ballinamore. Elizabeth at Cody's of Ballinamore. Mary A. and Thomas at Toher's of Ballynagoshen. Andrew at O'Connor's of Conroy's Court, Longford Town. Patrick at Taaffe's of Dublin Street, Longford Town. Bernard at Rafferty's of St. Michael's Road, Longford Town.

CONNOR:(54): Edmond at Drumanure. Patrick at Currycreaghan. James at Ballyclamay. John at Cornamucklagh. Thomas, Mary, Catherine at Forgney. Thomas at Pallas More. Patrick at Ballycloghan. Anne, Elizabeth at Keel (Kilglass D.E.D.). Bridget at Tennalough. John at Kilcurry. Patrick at Ballymahon Town. Michael at Carrowdunican. James at Carrowrory. John at Cloonmee. John at Derrydarragh. Daniel at Tipper (Cashel West D.E.D.). Patrick at Coolnahinch (Kilcommock D.E.D.). James at Ledwithstown (Kilcommock Civil Ph.). Patrick at Aghakilmore. Peter at Molly. John at Aghakine. James at Sonnagh. Anne at Kilbride. John at Halfcartron. Catherine at Mollyglass. Owen at Smear. Peter, Rose at Kilsallagh. Michael at Cloonback. John at Creelaghta. Andrew at Cloonagh (Breanrisk D.E.D.). James at Kilnashee. James, Andrew at Briskil. Thomas at Cloonfiugh. Hugh at Newtown (Killashee D.E.D.). Bridget, James at Agharanagh (Rathcline D.E.D.). Edward, Michael at Cashelbeg. James at Barney. James at Cornapark. Patrick at Crossea South. Patrick at Glen. Michael at Laughil (Ardagh West D.E.D.). Patrick at Rabbitpark. Patrick at Feraghfad. John, Andrew at Knockahaw. Joseph at Coach Yard, Longford Town. Catherine at Great Water Street, Longford Town. *ALSO:* Michael at Thomas Burke's (3) of Ballymaclifford. John et al. at Toole's of Tirlickeen. Mary at Henry S. Burd's of Ballymahon Town. Lizzie at Kate Whelan's of Ballymahon Town. Thomas et al. at Rush's of Carrowdunican. Mary and Patrick at Edward Egan's of Derrylough. Patrick at Hutchinson's of Firmount. Mary A. at Joseph Kiernan's of Aghakeeran. John at Patrick O'Reilly's of Main Street, Granard Town. John at Matthew McNamara's of Kilsallagh. John at Edgeworthstown Barracks (?). Molly and Kate at Farrington's of Newtownforbes Village. John of Nevin's of Kilmore Upper. Bridget et al. at Julia McLoughlin's of Crossea South. Patrick at Dooris's of Corboy. Thomas at Mary Barden's of Feraghfad. William at Farrell's of Lisduff (Longford Rural D.E.D.). Patrick at James Quinn's of Cooleeny. John at Rachel Farrell's of Glack (Longford Rural D.E.D.). Mary A. et al. at Rose Kelly's of Great Water Street, Longford Town. Thomas at Gordon's of Demesne.

O'CONNOR:(11): Thomas, Julia at Currycreaghan. Thomas at Newpark. Catherine at Breaghy. Mathew R. at Cloonfin. James at New Road, Granard Town. Bridget at Ballymahon Street, Longford Town. Peter at Conroy's Court, Longford Town. Francis at Earl Street, Longford Town. Michael at Main Street, Longford Town. Edward at St. Michael's Road, Longford Town. *ALSO:* Mary A. at Patrick Kiernan's of Clogh (Dalystown D.E.D.). James at Devany's of Treel (Newtownforbes D.E.D.). Sr. Teresa at Sr. Green's of Convent Lane, Longford Town. Patrick at O'Connell's of Dublin St., Longford Town. Kate at Skelly's of Main St., Longford Town.

CONNORTON: See Connaughton.

McCONOHY: See McConaghy.

CONROY:(11): Peter at Legan. Charles at Ballymahon Town. John at Prucklishtown. James at Drummeel. Patrick at Aghnacliff. Michael at

Ballinrud East. Matthew at Cloghchurnel. Michael at Bracklon. Patrick at Aghaboy (Aghaboy D.E.D.). John at Aghanahown. Julia at Abbeycartron. *ALSO:* Edward and John at Farrell's of Ballagh (Cashel West D.E.D.). Anne at Michael Farrell's of Edgeworthstown Town. John at Thomas Farrell's of Carrowstrawly. Daniel at Dublin Street Barracks, Longford Town. Margaret at Cully's of Richmond Street, Longford Town. Teresa at Harris's of Abbeycartron.

CONRY: William at Pallas More. *ALSO:* Bridget and Ellen at Shaw's of Rath.

CONWAY: William at Deerpark (Kilglass D.E.D.). Thomas at Tennalough. Peter at Main Street, Keenagh Village. James at Lissameen. Michael at Cloonbearla. Thomas at Moor. Maria at Ardnacassagh. James at St. Michael's Road, Longford Town.

COOGAN: Mary A. and Agnes at Gilhooly's of Keon's Terrace, Longford Town. (See Cogan).

COOKE, COOK: Mary A., James at Tober. John at Ballinulty Upper. Arthur, Anne at Cloonelly. Anne at Cornacullew. *ALSO:* Anthony at Kilby's of Cornamucklagh. Mary A. at James Sheridan's of Aghakine. G. at Duncan McGregor's of Lisbrack (Longford Rural D.E.D.).

COOLE: William at Fee's of Church Street, Longford Town.

COOLIHAN: Kate at Johnson's of Main Street, Longford Town.

COONEY:(19): Laurence at Daroge. Catherine at Main Street, Keenagh Village. Michael, John, Patrick at Breanriskcullew. Edward at Carrowbeg (Drumlish D.E.D.). William, John, Thomas, Margaret, Patrick at Barragh Beg. Francis at Barragh More. Francis at Cartrongolan. Hugh, John at Dooroc. Michael at Curry (Moydow D.E.D.). John at Gorteenboy. Michael at Lanesborough Village. Kate at Main Street, Longford Town. *ALSO:* Margaret at Joseph Gannon's of Ballymahon Town. Lizzie at Peter Sheridan's of Breanriskcullew. Bridget at Cummins's of Cornacullew. Mary at Creighton's of Bog Lane, Longford Town. Anne at Quinn's of Earl Street, Longford Town.

COOPER: William at Chapel Lane, Longford Town. *ALSO:* Mary A. at Molloy's of Ballymahon Street, Longford Town.

McCOPPIN: William at Kinard. Edward at Cloontirm.

CORBETT, CORBITT: Mary at Plant's of Ballymahon Town.

CORCORAN:(28): John at Cartrons (Kilcommock D.E.D.). Patrick at Island. Peter at Molly. Philip at Aghakeeran. John, Bridget at Sonnagh. Annie at Abbeylara Village. Thomas at Bunlahy. Thomas, James, Patrick at Clooneen (Creevy D.E.D.). Owen at Carrickduff. Mary at Tromra (Granard Rural D.E.D.). Laurence at Crott. John at Aghanoran. Mary at Cloonagh (Mullanalaghta D.E.D.). John at Cam. Michael at Edgeworthstown Town. Thomas at Moyne. Bridget at Clooncolligan. Henry at Brianstown. Mary, Michael at Carrowroe. John at Esker South. James, Hugh at Rabbitpark. John at Graffoge (Ardagh West D.E.D.). James at Cloonahussey. *ALSO:* Anne at Goldsberry's of Forgney. Sr. Augustine at Rev. Mother Whelan's of Ballymahon Town. Elizabeth at Hayes's of Main St., Keenagh Village. Henry at McCabe's of Culleenmore. John at Edgeworth's of Edgeworthstown. Susan and Edward at Garrett Murtagh's of Fostragh. Sr. Jane at Rev. Mother Farrington's of Newtownforbes Village. Margaret at McGuire's of Cloonbalt. Thomas at McLoughlin's of Cloonahard. Anne at McLoughlin's of Clooneeny. James at Eakins' of Coolnahinch (Longford Rural D.E.D.). Kate at Fee's of Church St., Longford Town.

McCORD: James, Alexander at Mullawornia. Charles at Aghintemple. William at Cordivin. Charles at Allenagh. Alexander at Corboy. Forster at Cloonturk. *ALSO:* Thomas A. and Arthur C. at Fee's of Trillickatemple.

CORDIAL: John at Conroy's of Ballinrud East.

CORDNER: Frances K. at Mullagh.

CORMACK, CORMICK: Peter at Agharra. *ALSO:* Patrick at John Hughes's of Drumanure. John at Michael Lee's of Forgney.

McCORMACK, McCORMICK:(110): Rose, John at Ratharney. Michael at Agharra. John at Cloonfide. John at Listobit. Joseph at Clooncallow. Elizabeth at Forgney. Patrick at Keel (Forgney D.E.D.). Michael, Anne at Clygeen. Patrick, James at Killeen (Foxhall D.E.D.). Ellen at Garrycam. Patrick at Keel (Kilglass D.E.D.). Michael at Ballynamanagh. James at Lisnacreevy. Mary at Loughsheedan. Bryan at Deerpark (Kilglass D.E.D.). Michael at Ballyglassin. John R., John, James at Kilcurry. Honor at Killinbore. James, Edward at Taghshinny. Mary, John at Tennalick. Catherine at Ballymahon Town. Anne, William at Cloonard (Ballymahon D.E.D.). Catherine at Cleraun. John at Glenmore (Kilcommock D.E.D.). James at Cartronbrack. Thomas at Clogh (Kilcommock D.E.D.). Michael at Creagh. John at Longford Road, Keenagh Village. Thomas at Derryad (Ledwithstown D.E.D.). James at Foygh. Michael at Ledwithstown (Kilcommock Civil Ph.). Margaret at Laughil (Adair). Joseph at Molly. Peter at Carrowlinan. John, Patrick at Billywillin. Patrick at Ballinulty Lower. Patrick at Cloonaghmore. John at Derragh. John at Smear. John at

Ballyduffy. John at Farmullagh. John at Cloonagh (Mullanalaghta D.E.D.).
Patrick at Derrycassan. William at Barne. Bridget at Ringowny. John at
Cranalagh More. Michael at Lisnageeragh. Bridget at Longfield. Catherine
at Garryandrew. John at Aghadowry. Patrick, James, Hugh at Fostragh.
Hugh, John at Glenmore (Ballinamuck East D.E.D.). Isabella, William,
Arthur at Leitrim (Breanrisk D.E.D.). Ellen at Prucklish. Michael at
Cloonagh (Breanrisk D.E.D.). Patrick at Annagh (Drumgort D.E.D.).
Thomas, Patrick at Cornacullew. Thomas at Garrowhill. John at Greagh.
Thomas at Derrynacross. Thomas at Cahanagh. Sarah at Tully (Cloondara
D.E.D.). Michael, Patrick, Francis at Cartronlebagh. James at Annaghbeg.
John at Killashee and Aghakeeran. Denis at Derryad (Mountdavis D.E.D.).
Bernard at Cloonevit. Patrick at Lisgurry. John at Moydow Glebe. Mary at
Toneen (Moydow D.E.D.). Anne at Ballygar. Mary, Mary at Crossea South.
William at Glen. Robert at Aghintemple. Peter, Bernard at Rabbitpark.
Cornelius at Cartrongarrow. Owen S. at Bawn Mountain. William, Moffett
at Clooncoose (Cloonee D.E.D.). Gilbert at Kilmoyle. Thomas at Kiltyreher
(Templemichael Civil Ph.). Matthew at Feraghfad. Maria at Garvagh
(Longford Rural D.E.D.). John, Bernard at Dublin Street, Longford Town.
Thomas, Patrick, Michael at Great Water Street, Longford Town. Thomas
at Hyde's Yard, Longford Town. Mary at Little Water Street, Longford
Town. Catherine at O'Donnell's Yard, Longford Town. *ALSO:* Bridget at
Bernard Kenny's of Killeen (Foxhall D.E.D.). John and Mary of Larkin's
of Corry (Kilglass D.E.D.). Mary A. at Payne's of Tennalick. Kate at
Conlon's of Rathmore (Ballymahon D.E.D.). Mary at Rogers' of Ards.
Margaret at Garahan's of Abbeyderg. John at Lennon's of Cartronawar
(Kilcommock D.E.D.). Thomas at Miller's of Cartronawar (Kilcommock
D.E.D.). Ned at McGovern's of Ballinulty Upper. Margaret and Elizabeth
at O'Dwyer's of Carragh (Granard Urban D.E.D.). John at Markey's of
Ball Alley Street Upper, Granard Town. Patrick and James at Grehan's of
Main Street, Granard Town. Elizabeth J. at Annie E. at Reilly's of
Cornadrung. Mary at Jones's of Birrinagh. Michael at Murphy's of
Cloonagh (Mullanalaghta D.E.D.). William at Mahady's of Kilsallagh. Peter
at Meehan's of Ballindagny and Cullyvore. Patrick at Sheridan's of
Edgeworthstown Town. Patrick at Farrell's of Carrowbeg (Drumlish
D.E.D.). James at Farrell's of Enybegs. Michael at Spearman's of
Annaghmore. Ellen at Lally's of Lanesborough Village. Mary at Short's of
Cross (Ardagh East D.E.D.). Michael and Maggie at Heavey's of Crossea
North. Owen at Newman's of Nappagh. Bridget at Bridget Heany's of
Aghadegnan (Longford Rural D.E.D.). Edward at O'Connor's of Conroy's
Court, Longford Town. Charles at Charles Sheridan's of Dublin Street,
Longford Town. Lizzie at Clyne's of Great Water Street, Longford Town.
James at Dempsey's of Great Water Street, Longford Town. Jane at
Armstrong's of Main Street, Longford Town. Michael at Myles' of New
Street, Longford Town. John at Mayne's of Abbeycartron (?).

CORR: John at Clooncoose (Ballinalee D.E.D.). Bernard at Ballybrien.

Mary at Prucklish. Charles at Corglass. Francis, Lawrence, Patrick at Brocklagh. *ALSO:* Edward at John O'Reilly's of Cornacullew. (See Carr).

CORRIGAN:(30): John at Curraghmore. Patrick at Ballymahon Town. Owen at Abbeyderg. Martin at Cloonfin. Anna M. at Grassyard. James, James, Bernard at Lettergullion. Anne at Melkagh. Bernard at Tawnagh. John at Aghnamaddoo. Patrick at Cloonelly. Patrick, Mary at Corglass. Patrick, John, Mary at Barragh More. Michael, Anne at Monaduff. John at Drumlish Village. Patrick at Ballinamore. James at Barroe. James at Aghaboy (Aghaboy D.E.D.). Patrick, James, Peter at Esker South. Patrick at Bohernacross (?). Teresa at Glebe (Longford Rural D.E.D.).. Andrew at Cooleeny. Thomas at McLoughlin's Yard. Longford Town. *ALSO:* Rosey at Gannon's of Carrigeen (Foxhall D.E.D.) (?). Michael at Murphy's of Coolnahinch (Kilcommock D.E.D.) (?). Annie at Rogers' of Annagh (Drumgort D.E.D.). John et al. at Patrick Collum's (11) of Barragh More. Mary at Thomas Heaney's of Barragh More. Mary at Farrington's of Newtownforbes Village. William at Yorke's of Dublin Street, Longford Town. Bernard at King's of Main Street, Longford Town.

CORRY: Sarah, Thomas, Newcomen at Keel (Kilglass D.E.D.). George at Ballybeg. *ALSO:* Sarah at Dickson's of Kinard.

CORVAN, CORVEN: Patrick at Rosduff. (See Curivan).

COSGROVE, COSGRAVE:(23): Patrick, James, Cornelius at Aghacordrinan. James at Gelshagh. James, Patrick at Main Street, Granard Town. Thomas at The Hill, Granard Town. Owen at Crott. Peter, James, Mary at Birrinagh. John, Thomas, James at Derrynacrit. Anne at Ballincurry. Patrick at Bawn (Breanrisk D.E.D.). Patrick, John at Cornacullew. Patrick at Derryad (Mountdavis D.E.D.). Daniel at Ballintempan. Bridget at Soran. Patrick at Aghintemple. John at Harbour Row, Longford Town. *ALSO:* Anne at McNally's of Gelshagh. Lizzie at Mullen's of Main Street, Granard Town. Annie at John Kiernan's of Main Street, Granard Town. Annie at John Sheridan's (15) of Leggagh. Lawrence at Bridget Prunty's of Dooroc. Ellie at Peter Maguire's of Drumnacooha. Mary and James at Kirkland's of Rabbitpark. Lizzie at Murphy's of Cooleeny. Patrick at Mathew Farrell's of Main Street, Longford Town.

COSTELLO: James, Catherine, William at Cleraun. Michael, James at Pollagh. Bridget at Enaghan. Anne, Michael at Carrowroe. Michael at Chapel Lane, Longford Town. *ALSO:* Margaret at Skelly's of Portanure. John at Hanly's of Tipper (Cashel West D.E.D.).

COTTER: Lizzy at Wilson's of Currygrane.

McCOTTER: G. at Hewetson's of Church Street, Longford Town.

COTTON: James at Kilmakinlan.

COUGHLAN, COUGHLIN, COGHLAN:(12): William at Clooncallow. Bridget, Edward at Cloonkeen (Ballymahon D.E.D.). James at Daroge. Bartley at Rathmore (Ballymahon D.E.D.). Margaret, William, John at Derrydarragh. John at Tipper (Cashel West D.E.D.). Patrick at Coolnahinch (Kilcommock D.E.D.). Anne at Cloonbreany. Thomas at Oldtown. *ALSO:* James at Orr's of Newcastle. Margaret at Nolan's of Glenmore (Kilcommock D.E.D.). Hugh at Histon's of Ballywillin. Catherine at O'Connor's of St. Michael's Road, Longford Town.

COURIGAN, COURICAN: Patrick at Bohernacross. *ALSO:* Rosey at Gannon's of Carrigeen (Foxhall D.E.D.).

COURTNEY, COURTENAY:(15): Peter at Mornin. James at Garrycam. Elizabeth at Keel (Kilglass D.E.D.). William at Lisnacreevy. Patrick at Cloonkeen (Ballymahon D.E.D.). James, James at Larkfield. Michael at Edgeworthstown Town. Bernard at Lettergullion. Mary at Cloonmacart. Patrick at Kilnashee. Patrick at Cornacullew. Michael, Patrick at Drumlish. Owen at Minard. *ALSO:* John at Ward's of Drinan. William at Noble's of Tonymore North. Mary A. at James McDowell's (61) of Smear. James at Dopping - Hepenstal's of Derrycassan.

COVIGAN: Michael at Murphy's of Coolnahinch (Kilcommock D.E.D.).

COWAN, COWEN: James at Ballymahon Town. Thomas at Barrack Street, Granard Town. James at Kilsallagh. Edward at Chapel Lane, Longford Town. *ALSO:* Thomas at James Kelly's of Legan. Edward at Magan's of Aghnaskea.

COX:(35): James at Corrycorka. Patrick at Tully (Agharra D.E.D.). Michael at Cloonscott. Peter at Mornin. William at Ballyclamay. Jane at Clontymullan. James at Killeen (Foxhall D.E.D.). John at Lisnacreevy. Julia at Ballymacshane. Michael at Carn. John at Ballymahon Town. James at Kilmakinlan. William at Cranally. Ambrose at Culray. Thomas at Shantum. James, Bridget, John at Leitrim (Breanrisk D.E.D.). Bernard at Deerpark (Newtownforbes D.E.D.). Margaret at Kilmacannon. Jane at Ahanagh. Patrick, John, Christopher at Cloonart North. Thomas at Clooncolligan. Thomas, John at Clooneen (Cox). Thomas at Edercloon. William at Clogher and Rinn. Patrick at Corragarrow (Killashee D.E.D.). Jane at Trillickacurry. Michael, Patrick at Killinlastra. Michael at Ballymahon Street, Longford Town. Mary A. at McLoughlin's Yard, Longford Town. *ALSO:* Richard and Hannah at William Doran's of Ardanragh. Mary at Farrell's of Garrycam. Julia at McCann's of Tirlickeen. Michael at Farrelly's of Corclaragh. Teresa and Mary E. at Farrington's of Newtownforbes Village. William at Bridget Keane's of Ballynakill. John at Mahary's of Barneygole.

Andrew at Dinnigan's of Crossea North. John et al. at Catherine Reilly's of Lisduff (Ardagh East D.E.D.). Peter at Plunkett's of Main St., Longford Town. John at Shanley's of Main St., Longford Town. Patrick at Guinan's of Main St., Longford Town. Mary A. at Thompson's of Demesne.

McCOY: John at Carrickateane. Bridget, Patrick at Lislea (Lislea D.E.D.). Anne, Amelia at Smear. Bridget at Glack (Longford Rural D.E.D.).

COYLE:(23): Patrick at Aghamore Upper. Henry at Carrickadorrish. John at Abbeylara Village. Thomas, William, Bridget, Patrick at Springtown. Patrick at Cartronamarkey. Thomas, Terence at Culleenmore. Patrick at Aghnagarron. Edward at Dalystown. Francis at Ballinulty Lower. Bridget at Main Street, Granard Town. Patrick at Camagh (Newgrove D.E.D.). Anne, Hugh at Enaghan. Anne at Lisraherty. Mary at Drumhalry. James, John, John at Esker South. Edward at Soran. *ALSO:* James at Dunne's of Elfeet (Adamson). Kate at O'Ferrall's of Corbeagh. Michael and Mary at Hanlon's of Ballinrooey. Bridget at Bridget Corcoran's of Sonnagh. Peter at Brady's of Tonymore North. John at Mallon's of Springtown. Patrick at James Treacy's of Bunlahy. Hugh at Wrenn's of Coolcor. Mary A. at McNally's of Killasona. John et al. at Hyland's of Barrack Street, Granard Town. Catherine at Philip Duffy's of Carrickmaguirk. Annie at O'Brien's of Smear. Matthew at Bridget McNamara's of Kilsallagh. Bridget and Henry at Anne Wiggins's of Rathmore (Ballinamuck East D.E.D.). Srs. Mary and Rosa at Rev. Mother Farrington's of Newtownforbes Village. Margaret at Anne Hughes's of Rhine.

COYNE: Rose at Ballymahon Town. Joseph at Castlenugent. Martin at St. Mel's Road, Longford Town.

CRAIG: Freddy at Mason's of Corry. (Kilglass D.E.D.).

CRAIN: See Crean, Crane.

CRAMER: Anne, Thomas at Ballymaurice. (Granard Rural D.E.D.). *ALSO:* Mary at McGivney's of Lechurragh.

CRANE: Michael at Michael Murtagh's of Cloonard (Cloondara D.E.D.). (See Crean).

McCRANN: Thomas at Patrick Lynch's of Ballywillin (?). Patrick at Burns' of Main Street, Longford Town. James at Trimble's of Main Street, Longford Town. Maggie at Harris's of Abbeycartron (?).

CRAWFORD: Bridget at Abbeylara Village. John at Ballymacroly. Mary A. at Newtownforbes Village. Elizabeth at Keeloges. George at Rhine. Robert at Corrabaun (Longford Rural D.E.D.). Thomas at Aghadegnan

(Longford Rural D.E.D.). Catherine at Bridge Street, Longford Town. *ALSO:* Mary at Dodd's of Druming. Martha at Plant's of Ballymahon Town. Mary A. at Mansergh's of Ballinalee Village. William at Gilligan's of Cloonaghmore. Isabella at Pollard's of Templeton Glebe. Mary at Donnelly's of Aghaboy (Aghaboy D.E.D.).

McCREA: Henry at Abbeycartron.

CREAGHTON: See Creighton.

CREAN, CREANE: Richard W. at Main Street, Keenagh Village. Mary at Ball Alley Street Upper, Granard Town. Bridget, Mary at Soran. *ALSO:* Kate at O'Ferrall's of Corbeagh (?). (See Crane).

McCREANOR: Rose at Lissavaddy.

CREATON: See Creighton.

CREDDIN: James at Howard's of Great Water Street, Longford Town. (see Crudden).

CREE: Marion at John P. Shaw's of Ballymahon Town.

CREED: Teresa at Clooneen (Cox). *ALSO:* Christopher at Guinan's of Main Street, Longford Town.

CREEGAN: Patrick at Carrickedmond. Thomas at Derryveagh. Patrick at Ball Alley Street Upper, Granard Town. Patrick at Creelaghta. Myles at Leggagh. Catherine at Barragh More. Hugh at Monaduff. Henry at Drumlish Village. *ALSO:* Ellen at Duggan's of Gorteenclareen. Mary at Flynn's of Creelaghta. Patrick at Ellen Donnelly's of Kiltycreevagh. Mathew at Patrick McKenna's of Kiltycreevagh. Margaret at Forbes's of Campbell's Row, Longford Town.

CREHAN: Michael at Killashee Barracks.

CREIGHTON, CREATON, CREAGHTON: Sylvester at Birrinagh. Patrick at Bog Lane, Longford Town. John at Healy's Terrace, Longford Town. John at Little Water St., Longford Town. Peter at McLoughlin's Yard, Longford Town. *ALSO:* John J. at Nolan's of Ballyglassin. Kate at McCann's of Abbeycartron.

CRINIGAN, CRINNIGAN: Mary at James Nally's of Ballymahon Town. Peter at Michael Mullooly's at Lehery.

CROCKER: W. at Hewetson's of Church Street, Longford Town.

CROGHAN: Bridget, William at Bog Lane, Longford Town. Patrick at Chapel Lane, Longford Town. *ALSO:* Mary A. at Burke's of Glebe (Cloondara D.E.D.). Mary E. et al. at Gill's of Great Water Street, Longford Town.

McCRONE, MULCRONE: Nicholas at Drumanure.

CRONOGUE: Matthew at Cartronamarkey. John at Ballinlough. Bridget at Bunlahy. Anne at Killasona. Mary at Gaigue. Margaret at Bog Lane, Longford Town. Bartholomew at St. Michael's Road, Longford Town. *ALSO:* John at Mahady's of Cranally. Patrick at Percival's of Crowdrumman. William and Rose at Farrell's of Garvey's Yard, Longford Town.

CROOKE, CROOKES: Martha at Clogh (Kilcommock D.E.D.). *ALSO:* Jannie and Sarah J. at John P. Shaw's of Ballymahon Town. R. at Dowler's of Edgeworthstown Town.

CROSBIE, CROSBY: Michael, Bridget at Bog Lane, Longford Town. John at Dublin Street, Longford Town. *ALSO:* Bridget at Peter J. Joyce's of Edgeworthstown Town. Mary at James Farrell's of Glack (Longford Rural D.E.D.).

CROSKERY: William D. at Ardagullion.

McCROTHERS: John at Abbeycartron. (See Carothers).

CROWE: Patrick at Aghakeeran. Michael at Carrickmaguirk. James at Larkfield. Laurence at Derawley. *ALSO:* Patrick at Gray's of Leggagh.

CRUDDEN: Margaret at Abbeylara Village. *ALSO:* Margaret at Brady's of Rathbrackan. (See Creddin).

CRUISE: Susan at Flanagan's of Killashee Village.

CRYAN: Patrick at Newtownforbes Village.

McCUE: See McHugh.

CUFFE: Patrick et al. at Bernard Lynch's of Castlenugent.

CUGGY: Michael at Treel (Foxhall D.E.D.). Thomas at Killeen (Foxhall D.E.D.). Michael at Craane. *ALSO:* Marcella at Moran's of Carrigeen (Foxhall D.E.D.).

McCULLAGH: John at Killashee Street, Longford Town.

CULLEN:(13): Patrick at Creevagh Beg. Honor at Creevaghmore (Noughaval Civil Ph.). James at Kilcourcey. James at Lisnageeragh. Patrick at Longfield. John, Patrick at Bracklon. Charles, Anne, Patrick at Edgeworthstown Town. Thomas at Lettergeeragh. Michael, Daniel at Brocklagh. *ALSO:* Bessie and Rosy at Blanford's of Clynan. Andrew at William Rickard's of Ballymahon Town. Katherine at Phillips's of Glenmore (Kilcommock D.E.D.). James at Farrell's of Corclaragh. Patrick at Michael Grimes' of Edgeworthstown Town. Mary at Lennon's of Cloonelly. Jane and Mary at Farrington's of Newtownforbes Village. Sr. Kate at St. Green's of Convent Lane, Longford Town. Mary at Cameron's of Main Street, Longford Town.

CULLIGAN: Edward at Larkfield. (See Colligan).

CULLIM, CULLUM: See Collum.

CULLY: Peter at Aghaboy (Milltown D.E.D.). Rose at Richmond Street, Longford Town. *ALSO:* Francis at Gettings' of Tully (Milltown D.E.D.).

CULREAVY: See Colreavy.

CUMISKEY, CUMMISKEY: See Comiskey.

CUMMINS: Peter at Rath. Martin at Carrickedmond. James at Kilcurry. James, Richard at Ballymahon Town. John at Cornacullew. *ALSO:* Joseph at William Seales' of Ballymahon Town. Michael at Peter Kiernan's of Main St., Granard Town. John at Johnson's of Main St., Longford Town.

CUNDLON, CUNDELAN: Charles at Drumlish Village. *ALSO*: Patrick at Anne Davis's of Drumlish Village. Bridget at Whitney's of Barragh More (?).

CUNNINGHAM:(27): Thomas at Ballymahon Town. James at Creevagh Beg. Thomas at Rathmore (Ballymahon D.E.D.). Patrick at Barry (Ballymahon D.E.D.). Bridget, James at Caltragh More. John, Thomas at Carrow Beg (Cashel West D.E.D.). Patrick at Corrool (Brennan). John at Loughfarm. Thomas at Pollagh. Martha at Drummeel. Bernard at Aghacordrinan. Eugene at Clooneen (Creevy D.E.D.). Patrick at Cartroncar. Margaret, Catherine at Derragh. John, Thomas at Cam. Owen at Lettergullion. James, Patrick, Thady at Gaigue. James at Cloonbearla. Sarah at Cloontamore. Daniel at Knock. James at Healy's Terrace, Longford Town. *ALSO:* Kate at Joseph Shore's of Rathmore (Ballymahon D.E.D.). John and Mary at Hopkins' of Corrool (Brennan). Kate at Ward's of Fortwilliam. James et al. at Clarke's of Druminacrehir. James at Mary Dolan's of Carrickduff. Owen at James Burns' of Main St., Granard Town. Katie at Keatings' of Cartroncar. Mary at Kate Reilly's of Cranalagh More.

John et al. at John Sheeran's (11) of Lettergeeragh. John at Patrick McWade's of Lettergullion. Mary A., Srs. Ellen and Jane at Farrington's of Newtownforbes Village. Eileen and Joseph at Mary Bourke's of Cloondara.

CUNNION: Alicia at Dan Monaghan's of Ballyduffy.

CURIVAN: John at McGrath's of Ballinalee Village. Patrick at Farrell's of France. (See Corvan, Kirwan).

CURLEY: Mary at Drumnacross. Thomas at Banghill. *ALSO:* Anne at Farrington's of Newtownforbes Village.

CURNEEN: Luke at Aghnagarron. Patrick at Tromra (Granard Rural D.E.D.). Bernard at Barrack Street, Granard Town. Francis at Dring.

CURRAN:(13): Jane at Taghshinny. Michael at Newpark. Patrick at Cloonmee. Robert at Tullybaun. Patrick at Garvagh (Currygrane D.E.D.). Catherine at Clooneen (Creevy D.E.D.). Bridget at Carrickduff. Elizabeth at Ball Alley St. Upper, Granard Town. Charles at Annagh (Drumgort D.E.D.). James at Begnagh. Owen at Killinure. James at Knockahaw. Patrick at Chapel Lane, Longford Town. *ALSO:* Kate at Stoney's of Glebe (Kilglass D.E.D.). James at Rose Coyne's of Ballymahon Town. Catherine and Mary at Cox's of Kilmakinlan. Mary and James J. at Luke Kiernan's of Clogh (Dalystown D.E.D.). Anne at Mary McKeon's of Smear. Catherine and Michael at Doogan's of Crott. Bridget at Philip Sheridan's of Farmullagh. Patrick at Owen Noonan's of Cam. Francis and Annie at Campbell's of Clonca. James and Christopher at Patrick Farrell's of Longfield. Elizabeth at Corcoran's of Edgeworthstown Town. James at Devine's of Bawn (Breanrisk D.E.D.). Bernard at Donohoe's of Annagh (Drumgort D.E.D.). Bridget at Leavy's of Cross (Ardagh East D.E.D.).

CURRY: Peter at Clooneen (Creevy D.E.D.). John at Aghanoran. Patrick at Cloonagh (Mullanalaghta D.E.D.). John at Kilmore. *ALSO:* Joseph at William Jones's of Larkfield.

CURWIN: See Kirwan.

CUSACK: Andrew at Main Street, Granard Town. *ALSO:* Thomas at O'Connor's of Conroy's Court, Longford Town.

CUSKER: John at Ballybrien.

McCUSKER: Catherine at Harbour Row, Longford Town. *ALSO:* John at Thomas Reilly's of Moyne.

McCUTCHEON: Katie at Bernard Smith's of Cloonaghmore. Kate at Dermody's of Freaghmeen.

CUTHBERT: Maggie at Ballyclamay.

DAIN: John at Knockloughlin Barracks (See Deane).

DALAN: Kate at Andrew King's of Main Street, Keenagh Village.

DALE, DALES: Matthew, Francis at Aghnagarron. John at Ballygilchrist.

DALLON: Simon D. at Harris's of Bridge Street, Longford Town.

DALTON:(26): Bridget at Drumanure. James at Lissawarriff. John at Cloghan (Forgney D.E.D.). Mary at Clooneen (Forgney D.E.D.). Cathcrine, James at Aghnavealoge. Patrick at Collum. Owen, Anne at Kilcommock Glebe. Peter at Ledwithstown (Shrule Civil Ph.). Julia at Ballyreaghan. Michael at Drummeel. William at Lisnanagh. Joseph, Andrew at Newtownbond. Mary at Aghnagarron. Anne at Camagh (Newgrove D.E.D.). Mary A. at Edgeworthstown Town. John at Rathcline. James at Clontumpher. James at Coolcaw. Anne, Thomas, Patrick at Breany. James at Cartronawar (Corboy D.E.D.). William at St. Mel's Road, Longford Town. *ALSO:* Michael et al. at Connor's of Currycreaghan. Patrick at Lyons's of Rockpeyton. William at Flood's of Foxhall. Margaret at Yorke's of Ballintober (Bonny). Hannah at Egan's of Cornahoo. Mary at Perry's of Foygh. Kate at Donnelly's of Moatfarrell. Kate at O'Hara's of Aghamore (Coolamber D.E.D.). Bridget at Phoebe Harris's of Enybegs. Christopher at Michael Lee's of Soran. Mary J. and Thomas J. at James Farrell's of Laughil (Ardagh West D.E.D.). James at Mallon's of Ballygarve.

DALY:(29): Catherine at Tennalick. Elizabeth, Gerald, James at Ballymahon Town. Rose at Creevagh Beg. Patrick, Owen at Coolnahinch (Kilcommock D.E.D.). Thomas at Glenmore (Kilcommock D.E.D.). Richard at Laghlooney. Anne at Doonacurry (Kilcommock Civil Ph.). James, Thomas at Barnacor (Ledwithstown D.E.D.). Thomas at Molly. Margaret at Aghaward. Hugh at Abbeylara. John at Abbeylara Village. Philip at Ballywillin. Luke at Clooneen (Creevy D.E.D.). Peter, Michael, Michael at Aghnagarron. Peter at Clogh (Dalystown D.E.D.). Michael, John at Barrack Street, Granard Town. Owen at Tuite's Lane, Granard Town. William at Bracklon. Luke at Drumlish Village. Stephen at Clontumpher. Mary at St. Michael's Road, Longford Town. *ALSO:* Mary at Bole's of Parkplace. Ellen at Catherine Flynn's of Ballymahon Town. Thomas at Greene's of Lissameen. Margaret at Wallace's of Aghagreagh. Francis at McLoughlin's of Lisnanagh. Bridget at Lynch's of Granardkill (Granard Rural D.E.D.). Bernard at Martin's of Monadarragh. Bridget at James Nolan's of Corralough. Rosanna at Bond's of Ballygarve. E. at Hewetson's of Church

Street, Longford Town.

McDANIEL: Luke at Currygrane. Hugh at Drummeel. Bridget at Ball Alley Street Upper, Granard Town (?). (See McDonnell).

DANN: William T. at Market Square, Longford Town. *ALSO:* Emily at Fetherston's of Newtownforbes Village.

DANNIN: James and Mary at McCormack's of Longfield. (See Dennan, Dinnan).

DANTZIG: Mary L. and Rosaline at Farrington's of Newtownforbes Village.

DARCY, DARCEY: Bridget at Ballybranigan. Anne at Lissanure.

DARDIS: Patrick at Leggagh. *ALSO:* Patrick at Markey's of Ball Alley Street Upper, Granard Town.

DAVID: Christopher at Lissanure.

DAVIES: G. at Hewetson's of Church Street, Longford Town.

DAVIS, DAVYS:(13): William at Glenoghil. Richard at Bank Street, Granard Town. Patrick at Lettergullion. Anne, John at Drumlish Village. Thomas, John at Cornafunshin. Margaret at Gaigue. George M. at Cloonbony. Jane at Lanesborough Village. Patrick at Ballymahon Street, Longford Town. Catherine at Main Street, Longford Town. William at Noud's Yard, Longford Town. *ALSO:* Philip et al. at O'Neill's of Shanmullagh. May R. at Patrick Kane's of Drumlish Village. Ellen and Thomas at Denigan's of Mullolagher. Elizabeth and Anna E. at Kelly's of Mucknagh.

DAWSON: Bridget, Catherine, Thomas at Leitrim (Granard Rural D.E.D.). William at Barrack Street, Granard Town. John at Lisryan. Rev. James at Shanmullagh. *ALSO:* Bridget at Joseph Gannon's of Ballymahon Town. Frances at Croskery's of Ardagullion. Rose at McGivney's of Lanesborough Village.

DAYNES: F. at Hewetson's of Church Street, Longford Town.

DEACON: John at Moxham Street, Granard Town. *ALSO:* Maggie at Kavanagh's of Ball Alley Street Lower, Granard Town.

DEALE, DEAL: Alice at Carragh (Granard Rural D.E.D.).

DEAN, DEANE: Thomas at Cloonmore. Joseph at Townparks (Longford Urban No. 1 D.E.D.). (See Dain).

DE BURG-SIDLEY: Rev. Henry F. at Granard.

DEEHAN: Thomas at Creed's of Clooneen (Cox).

DEGNAN, DEIGNAN: See Duignan.

DELAHUNTY: Patrick at Main Street, Granard Town. Thomas at Killashee Village.

DELAMERE: See Delmer.

DELANEY, DELANY:(10): William at Aghnavealoge. James at Carrigeen (Foxhall D.E.D.). Michael, Teresa at Drinan. Mary at Lislom. Mary, Daniel at Ballynahinch. Patrick at Carrow Beg (Cashel West D.E.D.). Patrick at Ballinroddy. Margaret at Church Street, Longford Town. *ALSO:* Patrick at Mullooly's of Tirlickeen. Rose at McCormack's of Derrycassan. Elizabeth at Corrigan's of Drumlish Village. Anne and Elizabeth at Farrington's of Newtownforbes Village. Winifred at Noud's of Main Street, Longford Town (?). Austin at Mary A. Callaghan's of Dublin Street, Longford Town.

DELMER, DELMORE: Mary and Kate at Macken's of Clonwhelan. Walter at Stephenson's of Dublin Street, Longford Town.

DEMPSEY:(15): Bridget at Kilnacarrow (Kilglass D.E.D.). Bridget at Derryoghil. Richard at Leitrim (Granard Rural D.E.D.). Kate at Lisnagrish. Michael at Aghafin. Terence, Ellen, James, Elizabeth at Edgeworthstown Town. James at Barnacor (Rathcline D.E.D.). Bridget at Cartrongarrow. John at Chapel Street, Longford Town. William at Great Water Street, Longford Town. Henry, Thomas at Little Water Street, Longford Town. *ALSO:* Ellen at Greene's of Lissameen. Joseph at McCauley's of Coolagherty.

DEMPSTER: Mary and Francis at McGowan's of St. Michael's Road, Longford Town.

DENIGAN: See Dennigan.

DENISTON: See Denniston.

DENNAN, DENNEN, DENNIN: Philip at Barrack Street, Granard Town. Patrick at Main Street, Granard Town. Bridget, Mary at Derrycassan. Catherine at Freaghmeen. Margaret at Cooleeny. *ALSO:* Patrick at Bernard McCormack's of Dublin Street, Longford Town. (See Dannin, Dinnan,

Denning).

DENNEHY: James at Glenmore (Kilcommock D.E.D.).

DENNENY, DENNANY: William at Ballyboy. Michael at Kiltycreevagh.
Mary at Cahanagh. *ALSO:* Owen and Elizabeth et al. (?) at Anne
McNerney's of Molly.(See Dinnany).

DENNIGAN, DENIGAN, DINNEGAN, DINNIGAN:(34): John at
Ardanragh. James at Sleehaun. James at Derrygowna. John at Derryart.
Laurence at Tomisky. Patrick, Thomas, William at Kilmore Lower. James,
John at Knappoge (Cloondara D.E.D.). James at Mullolagher. James at
Ballyclare (Killashee D.E.D.). Edward at Moygh (Killashee D.E.D.). Anne
at Cloonbrock. Peter at Cloonfore. Patrick, James at Magheraveen. William
at Barroe. Mary at Ardboghil. Peter at Crossea North. Michael, John,
Edward, Thomas at Cartronageeragh. William, William, Samuel at
Clooneeny. Lewis, Thomas at Cloontirm. Michael at Knockanboy. James
at Chapel Lane, Longford Town. Frederick, Andrew, Mary at Great Water
Street, Longford Town. *ALSO:* Mary at Joyce's of Smithfield. Jane at
Martin's of Moneylagan. Elizabeth at Elizabeth Burke's of Cloondara. Mary
at Hopkins' of Killeeny. Celia at Denis Casey's of Magheraveen (?).
Thomas at Hynes's of Barnacor (Rathcline D.E.D.). Anne at McGovern's
of Cloontirm.

DENNIN: See Dennan.

DENNING, DINNING: John at Lisnagrish. Joseph at Creeve. *ALSO:*
Patrick and Edward et al. (?) at Anne McNerney's of Molly. Maggie and
Molly at Killean's of Edgeworthstown Town. Mathew at Ward's of Dublin
Street, Longford Town. Bridget at Cameron's of Main Street, Longford
Town. (See Dennan etc).

DENNIS: Emily at Wilson's of Currygrane.

DENNISTON, DENISTON:(10): Thomas at Clontymullan. William,
Edward at Drumnacross. William, William at Drummeel. Michael at
Lisnanagh. Alexander of Ballagh (Newtownforbes D.E.D.). Patrick at
Cahanagh. James at Cloonrallagh. Joseph at Hyde's Yard, Longford Town.

DENNY: Daniel and Mary at Stanley's of Cloonshannagh or Coolamber
Manor Demesne.

DERMODY:(11): John at Ballinrooey. James at Tober. James at Mullinroe.
Bridget at Ballinulty Lower. Patrick at Melkernagh. William at
Ballymaurice (Granard Rural D.E.D.). Patrick at Tonywardan. Patrick at
Cloonagh (Mullanalaghta D.E.D.). Charles at Freaghmeen. Patrick at

Creeve. Michael at Chapel Lane, Longford Town. *ALSO:* Mary at Tyrrell's of Lissawarriff. James at Leavy's of Melkernagh. Lizzie at Masterson's of Coolagherty. Lizzie at Philip Quinn's of Aghadowry.

McDERMOTT, McDERMOT:(33): Anne at Tully (Agharra D.E.D.). James at Castlerea Mountain. Nabby at Aghanvally. John at Ballymahon Town. Robert at Barry (Ballymahon D.E.D.). John, Thomas at Toome (Ballymahon D.E.D.). Charles at Newpark. Mary at Curry (Kilcommock D.E.D.). John at Kilmakinlan. Thomas at Abbeyderg. John at Lisduff (Drummeel D.E.D.). John at Springtown. Thomas at Smear. William at Tinnynarr. Thomas at Edgeworthstown Town. John at Carrickmoyragh. William at Lissagernal. Mary at Sragarrow. James at Cornollen. Thomas, James, William at Killashee Village. Michael at Corralough. Michael at Mount Davis. Owen at Cloonmucker. Joseph at Lisnacush. Patrick at Crossea North. Elizabeth, Michael at Chapel Lane, Longford Town. Patrick at St. Michael's Road, Longford Town. Bridget, Henry R. at Abbeycartron. *ALSO:* Francis at Kenny's of Castlewilder. Sarah at Margaret Flower's of Barry (Ballymahon D.E.D.). Mary J. at John Yorke's of Barry (Ballymahon D.E.D.). Maggie at Hanly's/Haney's (?) of Cornadowagh. Thomas at Garrahan's of Ballyknock. Bernard at Quinlan's of Main Street, Keenagh Village. Margaret at John Reilly's of Aghagreagh. Peter at James Duffy's (20) of Fihoragh. John at Patrick Greene's of Shantum. Patrick at Rhatigan's of Camlisk More. Thomas at Donovan's of Edgeworthstown Town. Alice M. at Daly's of Drumlish Village. Catherine at Mullally's of Newtownforbes Village. Martin at Davys's of Lanesborough Village. Kate at Kiernan's of Ballinree and Ballymoat. Owen at John Kennedy's of Crossea South. Kate at Patrick Flood's of Glen. Margaret at Mary Hegarty's of Ballymahon Street, Longford Town. James at Ryan's of Broderick's Yard, Longford Town. Sr. Frances at Sr. Green's of Convent Lane, Longford Town. Annie at Laughlin's of Deanscurragh. Thomas at King's of Main Street, Longford Town.

DERWIN: Catherine at Forgney. Michael, James at Cartrons (Kilcommock D.E.D.). Anne at Aghinaspick. Peter at Bawn (Ardagh West D.E.D.). *ALSO:* Mary at Edward Egan's of Derrylough. John at Patrick Gerety's of Derrylough. Patrick et al. at McGeoy's of Caldraghmore. John and Patrick at Geraghty's of Bawn (Ardagh West D.E.D.).

DEVANEY, DEVANY:(15): Thomas at Main Street, Granard Town. John at Ferskill. John at Longfield. Patrick at Aghadowry. Peter, Patrick, James at Kilmahon. John at Treel (Newtownforbes D.E.D.). John at Aghaboy (Aghaboy D.E.D.). Elizabeth, James, Owen, Owen, Patrick, Catherine at Corneddan. *ALSO:* Winifred at Noud's of Main Street, Longford Town (?).

DEVEN: See Devins.

DEVENISH: Rev. William at Kilbride.

DE VERE: Alice at Shanmullagh.

DEVINE:(25): Ellen at Ballymahon Town. Catherine at Caltragh More. James at Ballinalee Village. Bridget at Aghamore Upper. Philip at Carrickateane. Thomas at Castlebaun. John at Lislea (Lislea D.E.D.). James at Barrack Street, Granard Town. John at Edgeworthstown Town. Michael at Kiltycreevagh. Thomas at Bawn (Breanrisk D.E.D.). Patrick, John, Patrick at Derawley. James, Patrick at Lettergonnell.Mary A. at Esker South. Catherine at Kilnacarrow (Aghaboy D.E.D.). Andrew J. at Ballymahon Street, Longford Town. Anne at Chapel Lane, Longford Town. Michael at Main Street, Longford Town. John at New Street, Longford Town. Andrew at Richmond Street, Longford Town. John J. at Sandy Row, Longford Town. James at Townparks (Longford Urban No. 1 D.E.D.). *ALSO:* Thomas and Elizabeth at Casey's of Healy's Terrace, Longford Town. (See Devins).

DEVINS, DEVIN, DEVEN: John at Ballymahon Town. *ALSO:* Elizabeth at Patrick Reynolds's (7) of Cloncowley. Mary at Mahon's of Abbeycartron. (See Devine).

DEVLIN:(14): Bridget at Listraghee. Bridget at Gorteenorna. Patrick at Cloonmore. Catherine at Drumlougher. Francis, Francis, Bridget, Arthur, Daniel at Derrymore. Sarah at Bawn (Ardagh West D.E.D.). James at Cloonahussey. Joseph at Lisbrack (Longford Rural D.E.D.). Patrick at Coach Yard, Longford Town. Owen at St. Michael's Road, Longford Town. *ALSO:* Thomas F. at Farrell's of Trillickacurry. Bridget at Coleman's of Derrymore.

DIAMOND, DIMOND: Major at Abbeyshrule. Francis at Tully (Agharra D.E.D.). Edward at Cornacarta. Jane at Cormaglava. Annie at Derrynabuntale. Robert at Lisnanagh. *ALSO:* Margaret at Lennon's of Rathsallagh. James at Teresa Delaney's of Drinan. Robert and Mary A. at Dawson's of Lisryan. Mary and Katie at Patrick Reynolds's (1) of Cloncowley.

DICKINSON: Francis M. at Main Street, Longford Town.

DICKSON: See Dixon.

DIFFLEY: Martin at Clooneen (Shanly). James at Lismoy. John, Patrick at Begnagh. John at Cloonbearla. Michael, Lawrence at Cloonbrock. Peter at Knock. James at Conroy's Court, Longford Town. *ALSO:* Michael at Lally's of Lismoy. Patrick at Magan's of Ballynakill. Ellen at John Farrell's of Derryad (Mountdavis D.E.D.). John at Reilly's of Cloonbony. John at

Michael Mullooly's of Lehery. Francis at Thomas Farrell's of Lanesborough Village. Kate at John Leavy's of Lanesborough Village. Mary A. at Connolly's of Canal Harbour, Longford Town. Maggie at Harris's of Abbeycartron.

DILLON:(13): Elizabeth at Forgney. George at Newcastle. Thomas at Clooncullen. William at Kilnacarrow (Kilglass D.E.D.). John, John at Ballyreaghan. Ellen at Ballinalee Village. John H., John at Gelshagh. John at Dring. Maria at Drumlish Village. Catherine at Drumbaun. William T. at Main Street, Longford Town. *ALSO:* John at Rhatigan's of Lislom. Ellen at Thomas Doyle's of Molly. Michael at Edward Tracey's of Lislea (Lislea D.E.D.).

DIMOND: See Diamond.

DINNAN, DINNEN: Mary at Carrickmaguirk. Michael at Toome (Mullanalaghta D.E.D.). John at Kilfintan. Joseph at Edgeworthstown Town. (See Dannin, Dennan).

DINNANY: Michael at Creevaghmore (Forgney Civil Ph.). *ALSO:* Mary at Gillan's of Ballymaurice (Granard Rural D.E.D.). (See Denneny).

DINNEGAN, DINNIGAN: See Dennigan.

DINNING: See Denning.

DIXON, DICKSON: John at Kinard. Michael at Bunlahy. Catherine at Aghareagh (Cloondara D.E.D.).

DOBBIN: Harriet at Glack (Longford Rural D.E.D.).

DOBSON: Michael at Edward Donohoe's of Aghamore Lower.

DOCKERY: John at Pettit's of Main Street, Granard Town. Winifred at Farrington's of Newtownforbes Village.

DODD: Michael at Druming. John at Ballynahinch. James at Healy's Terrace, Longford Town. *ALSO:* Mary A. at Devine's of Caltragh More.

DODSON: Anne at Bridge Street, Longford Town.

DOHERTY, DOGHERTY:(33): Patrick at Kilcurry. John at Taghshinny. Patrick at Aghnashannagh. Patrick at Ballinalee Village. John at Currygrane. Thomas at Molly. John at Ball Alley Street Upper, Granard Town. Eugene at Granardkill (Granard Urban D.E.D.). Patrick at New Road, Granard Town. Michael at Ardagullion. Mary at Willsbrook. Mathew at Barne.

Edward, Mary K. at Edgeworthstown Town. Catherine at Carrowbeg (Drumlish D.E.D.). James at Gaigue. Peter at Newtown (Moydow D.E.D.). Garratt, Thomas at Clontumpher. James, Edward, Terence, Terence, John, John at Esker South. James at Soran. Teresa at Drumhaughly. John at Kilmoyle. Thomas, Mary at Rhine. Stephen at Conroy's Court, Longford Town. Patrick at Harbour Row, Longford Town. Mary A. at Market Square, Longford Town. *ALSO:* Catherine at Monahan's of Killeendowd. Margaret et al. at Farrell's of Taghshinny. James at John McDermott's of Ballymahon Town. Garry at Mansergh's of Ballinalee Village. William and Elizabeth at Soden's of Glenoghil. Ellen at Shaw's of Drummeel. Annie and Edward at Murtagh's of Ballinlough. Catherine at Cooke's of Ballinulty Upper. Sr. Teresa at Sr. Hoare's of Grassyard. Eugene at John Kelly's of Main Street, Granard Town. Catherine at Reynolds's of Ferskill. Annie at Sullivan's of Willsbrook. Maggie at Greene's of Lisnagrish. Sr. Susan, Mary at Rev. Mother Farrington's of Newtownforbes Village. Mary and Maria at Peter Hughes's of Back of the Hill. Kate at James Dunne's of Kiltyreher (Templemichael Civil Ph.). John at Toole's of Dublin Street, Longford Town. Anne and Bridget at Toole's of Great Water Street, Longford Town. Maria at King's of Main Street, Longford Town.

DOLAN:(58): Margaret at Castlewilder. Patrick at Legan. Michael at Cloonagh (Kilglass D.E.D.). Patrick at Ballybeg. Patrick at Screeboge.Peter at Tennalick. Patrick at Derryoghil. Thomas, Patrick at Cross (Cashel West D.E.D.). Patrick, Mary, Lawrence, Catherine, Thomas at Drumnee. Lawrence at Pollagh. James at Edera. John at Aghamore (Ballinalee D.E.D.). Francis at Ballinalee Village. Julia at Aghakilmore. Margaret, Thomas at Coolcor. James, Patrick, Julia at Mullinroe. Patrick, John, Mary at Carrickduff. Catherine at Aghabrack. Catherine at Leitrim (Granard Rural D.E.D.). Mary at Main Street, Granard Town. Peter at Graffoge (Milltown D.E.D.). Hugh at Farmullagh. Peter at Lisnageeragh. Edward at Monadarragh. Thomas at Bracklon. James, Margaret at Edgeworthstown Town. Margaret, John, Felix at Aghadowry. Patrick, Michael, Peter, Patrick, Bridget at Kiltycreevagh. James at Cloonelly. Peter at Lettergonnell. Thomas at Newtownforbes Village. Patrick at Killashee Village. William, Patrick at Trillickacurry. Patrick at Cloonker. James at Aghaloughan. Patrick at Moyra and Fortmill. John at Broderick's Yard, Longford Town. James, Rev. Patrick at Dublin Street, Longford Town. *ALSO:* Thomas at Fitzgerald's of Smithfield. Margaret at Gannon's of Carrigeen (Foxhall D.E.D.). Patrick at John Carroll's of Clontymullan. Annie and Bridget at Hughes's of Sleehaun (Sankey). John at Gerety's of Killinbore. Bessy at Elizabeth Mulvihill's (109) of Ballymahon Town. Mary at Michael Derwin's of Cartrons (Kilcommock D.E.D.). Terence at Moore's of Cartronawar (Kilcommock D.E.D.). Kate at Andrew King's of Main Street, Keenagh Village (?). Patrick at Brady's of Cartronamarkey. Rose A. at Mulligan's of Ballinulty Lower. James at Flood's of Ballymore. Richard at Clark's of Leitrim (Granard Rural D.E.D.). Sr. Julia at Sr. Hoare's of

Grassyard. Patrick at Bridget Reilly's of Toome (Mullanalaghta D.E.D.). John at Denneny's of Kiltycreevagh. Rose at Patrick Donnelly's (40) of Kiltycreevagh. Michael at Bridget McNamee's of Cloonelly. Annie at Davis's of Gaigue. Kate at Telford's of Grillagh (Killashee D.E.D.). James et al. at Mary Farrell's (5) of Caldraghmore. John at Luke Farrell's of Lisnacush. Martha at John Genty's of Corneddan. John at Keegan's of Corboy. Maria at Mallon's of Dublin Street, Longford Town. Lizzie at Elizabeth Kelly's of Dublin Street, Longford Town. Bridget at Boyers' (4) of Main Street, Longford Town. Mary A. at Fee's of Church Street, Longford Town.

McDONAGH, McDONOUGH:(14): Thomas, Francis at Cloonard (Ballymahon D.E.D.). Peter at Lismacmurrogh. Hugh at Kilshruley. Patrick at Drummeel. Joseph at Creevy. Patrick at Lisryan. Thomas at Cartronlebagh. Patrick at Ballyclare (Moydow D.E.D.). Arthur at Cloonbony. Thomas at Derrygeel. John at Cloonahard. Martin at Bog Lane, Longford Town. Francis at Bridge Street, Longford Town. *ALSO:* James at Kate Whelan's of Ballymahon Town. Ellen and Mary at Skelly's of Lisnanagh. Florence at Martha Beatty's of Cleggill. Patrick at Gannon's of Glack (Longford Urban No. 1 D.E.D.).

McDONALD: Ellen at Clooneen (Forgney D.E.D.). John at Sleehaun. Patrick at Ball Alley Street Upper, Granard Town. Mary at Agnagore (?). *ALSO:* Michael at Regan's of Smithfield. Edward at Joyce's of Smithfield. James et al. at Clines' of Cleenrah. Michael at Michael Reilly's of Enaghan. Anne at Garrahan's of Bohermore. Jane at Patrick Kelly's of Dublin Street, Longford Town. Nannie at Jane Donnelly's of Great Water Street, Longford Town (?). Maggie at Cooney's of Main Street, Longford Town. (See McDonnell).

DONALDSON: Mary A. at Mansergh's of Ballinalee Village.

DONEGAN, DUNIGAN, DUNICAN:(12): John, Michael at Listobit. William at Drumnacor. Michael, Elizabeth at Lisnagrish. Patrick, James, Patrick at Carrickmoyragh. Patrick at Annaghmore. Winifred, Ann (?), Patrick at Derrygeel. *ALSO:* William and Ellen at Moughty's of Daroge. Mary at Richard Cummins's of Ballymahon Town. Michael at McKenna's of Leitrim (Breanrisk D.E.D.). Celia at Denis Casey's of Magheraveen (?). Winifred at John Leavy's of Lanesborough Village. James at Ellen Hughes's of Back of the Hill. Margaret of Hoare's of Deanscurragh.

DONLON:(50): John, Peter at Castlerea Mountain. Bernard at Doory. Elizabeth at Forgney. John at Newcastle. Michael, John at Clooncullen. William at Keel (Kilglass D.E.D.). James at Ballymahon Town. Thomas at Derraghan Beg. Michael at Derrygowna. John at Corlea. Michael at Ards. Peter at Laughil (Kilcommock D.E.D.). John at Doonacurry

(Kilcommock Civil Ph.). Winford at Ledwithstown (Kilcommock Civil Ph.). James at Cartronamarkey. Bridget at Clooneen (Creevy D.E.D.). Anne at Corbaun or Leitrim. John at Kilmore. Margaret at Kilmore Lower. Jane at Aghnaskea. Thomas at Ballyclare (Killashee D.E.D.). Peter at Sharvoge. Andrew at Derryad (Mountdavis D.E.D.). Peter, Patrick at Cloonker. John at Meeltanagh (Moydow D.E.D.). Jane at Monascallaghan. Timothy, James, John, Bridget, Peter at Derryshannoge. James, Bridget at Aghaloughan. Bridget at Carrowstrawly. Catherine, Owen at Ardboghil. Catherine at Barneygole. Elizabeth, John at Garryconnell. Edward at Clooncaulfield (?). John at Drumlougher (?). Anne at Aghanahown. James at Ballymakeegan. James at Farnagh. Patrick at Fee's Terrace, Longford Town. Michael at Great Water St., Longford Town. Michael at Abbeycartron. *ALSO:* Bridget at Austin's of Drumanure. John at Farrell's of Carrickedmond. Mary at Albert Shaw's of Ballymahon Town. Teresa at John Yorke's of Barry (Ballymahon D.E.D.). Cecilia at Thomas Yorke's of Barry (Ballymahon D.E.D.). Catherine at Killian's of Derrygowna. Mary at Hanly's of Corrool (Kenny). Mary at Davis's of Bank Street, Granard Town. Margaret at Michael Kelly's of Main Street, Granard Town. Thomas at Boyce's of Lissanure. Peter at Elizabeth Holmes's of Kilmore Lower. Anne M. at Bridget Regan's of Cloonmore. Patrick at John Skelly's of Carrigeens. Catherine at Dwyer's of Bohernacross. John at Coffey's of Drumlougher. Annie at Bridget Lenahan's of Lisduff (Montgomery). John at Nixon's of Dublin St., Longford Town. Anne at Howard's of Great Water St., Longford Town. James at Shanley's of Main St., Longford Town. Patrick at Mathew Farrell's of Main Street, Longford Town. John H. and Alice J. at Devine's of Townparks (Longford Urban No. 1 D.E.D.). (See Donnellan).

McDONNELL:(24): Michael at Ratharney. John at Mornin. John at Forgney. John at Kilglass and Cloonagh. John at Aghnavealoge. Patrick at Sleehaun (Sankey). Francis at Toome (Ballymahon D.E.D.). James at Cross (Cashel West D.E.D.). Margaret at Corbeagh. Roger at Ballinulty Lower. Elizabeth at Rossan. Bridget at Ball Alley Street Upper, Granard Town. John at New Road, Granard Town. John at Rathcronan. Bridget at Melkagh. Bridget at Drumlish. Hugh at Lisnabo. Mary at Aghnagore. Thomas at Finnaragh. Mary at Feraghfad. James at Garvagh (Longford Rural D.E.D.). Michael at Campbell's Row, Longford Town. Charles at Healy's Terrace, Longford Town. Margaret at St. Michael's Road, Longford Town. *ALSO:* Patrick at Cahill's of Ardanragh. Mary A. at Clarke's of Mornin. Peter at Ledwith's of Sleehaun. John at Elizabeth Mulvihill's (106) of Ballymahon Town. Mary at Patrick Smyth's of Culray. Annie at Reilly's of Rossan. Bridget at Donohoe's of Ballymaurice (Granard Rural D.E.D.). Mary at Pettit's of Main Street, Granard Town. Elizabeth at Keegan's of Main Street, Granard Town. Patrick and Jane at Anne Mahon's of Farmullagh. Georgina at Farrington's of Newtownforbes Village. Owen at Allen's of Lismoy. Mary and Emily at Gutherie's of Aghnagore. Kate at

Kearney's of Crossea North (?). Patrick at Michael Kenny's of Moor. Annie at Jane Donnelly's of Great Water Street, Longford Town. F. at Hewetson's of Church Street, Longford Town. (See McDonald, McDaniel).

O'DONNELL:(12): Michael at Kilcommock Glebe. Hugh, Patrick at Molly. Jane, Patrick at Cam. Michael at Dunbeggan (Moydow D.E.D.). Bernard at Moydow Glebe. Thomas at Soran. Patrick at Lyanmore. Bridget at Chapel Lane, Longford Town. Joseph at Dublin Street, Longford Town. Susan at Abbeycartron. *ALSO:* Patrick at Peter Kiernan's of Main Street, Granard Town. Mary at James Devany's of Corneddan. Robert of Lanesborough Barracks. Mary at McElnea's of Main Street, Longford Town.

DONNELLAN, DONOLAN:(11): Thomas at Ballinamore. Thomas, Anne, Peter, Rose at Lehery. Michael at Tullyvrane. John at Lanesborough Village. Edward, Edward at Clooncaulfield. John at Drumlougher. Anne at Aghanahown (?). *ALSO:* Anne at Berrane's of Carrickglass Demesne (Templemichael Civil Ph.). (See Donlon).

DONNELLY, DONNOLLY:(52): John at Torboy. Patrick at Corrabola (Dorry D.E.D.). Thomas at Smithfield. Edward at Daroge. Bridget at Ballagh (Cashel West D.E.D.). William at Cashel. Edward at Cartronbrack. Bernard at Ballyreaghan. John at Drumnahara. James at Moatfarrell. Anne at Bunlahy. John at Ballinrud Glebe. Owen at Cloonaghmore. Patrick at Carrickmaguirk. Catherine at Edenmore. William, Felix at Glenmore (Ballinamuck East D.E.D.). Margaret, James, Ellen, Michael, Bridget, Patrick, Owen, Patrick, Anne, Patrick at Kiltycreevagh. Edward, Felix, Bridget, James at Shanmullagh. Edward, Edward at Currygranny. Michael at Gaigue. Thomas at Briskil. Catherine at Lissanurlan. Ellen, Ann at Cloonfore. John at Magheraveen. John at Trillickacurry. Margaret at Aghaboy (Aghaboy D.E.D.). Patrick at Esker South.Elizabeth at Rabbitpark. Elizabeth at Cartronawar (Corboy D.E.D.). Patrick at Cooleeny. Mary at Bog Lane, Longford Town. Anne, Daniel, Margaret at Chapel Lane, Longford Town. Sarah at Convent Lane, Longford Town. Daniel, Jane at Great Water Street, Longford Town. *ALSO:* Bridget at Moran's of Carrigeen (Foxhall D.E.D.). Thomas at Moughty's of Daroge. Anne at Dinnigan's of Derryart. Julia at Duffy's of Rinroe. Mary at Michael Galligan's of Derragh. Michael at McConkey's of Cornacullew. Bridget at Mimnagh's of Derrynacross. Maria at Peter Donlon's of Derryshannoge. Elizabeth at John Genty's of Corneddan. Elizabeth at James Mahon's of Killeenatruan. Nannie at Skelly's of Main Street, Longford Town. Rose at Healy's of Market Square, Longford Town.

DONOHOE:(76): Mary at Smithfield. Bridget at Ballyglassin. Bernard at Glenoghil. Michael at Lissameen. Thomas at Laughil (Edgeworth). Catherine at Aghacordrinan. John at Lislea (Lislea D.E.D.). James at

Cranally. Bernard at Aghakeeran. Thomas, Michael, Michael, Thomas, Bernard, Matthew at Aghakine. Thomas, Catherine, Mary at Sonnagh. Lawrence at Ballywillin. Maria, Owen, John at Springtown. Hugh at Bunlahy. Patrick at Cloonfin. Mary, Patrick at Mullinroe. Thomas at Ballyboy. Patrick at Killasona. Farrel at Ballymaurice (Granard Rural D.E.D.). John at Ballynacross (Granard Rural D.E.D.). Bridget at Ball Alley St., Lower, Granard Town. Michael at Ball Alley St., Upper, Granard Town. Peter at Ballynacross (Granard Urban D.E.D.). Charles at Barrack Street, Granard Town. Mary, Michael at Carrickmaguirk. Thomas at Cleenrah. Patrick, Hugh, James at Smear. Owen, John at Ballyduffy. William, James, Hugh, Edward, Patrick, Mary, Edward, John, Ellen, John at Drumard. Michael, Patrick, John at Farmullagh. Bernard, James at Derrycassan. Patrick at Larkfield. Peter at Rinnenny. Joseph at Fostragh. John at Cloonellan. Edward, Michael, James, Owen at Aghamore Lower. Thomas at Annagh (Drumgort D.E.D.). Mary, James, John at Corglass. John at Kiltycon. Peter, Patrick at Leggagh. Edward at Grillagh (Ardagh West D.E.D.). Bernard at Killoe Glebe. John at Rhine. Jane at Great Water Street, Longford Town. *ALSO:* Bernard at William Farrell's of Ardanragh. Mary A. and Hugh at Julia Fox's of Aghakilmore. Bridget at John Brady's of Gelshagh. Bernard at John McNerney's of Aghakine. Rose at Seery's of Aghakine. Patrick at Anne McCabe's of Aghakine. Philip at Owen Reilly's of Carrickadorrish. Annie at Bridget Doyle's of Sonnagh. James at John Doyle's of Sonnagh. Patrick at Briody's of Cartronbore. John at Plunkett's of Bunlahy. Mary at Cassidy's of Mullinroe. Joseph and John at Laurence Early's of Creevy. Farrel at Pollard's of Leitrim (Granard Rural D.E.D.). Maggie at Lizzie Brady's of Main Street, Granard Town. Michael at Flood's of Main Street, Granard Town. Mary at John Kelly's of Main Street, Granard Town. Anne at James Smyth's (56) of Main Street, Granard Town. Kate at Hinds's of Cooldoney. Annie at Ginty's of Dunbeggan (Columbkille D.E.D.). James at Catherine Curwin's of Mollyglass. Edward at Patrick Gormley's of Polladooey. Edward at Mary Mulligan's of Crott. Edward at Patrick Mulligan's of Birrinagh. Patrick at Boyle's of Drumard. James et al. at Gray's of Farmullagh. Annie at Bernard Masterson's (23) of Farmullagh. Mary at Dopping-Hepenstal's of Derrycassan. Rose at McGuiness's of Derrycassan. Mary F. at Tynan's of Castlenugent. John at Fegan's of Ballaghgowla and Froghan. George at Kiernan's of Curry (Coolamber D.E.D.). Michael et al. at James Wiggins's of Rathmore (Ballinamuck East D.E.D.). James at Morrison's of Glenmore (Ballinamuck East D.E.D.). Anna at Peter Mulligan's of Moyne. Francis at McNamee's of Leggagh. Bridget at McGivney's of Lanesborough Village. Peter and John at Malachy Kelly's of Bog Lane, Longford Town. Anne at Mulheran's of Conroy's Court, Longford Town. Annie at Mayne's of Abbeycartron. Rose at McDermot's of Abbeycartron.

DONOLAN: See Donnellan.

McDONOUGH: See McDonagh.

DONOVAN: Mary at Carrigeen (Foxhall D.E.D.). John at Ballycloghan. Catherine at Druming. Jeremiah at Barrack Street, Granard Town. Thomas H. at Edgeworthstown Town. *ALSO:* Patrick at McCormack's of Feraghfad.

DOOGAN: See Duggan.

DOOLADY: Mary at Tawnagh.

DOOLEY, DOOLY: John at Doory. James at Coolnafinnoge. Patrick at Treel (Foxhall D.E.D.). Mary at Ledwithstown (Kilcommock Civil Ph.). Mary at Barnacor (Rathcline D.E.D.). *ALSO:* Bridget et al. at Julia O'Connor's of Currycreaghan. Elizabeth at Margaret Newman's of Lisnacreevy. William at O'Brien's of Daroge. Michael at John Feeney's of Creevagh Beg, Ballymahon Town. Michael at Wilson's of Currygrane. Thomas at Edward Donohoe's (8) of Drumard. Michael at Devine's of Sandy Row, Longford Town. Michael at Stewart's of St. Michael's Road, Longford Town.

DOOLIN: William at Loughan.

DOONAN: Mary, Thomas, Stephen at Leitrim (Breanrisk D.E.D.). Hugh at Enybegs. *ALSO:* Mary at Michael Rodgers' of Cloonellan.

DOONER:(11): Patrick at Lislea (Doory D.E.D.). Mary E. at Sragarrow. Patrick at Cloonart North. Edward at Lismore. Thomas at Templeton Glebe. Lizzie at Curry (Moydow D.E.D.). Joseph at Dunbeggan (Moydow D.E.D.). Patrick at Ballygar. William, John, Elizabeth at Cartrongarrow. *ALSO:* Hugh at Duffy's of Cartrongarrow.

DOONIGAN: See Donegan.

DOORIGAN, DORIGAN, DURIGAN, DOURIGAN: Charles at Annaghcooleen. Francis at Cloonageeher. Charles at Magheraveen.

DOORIS, DORIS:(25): Bernard at Aghnashannagh. James at Aghakeeran. Patrick, Catherine at Edgeworthstown Town. John, Michael, Ellen, Daniel at Kiltycreevagh. Margaret at Leitrim (Breanrisk D.E.D.). Anne, John at Ballincurry. Michael, Daniel at Kilnashee. Patrick at Garrowhill. John at Cartrongolan. Elizabeth at Enybegs. Mary at Brianstown. Francis at Cornollen. Matthew at Kilmore Lower. Mary, Peter at Aghaboy (Aghaboy

D.E.D.). Thomas, Anne at Corneddan. Patrick at Killeter. Denis at Corboy. *ALSO:* James at O'Farrell's of Drummeel. Peter at Elizabeth McCann's of Carrowbeg (Drumlish D.E.D.). Daniel at Golden's of Drumlish Village.

Francis at Bridget Molloy's (7) of Derryheelan. Bridget at Musters' of Brianstown. Rose at James Hughes's of Rhine. John at Fullam's of Deanscurragh.

DOORLY: Thomas at Plunkett's of Main Street, Longford Town.

DOPPING-HEPENSTAL: Susanna at Derrycassan. *ALSO:* Maxwell E. at Fox's of Foxhall.

DORAN: William, John at Ardanragh. Henry at Treel (Foxhall D.E.D.). Annie at Claras. Joseph at Moxham Street, Granard Town. Elizabeth at Ringowny. John at Moatavally. Elizabeth at Glack (Longford Rural D.E.D.). *ALSO:* William at Peter Kiernan's of Main Street, Granard Town.

DORIS, DORRIS: See Dooris.

DOURIGAN, DORIGAN: See Doorigan.

DOVEY: G.W. at Hewetson's of Church Street, Longford Town.

DOWD:(43): Bernard at Lightfield. Michael, Bernard, Mary at Aghnacross. Bernard at Fortwilliam. Mary at Curry (Kilcommock D.E.D.). Peter at Lislea (Lislea D.E.D.). Patrick at Ballybrien. Edward at Ballymore. Michael at Cloontagh. Ellen at Kilnashee. John, Mary at Drumnacooha. John at Cahanagh. Denis, Catherine, Patrick at Kilmore Upper. Michael at Templeton Glebe. James at Carrowmanagh. Timothy at Crockaun. Richard at Gowlan. Bernard at Newtown (Moydow D.E.D.). Peter at Cloonevit. James at Commock. James at Lisgurry. James at Toneen (Moydow D.E.D.). Patrick at Carrowstrawly. John, Hanora at Commons South. Elizabeth at Killinure. Mathew at Lehery. Thomas, James at Turreen. Patrick at Esker South. John, John at Gorteenagloon. Michael at Feraghfad. John at Mullaghavorneen. John at Ballymahon Street, Longford Town. Thomas, Mary at Bog Lane, Longford Town. Anne at Great Water Street, Longford Town. Patrick at Killashee Street, Longford Town. *ALSO:* Kate at Ledwith's of Sleehaun. Bernard at John Majore's of Cartron (Granard Rural D.E.D.). John at Colsten's of Ballaghgowla and Froghan. Michael at Tally's of Drumnacooha. Teresa and Anne at Farrington's of Newtownforbes Village. Ellen at Corcoran's of Brianstown. Kate at Reynolds's of Cloonmore. Patrick et al. at Stephen's of Moydow Glebe. Martin and Margaret at Patrick Murphy's of Esker South. John at Greene's of Cornapark. Francis at Rodgers' of Killinlastra. Anne at Lamb's of Earl Street, Longford Town. Francis at McNerney's of New Street, Longford Town.

O'DOWD: Catherine at Bridge Street, Longford Town.

DOWDALL: Rev. James J. at Cloonagh (Mullanalaghta D.E.D.). Henry at Ballinamore. *ALSO:* Anne and Bridget at Fox's of Foxhall. May at Gerety's of Killinbore. James at John McHugh's of Tennalick. Francis at Mathew Farrell's of Main Street, Longford Town.

McDOWELL:(14): William at Cartrons (Kilcommock D.E.D.). Alexander at Glenmore (Kilcommock D.E.D.). Mathew at Ballynascraw. Elizabeth at Listraghee. Anne, John at Drumnacross. Patrick at Castlebrock. Alice A. at Granardkill (Granard Urban D.E.D.). James, James at Smear. Mathew at Castleforbes Demesne. Robert at Creenagh. Maria at Gorteenorna. Jane at Cross (Ardagh East D.E.D.). *ALSO:* Roseanne at Killaine's of Kilshruley. Elizabeth at Cavanagh's of Ballynascraw. James at Smith's of Listraghee. Mary at Smith's of Coolagherty. Kate at Kearney's of Crossea North (?). Donald at McManus's of Main Street, Longford Town.

DOWLER: Bryan at Tennalough. John at Screeboge. Mary at Knockagh. John at Edgeworthstown Town. Elizabeth at Moor. George at Ballynagoshen. John at Corboy. Jane at Lisnamuck. *ALSO:* William at Kenny's of Churchquarter.

DOWLING: Timothy at Corlea. Mary A. at Kilshruley. *ALSO:* James at King-Harman's of Newcastle. George at Lynch's of Listraghee. Johanna at Whyte's of Clonwhelan. Mary A. at Farrington's of Newtownforbes Village.

DOWNES: Patrick at Forgney. Patrick at Barrack St., Granard Town. *ALSO:* Elizabeth and Margaret, Bridget at Farrington's of Newtownforbes Village.

DOWNEY: James, John at Ballymahon Town. *ALSO:* M. at Hewetson's of Church Street, Longford Town.

DOYLE:(51): Anne at Doory. Thomas at Clooncallow. Catherine at Keel (Forgney D.E.D.). George at Clontymullan. Patrick at Ballymahon Town. John at Ballynascraw. James, Bernard at Ballyreaghan. Patrick at Tullybaun. James at Aghagreagh. John at Aghamore Upper. James, Thomas at Molly. Patrick at Cranally. Thomas at Aghakine. Francis at Carrickadorrish. Bridget, John at Sonnagh. Thomas at Ballinulty Lower. John at Mollyglass. Patrick, John, Patrick at Rosduff. Owen, Kate, John, Michael, Patrick at Smear. Patrick at Aghagah. John, John at Drumhalry. Thomas at Farmullagh. William at Cam. Patrick at Glenmore (Ballinamuck East D.E.D.). Hugh at Cloncowley. John at Aghnamaddoo. Thomas at Moyne. Michael at Annagh (Drumgort D.E.D.). Elizabeth at Newtownforbes Village. James, John at Creenagh. Owen at Moneylagan. Joseph at Cloonrallagh. Thomas at Newtown (Moydow D.E.D.). Michael at Soran. Patrick at Ballinroddy. Marcella at Lenaboy. Alice, Bernard at Garvagh

(Longford Rural D.E.D.). James at St. Mel's Road, Longford Town. Bridget at Abbeycartron. *ALSO:* John at Jessop's of Doory. Julia at Noragh Ryan's of Barnacor (Ledwithstown D.E.D.). Anne at Kiernan's of Culray. William at Thomas Donohoe's (3) of Aghakine. Rose at Reilly's of Mollyglass. James at Catherine Kiernan's of Smear. Patrick at Molphy's of Gneeve. Rose and Kate at James Duffy's of Kilsallagh. Mary at McGrath's of Ringowny. Patrick at Cullen's of Longfield. Mary A. at John Murtagh's of Cloonback. William at James Duffy's of Moyne. James at Quinn's of Banghill. Joseph at Flattery's of Barney. Ellen and Mary at Cordner's of Mullagh. Michael at Cox's of Ballymahon Street, Longford Town. James at Boyd's of Main Street, Longford Town. Mary A. at McElnea's of Main Street, Longford Town. Edward at Fleming's of Abbeycartron.

DRAKE: Mary at Carrickduff. Anne, Edward at Ballinulty Upper. *ALSO:* Mary at John Lynch's of Dring.

DRAPER: Thomas at Clooncullen. Thomas at Cloonard (Ballymahon D.E.D.). John at Island.

DRENNAN: Joseph at Barrack Street, Granard Town.

DREW: Isabella D. at Carrickmoyragh. Maria, Thomas, James at Ballagh (Newtownforbes D.E.D.). *ALSO:* Mary et al. at Keena's of Tennalick.

O'DRISCOLL: M. at Hewetson's of Church Street, Longford Town.

DROUGHT: Elizabeth at Stewart's of Edgeworthstown Town.

DRUM: Eugene, Michael at Main Street, Granard Town. William at Cloonellan. John at Ahanagh. James at Edercloon.

DRUMMOND: Margaret at Bond's of Newtownbond.

DUCK: See Duke.

DUDLEY: D. at Muir's of Edgeworthstown Town.

DUDSEM: Bridget at Hugh Flood's of Ballymahon Town.

DUFF: Joseph N. at Mornin. Edward at Ballymacshane. Margaret at Killinbore. Thomas at Tennalick. Thomas at Ballymahon Town. *ALSO:* Lizzie at McCormack's of Killinbore.

DUFFY:(78): Thomas at Killeen (Foxhall D.E.D.). Michael, Patrick at Garrycam. John at Kilcurry. Patrick at Cavan. Patrick at Ballinalee Village. Philip at Aghamore Upper. James at Derreenavoggy. Catherine at Molly.

Patrick at Kilbride. Patrick at Coolcor. Mary at Cloonaghmore. Patrick at
Rinroe. Philip, Bridget at Carrickmaguirk. John at Smear. Patrick, Mary,
Ellen, James, Michael, James at Aghagah. John, Mathew, John, Owen at
Ballyduffy. John, William, Bernard, Catherine, Rose, Anne at Drumhalry.
John, Michael, James, James, James, Catherine, Bridget, Margaret, Michael
at Fihoragh. Michael, Michael at Kilmore. James, Mary at Kilsallagh.
Daniel at Monadarragh. Mary at Lackan. William J. at Edgeworthstown
Town.   Philip at Cloonback. Philip at Cuingareen. Felix, Bernard at
Aghadowry. Elizabeth at Lettergullion. John at Cloontagh. John, Charles,
Catherine, James at Moyne. Charles at Annagh (Drumgort D.E.D.). Rose
at Cornacullew. Thomas at Leggagh. John at Brocklagh. Francis at Mullagh
Bog. William at Cloontamore. Mary at Aghaboy (Aghaboy D.E.D.).
Bernard at Ballinree and Ballymoat. Thomas, James, Michael, John at
Crossea South. John at Aghintemple. William at Cartrongarrow. Michael,
Annie, John at Cloonee. Mary at Drumhaughly. Thomas at Lisnamuck.
Thomas (absent from No. 32) at Ballymahon Street, Longford Town.
ALSO: Bernard at Edward Monaghan's of Aghagreagh. James at Quinn's
of Carrowlinan. James at Doyle's of Ballinulty Lower. Susan at Boylan's
of Cleenrah. Catherine at Mary McKeon's of Smear. Rose at Carolan's of
Farmullagh. Kate at Gormley's of Shanmullagh. Edward and Anne M. at
Peter Mulligan's of Moyne. May at Marsden's of Glebe (Cloondara
D.E.D.). James at Gunshenan's of Killashee Village. Elizabeth at Kelly's
of Trillickacurry. James at Kiernan's of Carnan. Joseph at Peter Igoe's of
Ballymahon Street, Longford Town. Francis at Molloy's of Ballymahon
Street, Longford Town. William J. at Lizzie Hagarty's of Ballymahon
Street, Longford Town. Elizabeth and Kate at Kelly's of Richmond Street,
Longford Town. Mary at Dunne's of St. Mel's Road, Longford Town.

DUGDALE: Thomas at Craane. Joseph at Esker South.

DUGGAN, DOOGAN: Edward at Gorteenclareen. Terence at Clooneen
(Creevy D.E.D.). Mary at Crott. Thomas at Farmullagh. Daniel at
Cloonbearla. John at Knockatarry Poynton. Ellen at Dwyer's Yard.
Longford Town. *ALSO:* Michael at Airlie's of Main Street, Longford Town.
John at Devine's of Main Street, Longford Town.

DUIGAN: Anne at Derrygeel.

DUIGNAIM: Mary at Lyon's of Kilcommock Glebe.

DUIGNAN, DEGNAN, DEIGNAN:(24): Bridget at Creevagh Beg. Patrick
at Aghakine. John at Rosduff. Francis at Edenmore. John at Kiltycreevagh.
Jane at Shanmullagh. Patrick, Francis at Corglass. Paul, Peter, Paul,
Thomas, Patrick at Leggagh. Peter at Derawley. Rose A. at Kilmacannon.
James at Creenagh. Andrew at Cornollen. John at Knockatarry Poynton.
Michael at Knock. Michael at Kiltybegs. Patrick, James at Cloonee.

Michael, James at Kiltyreher (Killoe Civil Ph.). *ALSO:* Michael at Harman's of Glenmore (Kilcommock D.E.D.). Mary at Lyon's of Kilcommock Glebe (?). Mary at James Gormley's of Cornadrung. John at Bernard Berry's of Enaghan. Mary A. at O'Hara's of Drumlish. Patrick at Percival's of Minard. Thomas at Kelly's of Cloonmucker. James at Thomas Quinn's of Kiltyreher (Killoe Civil Ph.). Peter at O'Neill's of Main Street, Longford Town.

DUKE, DUCK: Albert at Mosstown (Rathcline Barony). John, John at Dwyer's Yard, Longford Town. *ALSO:* Anne and Francis at Patrick Clarke's of Clontymullan. Kate at Nolan's of Kilsallagh.

DUNCAN: James, Thomas, Patrick at Ballymahon Town.

DUNICAN, DUNIGAN: See Donegan.

DUNLEAVY, DUNLEAVEY:(11): Michael F. at Lislea (Lislea D.E.D.). Christopher at Culleenmore. James at Killasona. John, Patrick, Bridget, Anne, Patrick at Oghil. Bryan at Clontumpher. Jane at Great Water Street, Longford Town. Bridget at Hyde's Yard, Longford Town. *ALSO:* Denis at Early's of Ringowny. Kate at Bridget Mimna's of Kilnashee. William at Keogh's of Cartrongolan. Mary and Margaret at Farrington's of Newtownforbes Village. Mary at Adam's of Craane. Alice and Bridget at Patrick Prunty's of Clontumpher.

DUNLOP: Lizzie at Lisduff (Longford Rural D.E.D.).

DUNNE, DUNN:(15): Lawrence at Ballymahon Town. Patrick at Derraghan Beg. Michael at Elfeet (Adamson). Daniel at Firmount. Edward, Hugh at Cooldoney. Mary at Dunbeggan (Columbkille D.E.D.). Patrick at Lanesborough Village. Maurice at Killeter. Michael, James at Kiltyreher (Templemichael Civil Ph.). James H. at Fee's Terrace, Longford Town. Mary, Edward at Great Water Street, Longford Town. Patrick at St. Mel's Road, Longford Town. *ALSO:* Maggie at Killian's of Derrygowna. Peter J. at Hevehan's of Derrygowna. Margaret and Mary at Bernard Dowd's of Aghnacross. Patrick at Kearney's of Cornadowagh. Lizzie at McGovern's of Ballinulty Lower. Patrick at Thomas Early's of Derragh. Bridget at McGuire's of Cleenrah. Kate at Duffy's of Monadarragh. Bridget at Egan's of Cloontagh. Michael at John Hopkins' of Cloonfore. John at Keenan's of Kiltyreher (Killoe Civil Ph.). Michael at Brady's of Ballymahon Street, Longford Town. James at Cox's of Ballymahon Street, Longford Town. Agnes M. at Green's of Convent Lane, Longford Town. Heline at McNeill's of St. Mel's Road, Longford Town.

DUNNION: Hanora at Ann Walsh's of Knock.

DUNPHY: Clara J. at Wilson's of Main Street, Keenagh Village.

DURIGAN: See Doorigan.

DURKAN: Hugh at Leonard's of Main Street, Granard Town. Bernard et al. at Moraen's of Coach Yard, Longford Town.

DURRANT: J.C. at Hewetson's of Church Street, Longford Town.

DWYER: Margaret at Kilnacarrow (Kilglass D.E.D.). John at Lissanure. Patrick at Toneen (Moydow D.E.D.). Rose at Bohernacross. Michael at Sandy Row, Longford Town. *ALSO:* Anne at William Greene's of Lissanure.

O'DWYER: James at Carragh (Granard Urban D.E.D.). *ALSO:* William at Francis Cahill's of Ballymahon Town.

DYAS: Michael at Cloonkeen (Ballymahon D.E.D.). *ALSO:* Mary A. at Edward Kenny's of Main Street, Longford Town.

EAKINS: Joseph at Coolnahinch (Longford Rural D.E.D.).

EARLY, EARLEY:(17): John at Clooncoose (Ballinalee D.E.D.). Patrick at Ballinalee Village. Patrick at Abbeylara Village. Michael at Cloghchurnel. Laurence, Bernard at Creevy. Michael at Bank Street, Granard Town. Patrick at The Hill, Granard Town. Patrick at Tonywardan. Edward, Thomas, Peter at Derragh. Patrick at Toome (Mullanalaghta D.E.D.). James at Ringowny. James at Kilfintan Lower or Crancam. Mary at Sragarrow. Annie at St. Mel's Road, Longford Town. (?) *ALSO:* Bridget at Patrick Geraghty's of Ballymore. Catherine at Carroll's of Aghaboy (Milltown D.E.D.). Patrick at Farrell's of Graffoge (Milltown D.E.D.). James at Green's of Corclaragh. Rosanna at Boyle's of Corglass (?). Annie at Caldwell's of Corboy. Mary at Ward's of Dublin Street, Longford Town. Martin at Irwin's of Main Street, Longford Town. (See Airlie).

EBBITT: Mary A. at Drumlish Village. *ALSO:* Francis at Boyers' (2) of Main Street, Longford Town.

EDGELY: Catherine at Kate Cassedy's of Ballyduffy. Mary at Maher's of Glenmore (Ballinamuck East D.E.D.). John and William at Berry's of Glenmore (Ballinamuck East D.E.D.). Peter at Hogan's of Glenmore (Ballinamuck East D.E.D.).

EDGEWORTH: Rev. John E. at Gorteen. Thomas N. at Kilshruley. Antonio E. at Edgeworthstown. John N. at Lisbrack (Newtownforbes D.E.D.). Matthew at Ballycore. Thomas at Newtown (Killashee D.E.D.).

EDMONDS: Margaret J. at Acheson's of Derawley.

EGAN:(46): George at Drumanure. Patrick at Cloonfide. Richard, Denis at Mornin. Edward at Clooneen (Forgney D.E.D.). James at Forgney. Bridget, Mary at Tennalick. Bridget at Ballymahon Town. Francis at Creevagh Beg. Patrick at Derrindiff. Michael at Corlea. Bridget at Carrow Beg (Cashel West D.E.D.). Francis at Elfeet (Burke). Annie at Cornahoo. Edward at Kilmakinlan. Edward, Michael at Creagh. Michael at Kilcommock Glebe. Edward, Michael at Derrylough. Edward at Ball Alley Street Upper, Granard Town. Daniel at Birrinagh. Patrick at Cloontagh. Michael, Peter at Aghnagore. James at Aghareagh (Cloondara D.E.D.). Mary, Maria at Begnagh. Patrick at Cloonbrock. James at Cloonfore. Patrick at Gowlan. Edward, Catherine at Garranboy. Mary at Derrygeel. Mary at Coolcaw. Lawrence at Drumroe. James at Rathvaldron. Peter at Treel (Corboy D.E.D.). Mary at Healy's Terrace, Longford Town. Patrick at Hyde's Yard, Longford Town. James, Peter at Main Street, Longford Town. Thomas, Bernard (both absent from home) at Richmond Street, Longford Town. Fanny at Abbeycartron. *ALSO:* Anne at Eivers' of Lissawarriff. Annie at McGoey's of Cloghan (Doory D.E.D.). Mary at Loughran's of Lissakit. Mary at Farrell's of Loughan. John at Duffy's of Kilcurry. Winnie at Teresa Delaney's of Drinan. Christy at Margaret Fox's of Mullawornia. Hester at John P. Shaw's of Ballymahon Town. Fr. Robert at Rev. James Smyth's (56) of Main Street, Granard Town. Catherine at Farrington's of Newtownforbes Village. Thomas at McNally's of Lisbrack (Longford Rural D.E.D.). Mathew at Moran's of Main Street, Longford Town. Thomas and Bernard at Flanagan's of Richmond Street, Longford Town.

EGINTON: Daniel at Bridge Street, Longford Town. *ALSO:* George at Free's of Cooleeny.

EIVERS, EVERS:(27): Timothy at Lissawarriff. John, Catherine at Pallas More. James at Keelbaun. Patrick at Ballyglassin. Mary at Carrickboy. Denis at Kilcurry. Thomas at Daroge. Julia, William at Cloonard (Ballymahon Town D.E.D.). Patrick, Denis at Kilcourcey. Michael, Denis at Glannagh. Denis at Asnagh. James at Lissanure. Felix, Michael, Patrick, Felix, Michael at Cloonagh (Breanrisk D.E.D.). Bernard at Cloonmacart. Michael at Enybegs. Patrick at Oghil. John at Drumlish Village. Catherine at Newtownforbes Village. John at Lisdreenagh. *ALSO:* Mary at Mahedy's of Ballina. Mary at Patrick Burns' of Edera. John at Edward Murphy's of Glenmore (Ballinamuck East D.E.D.). Patrick at John McAvey's of Bawn (Breanrisk D.E.D.). Michael at McManus's of Drumlish. John at Mayne's of Abbeycartron.

ELAM: Vallence at Derrydarragh.

McELINEY: James at Sonnagh. *ALSO:* James at John Corcoran's of

Sonnagh. (See McAliney, McLiney).

McELLIGOTT: Lizzie A. at Belton's of Ballymahon Street, Longford Town. Lizzie at Cody's of Church Street, Longford Town.

ELLIOTT: William, Hannah at Drummeel. William at Fihoragh. Elizabeth at Gorteenorna. Thomas at Ardagh Demesne. *ALSO:* Albert at Stephenson's of Dublin Street, Longford Town.

ELLIS: Thomas at Ratharney. James at Edgeworthstown Town. Ellen, Michael, Teresa at Cloonellan. John at Leitrim (Breanrisk D.E.D.). Anne at Creenagh. John at Kilmore Upper. Catherine at St. Michael's Road, Longford Town. *ALSO:* Bridget at Ghee's of Cloonellan. Henry at Anne Walsh's of Treel (Newtownforbes D.E.D.). Anna at Adams's of Craane (?).

ELMS: A.M. at Hewetson's of Church Street, Longford Town.

McELNEA: Kate at Main Street, Longford Town.

EMMETT: R.W. at Hewetson's of Church Street, Longford Town.

ENGLISBY, ENGLISHBY: Thomas at Creeve. *ALSO:* Margaret at Allen's of Abbeycartron.

ENRIGHT: Elizabeth at Farrington's of Newtownforbes Village.

McENROE: Hugh at Grehan's of Main Street, Granard Town.

McENTEE, McINTEE: Patrick at Bank Street, Granard Town. *ALSO:* Lizzie at Parks' of Ball Alley Street Upper, Granard Town.

McENTIRE: See McIntyre.

ENTWISTLE: W. at Hewetson's of Church Street, Longford Town.

ESTRANGE: See L'Estrange.

EUSTACE: John at Gorteenclareen. *ALSO:* G. at Duncan McGregor's of Lisbrack (Longford Rural D.E.D.).

EVANS: Margaret at Irwin's of Colehill. J. at Hewetson's of Church Street, Longford Town.

EVERARD: Mary at Delany's of Church Street, Longford Town.

EVERS: See Eivers.

McEVOY, McVOY: James at Lislea (Lislea D.E.D.). Edward, James, Philip at Sonnagh. Michael at Tonymore North. John at Springtown. Michael at Killeenatruan. *ALSO:* Bridget at John Corcoran's of Sonnagh. Bridget at Patrick Ginty's of Shanmullagh. M.J. and T. at Hewetson's of Church Street, Longford Town.

EYERS, EYRE: Patrick at Ballywillin.

FAGAN, FEGAN:(27): John, Thomas, James at Drumanure. Lawrence at Clooncullen. John at Ballymacclifford. Patrick at Ballybranigan. John at Shrule. Laurence at Ballymahon Town. Thomas at Rathmore (Ballymahon D.E.D.). Edward at Drumnee. Thomas, James at Saints Island. Michael, James at Derrymacar. Elizabeth at Moatfarrell. John at Killeen (Bunlahy D.E.D.). Peter at Killasona. Michael, Matthew at Rincoolagh. Mary at Aghabrack. James at Gallid. John at Ball Alley Street Upper, Granard Town. Thomas at Tonywardan. Christopher at Derragh. James at Corbaun or Leitrim. Charlies at Derrycassan. Felix at Ballaghgowla and Froghan. *ALSO:* Anne at Murphy's of Creevaghmore (Forgney Civil Ph.). Patrick and Michael at James Reilly's of Killeen (Bunlahy D.E.D.). Bridget at Cahill's of Killasona. James at Caffrey's of Carragh (Granard Urban D.E.D.). John at Flynn's of Barrack Street, Granard Town. Joseph at O'Flanagan's of Main Street, Granard Town. Mary at Reilly's of Cleenrah. Bernard at O'Hara's of Aghamore (Coolamber D.E.D.). Annie at Kilkelly's of Lisnamuck. Mary at Skelly's of Main Street, Longford Town.

FAHEY, FAHY: Bridget at Claras. James at Drumlish Village. Rose at Chapel Lane, Longford Town. Thomas at Sandy Row, Longford Town.

FALLON:(27): Catherine at Drinan. Francis at Ballynahinch. Catherine at Ballyrevagh. Thomas at Drumnee. Michael at Fortwilliam. Patrick, Elizabeth at Cullentragh (Rathcline Civil Ph.). Edward at Lyneen. Bridget, Mary, Michael at Cloonard (Cloondara D.E.D.). Michael at Glebe (Cloondara D.E.D.). Michael at Cloonsheerin. Michael, Mary at Sharvoge. Anne, Bernard at Derryad (Mountdavis D.E.D.). John at Craane. Thomas at Aghaloughan. Patrick at Commons South. Michael at Lismacmanus. Thomas, Patrick at Lisrevagh. John at Moyra and Fortmill. Thomas at New Street, Longford Town. Michael at St. Mel's Road, Longford Town. Maria at Dublin Street, Longford Town. *ALSO:* Mary at Feeney's of Moneyfad. John at Lennon's of Derrynagalliagh. Joseph at Thompson's of Newtownforbes Village. Sr. Mary at Rev. Mother Farrington's of Newtownforbes Village. Patrick at Denis Dowd's of Kilmore Upper. Anne at James Casey's of Derryloughbannow. Rose at Murray's of Corlagan.

FANCLEY: Mary at Abbeyderg. (See Finsley).

FANNIN: Edward at Cartronageeragh. James at Mullaghavorneen.

FANNING: John at Cartronlebagh. Patrick at Mullolagher. *ALSO:* Agnes at Free's of Dublin Street, Longford Town.

FANNON: Michael at Ballymahon Town.

McFARLAND: S. at Hewetson's of Church Street, Longford Town.

FARMER: James at Lissanure.

FARRELL:(337): Margaret, William at Ardanragh. John, John, Richard at Lissawarriff. Mary, Anne, Mary at Castlerea Mountain. Timothy, James, Patrick, Patrick, Kate at Cloghan (Doory D.E.D.). Patrick, Julia, Peter at Cloonscott. John at Loughan. Michael, Michael, John at Mornin. Catherine at Torboy. Catherine, William, Francis, Patrick, Patrick at Cloghan (Forgney D.E.D.). Edward at Clooncallow. Kate at Forgney. Francis at Carrigeen (Foxhall D.E.D.). Honoria, Patrick at Killeen (Foxhall D.E.D.). Peter at Kinard. Mary at Aghnasillagh. John at Garrycam. Patrick at Keel (Kilglass D.E.D.). Michael, Edward at Ballintober (Bonny). Edward at Ballynamanagh. John at Carrickedmond. Luke at Liscormick. Hugh at Tennalough. James, James at Ballyglassin. Michael at Lisaquill. Peter, William at Kilcurry. Patrick at Taghshinny. Anne at Ballybranigan. Thomas at Ballymulvey. Christopher, Anne, Timothy, Timothy at Tirlickeen. Patrick, Rose, Gerald, Marcella, Mary at Ballymahon Town. Thomas at Lislom. Patrick at Agharanagh (Ballymahon D.E.D.). Thomas, Francis at Barry (Ballymahon D.E.D.). Thomas at Derryoghil. Mary at Ballina. Hannah at Caltragh Beg. Mary, James, Francis at Derraghan Beg. Patrick, Catherine at Derryglash. Daniel, John at Derrygowna. Margaret at Forthill. Peter at Streamstown (Cashel East D.E.D.). Thomas at Ballagh (Cashel West D.E.D.). Michael at Ballyrevagh. Patrick at Carrowrory. Thomas, James, Bernard, Daniel at Cloonmee. James, Thomas at Cornadowagh. Patrick, Patrick at Corrool (Fox). Peter at Cross (Cashel West D.E.D.). James at Derrydarragh. Patrick at Elfeet (Adamson). Bridget at Elfeet (Burke). Patrick at Greenhall Lower. Michael at Greenhall Upper. John, Catherine at Leab. James at Inchcleraun Island (Cashel West D.E.D.). John at Portanure. James at Coolnahinch ((Kilcommock D.E.D.). William at Glenmore (Kilcommock D.E.D.). Patrick at Abbeyderg. John at Cartronbrack. Patrick at Laughil (Kilcommock D.E.D.). James at Longford Road, Keenagh Village. Patrick at Main Street, Keenagh Village. Peter at Derrymany. Thomas at Foygh. Patrick, Mary A. at Barnacor (Ledwithstown D.E.D.). Thomas at Aghamore (Ballinalee D.E.D.). John at Ballyreaghan. Patrick at Derryneel. Daniel at Drumnahara. Anne at Kilshruley. Thomas at France. Gerald at Kilderreen. Michael at Roos. Michael at Aghagreagh. Rose, Patrick, Mathew at Gelshagh. Peter at Firmount. Bridget at Aghakeeran. John at Coolcor. James at Rathcor. Henry at Ballymore. Michael, Michael, Peter, Garrit at Cartron (Granard Rural D.E.D.). William at Grassyard. Michael at Graffoge (Milltown D.E.D.). Peter at Cooldoney.

James at Derragh. Mary at Cleenrah. John at Dunbeggan (Columbkille D.E.D.). Laurence at Rosduff. Fanny at Crott. Thaddeus at Birrinagh. Michael at Farmullagh. Francis, Elizabeth at Cloonagh (Mullanalaghta D.E.D.). Thomas at Kilsallagh. Catherine at Ringowny. Peter at Corclaragh. Thomas at Lissanore. Thomas, Patrick at Longfield. Catherine at Aghafin. Patrick at Lackan. Peter, James at Tinnynarr. Michael, Christopher, Mary, Patrick at Edgeworthstown Town. Francis at Aghadowry. Owen at Fostragh. Thomas at Glenmore (Ballinamuck East D.E.D.). James at Cloncowley. James at Lettergullion. William at Carrickmoyragh. Patrick at Cloontagh. Thomas at Leitrim (Breanrisk D.E.D.). Bernard, Catherine, Patrick, Francis at Cornacullew. Michael at Carrowbeg (Drumlish D.E.D.). Michael, Anne at Bohernameeltoge.Denis, John at Derawley. Patrick at Enybegs. William Patrick, John at Brocklagh. Bernard at Derrynacross. James at Gaigue. John at Bunanass. Thomas at Edercloon. Thomas at Killeen (Caldragh D.E.D.). John at Cloonbalt. Daniel, Patrick, Daniel at Cloonrallagh. Patrick, Joseph at Aghnagore. Luke at Cloonard (Cloondara D.E.D.). Patrick at Brownbog. Bridget, Maria at Lissanurlan. Patrick at Cloonmore. Patrick at Templeton Glebe. John, Michael, Patrick at Derryad (Mountdavis D.E.D.). Patrick at Cloonfore. James, Michael at Ballintempan. Michael at Brickeens. Mary, Mary at Caldraghmore. Charles at Carrowmanagh. Patrick, Thomas at Knockatarry Poynton. Daniel at Newtown (Moydow D.E.D.). Thomas at Trillickacurry. Winifred at Aghinaspick. Bridget at Aughine. Anne at Barroe. Ellen at Cloonevit. Thomas at Commock. John at Garranboy. Peter at Mollyroe. James at Toneen (Moydow D.E.D.). Mary at Carrowroe. Catherine, John, Thomas, Catherine at Carrowstrawly. Michael at Cloonbony. Michael at Derrygeel. John T., William, Elizabeth, Patrick, Catherine, Ellen, John, Thomas, Peter at Lehery. Patrick at Lismacmanus. Luke, Edward, Edward at Lisnacush. John, Catherine at Lisrevagh. John at Rathcline. Honoria, Luke, Patrick, Patrick at Tullyvrane. John, Edward, at Turreen. Mary, Michael, Mary, Catherine, Maria, Thomas, Patrick, Terence, John at Lanesborough Village. Lawrence at Ardagh Demesne. Michael at Back of the Hill. Ellen at Ballinree and Ballymoat. Bernard at Carnan. Francis, Peter at Coolcaw. Mary at Crossea South. Catherine at Drumroe. John at Garryconnell. Anne, Christopher, William, Elizabeth at Glen. John at Lissanisky (Ardagh East D.E.D.). James at Lisdreenagh. Kieran at Cooleeshil or Richfort. James at Drumbaun. Thomas at Grillagh (Ardagh West D.E.D.). Peter, James at Laughil (Ardagh West D.E.D.). Thomas at Rabbitpark. Denis, James, Garrett at Cartrongarrow. Mary at Derrymore. Thomas, Mary at Graffoge (Ardagh West D.E.D.). Mary at Cloonkeen (Ardagh West D.E.D.). Thomas, Garrett at Gorteenagloon. John, William at Bawn (Ardagh West D.E.D.). Thomas, James at Bawn Mountain. John at Cloonee. Edward at Farraghroe. James at Aghanageeragh. Thomas at Treel (Corboy D.E.D.). Rose, Thomas at Cloonahard. Thomas at Ballynagoshen. John at Corboy. Bridget at Ballymakeegan. Mary at Cartronageeragh. Joseph at Cloonturk. Thomas, Thomas at Feraghfad. Ellen at Knockanboy. William at Lisduff (Longford Rural D.E.D.). Patrick at

Mullaghavorneen. John, Thomas at Stonepark (Longford Rural D.E.D.).
Mary, James at Cooleeny. Catherine, Rachel, James at Glack (Longford
Rural D.E.D.). Mathew at Townparks (Longford Rural D.E.D.). Patrick,
Patrick, John at Whiterock. Patrick, James at Ballymahon Street, Longford
Town. Mary at Broderick's Yard, Longford Town. Rose, John at Chapel
Lane, Longford Town. Mary at Conroy's Court, Longford Town. Patrick
at Dwyer's Yard, Longford Town. Thomas, Anne at Earl Street, Longford
Town. Michael at Garvey's Yard, Longford Town. William, William, Peter,
John at Great Water Street, Longford Town. Mathew (absent from No. 18),
Patrick at Main Street, Longford Town. James P. at Market Square,
Longford Town. Patrick, James, James at Richmond Street, Longford Town.
Patrick at St. Mel's Road, Longford Town. Patrick, Patrick, Peter, John at
Townparks (Longford Urban No. 1 D.E.D.). Denis at Bridge Street,
Longford Town. *ALSO:* Mary at McDermott's of Aghanvally. Margaret at
Bole's of Parkplace (?). Kate at Clyne's of Listobit. Mary at Fitzgerald's
of Smithfield. Bridget at Keena's of Treel (Foxhall D.E.D.). Mary at
Newcomen Corry's of Keel (Kilglass D.E.D.). Edward and Patrick at
Maguire's of Ballybeg. Michael at Nulty's of Ballybeg. Bridget and Patrick
at McGarry's of Kilnacarrow (Kilglass D.E.D.). Bridget at Higgins's of
Cartronboy. John at Casey's of Tirlickeen. Michael at Elizabeth Mulvihill's
(106) of Ballymahon Town. Catherine at Duignan's of Creevagh Beg.
Richard at Concannon's of Creevagh Beg. Mary at John Walsh's (3) of
Toome (Ballymahon D.E.D.). Maria at Malone's of Derryoghil. Edward at
Regan's of Derryoghil. Thomas at Stanley's of Forthill. Patrick at
McGrain's of Newtownflanigan. John at Shanley's of Cornadowagh. Kate
at Connaughton's of Loughfarm. Francis at Skelly's of Portanure. Mary et
al. at Connor's of Coolnahinch ((Kilcommock D.E.D.). John at Corr's of
Clooncoose (Ballinalee D.E.D.). Patrick at Reynolds's of Ballinalee Village.
Kate et al. at John Hetherton's of Aghacordrinan. Patrick at Fullam's of
Druminacrehir. Elizabeth at Early's of Cloghchurnel. Ala (?) at Laurence
Early's of Creevy. James at Deal's of Carragh (Granard Rural D.E.D.).
Charles at Lee's of Balnagall (Granard Urban D.E.D.). Rose A. at Slevin's
of Main Street, Granard Town. Margaret at Kilduff's of Main Street,
Granard Town. Elizabeth at Mulhare's of Ferskill. Joseph at Dalton's of
Camagh (Newgrove D.E.D.). Mary at Leavey's of Liscahill. Michael at
James Victory's of Corclaragh. Mary at Victory's of Longfield. Mary at
Peter McLoughlin's of Bracklon. Francis at Killean's of Edgeworthstown
Town. Mary A. and Mary at Kate Finlan's of Edgeworthstown Town.
Katie and John at Hosey's of Edgeworthstown Town. James at Reynolds's
of Edgeworthstown Town. Sarah at Rose Jordan's of Cloncowley. John et
al. at John McGeoy's of Currygranny. John at William McNamee's of
Corglass. Thomas at John Taaffe's (6) of Leggagh. James at Bridget
Heaney's of Oghil. Kate at Keville's of Drumlish Village. William at
McGuirk's of Brocklagh. Catherine and John at Hughes's of Ballagh
(Achmuty). Mary at Hopkins' of Cleggill. Kate at Moffett's of Cloonfiugh.
Thomas at Pollard's of Templeton Glebe. Theresa at Rhatigan's of

Killashee Village. John at Michael Casey's (9) of Cloonbrock. John at Patrick Cassidy's of Derryad (Mountdavis D.E.D.). Patrick et al. at James McGuire's (2) of Cloonfore. Thomas at Bridget Murtagh's of Cloonfore. Peter J. at James Dennigan's of Magheraveen. Catherine at Dowdall's of Ballinamore. John at Ward's of Brickeens. Margaret at Dowd's of Carrowmanagh. Thomas at Dowd's of Gowlan. Catherine at George Carey's of Monascallaghan. Daniel at Mulvihill's of Toneen (Moydow D.E.D.). James at Anne Costello's of Carrowroe. Elizabeth at Mathew Kearney's of Formoyle (Farrell). Elizabeth at Dowd's of Killinure. Lizzie at Flood's of Cornapark. Peter at John Ryan's of Cross (Ardagh East D.E.D.). Mary at Lyons's of Lenaboy. Bernard at O'Farrell's of Moor. Thomas and William at Margaret Thompson's of Cartrongarrow. Kate at McIntyre's of Farraghroe. James et al. at McNabo's of Kiltyreher (Killoe Civil Ph.). Rose A. at Michael Dunne's of Kiltyreher (Templemichael Civil Ph.). Patrick at Egan's of Treel (Corboy D.E.D.). Mary K. at Bond's of Ballygarve. Patrick at Keegan's of Corboy. Patrick at Dowler's of Lisnamuck. Elizabeth at McNally's of Lisbrack (Longford Rural D.E.D.). Peter at O'Connor's of Conroy's Court, Longford Town. Elizabeth at Fullam's of Deanscurragh. James at Ward's of Dublin Street, Longford Town. Ellie at Lynn's of Dublin Street, Longford Town. Thomas at Patrick Dolan's of Dublin Street, Longford Town. Agnes at Latimer's of Earl Street, Longford Town. Christopher J. at Lamb's of Earl St., Longford Town. John at King's of Main Street, Longford Town. Mary at Burke's of Main Street, Longford Town. Mary at Waters' of Main Street, Longford Town. Annie at Trimble's of Main Street, Longford Town. Michael at Maxwell's of Main Street, Longford Town. Mary at Gallagher's of Main Street, Longford Town. Maria at Moore's of New Street, Longford Town. Mary at Toole's of O'Donnell's Yard, Longford Town. Joseph at Callaghan's of Richmond Street, Longford Town.

O'FARRELL, O'FERRALL: John F. at Corbeagh. Rev. Canon Francis at Drummeel. Charles at Barrack Street, Granard Town. Conal at Camlisk More. Alicia at Aghadowry. Very Rev. James at Moor. *ALSO:* Kathleen at Philip Brady's of Gaigue. Mary at James Farrell's of Glack (Longford Rural D.E.D.). (See More O'Ferrall).

FARRELL-McAULIFFE: James J. at Maria Farrell's of Lanesborough Village.

FARRELLY, FERRALLY:(33): Thomas at Currygrane. Edward, Anne, Francis at Carrickadorrish. Owen at Sonnagh. Mary at Abbeylara Village. Terence at Springtown. Edward, Henry at Ballinulty Lower. Margaret at Moxham Street, Granard Town. Patrick at Coolcraff. Patrick, Patrick at Enaghan. Michael at Drumhalry. Patrick, Mathew at Drumury. Ellen, Thomas, Luke, Owen at Fihoragh. John at Corclaragh. Thomas at Cranalagh More. Bernard at Longfield. Mary at Bracklon. James at Bawn

(Breanrisk D.E.D.). James at Cloonelly. Michael at Kiltycon. John at Carnan. Anne at Coolcaw. Elizabeth at Glen (?). Michael at Lenaboy. Thomas at Moyra and Fortmill. Mathew at Townparks (Longford Rural D.E.D.). (?). *ALSO:* Margaret at Bole's of Parkplace (?). Maria at James Duncan's of Ballymahon Town. John at James Macken's of Cranally. John at Carters' of Ball Alley Street Upper, Granard Town. Peter at Patrick Duffy's of Aghagah. Peter at Charles Sheridan's of Ballyduffy. Bridget at Fleming's of Drumhalry. Patrick et al. at Francis Reilly's of Fihoragh. Bridget at Edward Kiernan's of Cloonagh (Mullanalaghta D.E.D.). Edward and Anne at Margaret Reilly's of Cloonagh (Mullanalaghta D.E.D.). Ellen at Wiggins's of Moatavally. Maria at Farrington's of Newtownforbes Village. Mary K. at Green's of Keeloges. Anne at Skeffington's of Earl Street, Longford Town.

FARRINGTON: Rev. Mother Elizabeth at Newtownforbes Village.

FAUGHNAN: Patrick at Breanrisk. Thomas at Cloontagh. Bernard at Currygranny. Mary at Ballagh (Newtownforbes D.E.D.). Margaret, John, James at Briskil. *ALSO:* Hugh at Margaret Manning's of Cloonellan. Catherine at Small's of Cloonageeher. John at Tapp's of Bridge Street, Longford Town (?).

FAULKNAN: John at Tapp's of Bridge Street, Longford Town.

FAWARY: C.R. at Hewetson's of Church Street, Longford Town.

FAY: Peter at Barnacor (Ledwithstown D.E.D.). Luke at Ballinulty Upper. Bridget at Rinroe. James at Cloonagh (Mullanalaghta D.E.D.). Thomas at Glebe (Cloondara D.E.D.). *ALSO:* Catherine at O'Reilly's of Granard. Eugene at Mallon's of Aghanoran. Gerald at Whyte's of Clonwhelan.

FAYLE: William at Creeve.

FAYNE: Patrick, Anne at Cullentragh (Rathcline Civil Ph.). *ALSO:* Thomas et al. at Bridget Cunningham's of Caltragh More.

FEALY, FEELY: John at Clooncoose (Ballinalee D.E.D.). John at Lissameen. Thomas at Drummeel. John at Drumderg. James at Drumhaughly. Elizabeth at Farraghroe. Peter at Killyfad. Owen at Mucknagh. William at Stonepark (Longford Rural D.E.D.). *ALSO:* Jane at James Cassidy's of Ballymahon Town (?). Mary A. at Anne Whelan's of Glenoghil. Kate at Fagan's of Moatfarrell. John at Patrick Gavagan's of Rinroe. Catherine at Farrington's of Newtownforbes Village. Martin J. and Mary K. at Hughes's of Drumbaun. Mathew at Farrell's of St. Mel's Road, Longford Town. (See Feehily).

FEAVER: G. at Hewetson's of Church Street, Longford Town.

FEE:(11): Charles at Keel (Kilglass D.E.D.). Charles, Anne at Deerpark (Kilglass D.E.D.). John at Carrickboy. Joseph at Killinbore. Mary J. at Ballybranigan. Mary at Trillickatemple. John, George at Creeve. Henry S. at Lisduff (Longford Rural D.E.D.). Mary at Church Street, Longford Town. *ALSO:* Sarah at Sarah Corry's of Keel (Kilglass D.E.D.). Harriett at John H. Plant's of Ballymahon Town. Jack H. at Wilson's of Main Street, Keenagh Village.

FEEHAN: See Feighan.

FEEHILY, FEHILY, FEEHILLY:(14): Andrew, Thomas at Aghnasillagh. Edward at Knocknaskea. James at Edgeworthstown Town. Thomas at Cloncowley. Michael at Cloonagh (Breanrisk D.E.D.). Maria, Thomas at Cloonmacart. Patrick at Monaduff. Ellen at Drumlish Village. Michael at Gaigue. Patrick at Magheraveen. Thomas at Ballywalter. Thomas at Sandy Row, Longford Town. *ALSO:* Maggie R. at Denis Tally's of Castlebaun. Ellen J. at Margaret Quinn's of Drumlish. (See Fealy).

FEELY: See Fealy.

FEENEY, FEENY:(26): Charles at Ballybranigan. Thomas at Moneyfad. John at Moygh (Ballymahon D.E.D.). James at Mullawornia. James at Ballymahon Town. John at Creevagh Beg, Ballymahon Town. Michael at Creevagh Beg. James at Rathmore (Ballymahon D.E.D.). Bernard at Foygh. Patrick at Gorteenclareen. Elizabeth at Killasona. Michael at Ballymore. Patrick at Breanrisk. Joseph at Cloonart South. William at Aghnagore. John, Patrick at Cloondara. James at Glebe (Cloondara D.E.D.). Bernard at Ballymichan. John at Barnacor (Rathcline D.E.D.). Michael at Tullyvrane. Michael at Lisduff (Montgomery). John at Coach Yard, Longford Town. Edward at Earl Street, Longford Town. Thomas at Great Water Street, Longford Town. Michael at St. Michael's Road, Longford Town. *ALSO:* Mary J. at Dolan's of Castlewilder. Kate at Skelly's of Cornacarta. Mary at Poynton's of Cornacarta. Michael at James Cassidy's of Ballymahon Town. Elizabeth at John Lynch's of Tonymore North. Kate at Hugh Briody's of Killasona. Patrick at Reid's of Killasona. Elizabeth at Gillan's of Ballymaurice (Granard Rural D.E.D.). William et al. at Bartholomew Mulligan's of Dunbeggan (Columbkille D.E.D.). Patrick at Hughes's of Cahanagh. Patrick at Murtagh's of Cloondara. Michael at Gaughran's of Kilnacarrow (Mountdavis D.E.D.). Margaret at Garrahan's of Cloonevit. Anne at John Carney's of Cartronawar (Corboy D.E.D.). Kate at Shaw's of Cloonturk. James at McDonnell's of Healy's Terrace, Longford Town. James at McGarry's of Main Street, Longford Town. Katie at Skelly's of Main Street, Longford Town.

FEGAN: See Fagan.

FEHILY: See Feehily.

FEIGHAN: John at Peter J. Joyce's of Main Street, Longford Town.

FENLON, FINLON, FENELON: Thomas, Kate at Edgeworthstown Town. *ALSO:* James at O'Connor's of Conroy's Court, Longford Town.

FENNAN: See Finnan.

FENNELL, FENNEL: Annie at Jessop's of Doory. Edward at Thomas Clarke's of Oghil.

FENNELLY: Letitia at James Farrell's of Glack (Longford Rural D.E.D.).

FENNER: Elizabeth at Farrington's of Newtownforbes Village.

FENNIN, FENNON: See Finnan.

O'FERRALL: See O'Farrell.

FERRALLY: See Farrelly.

FERRIS, FERIS: William J. at Boyers' (2) of Main Street, Longford Town.

FETHERSTON: Seward at Newtownforbes Village. Rev. Sir George R. at Ardagh Demesne. *ALSO:* Mary at Macken's of Edgeworthstown Town.

FILAN: See Whelan.

FINEGAN: See Finnegan.

FINLAN: See Fenlon.

FINLAY: Thomas at Mosstown (Moydow Barony). Margaret at Glebe (Cloondara D.E.D.). Maria at Clooncoose (Cloonee D.E.D.). James at Fee's Terrace, Longford Town.

FINN: Bridget at Cornamucklagh. Catherine, Catherine at Moygh (Ballymahon D.E.D.). Maria at Shrule. Michael, Patrick at Rathmore (Ballymahon D.E.D.). Bridget at Caldraghmore. James at Meeltanagh (Moydow D.E.D.). Mary at Glack (Longford Rural D.E.D.). *ALSO:* Kate at Owen Hourican's of Aghnacliff. Bridget at John Skelly's of Knappoge (Cloondara D.E.D.). Mary at Donlon's of Monascallaghan. Delia at Little's of Main Street, Longford Town.

FINNAN, FINNEN, FENNAN:(11): James at Rincoolagh. Lawrence at Ballymaurice (Granard Rural D.E.D.). Bernard, Patrick at Barrack Street, Granard Town. Michael at Liscahill. Bridget at Corralough. James at Cornapark. Mary at Cordivin. Thomas at Bawn (Ardagh West D.E.D.). John at Bawn Mountain. Michael at Lisduff (Longford Rural D.E.D.). *ALSO:* Mary A. at Hanlon's of Tipper (Ballymahon D.E.D.). Hugh at McCabe's of Clooneen (Creevy D.E.D.). Lawrence at Smith's of Coolagherty.

FINNEGAN, FINEGAN:(10): John at Vicarstown. Michael at Pallas More. Catherine at Cornaguillagh. John at Molly. James at Ballywillin. Margaret at Aghnagarron. Michael at Grassyard. John at Ferskill. William at Willsbrook. Catherine at Rathcline. *ALSO:* Patrick at Sullivan's of Main Street, Granard Town. Annie at Telford's of Grillagh (Killashee D.E.D.).

FINNERAN: Thomas at Portanure. Mary at Lyanmore.

FINSLEY: Elizabeth at Keelogalabawn. (See Fancley).

FINUCANE: James at Church Street, Longford Town.

FISHER: J. at Hewetson's of Church Street, Longford Town.

FITZGERALD: Rev. Patrick at Smithfield. William at Ballymahon Town. Patrick, Patrick E. (absent from No. 6) at Main Street, Longford Town. *ALSO:* Angela at Bernard Kenny's of Keel (Kilglass D.E.D.). Rose at Leahy's of Ballyclare (Killashee D.E.D.). Thomas at Maxwell's of Main Street, Longford Town.

FITZMAURICE, FITZMORRIS: William at Ballymahon Town. Thomas at Creevagh Beg. *ALSO:* Ellen at Nolan's of Ballybranigan.

FITZPATRICK:(19): Thomas at Druming. Edward at Drinan. James at Ballymahon Town. Bernard at Aghnacliff. Mary at Springtown. Patrick at Dunbeggan (Columbkille D.E.D.). Terence at Mollyglass. James at Polladooey. Patrick at Rosduff. Michael at Smear. Philip, Philip, Annie at Drumhalry. Fanny at Kilmore. Owen at Toome (Mullanalaghta D.E.D.). Patrick at Lisryan. Charles at Aghafin. John at Aghinaspick. Thomas at Killeter. *ALSO:* Annie at Jessop's of Doory. John at Doherty's of Taghshinny. Elizabeth at Dimond's of Cornacarta. James at Hewitt's of Ballymulvey. William et al. at Flood's of Cloonard (Ballymahon D.E.D.). Christopher at Mulligan's of Cloonard (Ballymahon D.E.D.). Patrick at Auchmuty's of Garrynagh. Mary at Rorke's of Ledwithstown (Shrule Civil Ph.). Elizabeth at Ellen Kiernan's of Aghnacliff. Abigail at Amelia

McCoy's of Smear. James at Brennan's of Cloonart South. Joseph and Jane A. at Leonard's of Trillickatemple. Lizzie at Garrahan's of Cloonker. John at Dowler's of Moor. Michael at Patrick Fitzgerald's (1) of Main Street, Longford Town. Mary K. at Boyers' (4) of Main Street, Longford Town.

FITZSIMONS:(19): John at Abbeyshrule. John at Aghagreagh. William at Carrickateane. Bridget at Abbeylara Village. Bridget, Patrick, Joseph at Culleenmore. Mathew at Mullinroe. Elizabeth at Creevy. Patrick at Killasona. Mary at Ballymore. Julia at Corbaun or Leitrim. Anne, Mary at Toome (Mullanalaghta D.E.D.). Catherine, Bridget at Kilsallagh. Margaret at Kilfintan. Anne at Lisnageeragh. Edward at Lisduff (Montgomery). *ALSO:* Margaret at Kelly's of Moygh (Ballymahon D.E.D.). Thomas at James Nally's of Ballymahon Town. Bernard at Joseph Gannon's of Ballymahon Town. Thomas at Rose Flood's of Ballinrooey. Bridget at Michael Farrell's (5) of Cartron (Granard Rural D.E.D.). Margaret at Markey's of Main Street, Granard Town. Eugene at Michael Kelly's of Main Street, Granard Town. Maria at Leonard's of Main Street, Granard Town. Kate at Patrick Cosgrove's of Main Street, Granard Town.

FLAHERTY:(14): Maria at Rathmore (Ballymahon D.E.D.). Henry at Kilshruley. Anne at Culray. Michael at Aghakine. Thomas at Ballinulty Lower. Jane at Castlenugent. Patrick, Thomas, James at Edenmore. Margaret at Glenmore (Ballinamuck East D.E.D.). John at Kilnashee. Michael at Leggagh. Mary E. at Newtownforbes Village. James at Cloontirm. *ALSO:* Patrick at Mulligan's of Ballinulty Lower. Mary at Kiernan's of The Hill, Granard Town (?). Ellen at Margaret Gormley's (8) of Polladooey. James at Newtownforbes Barracks. Peter et al. at Mulligan's of Templeton Glebe. Mary at Coleman's of Lanesborough Village.

FLANAGAN:(18): Luke at Cloghan (Forgney D.E.D.). Michael at Cornamucklagh. Michael at Aughnavealoge. Kate at Derrindiff. Michael at Corrool (Fox). James at Lyneen. Thomas at Derryad (Ledwithstown D.E.D.). Thomas at Ledwithstown (Kilcommock Civil Ph.). Marian J. at Main Street, Granard Town. Francis at Kilsallagh. Patrick at Aghnagore. Bridget at Ballyclare (Killashee D.E.D.). Marcella at Killashee Village. Celia at Dublin Street, Longford Town. John at Fee's Terrace, Longford Town. Patrick at Market Square, Longford Town. Thomas at Richmond Street, Longford Town. James at St. Michael's Road, Longford Town. *ALSO:* Patrick at Fox's of Foxhall. Thomas at Gerety's of Killinbore. Anne at John Devins's of Ballymahon Town. Mary et al. at Steele's of Derrindiff. John at Hannigan's of Aghnashannagh, Ballinalee Village. Thomas at O'Neill's of Ballywillin. Bernard P. at Larkfield Barracks. Margaret at Early's of Sragarrow. Patrick at Addy's of Richmond Street, Longford Town. Agnes at Fleming's of Abbeycartron.

O'FLANAGAN: William J. at Toneen (Firry D.E.D.). Marian J. at Main

Street, Granard Town (?).

FLARTY: Mary at Kiernan's of The Hill, Granard Town.

FLATTERY: Elizabeth at Clooneen (Forgney D.E.D.). Mary at Barney.

FLEMING, FLEMMING: John at Leitrim (Ballinalee D.E.D.). James R. at Killeen (Bunlahy D.E.D.). Frances at Granard. James at Drumhalry. Hugh at Fihoragh. William at Cloondara. Leslie M. (absent from home) at Abbeycartron. *ALSO:* Catherine at Fagan's of Moatfarrell. Sarah at Stephenson's of Ballinlough. Michael at Luke Farrelly's of Fihoragh.

FLETCHER: Mary A. at Farrington's of Newtownforbes Village. Barbara at Terence Doherty's (14) of Esker South.

FLEURY, FLUERY: Michael at Smear. *ALSO:* Rose at Corrigan's of Curraghmore. (See Furey).

FLOOD:(39): Anne at Ratharney. Michael, Elizabeth at Agharra. Christopher at Legan. Marcella, Thomas at Rath. John at Foxhall. Kate at Lissanisky (Ballymahon D.E.D.). Hugh at Ballymahon Town. James at Cloonard (Ballymahon D.E.D.). Connor at Knappoge (Ballymahon D.E.D.). John at Greenhall Upper. Connor at Derrymacar. James, Rose, James at Ballinrooey. Thomas at Culleenmore. James at Ballinrud West. Anne at Rathbrackan. Catherine, Mary at Ballinulty Lower. Patrick at Killasona. Hugh at Rincoolagh. Maria at Ballymaurice (Granard Rural D.E.D.). Terence at Ballymore. Patrick at Barrack Street, Granard Town. Peter at Main Street, Granard Town. Bernard at Dring. Anne at Ringowny. Nicholas at Cloonshannagh or Coolamber Manor Demesne. Annie, Bernard, John at Edgeworthstown Town. Terence at Glenmore (Ballinamuck East D.E.D.). Mary A. at Drumbad. Patrick at Cloonrallagh. Michael at Cornapark. Thomas, Patrick at Glen. *ALSO:* Ellen at Lynch's of Curraghmore. Bridget at Feeney's of Moygh (Ballymahon D.E.D.). James at McGoey's of Abbeyderg. Annie at Jordan's of Ardoghil. Patrick at Granard Barracks. James at John Macken's of Muckerstaff. Patrick at John Cosgrove's of Cornacullew. Sr. Bridget at Rev. Mother Farrington's of Newtownforbes Village. Sr. Ellen at Sr. Green's of Convent Lane, Longford Town. William P. at Gilhooly's of Keon's Terrace, Longford Town. Eily at Gallagher's of Main Street, Longford Town.

FLOWER: Maria, Francis, Margaret, Elizabeth, Robert at Barry (Ballymahon D.E.D.). *ALSO:* Susan at Francis Armstrong's of Main Street, Keenagh Village.

FLUERY: See Fleury.

FLYNN:(41) Mary at Drumanure. Catherine, Marcella at Ballymahon Town. Michael at Corrool (Fox). Thomas at Lissameen. Bridget at Aghacordrinan. Thomas at Lislea (Lislea D.E.D.). Mary at Ballymacroly. Edward at Cartron (Granard Urban D.E.D.). John at Ball Alley Street Lower, Granard Town. Owen at Barrack Street, Granard Town. John at Tromra (Granard Urban D.E.D.). Patrick at Ardagullion. John, James at Aghanoran. Patrick, John, Patrick, Hugh, Patrick at Corbaun or Leitrim. John at Creelaghta. Michael, Connor at Crowdrumman. Francis at Fardrumman. Peter at Lettergeeragh. James, Patrick at Cartrongolan. Mary at Brocklagh. John at Ballagh (Newtownforbes D.E.D.). John at Newtownforbes Village. Michael at Lismoy. Michael, Peter at Clontumpher. John at Kilnacarrow (Aghaboy D.E.D.). Hugh, John at Killeenatruan. Francis at Cloonahussey. Annie at Ballygarve. Fanny at Glack (Longford Rural D.E.D.). Mary, James at Abbeycartron. *ALSO:* James at Gerald Daly's of Ballymahon Town. Gerald at Kate Whelan's of Ballymahon Town. Patrick at Hannigan's of Aghnashannagh, Ballinalee Village. Hugh at Robinson's of Gorteenrevagh, Ballinalee Village. Thomas at James Flood's (2) of Ballinrooey. Ellen at Donohoe's of Ball Alley Street Upper, Granard Town. Bridget at John Reilly's of Barrack Street, Granard Town. Bridget and Mary J. at Henry Reilly's of Aghanoran. Francis at Bridget Reilly's of Toome (Mullanalaghta D.E.D.). John at Terence Lennon's of Fardrumman. Mary and Anne at Farrington's of Newtownforbes Village. Mary at Percival's of Minard. Peter at James McGee's (4) of Derryharrow. Mary at Fullam's of Rhine. Ellen at Shaw's of Glack (Longford Rural D.E.D.). William at Ussher-Roberts' of Knockahaw. Hugh and Patrick at John Farrell's of Chapel Lane, Longford Town. Mary at Green's of Convent Lane, Longford Town.

FOILAN: See Whelan.

FOLEY: Michael at Newtownbond. Patrick at Clonwhelan. Michael at Bridge Street, Longford Town. *ALSO:* Jane at James Cassidy's of Ballymahon Town.

FOLLARD: John A. at James Daly's of Ballymahon Town.

FORAN: Patrick J. at Great Water Street, Longford Town.

FORBES: Joseph at Drummeel. Charles at Aghaward. Samuel at Abbeylara Village. Frances (Countess of Granard) at Castleforbes Demesne. Robert at Farraghroe. Margaret at Campbell's Row, Longford Town.

FORDE, FORD:(12): Patrick at Derrindiff. Mary at Forthill. Patrick at Cleraun. Patrick, Honor at Derrynagalliagh. Francis, Thomas at France. Michael at Bunlahy. James, Patrick at Derawley. Michael at Kilmahon. Thomas at Richmond Street, Longford Town. *ALSO:* Maggie and Joseph

F. at Nolan's of Glebe (Kilglass D.E.D.). Mary at Mulvihill's of Corrool (Fox). Sarah at James Ryan's of Barnacor (Ledwithstown D.E.D.). James at McGovern's of Cartronamarkey.

FORREST: Robert at Abbeycartron. *ALSO:* Elizabeth J. and Margaret F. at Finlay's of Clooncoose (Cloonee D.E.D.).

FORSTER: Sarah at Aghnashannagh. Thomas E. at School Land. John at Sharvoge.

FOSTER: Denis at Killeen (Foxhall D.E.D.). Donald at Lissagernal. James at Moor. *ALSO:* Samuel at Gerety's of Main Street, Kennagh Village. Margaret at Morrow's of Drumderg.

FOWLER: Mary and Jerry at Patrick McCarthy's of Aghadowry.

FOX, FOXE:(41): Bernard at Torboy. Daniel at Forgney. John at Kildordan. William W. at Foxhall. John, Michael, Margaret, Andrew at Mullawornia. Mary at Tirlickeen. James, Mary at Ballymahon Town. Patrick at Newpark. Michael at Corrool (Fox). Anna at Corryena. Bernard, John at Derrynagalliagh. Michael, Thomas at Annagh (Ledwithstown D.E.D.). Patrick at Derrynabuntale. Mary at Prucklishtown. Eugene at Ballinalee Village. Julia, Charles at Aghakilmore. Bridget, Matthew at Abbeylara Village. Mary at Ballywillin. Charles at Ballinlough. James at Rathbrackan. Bridget at Rossan. Patrick at Melkernagh. John at Barrack St., Granard Town.   Bridget at Derragh. Patrick at Ballyduffy. Anne, Cornelius at Edgeworthstown Town. Elizabeth at Kilmahon. Anne at Cahanagh. Patrick at Magheraveen. Margaret at Knockagowny. James at Cloonmucker. Bridget at Lisrevagh. *ALSO:* Kate at Farrell's of Forgney. William at Hanly's of Corlea. Mary at Armstrong's of Glenmore (Kilcommock D.E.D.). John at Lynam's of Derryart. Edith at Edgeworth's of Gorteen. James at Patrick Cahill's of Aghagreagh. Michael at Treacy's of Gelshagh. Jane at Murphy's of Drumderg. Patrick at Treacy's of Newtownbond. John at Cox's of Cranally. Mary at Kiernan's of Ballinlough. John at Masterson's of Rinroe. Bridget at Pettit's of Main St., Granard Town. Ton (?) at Hinds's of Cooldoney. Francis at John Reilly's of Shanmullagh. Agnes and Margaret at Farrington's of Newtownforbes Village. Thomas at Bridget Regan's of Cloonmore. John at Farrell's of Carnan. John at O'Connor's of Conroy's Court, Longford Town.

FOYLAN: See Whelan.

FRARY: See Friary.

FRAWLEY: John at Daroge. *ALSO:* Mary B. at John Brady's of Kilmore.

FRAYNE: Ambrose at Curraghmore. Alexander at Torboy. Alexander at Abbeyderg. John at Main Street, Keenagh Village. *ALSO:* Margaret at Anne McDowell's of Drumnacross. Rose A. at Mulhill's of Kilfintan.

FREE: Richard at Cooleeny. Thomas at Dublin Street, Longford Town.

FREEMAN: Sr. Mary at Sr. Green's of Convent Lane, Longford Town.

FRIARY: John at Cloonagh (Mullanalaghta D.E.D.). Anne, John at Bog Lane, Longford Town. *ALSO:* Mary at James Cosgrove's of Main Street, Granard Town. Kate at Laurence Cluskey's of Kilmore.

FRIZZELL: Anne at Cartron (Granard Rural D.E.D.).

FROST: Sr. Mary at Rev. Mother Farrington's of Newtownforbes Village.

FRY: Alexander at Cloonbrin. *ALSO:* William at Bogan's of Aghaboy (Milltown D.E.D.). Jane and Annie at Wilson's of Ballydrum.

FULLAM, FULHAM, FULLUM: Thomas at Cloonfin. James at Druminacrehir. Anne, Patrick at Mullinroe. James at Creevy. Mathew at Clonwhelan. Maria at Rhine. Rev. James J. at Deanscurragh. *ALSO:* Bernard at Edward Drake's of Ballinulty Upper. Julia at Francis Farrell's of Cloonagh (Mullanalaghta D.E.D.) (?).

FULLAN: Julia at Francis Farrell's of Cloonagh (Mullanalaghta D.E.D.).

FULLARD: See Follard.

FUREY, FURY:(11): Patrick at Sleehaun (Sankey). Cormack at Kilmore. Francis, James at Esker North. Patrick, Francis at Kiltycreevagh. Patrick at Garvary. Patrick, Patrick at Monaduff. Mary at Cloonmucker. Margaret at Bog Lane, Longford Town. *ALSO:* Margaret at Carty's of Kilglass and Cloonagh. (See Fleury).

GAFFNEY:(14): John at Ballywillin. Michael at Cartronamarkey. Owen, Owen at Ballinulty Upper (?). Mary at Cartron (Granard Rural D.E.D.). Margaret at Robinstown. Cornelius at Main Street, Granard Town. Owen at Derragh. Patrick at Toome (Mullanalaghta D.E.D.). Thomas at Cam. Anne at Aghafin. Thomas at Rathmore (Ballinamuck East D.E.D.). Rebecca at Lanesborough Village. Anne at Ballyminion. *ALSO:* Catherine at Murphy's of Coolnahinch (Kilcommock D.E.D.). Bernard et al. at Quinn's of Kilcourcey. Peter at Bartley's of Abbeylara Village. Julia at Laurence Mulligan's of Ballywillin. James and Bridget at O'Brien's of Drumlish Village. Lizzie at Peter Bannon's of Barney. Francis at Michael Thompson's of Ballymahon Street, Longford Town. John at Mary A.

Callaghan's of Dublin St., Longford Town. Catherine at Michael Maguire's of Great Water St., Longford Town. Patrick at Reilly's of Great Water St., Longford Town. Charles at Nevin's of Market Square, Longford Town.

GAHAN: Bridget at Garryandrew.

McGAHERN, McGAHARAN: Thomas at Lisraherty.

GAINTY: See Ginty.

GALLAGHER:(13): John at Cloonbreany. William at Glenoghil. John at Drummeel. Patrick at Tober. Peter at Dalystown. Edward at Barrack Street, Granard Town. Thaddeus at Ballyduffy. Thomas at Lisnagrish. Bernard at Aghafin. John at Carrickmoyragh. Peter at Drumlish Village. Patrick at Lismoy. Teresa at Main Street, Longford Town. *ALSO:* Mary at Wilson's of Main Street, Keenagh Village. Anne at Newman's of Ballinalee Village. Bridget at Bridget Loughery's (14) of Greagh. Sarah at McQuaid's of Drumlish Village. Anna at Sullivan's of Creenagh. John at Quinn's of Drumure. John at O'Connor's of Conroy's Court, Longford Town. Sr. Margaret at Sr. Green's of Convent Lane, Longford Town. Anne at Free's of Dublin Street, Longford Town. Nanny at Ross's of Dublin Street, Longford Town.

GALLIGAN: Thomas at Mullinroe. John at Rinroe. Thomas, Michael at Derragh. Rose at Smear (?). *ALSO:* Kate at Ryder's of Aghakeeran. Mary and Eugene at Lynch's of Kilfintan. Thomas at Brady's of Fostragh. James at Patrick Higgins's of Aghamore Lower. Patrick at Peter J. Joyce's of Main Street, Longford Town. (See Gilligan).

GALVIN, GALVAN: Michael at Chapel Lane, Longford Town. *ALSO:* Patrick at Burns' of Newtownforbes Village. John et al. at McCusker's of Harbour Row, Longford Town.

GALWAY: Hester at Higgins's of Keon's Terrace, Longford Town.

GAMBLE: Edward at Cooleeny.

GANLY: William at Cloonscott. Thomas at Mornin. John at Ballyclamay. Thomas at Toome (Ballymahon D.E.D.). Bernard at Portanure. *ALSO:* Joseph at Lennon's of Derrynagalliagh. (See Garly).

McGANN: Henry at Newcastle. Patrick at Corlea. Francis at Knockavegan. Patrick, Thomas at Derrylough. Francis, Michael at Kilmahon. Bridget at Cloonahard. *ALSO:* James et al. at Bellew's of Creevaghmore (Forgney Civil Ph.). Daniel and Ellen at Keegan's of Corboy. James at Quinn's of Whiterock (?). (See McCann).

MAGAN, MAGANN: Martin at Aghnaskea. Margaret at Killashee Village. Mary A. at Ballynakill. *ALSO:* John at William Rickard's of Ballymahon Town.

GANNON:(15): Bernard at Taghsheenod Glebe. Patrick at Carrigeen (Foxhall D.E.D.). James at Clontymullan. Bernard at Taghshinny. Joseph at Ballymahon Town. Mary at Creevagh Beg. James at Derrindiff. John at Kilcommock Glebe. Michael at Kilsallagh. Michael at Lisnagrish. Michael at Corry (Caldragh D.E.D.). James, Catherine at Cloonahard. Bridget at Dublin Street, Longford Town. Catherine at Glack (Longford Urban No. 1 D.E.D.). *ALSO:* Mary at Ganly's of Cloonscott. Patrick at Farrell's of Loughan. John at Keegan's of Loughan. Nannie at Mulvihill's of Moygh (Ballymahon D.E.D.). Michael at James Feeney's of Ballymahon Town. Ellen at Peter Connor's of Kilsallagh. Mary at Farrington's of Newtownforbes Village. Joseph at Brett's of Derryad (Mountdavis D.E.D.). Patrick and Anne at Lamb's of Earl Street, Longford Town.

McGANTY: See McGinty.

O'GARA: Charles at St. Mel's Road, Longford Town.

McGARAHAN: John at Farmullagh. (See Garrahan).

GARDINER: F. at Hewetson's of Church Street, Longford Town.

McGARLE: See McGarrell.

GARLY: Sarah at Fagan's of Moatfarrell. (See Ganly).

McGARR: Patrick at Tawnagh. Catherine at Corglass. *ALSO:* James at Quinn's of Whiterock (?).

GARRAHAN, GARAHAN, GARRAGHAN:(15): Margaret, John at Lissawarriff. John at Legan. John at Ballyknock. Michael, Peter, Patrick at Laghlooney. Patrick at Abbeyderg. Daniel at Cloonbreany. James at Kilsallagh. Catherine at Edgeworthstown Town. Jane at Cloonevit. Mary at Cloonker. Michael at Bohermore. Susan at Chapel Lane, Longford Town. *ALSO:* Thomas and Lizzie at Donovan's of Carrigeen (Foxhall D.E.D.). Maggie et al. at Ward's of Kinard. Mary A. at Gill's of Lisom. Annie at Duignan's of Creevagh Beg. Ellen at Casey's of Rappareehill. Catherine at Clarke's of Lanesborough Village. Margaret at Farrelly's of Moyra and Fortmill. John J. at Brady's of Ballymahon Street, Longford Town. Brian at O'Connor's of Conroy's Court, Longford Town. William at Rose Kelly's of Great Water Street, Longford Town. Bridget at Nolan's of New Street, Longford Town. Peter at Dunne's of St. Mel's Road, Longford Town. (See McGarahan).

McGARRELL: Patrick at Gorteenclareen. Myles at Soran. *ALSO:* Francis at James Ryan's of Barnacor (Ledwithstown D.E.D.). Kate at Noragh Ryan's of Barnacor (Ledwithstown D.E.D.). Michael at Ryan's of Drumnacor.

GARRY, GARY: Edward at Abbeylara. Richard at Kilbride.

McGARRY:(24): Rose at Castlerea Mountain. Mary, Michael, Thady, Owen at Cloghan (Doory D.E.D.). Thomas at Tagsheenod Glebe. Margaret at Kilnacarrow (Kilglass D.E.D.). Charles at Knockavegan. Bridget at Abbeyderg. James, Francis, Anne, Julia at Aghamore Upper. Bridget, Patrick, John at Cloonellan. Patrick, Bernard at Leitrim (Breanrisk D.E.D.). Bernard at Enybegs. Patrick at Ballagh (Newtownforbes D.E.D.). Thomas at Lissagernal. James at Trillickatemple. Peter at Aghalust. Patrick at Main Street, Longford Town. *ALSO:* Margaret at McGinn's of Derragh. Elizabeth at Murphy's of Newtownforbes Village. Margaret at Walsh's of Moygh (Killashee D.E.D.). Owen at Catherine Donlon's of Ardboghil. Dominick at Owen Donlon's of Ardboghil. John at Lefroy's of Carrickglass Demesne (Templemichael Civil Ph.). Sr. Mary E. at Sr. Green's of Convent Lane, Longford Town. Mary A. at Harris's of Main Street, Longford Town. Patrick at Cameron's of Main Street, Longford Town.

McGARTNA, McGARTNEY (?): Bridget at Water Lane, Granard Town. (See McCartney).

GARTY: James at Creevagh Beg. (See Carty).

GARVEY: John at Rinroe. Thomas at Crowdrumman. James at Coach Yard, Longford Town. *ALSO:* Julia at Patrick O'Reilly's of Main Street, Granard Town.

GARVIN: Anthony at Killasona.

GARY: See Garry.

GAUGHNEY: Owen, Owen at Ballinulty Upper.

GAUGHRAN: Joseph at Kilnacarrow (Mountdavis D.E.D.). Peter at Lanesborough Village. Thomas at Market Square, Longford Town. *ALSO:* Mary A. at Dillon's of Main Street, Longford Town.

McGAUVERN: See McGovern.

GAVAGAN, GAVIGAN, GAVACAN: James at Rincoolagh. Owen, Patrick at Rinroe. Catherine at Cloonbearla. Bridget at Turreen. *ALSO:* Rev. Thomas at Higgins's of Carragh (Granard Urban D.E.D.).

McGAVER: Thomas at Cloonsellan. Patrick at Cloontamore. Joseph at Bridge Street, Longford Town. *ALSO:* Sr. Rose at Rev. Mother Hampson's of Aghafin.

GAVIN, GAVAN: Michael at Kilnashee. Patrick at Rappareehill. John at Creeve. Bridget at Hyde's Yard, Longford Town. Patrick at Little Water Street, Longford Town. *ALSO:* William and Cornelius at Thomas Kiernan's of Barrack Street, Granard Town. Patrick et al. at Catherine Kane's of Bawn (Breanrisk D.E.D.).

McGAWLEY: Thomas at Cloonmore.

GAY, GAYE: See Gey.

GAYNOR: Anne at Kilcourcey. Margaret at Lisryan. Patrick, John at Cranalagh More. George at Ballindagny and Cullyvore. James at Bohermore. Margaret at Little Water Street, Longford Town.

GEARTY: John at Bank Street, Granard Town (?). Thomas at Cloonart North. John at Clooneen (Cox). John at Richmond Street, Longford Town. *ALSO:* Margaret at Sweeney's of Liscahill (?). John at Thomas McGlynn's (4) of Cloonart North. (See Geraghty).

McGEE, MAGEE:(27) Michael, Charles at Cloghan (Forgney D.E.D.). Andrew, Edward at Clooncullen. Thomas at Kinard. James at Tennalick. Margaret at Daroge. Margaret at Toome (Ballymahon D.E.D.). John at Corrool (Kenny). John at Ballymaurice (Granard Rural D.E.D.). Philip at Smear. Peter at Derrycassan. Patrick, Peter at Lettergullion. Daniel, James at Derawley. Bridget at Drumlish Village. Patrick at Dooroc. John at Newtownforbes Village. Owen at Cloonart North. John at Caldragh. Thomas, James, James at Derryharrow. Michael at Ballymahon Street, Longford Town. Catherine, Owen at Abbeycartron. *ALSO:* James at Mulvihill's of Clooncullen. John at Mulvihill's of Moygh (Ballymahon D.E.D.). Patrick at Kate Whelan's of Ballymahon Town. Matthew at Auchmuty's of Creevaghmore (Forgney Civil Ph.). Margaret at Richard Charters' of Garvagh (Currygrane D.E.D.). Daniel at Beatty's of Main Street, Granard Town. Daniel at Sesnan's of Newtownforbes Village. Elizabeth and Catherine at Farrington's of Newtownforbes Village. Sarah and Edward at Edward Morgan's of Fee's Terrace, Longford Town. Michael et al. at Dodd's of Healy's Terrace, Longford Town. (See Ghee).

GEELAN:(11): Robert at Currygranny. John at Drumlish. John at Kilmacannon. Francis at Ahanagh. Christopher, James, Henry, Coote, William, Arthur at Cloonageeher. James at Glebe (Cloondara D.E.D.). *ALSO:* Kate at Keena's of Glenoghil. John at Anne Walpole's of Greagh. Mary A. at Clabby's of Clogher and Rinn. Maria and Mary at Magan's of

Killashee Village. Patrick at Thompson's of Lissavaddy. John and Mary B. at Kelly's of Richmond Street, Longford Town.

GEHARTY, GEHERTY: John at Bank Street, Granard Town.

GELNAGH: See Gilna.

GELSHINAN, GELSINAN: See Gilsenan.

McGENNIS: Rachel at Farrington's of Newtownforbes Village. (See McGuinness).

GENTY: See Ginty.

GEOFFROY: George at Rathcline.

McGEOUGH-BOND: Mabel A. and Ralph S. at Bond's of Farraghroe.

McGEOY: See McGoey.

GERAGHTY, GERETY:(49): John at Rath. Catherine at Kilcurry. Patrick at Killinbore. James at Daroge. John at Moneyfad. Mortimer at Ballymahon Town. Mary at Creevaghmore (Forgney Civil Ph.). William at Derryoghil. Margaret at Derraghan Beg. Thomas at Derraghan More. Michael at Forthill. John at Derryart. Thomas at Main Street, Keenagh Village. Patrick, Bridget at Derrylough. Peter at Ledwithstown (Kilcommock Civil Ph.). Thomas at Derrynabuntale. Margaret at Edera. Anne, Laurence, Bridget, Margaret, John at Gorteenclareen. John at Sonnagh. Patrick at Coolcor. Patrick, Mary at Ballymore. John at Bank Street, Granard Town (?). John at Barrack Street, Granard Town. John J. at Main Street, Granard Town. James at Ferskill. Thomas at Balloo. Michael at Aghafin. Luke at Camlisk Beg. William at Edgeworthstown. James at Edgeworthstown Town. Patrick at Aghareagh (Cloondara D.E.D.). Thomas at Mullagh Bog. John at Cloonsheerin. Bridget at Knockatarry Poynton. James, Anne at Newtown (Moydow D.E.D.). James at Derrygeel. Laurence at Bawn (Ardagh West D.E.D.). Thomas at Allenagh. John, Michael at Great Water Street, Longford Town. Bridget at New Street, Longford Town. John at Abbeycartron. *ALSO:* John at Dowling's of Corlea. Patrick at Hopkins' of Ballagh (Cashel West D.E.D.). Mary at Notley's of Claras. Mary at Skelly's of Edera. Mary A. at McNamara's of Glannagh. Ellen at Monaghan's of Leitrim (Granard Rural D.E.D.). Thomas J. at Rose Reilly's of Water Lane, Granard Town. Margaret at Sweeney's of Liscahill. James at Carty's of Doonameran. James at Dooris's of Corboy. (See Gearty).

McGERR: Patrick at Killasona. Edward at Clontumpher. *ALSO:* Patrick at Pettit's of Main Street, Granard Town. John at William Masterson's of

Farmullagh.

GERRARD: William at Lissameen. *ALSO:* Archibald at John McDowell's of Drumnacross.

GETHIN: Michael at Killashee or Carrickboy Barracks.

GETTINGS, GETHINGS: Mary at Mornin. Andrew at Asnagh. Catherine at Tully (Milltown D.E.D.). John at Carnan. Ellen at Killyfad. *ALSO:* Michael at Brady's of Lisraghtigan. Denis at Cully's of Aghaboy (Milltown D.E.D.). Anne at Feehilly's of Ballywalter. Edward at Bond's of Farraghroe.

McGETTRICK: Matthew at Ward's of Edgeworthstown Town.

GEY: Mary A. at William Deniston's of Drumnacross.

GHEE: John at Cloonellan. Patrick at Cloonmacart. Thomas, Anne at Briskil. John at Corboy. John at Lisduff (Longford Rural D.E.D.). *ALSO:* Mary A. at William Deniston's of Drumnacross (?). Lizzie at Cahill's of Cornapark. James at Dowler's of Ballynagoshen. (See McGee).

McGHRAUN: See McGraun.

GIBBONS, GIBBINS: Margaret at Shrule. Thomas at Cloonfore. Edward N. at Curreen. *ALSO:* Maria at O'Brien's of Daroge.

GIBBS: Mary A. and Robert at Doherty's of Currygrane.

GIBLIN: Mary at Delany's of Church Street, Longford Town.

McGIBNEY: Kate at Ballymahon Street, Longford Town. *ALSO:* Henry and Annie at Michael Donohoe's of Farmullagh. (See McGivney).

GIBSON: Henry at Drumhalry. Frederick J. at Lisnabo. *ALSO:* William at Legge's of Main Street, Longford Town. William at McElnea's of Main Street, Longford Town.

GIDDINGS: George at Little Water Street, Longford Town.

McGIFF: Bridget at Cloonbrin. Patrick at Brickeens.

GILBERT: Mary and Henrietta at Farrington's of Newtownforbes Village.

GILBRIDE: See Kilbride.

GILCHRIEST, GILCHRIST:(12): Edward at Ballywillin. William at The Hill, Granard Town. John, John, James at Lissanure. Patrick at Shantum. Patrick at Cranalagh More. Ellen at Chapel Lane, Longford Town. William, James at Great Water Street, Longford Town. Michael at Market Square, Longford Town. Patrick at Noud's Yard, Longford Town. *ALSO:* Julia at Smyth's of Aghagreagh. Robert J. et al. at Mahon's of Deerpark (Newtownforbes D.E.D.). Francis at William McCormack's of Clooncoose (Cloonee D.E.D.). Bridget and John at McCormack's of Kiltyreher (Templemichael Civil Ph.).

GILDEA: James at Cloghchurnel.

GILHEANY: Patrick et al. at McCusker's of Harbour Road, Longford Town.

GILHOOLY: See Gillooly.

GILL:(39): Anne at Torboy. John at Keel (Kilglass D.E.D.). Peter at Killinbore. Owen at Taghshinny. John, Mary at Ballymahon Town. Kate at Cloonard (Ballymahon D.E.D.). Daniel at Lislom. Patrick at Barry (Ballymahon D.E.D.). James at Toome (Ballymahon D.E.D.). Peter, Thomas at Carrowdunican. Annie, Francis at Cleraun. Anne at Barne. Edward at Clonca. Patrick, John, Michael, James at Edenmore. James at Derawley. John, Patrick, Patrick at Brocklagh. James at Gaigue. Joseph at Lamagh. Peter at Corragarrow (Killashee D.E.D.). Betty at Derryaroge. Bernard at Commons North. Patrick at Derrygeel. Michael at Lisrevagh. Patrick at Lissawly or St. Albans. James at Ballinreaghan. Michael at Crossea South. William at Drumroe. Terence at Moyra and Fortmill. Richard at Ballymakeegan. Patrick at Great Water St., Longford Town. Mary at New St., Longford Town. *ALSO:* Mary at Elizabeth Mulvihill's (106) of Ballymahon Town. Margaret at Francis Flower's of Barry (Ballymahon D.E.D.). Anne at McNally's of Cornadowagh. Anne and Mary at Leavy's of Barne. Francis at Reynolds's of Barne. John at Mullen's of Lissanure. Kate at Molphy's of Edgeworthstown Town. Patrick J. at Peter J. Joyce's of Edgeworthstown Town. Patrick et al. at Bryan Keenan's (6) of Tawnagh. Katie at Rodgers' of Drumlish Village. Mary A. at Farrell's of Drumroe. Margaret at Gillan's of Mollyroe. Michael at Murphy's of Bundoon. Bridget at Michael Boyce's of Lissaghanedan. Michael at Casey's of Mullaghavorneen. Patrick at Shevlin's of Aghadegnan (Longford Rural D.E.D.).

GILLEESY, GILLEECE (?): Michael at Garrycam.

GILLELAND: See Gilliland.

GILLEN, GILLAN:(13): Margaret at Coolnafinnoge. Mary A. at

Ballymaurice (Granard Rural D.E.D.). John at Cam. Patrick, Bernard, James at Enybegs. Patrick at Mollyroe. Michael at Ardboghil. James at Barney. Patrick at Bohernacross. Thomas at Finnaragh. Richard at Glen. John at Broderick's Yard, Longford Town. *ALSO:* Christopher at Brady's of Ballyboy. Kate at Carrigy's of Tonywardan. Thomas at Beglin's of Lisryan. Peter et al. at Reynolds's of Lyanmore.

GILLERAN: Peter, Winifred at Cloonkeel. Patrick at Dublin Street, Longford Town. *ALSO:* Patrick at Conway's of Cloonbearla. Rebecka at Jackson's of Earl Street, Longford Town (?). Thomas at John Mathews' of Main Street, Longford Town.

GILLESPIE: Thomas at Derrycassan.

GILLIARD: Henry at Ballyreaghan. *ALSO:* Fanny E. at Bond's of Farraghroe.

GILLIGAN: Bernard at Cloonaghmore. Rose at Smear. Jane at Lisduff (Longford Rural D.E.D.). *ALSO:* Michael and Ellen at Crawford's of Abbeylara Village. Thomas at Gurd's of Templeton Glebe. (See Galligan).

GILLILAND, GILLELAND: William at Barry (Kilcommock D.E.D.).

GILLOOLY, GILLOOLEY, GILHOOLY: Patrick at Derawley. Catherine at Cloonfore. Fanny at Keon's Terrace, Longford Town. *ALSO:* Ellen at Mallon's of Derawley. Mary at Connaughton's of Inchenagh Island (Rathcline D.E.D.).

GILMARTIN: Mary T. at Drummeel.

GILMORE, GILMOUR: Patrick at Carrowrory. Thomas at Collum. Lucinda at Edgeworthstown Town. *ALSO:* William at Edgeworthstown Barracks.

GILMURRAY, GILMURRY: See Kilmurray.

GILNA, GILNAGH, GELNAGH: John, Anne, Ellen at Soran. Hugh at Rhine. *ALSO:* Teresa at Sullivan's of Willsbrook. Thomas and Sarah at Peter Quigley's of Soran.

GILPIN: John at Killeen (Bunlahy D.E.D.). *ALSO:* Charles at Abbott's of Drummeel. Jane at Anne Reilly's of Cartron (Granard Rural D.E.D.).

GILROY: James at Aghacordrinan. Hugh at Barragh Beg. John at Allenagh. *ALSO:* Sarah at O'Connor's of St. Michael's Road, Longford Town.

GILSENAN, GELSHINAN: John at Currycahill. Margaret at Kilbride. Mary at Robinstown. Patrick at Lettergullion. Patrick at Gaigue. Patrick at Mullolagher. *ALSO:* Francis at Mullen's of Main Street, Granard Town. Rose A. at Cunningham's of Lettergullion.

GINLOM (?): Michael at McClean's of Edgeworthstown Town.

McGINN: Owen at Derragh. *ALSO:* Bridget at Treacy's of Aghagreagh. Hugh at Doran's of Moxham Street, Granard Town.

GINTY, GENTY, GAINTY: Edward at Dunbeggan (Columbkille D.E.D.). Patrick, John, Thomas at Shanmullagh. Bridget, John at Corneddan. *ALSO:* Anne at Felix Donnelly's of Shanmullagh. John at Pettit's of Annagh (Drumgort D.E.D.).

McGINTY, McGANTY: Fred at Devine's of Chapel Lane, Longford Town. Teresa at Elizabeth Kelly's of Dublin Street, Longford Town (?).

McGIRL (?): See McGuirle.

McGIRR: See McGerr.

McGIVNEY:(18): Thomas at Kiltyclogh. Annie at Culray. Bernard at Sonnagh. Patrick at Culleenmore. Bridget at Ballinrud Glebe. Anne at Creevy. Patrick at Aghabrack. Edward at Ballybrien. Patrick at Ballynacross (Granard Rural D.E.D.). Patrick at Cartron (Granard Rural D.E.D.). Patrick at Ardagullion. Henry at Asnagh. Mary, Thomas, Rose at Corbaun or Leitrim. Bernard at Kilmore. Ellen at Lechurragh. Rev. John at Lanesborough Village. *ALSO:* Rev. Peter at Duffy's of Kilcurry. Rose at Crawford's of Ballymacroly. Mary at Eivers' of Asnagh. Ellen at Campbell's of Muckerstaff. (See McGibney).

McGLADE: Nicholas at Polladooey. Anne, Patrick at Smear.

GLANCY: Jane at Listraghee. Anne at Cloonfin. Mary at Clooneen (Creevy D.E.D.). Bridget at Moxham Street, Granard Town. Margaret at Ferskill. Ann at Gragh. Francis at Newtown (Moydow D.E.D.). Margaret at Aghaboy (Aghaboy D.E.D.). John at Dublin Street, Longford Town. *ALSO:* Bernard at Dooner's of Curry (Moydow D.E.D.). Mark and Annie at Dooner's of Dunbeggan (Moydow D.E.D.). James at McGeoy's of Newtown (Moydow D.E.D.). Bridget at Clyne's of Cloonevit. Mary at Moran's of Main Street, Longford Town. (See Clancy).

GLANFIELD: Robert at Clontymullan.

GLEESON: Catherine at Firmount.

GLENNON:(11): Patrick at Creevaghmore (Forgney Civil Ph.). Patrick at School Land. Patrick at Carragh (Granard Urban D.E.D.). William, Michael, James, Patrick, Thomas at Cranalagh More. Michael at Currygranny. Edward at Bank of the Hill. John at Ballygarve. *ALSO:* Bridget at Killian's of Forthill. Thomas at Sheridan's of Abbeylara. Bridget and John at Andrew Kiernan's of Edgeworthstown Town.

McGLINN: See McGlynn.

McGLONE: Thomas at Knockloughlin.

McGLORIAN: John at Larkin's of Drumlish Village.

McGLOUGLIN: See McLoughlin.

GLYNN, GLYNNE: Joseph at Cloonbrin. John at Edgeworthstown. *ALSO:* Annie at Rehill's of Ballinulty Lower. Sr. Julianna at Rev. Mother Hampson's of Aghafin. John at Toole's of Dublin Street, Longford Town.

McGLYNN, McGLINN:(31): Rose at Cavan. Michael, James at Kiltykeary. Patrick at Sheeroe (Knockanbaun D.E.D.) William at Glannagh. John at Cartronamarkey. Laurence at The Hill, Granard Town. Francis at Garryandrew. Margaret, Patrick at Edgeworthstown Town. James at Cloontagh. Francis, John at Drumlish. Hugh, James at Gaigue. Maria at Ballagh (Newtownforbes D.E.D.). James at Briskil. James at Ahanagh. Thomas, Thomas, Peter at Cloonart North. Joseph, Anne, Patrick at Cloonart South. Patrick, Lawrence, Thomas at Edercloon. Thomas at Newtown (Killashee D.E.D.). James at Killyfad. Thomas at Knockloughlin. Thomas at Little Water Street, Longford Town. *ALSO:* Lawrence et al. at Roarke's of Drummeel. Patrick at O'Connor's of Conroy's Court, Longford Town.

McGOEY, McGEOY:(15): Charles, William at Drumanure. Charles at Cloghan (Doory D.E.D.). Michael at Abbeyderg. Bernard, John at Currygranny. Bernard, John at Treel (Newtownforbes D.E.D.). Michael at Caldraghmore. Bernard at Newtown (Moydow D.E.D.). Christopher at Grillagh (Ardagh West D.E.D.). Patrick, Thomas at Bawn (Ardagh West D.E.D.). Mary at Killoe Glebe. Rose at Cartronageeragh. *ALSO:* Mary at Mulvihill's of Cloonbrin. Peter at Dowd's of Newtown (Moydow D.E.D.). Anne at Armstrong's of Main Street, Longford Town.

GOGARTY: James at Corrabaun (Breanrisk D.E.D.).

GOLDEN: Robert at Drumlish Village. *ALSO:* Margaret at Margaret Mathews' of Main Street, Longford Town.

GOLDING: Henry at Breaden's of Great Water Street, Longford Town.

GOLDRICK: Thomas at Agharanagh (Ballymahon D.E.D.).

McGOLDRICK:(11): Michael, Peter, William at Carrickmoyragh. Peter, Andrew at Currygranny. Mary at Prucklish. Teresa at Aghnamaddoo. Thomas at Enybegs. Thomas at Ballagh (Achmuty). Michael at Deerpark (Newtownforbes D.E.D.). Thomas at Creenagh. *ALSO:* Francis et al. at Sommers' of Kilmacannon.

GOLDSBERRY: See Gouldsbury.

GOODE: Harriet at Church Street, Longford Town.

GOODWIN: Patrick at Newtownforbes Village. *ALSO:* Joseph at O'Connor's of Conroy's Court, Longford Town. Annie C. at Lloyd's of Main Street, Longford Town.

GORDON, GORDAN: William at Ballymahon Town. Elizabeth at Kilmoyle. Patrick at Demesne. *ALSO:* Sr. Margaret at Rev. Mother Farrington's of Newtownforbes Village.

GORMALLY: See Gormley.

GORMAN:(23): John at Ballycloghan. William at Ballybranigan. James at Ballymahon Town. James at Foygh. John at Ballinalee Village. Bartholomew, Bartholomew at Garvagh (Currygrane D.E.D.). Patrick at Cloonfin. Charles at Ballymaurice (Granard Rural D.E.D.). Mathew, Timothy at Coolamber. John, John, Mathew, Peter, Thomas, Peter at Fardrumman. William, John at Kiltycreevagh. Bridget at Lettergonnell. Patrick at Corneddan. Michael at Chapel Lane, Longford Town. Denis at Dublin Street, Longford Town. *ALSO:* Edward at Abbeyshrule Barracks. Thomas at McGrath's of Garvagh (Currygrane D.E.D.). Francis at Flood's of Ballymaurice (Granard Rural D.E.D.). Bridget at Francis Connell's of Fardrumman. Ellen at Hanify's of Drumlish.

GORMLEY, GORMLY, GORMALLY:(19): Annie at Killeen (Bunlahy D.E.D.). Arthur at Kinkillew. James, Mary, Margaret at Cornadrung. James, Patrick, James, James, Margaret, Margaret, Francis, Peter at Polladooey. Francis at Birrinagh. Felix at Shanmullagh. Michael at Cornafunshin. Alice at Drumnacooha. Michael, Edward at Esker South. *ALSO:* Mathew at Brady's of Cornadrung. Mary A. at Fitzpatrick's of Polladooey. John at Kate Doyle's of Smear. Annie at Morgan's of Drumhaughly.

GOSNEY: H. at Hewetson's of Church Street, Longford Town.

McGOUGH: See McGeough.

GOULD: Jane at Fetherston's of Ardagh Demesne.

GOULDSBURY, GOLDSBERRY: John at Cornamucklagh. James at Forgney. Maria H. at Glebe (Cloondara D.E.D.). Joseph, John, Richard at Cloonbrock. *ALSO:* Isabella and Mary J. at Morrow's of Caldragh.

McGOVERN, MAGOVERN:(13): Rose, Peter at Aghakilmore. Thomas at Cartronamarkey. Hugh at Ballinulty Lower. James at Ballinulty Upper. Garret at Leitrim (Granard Rural D.E.D.). Charles at Ball Alley Street Upper, Granard Town. James at Main Street, Granard Town. Anne at The Hill, Granard Town. Margaret at Farmullagh. Edward at Corglass. Charles at Cloontirm. John at Cooleeny. *ALSO:* Bernard at McGivney's of Culray. Mary at Bernard Finnan's of Barrack Street, Granard Town. Sarah A. at Bridget Reilly's of Toome (Mullanalaghta D.E.D.). Francis at O'Donnell's of Dublin Street, Longford Town. John at Dempsey's of Great Water Street, Longford Town.

McGOWAN, McGOWN: James at Drumnee. Edward at Pollagh. Rose at Cloonfin. Michael at Leitrim (Breanrisk D.E.D.). Catherine at Drumlish Village. Patrick at Earl Street, Longford Town. Elizabeth at St. Michael's Road, Longford Town. *ALSO:* Isabella at McCann's of Keon's Terrace, Longford Town.

GRACE: John at Wilson's of Ballymahon Road, Keenagh Village.

GRADY: Thomas at Abbeyshrule Barracks.

GRAHAM: James at Drumury. *ALSO:* Mary A. at Fennon's of Cornapark.

GRANARD: See Forbes.

McGRANE, McGRAIN: John at Castlerea Mountain. Thomas at Newtownflanigan. Patrick at Corryena. Joseph at Ardoghil. James at Moydow Glebe. *ALSO:* Thomas at Frayne's of Torboy. John et al. at Kelly's of Torboy. Kate at O'Ferrall's of Corbeagh (?). Jane at Farrington's of Newtownforbes Village. Maggie at Harris's of Abbeycartron (?). Thomas at Patrick Lynch's of Ballywillin (?).

McGRANN, McGRAN: See McCrann.

McGRATH, MAGRATH:(24): Kate at Castlerea Mountain. Hugh at Currycreaghan. Michael at Lisnacreevy. Patrick at Tennalick. James at Toome (Ballymahon D.E.D.). Patrick at Ballina. Patrick at Ballagh (Cashel West D.E.D.). Michael at Main Street, Keenagh Village. Bryan, Patrick at

Edera. Thomas, Bernard, Hugh at Gorteenclareen. William at Ballinalee Village. Anne at Garvagh (Currygrane D.E.D.). Patrick at Ballinlough. Michael at Main Street, Granard Town. Owen at Enaghan. Elizabeth at Ringowny. Patrick at Bracklon. Bridget at Kiltycreevagh. Bridget at Bunalough. Mary at Derrygeel. Mary J. at Ballymahon Street, Longford Town. *ALSO:* Margaret at Maguire's of Tirlickeen. Mary and Maria at Connaughton's of Derryveagh. John at Thomas Fox's of Annagh (Ledwithstown D.E.D.). Mary at Dolan's of Edera. Michael at Treacy's of Aghagreagh. Patrick at Catherine Monaghan's of Aghagreagh. Anne at John Treacy's of Bunlahy. Bridget at Ledwith's of Edgeworthstown Town. Patrick at James Cunningham's of Gaigue. Kate at James Farrell's of Glack (Longford Rural D.E.D.). Peter at James Brady's of Main Street, Longford Town.

McGRAUN, McGHRAUN: Thomas at Patrick Lynch's of Ballywillin.

GRAY, GREY:(32): James at Kilcurry. William G. at Glenoghil. Laurence, Patrick at Aghagreagh. Patrick, Thomas at Aghamore Upper. Rev. William at Abbeylara. Owen at Ballinulty Upper. Catherine at Cleenrah. Mary at Dunbeggan (Columbkille D.E.D.). Thomas at Smear. Michael, Laurence, Daniel at Ballyduffy. Patrick at Birrinagh. John, Peter at Drumard. Mathew at Farmullagh. Owen, Laurence at Edenmore. Catherine at Cloncowley. Denis at Kiltycreevagh. Thomas at Corrabaun (Breanrisk D.E.D.). Mathew at Cornacullew. Michael at Kiltycon. Daniel at Leggagh. Thomas at Barragh Beg. John, Thomas, Matthew D. at Drumlish Village. Francis at Ballagh (Achmuty). Richard at Bridge Street, Longford Town. *ALSO:* Catherine at John Devins's of Ballymahon Town. Mary A. at William Deniston's of Drumnacross (?). Kate at Brady's of Cartronamarkey. Mary at Catherine Kiernan's of Smear. Mary A. at Morris's of Crott. Denis et al. at Kennedy's of Ballyduffy. Patrick at Patrick Mulligan's of Birrinagh. Ellen at Patrick Reynolds's (10) of Cloncowley. Anne at Patrick Dolan's (13) of Kiltycreevagh. Patrick and Annie at McGarr's of Tawnagh. Catherine at Bridget Healy's of Cloonagh (Breanrisk D.E.D.). Anne at Edward Masterson's of Corglass. Annie at Thady Cunningham's of Gaigue. Francis at Peter Devany's of Kilmahon. Peter and Bridget at Pinkman's of Clogher and Rinn. Patrick and Charles at O'Connor's of Conroy's Court, Longford Town. Michael at Thompson's of Great Water Street, Longford Town. Sarah at Burke's of Main Street, Longford Town. Lizzie at Thomas Stafford's of Main Street, Longford Town.

McGREAL: Christopher at St. Michael's Road, Longford Town.

GREALY, GREALLY: James at Tirlickeen. Margaret at Cullentragh (Rathcline Civil Ph.). Patrick at Cloonkeel. John at Rappareehill. John at Lehery. Bridget at St. Mel's Road, Longford Town. *ALSO:* Maria at Martin Casey's of Cloonbrock.

GREAN: Kate at O'Ferrall's of Corbeagh.

McGREAN: See McGrane.

GREAVES: See Greeves.

GREENAWAY: H. at Hewetson's of Church Street, Longford Town.

GREENE, GREEN:(41): John at Killeen (Foxhall D.E.D.). Catherine, Anne at Elfeet (Adamson). Patrick at Greenhall Lower. Mary at Cloonbreany. John at Lissameen. Bernard at Kilsallagh. Margaret at Liscahill. William at Lisnagrish. William, Mary, Michael at Lissanure. Charles, Patrick at Shantum. Bridget at Lisryan. John at Corclaragh. Edward at Longfield. Peter at Bracklon. Margaret at Lackan. Francis, Philip, Michael, John, Michael, Patrick, Margaret at Edgeworthstown Town. William at Ballagh (Achmuty). Elizabeth at Treel (Newtownforbes D.E.D.). Michael at Newtownforbes Village. Francis, James at Cloonart South. Patrick at Clooneen (Cox). Owen at Clooniher. Henry at Lisnabo. John at Newtown (Moydow D.E.D.). James at Cornapark. Mathew at Finnaragh. Thomas at Keeloges. Thomas at Templemichael Glebe. Edward at Chapel Lane, Longford Town. Sr. Elizabeth at Convent Lane, Longford Town. *ALSO:* Hannah at Mason's of Ballymacshane. William at Elizabeth Mulvihill's (106) of Ballymahon Town. Annie at Kenny's of Castlebrock. Kate at O'Ferrall's of Corbeagh (?). Eleanor F. at Bond's of Newtownbond. Mary A. at Flood's of Killasona. Mary A. at Browne's of Aghaboy (Milltown D.E.D.). Mary at Murphy's of Lisryan. Margaret at Farrelly's of Corclaragh. Mary A. at Anne Cullen's of Edgeworthstown Town. Margaret and Harriet at Farrington's of Newtownforbes Village. Maggie and James at McCormack's of Lisgurry. Maggie J. and Katie M. at Peter Kilduff's of Barney. Rose at Phillips's of Dublin Street, Longford Town.

GREER: See Grier.

GREEVES: Edward at Ballymahon Street, Longford Town.

McGREEVY: Patrick at Ballymahon Town.

GREGG: Richard at Prucklish. Richard, Peter, John, James at Garrowhill. James at Cloonbalt. *ALSO:* James at Casserly's of Ballagh (Newtownforbes D.E.D.).

McGREGOR: Duncan at Lisbrack (Longford Rural D.E.D.).

GREGORY: Bridget, Thomas at Carrickedmond. Thomas at Carrickmoyragh.

GREHAN: Patrick at Main Street, Granard Town. Bridget at Lenaboy.

GRENNAN: Daniel at Cloonart South. Thomas at Clooniher. Thomas at Bleanavoher (?). *ALSO:* Bridget and Catherine at Farrington's of Newtownforbes Village.

GREY: See Gray.

GRIER, GREER: Francis H., Edward at Roos. Thomas at Cloghchurnel. John at Leitrim (Granard Rural D.E.D.). Elanor at Main Street, Granard Town. Mary at Coolamber. *ALSO:* Henry at Miller's of Edgeworthstown Town. Ellie R. at Rodgers' of Drumlish Village. James W. at Dowler's of Lisnamuck.

GRIFFIN: Margaret, Ellen at Breanrisk. *ALSO:* Vincent at Newman's of Cartronboy. John at Mary A. Callaghan's of Dublin Street, Longford Town.

GRIFFITH: Thomas at Ferskill. William at Keelogenasause. Elizabeth at Kiltycreevagh.

GRIMES: Anne at Cloonagh (Mullanalaghta D.E.D.). Francis, Edward, Michael of Edgeworthstown Town. Catherine at Kiltycreevagh. Bridget, Daniel at Drumlish. Michael at Cartronawar (Corboy D.E.D.). *ALSO:* Mary A. at Julia McGarry's of Aghamore Upper. Patrick at Francis Kiernan's of Ballyduffy. John et al. at Anne Cullen's of Edgeworthstown Town. Bridget at Calwell's of Cloonmacart.

GROARKE: Thomas at Lisaquill.

GROGAN: Lizzie at Hanly's of Tipper (Cashel West D.E.D.). Michael at Egan's of Healy's Terrace, Longford Town.

GROOVES: W.H. at Duncan McGregor's of Lisbrack (Longford Rural D.E.D.).

GUCKIAN, GUCKION: James at Granard. *ALSO:* Ellen and Margaret at Farrington's of Newtownforbes Village. Mathew at O'Connor's of Main Street, Longford Town.

GUFF: John at Edward G. Joyce's of Edgeworthstown Town.

GUIHEN: Michael at Mulvihill's of Toneen (Moydow D.E.D.).

GUINAN: Martin at Main Street, Longford Town. *ALSO:* Thomas J. at Quinn's of Banghill.

McGUINNESS, McGUINESS:(10): Nicholas at Ballinalee Village. Bridget at Derrycassan. Thomas at Cranalagh More. James at Moyne. John at Leggagh. Michael at Aghinaspick. Patrick at Lanesborough Village. Thomas, Winifred at Aghaboy (Aghaboy D.E.D.). Joseph at Killashee Street, Longford Town. *ALSO:* Thomas et al. at Martin's of Drumard. Margaret at Boles' of Aghaboy (Aghaboy D.E.D.). Francis at McGarry's of Main Street, Longford Town. Martin at Mathew Farrell's of Main Street, Longford Town. (See McGennis).

GUINTY: See Ginty.

McGUIRE: See Maguire.

McGUIRK: Bridget at Brocklagh. (See McQuirk).

McGUIRLE: Nicholas at Brady's of Rathbrackan.

GUNN: Patrick at Ballymahon Town.

GUNNEN: Thomas at Bleanavoher.

GUNNING: Patrick at Kilmore Upper. William at Cloonmore.

GUNNIS: John W. at Demesne.

GUNSHINAN, GUNSHENAN: Terence at Lettergullion. John at Drumlish Village. James at Killashee Village.

GURD: Ellen at Templeton Glebe.

GURHY: Martin at Carrickboy or Killashee Barracks.

GURLEY, GURLY: See Garly.

GURRAN, GURREN, GURRIN: Francis at Doory. John at Clooneen (Forgney D.E.D.). Mathew at Lisnanagh. Joseph at Keelogenasause. *ALSO:* Anne at Gahan's of Garryandrew.

GURRY: Bridget at Knappoge (Ballymahon D.E.D.). *ALSO:* Jane at Mulvihill's of Moygh (Ballymahon D.E.D.).

McGUSHEN, McGUSHIN: Catherine at Prucklish. *ALSO:* Mary J. at Green's of Convent Lane, Longford Town.

GUTHRIE, GUTHERIE: John at Aghnagore.

GUY: Thomas at John R. McCormack's of Kilcurry.

GWYNNE: Margaret at Banghill.

HAAN: Alphonsus at Abbeycartron.

HACKETT: Robert at Ballymahon Street, Longford Town. Joseph at Chapel Lane, Longford Town. Frances at Demesne. *ALSO:* Michael at Brady's of Edgeworthstown Town. Anne at James Murray's of Great Water Street, Longford Town.

HAFFORD: Edward at Corryena. Bridget at Bohermore. *ALSO:* James at Killian's of Clooncallow. Patrick at Derwin's of Forgney. Lizzie at John Skelly's of Ballymahon Town. Elizabeth at Farrington's of Newtownforbes Village.

HAGAN:(26): Mary at Lissanisky (Ballymahon D.E.D.) (?). Patrick at Carrowlinan. John at Drumbad. James at Fardrumman. Bridget at Cloontagh. James at Ballincurry. John, Mary A. at Cloonagh (Breanrisk D.E.D.). Edward, Patrick, Michael, Mary A., Michael at Cornacullew. Mary at Newtownforbes Village. Felix at Lismoy. William at Aghaboy (Aghaboy D.E.D.). James at Cloonee. James at Killyfad. Peter, James, Ellen, Catherine, Patrick at Rhine. Peter, John, Bernard at Knockloughlin. *ALSO:* Nannie at Hannigan's of Aghnashannagh, Ballinalee Village. Mary A. at O'Reilly's of Drummeel. Lizzie K. at Michael Reilly's of Aghamore Upper. Margaret at James Cox's of Leitrim (Breanrisk D.E.D.). Margaret at McManus's of Corrabaun (Breanrisk D.E.D.). Peter at Owen Hughes's of Rhine. John and Kate at Simon Brady's of Rhine. Patrick at Fullam's of Rhine. Bridget et al. at McNerney's of Rhine. (See Hogan).

HAGARTY, HAGERTY: See Hegarty.

HAIGADON: See Hargadon.

HAIGH: Percy at Main Street, Longford Town.

HALE: Catherine at Farrington's of Newtownforbes Village.

McHALE: Mary at O'Connell's of Demesne.

HALEY: See Healy.

HALFPENNY: See Halpenny.

HALL:(16): William at Carrigeen (Foxhall D.E.D.). John at Killeen (Foxhall D.E.D.). Samuel at Ards. John at Ballyknock. Charles at

Coolnahinch (Kilcommock D.E.D.). James at Kilmakinlan. George, Margaret at Mosstown (Rathcline Barony). Mary E., Charles, John, Annabella at Cornadrung. Joseph at Tully (Cloondara D.E.D.). James at Meelick. Anne, William at Moor. *ALSO:* Sarah J. at Kingstone's of Mosstown (Rathcline Barony). James at Pollock's of Main Street, Keenagh Village. Anna at Edgeworth's of Gorteen. Ellen at Cassidy's of Kilshruley. John at Browne's of Vicarsfield Glebe. Mary A. at Peter Gormley's of Polladooey. Edward at Geraghty's of Edgeworthstown Town. Elizabeth and Esther at Fetherston's of Ardagh Demesne.

HALLIDAY, HALLIDY: William at St. Mel's Road, Longford Town. *ALSO:* William A. at Alexander Morrison's of Edenmore.

HALLIGAN: John at Killeen (Foxhall D.E.D.). Bernard at Sleehaun. James, Nicholas at Drumlougher. *ALSO:* Mary at Murtagh's of Toneen (Moydow D.E.D.). James and Kate at Francis Devlin's (2) of Derrymore. Thomas at Kearney's of St. Michael's Road, Longford Town.

HALLISSY: Phonsey at McGuiness's of Derrycassan.

HALLORAN: Thomas at Water Lane, Granard Town. *ALSO:* William at Mary Dennigan's of Great Water Street, Longford Town.

HALPENNY, HALFPENNY: William at Drumlish Village.

HALPIN: Peter at Meeltanagh (Ardagh East D.E.D.). John, James, Thomas at Richmond Street, Longford Town.

HALSAUL: R. at Duncan McGregor's of Lisbrack (Longford Rural D.E.D.).

HALTON, HAULTON: Philip at Drumhalry. *ALSO:* Charles at Julia Mulligan's of Culray. Laurence et al. at Anne Drake's of Ballinulty Upper. Laurence and James at Anne Cluskey's of Kilmore. Lawrence at Canavan's of Edgeworthstown Town.

HAM: John at Tennalick. Richard at Toome (Ballymahon D.E.D.).

HAMILTON: Mary at Cranalagh Beg. Elizabeth at Aghakeeran. John at Gorteenorna. Mary J., George at Kilnacarrow (Aghaboy D.E.D.). William at Moor. William at Lisduff (Montgomery). James at Ballymakeegan. *ALSO:* Mary J. at Browne's of Vicarsfield Glebe. James at McCormack's of Derrycassan. Mary at Philip Brady's of Kiltycon. Kate at Farrington's of Newtownforbes Village. Margaret at Lefroy's of Carrickglass Demesne (Templemichael Civil Ph.). Carter at Little's of Main Street, Longford Town. W. at Hewetson's of Church Street, Longford Town.

HAMPSON, HAMSON: Rev. Mother Sarah at Aghafin. James at Cloonee.

HANAFEE: See Hanify.

HANAFIN: Patrick at Dublin Street, Longford Town.

HAND: John at Newpark. James at Clooneen (Creevy D.E.D.). Mary at Culleenmore. Michael at Derrycassan. Peter, Patrick at Larkfield. *ALSO:* Kate et al. at Anne Rattigan's of Newpark. Mary A. at Casserly's of Loughfarm. Patrick at Dolan's of Killashee Village (?). Kate at Murray's of Derrygeel. Marianne at McNerney's of New Street, Longford Town.

HANEY: See Heaney.

HANIFY, HANAFEE, HANNIFY: John at Drumlish. Peter, Patrick at Treel (Newtownforbes D.E.D.). *ALSO:* John at Catherine Reilly's of Cranalagh More.

HANIGAN: See Hannigan.

HANLEY, HANLY:(30): James at Ballybranigan. Mary at Tirlickeen. James at Corlea. John at Carrowdunican. Agnes at Cornadowagh. James at Corrool (Kenny). Thomas at Fortwilliam. Thomas at Leab. James at Loughfarm. John at Tipper (Cashel West D.E.D.). Anne, Thomas at Kings Island (Cashel West D.E.D.). William at Foygh. James at Derrynabuntale. Mary at Monadarragh. John at Cloondara. Margaret at Barnacor (Rathcline D.E.D.). John at Bleanavoher. Edward at Formoyle (Newcomen). Luke at Lehery. Peter, Catherine at Lisnacush. Robert at Cooleeshil or Richfort. John at Cloonturk. Matthew at Bog Lane, Longford Town. John at Chapel Lane, Longford Town. Patrick at Dublin Street, Longford Town. Patrick at Garvey's Yard, Longford Town. John at Richmond Street, Longford Town. Michael at Church Street, Longford Town. *ALSO:* James and Anne at Farrell's of Derrydarragh. Mary at Kelly's of Ledwithstown (Kilcommock Civil Ph.). Bridget at Mulvihill's of Ardoghil. James at Fox's of Derrynabuntale. Thomas at John Mulleady's of Edera. Thomas and Rose at Conlon's of Edenmore (?). Michael at Catherine Quinn's of Oghil. John at Michael Egan's of Aghnagore. Mary and Kate at Martin's of Barnacor (Rathcline D.E.D.). Patrick at Rhatigan's of Rathcline. Catherine et al. at Campbell's of Killashee Street, Longford Town. Thomas at Boyhan's of Killashee Street, Longford Town.

HANLON: Francis at Tipper (Ballymahon D.E.D.). John at Castlebrock. Daniel at Ballinrooey. Peter at Clooneen (Creevy D.E.D.). Peter at Culleenmore. Anne at Kilmore. Thomas at Derrynacross. Margaret at Killeter. *ALSO:* Patrick at Patrick McCabe's of Aghanoran. John at Edward Gormley's of Esker South. Anne at Gaffney's of Ballyminion. Enna at

Felix Larkin's of Main Street, Longford Town.

O'HANLON: Margaret at Charles Cullen's of Edgeworthstown Town.

HANLY: See Hanley.

HANNA: W. at Hewetson's of Church Street, Longford Town.

HANNAN: Patrick and Stephen J. at Edward Kenny's of Main Street, Longford Town.

HANNDS: Patrick at Dolan's of Killashee Village.

HANNIFY: See Hanify.

HANNIGAN, HANIGAN: Patrick at Aghnashannagh. James at Aghnashannagh, Ballinalee Village. James at Springtown. Thomas at Ball Alley Street Lower, Granard Town. John at Soran. Bridget at Main Street, Longford Town.

HANRAHAN: Kate at Phillips's of Forgney.

HANRATTY: Bernard at St. Mel's Road, Longford Town.

HANSTON, HAUSTON (?): Teresa at Thomas Cunningham's of Ballymahon Town. (See Houston).

O'HARA:(29): Michael at Keel (Forgney D.E.D.). Edward, Daniel, Mary at Ballymahon Town. Patrick at Kings Island (Cashel West D.E.D.). Michael at Lismagoneen. Charles at Lislea (Lislea D.E.D.). John at Lisraghtigan. Jane at Graffoge (Milltown D.E.D.). Mary, John at Muckerstaff. Edward at Aghamore (Coolamber D.E.D.). Francis at Aghafin. Matthew, Francis, Mary at Bawn (Breanrisk D.E.D.). James, Ellen at Cloonagh (Breanrisk D.E.D.). Catherine, Francis at Cloonmacart. Mathew at Kilnashee. Anne at Drumlish. Bridget at Creenagh. Michael at Aghaboy (Aghaboy D.E.D.). Thomas at Corneddan. Patrick at Knockloughlin. John at Feraghfad. Thomas at Coach Yard, Longford Town. Kate at St. Michael's Road, Longford Town. *ALSO:* Patrick at Flanagan's of Main Street, Granard Town. Maria at Connor McKenna's of Cloonmacart. Bridget at Kellagher's of Greagh. Lizzie at Taylor's of Corboy. Kate at McCormack's of Feraghfad. Mary at Shanley's of Main Street, Longford Town. Shea at Felix Larkin's of Main Street, Longford Town.

HARE: William at Killashee Village.

HARGADON: Peter at Firmount. Margaret at Culray. *ALSO:* Michael at

Beglin's of Culray.

HARKINS, HARKIN: John at Cranally.

HARMAN: John at Glenmore (Kilcommock D.E.D.). (See King-Harman).

HARNAN, HEARNAN: Patrick at Ellen McLoughlin's of Lisfarrell.

HARNEY: Edward et al. at Margaret Hall's of Mosstown (Rathcline Barony (?).

HAROLD: Sr. Minnie at Rev. Mother Hampson's of Aghafin.

HARPER: James at Abbeycartron.

HARRIGAN: Ellen and Katie at Geelan's of Glebe (Cloondara D.E.D.).

HARRINGTON: Patrick at Lissawarriff. Edward at Smithfield. Thomas at Taghshinny. James at Garryandrew. *ALSO:* Mary A. at Flood's of Ratharney. Ellen at Cahill's of Ardanragh. Bernard at Murtagh's of Kilcurry. Mary at Patrick Oroho's of Lisdreenagh.

HARRIS:(11): Richard at Kildordan. David at Currycahill. John at Aghaward. David at Drumderg. Phoebe, Alexander at Enybegs. Morgan at Rhine. Annie M. at Main Street, Longford Town. Thomas L. at St. Mel's Road, Longford Town. Elizabeth at Abbeycartron. Isabella at Bridge Street, Longford Town. *ALSO:* Bridget at John Quinn's (46) of Dublin Street, Longford Town. Ellen at Samuel Wilson's of Main Street, Longford Town. Maggie at McElnea's of Main Street, Longford Town.

HARRISON, HARRISSON: John at Portanure. Mary J. at Main Street, Keenagh Village.

HARTE, HART:(16): John at Aghnavealoge. Catherine at Aghnashannagh. Anne at Ederland. John at Ardagullion. Owen at Tonywardan. Elizabeth at Kiltycreevagh. John at Lettergullion. Bridget at Shanmullagh. Elizabeth at Leitrim (Breanrisk D.E.D.). Michael at Prucklish. Patrick at Cornacullew. Margaret at Garvary. James at Dooroc. John at Cloonageeher. Lawrence at Creenagh. Anne at Ballymahon Street, Longford Town. *ALSO:* John at Carrickboy or Ballina Barracks. Mary at Farrington's of Newtownforbes Village. Lizzie at Gillen's of Bohernacross. George at Larkin's of Killeter. Anne at Clarke's of Bog Lane, Longford Town. Ellen at Farrell's of Broderick's Yard, Longford Town. John at McNamee's of Richmond Street, Longford Town. Patrick at Jordan's of Abbeycartron.

HARTEN, HARTON, HARTIN: Michael, Patrick, Hugh at Glenoghil.

Peter at Kiltyclogh. Patrick at Smear. Patrick, Bernard at Kilmore. *ALSO:* Margaret at McCabe's of Clooneen (Creevy D.E.D.). Mary at Newman's of Cloghchurnel. Mary at Roarke's of Creevy. Thomas at Esther Kiernan's of Clogh (Dalystown D.E.D.).

HARTIGAN: Ellen at King-Harman's of Newcastle (?).

HARVEY: Mary at Cloonagh (Kilglass D.E.D.). Michael at Tirlickeen. John, Francis, Thomas at Bog Lane, Longford Town. *ALSO:* Edward et al. at Margaret Hall's of Mosstown (Rathcline Barony) (?). Margaret at Donnelly's of Bog Lane, Longford Town. Mary at Mary Quinn's of Little Water Street, Longford Town. Marion E. at McElnea's of Main Street, Longford Town.

HASLER: W. at Hewetson's of Church Street, Longford Town.

HASSETT: Patrick at Lissanisky (Ballymahon D.E.D.).

HASTINGS: William at Newtownforbes Village.

HATCHEL: William at John Pakenham's of Lechurragh.

HATCHETT: Francis at Ballymahon Town.

HATTON: Mary A. at Ballyclare (Killashee D.E.D.). Mary at Aghantrah. *ALSO:* James at James Geraghty's of Newtown (Moydow D.E.D.).

HAULTON: See Halton.

HAUSTON: See Hanston.

HAWKINS: Johanna at Forbes's of Castleforbes Demesne.

HAYDE: Margaret at Bridget Kiernan's of Aghnacliff. Mary at Peter Sheridan's of Corrinagh.

HAYDEN: Patrick at Creevagh Beg, Ballymahon Town. Anne at Ballymaurice (Granard Rural D.E.D.). James at Broderick's Yard, Longford Town. John at Chapel Lane, Longford Town. *ALSO:* John and Rose A. at James Donlon's of Ballymahon Town. Mary at James Farrell's of Glack (Longford Rural D.E.D.). Bridget et al. at Carney's of Chapel Lane, Longford Town. Thomas at Bernard McCormack's of Dublin Street, Longford Town. Jane M. at O'Gara's of St. Mel's Road, Longford Town.

HAYES: Elizabeth at Main Street, Keenagh Village. Jane at Glenoghil. *ALSO:* Thomas J. at Armstrong's of Creevagh Beg, Ballymahon Town.

Mary A. at Thompson's of Newtownforbes Village. Patrick at O'Connor's of Conroy's Court, Longford Town. C. at Hewetson's of Church Street, Longford Town (?).

HEADON: Kate at Murray's of Main Street, Longford Town.

HEALY:(20): Michael at Cloghan (Doory D.E.D.). John at Cornaguillagh. John at Cleraun. Margaret, Michael at Corrool (Brennan). Michael at Drumnee. Bridget at Creagh. Maria at Ballincurry. Peter, Bridget at Cloonagh (Breanrisk D.E.D.). Thomas at Cloonelly. Patrick at Drumlish. James, Patrick at Oghil. Patrick at Drumlish Village. Michael at Kiltyreher (Templemichael Civil Ph.). Catherine at Cartron Big. Patrick at Farnagh. James at Little Water Street, Longford Town. Anne at Market Square, Longford Town. *ALSO:* Thomas and Margaret at Anne Farrell's of Tirlickeen. John at Dimond's of Cormaglava. Ellen at Ward's of Cloonmee. James et al. at Hoey's of Laughil (Kilcommock D.E.D.). Mary at Farrelly's of Cloonelly. James at John Taaffe's (9) of Leggagh. Thomas at Patrick Killimade's of Feraghfad. Sr. Frances A. at Sr. Green's of Convent Lane, Longford Town.

HEANEY, HEANY:(28): Isabella at Toome (Ballymahon D.E.D.). Agnes at Cornadowagh (?). Joseph at Currycahill. Alexander at Kilshruley. Robert at Currygrane. Thomas at Cartronamarkey. Thomas at Tober. William, Mary at Aghnagarron. Patrick at Cloghchurnel. Michael at Dalystown. Thomas at Granardkill (Granard Rural D.E.D.). James at Robinstown. Margaret at Moxham Street, Granard Town. William at Prucklish. James, William, Thomas at Barragh More. Bridget at Enybegs. Bridget, John, Elizabeth at Oghil. Bernard at Dooroc. William at Cahanagh. Bernard at Clontumpher. Rose, Bridget at Aghadegnan (Longford Rural D.E.D.). Julia at Dublin Street, Longford Town. *ALSO:* Teresa at Patrick Reilly's of Ballymahon Town. Kate at Clarke's of Roos. Mary at Peter Kiernan's of Main Street, Granard Town. Rose A. at Corcoran's of Aghanoran. Thomas and Rose at Conlon's of Edenmore (?). Mary E. and Patrick at Bernard Murphy's of Enybegs. George at Wilson's of Ballydrum. Patrick at McKeon's of Knockahaw. Mary H. at Cody's of Church Street, Longford Town (?).

HEAPHY: Delia at Heslin's of Drumlish Village.

HEARNAN: See Harnan.

HEART: See Harte.

HEARY: Margaret at Abbeylara Village. *ALSO:* Bridget at Dawson's of Barrack Street, Granard Town.

HEATH: E. at Hewetson's of Church Street, Longford Town.

HEATHERTON: See Hetherton.

HEAVEY, HEAVY: Mary at Crossea North. Thomas at Ballyminion. Michael at Clooneeny. Thomas, Owen at St. Michael's Road, Longford Town. *ALSO:* Mary J. at Leavy's of Kilsallagh. Mary H. at Cody's of Church Street, Longford Town (?).

HEFFERNAN: Catherine at Abbeyshrule. *ALSO:* John at O'Brien's of Clonca.

HEGARTY, HAGARTY, HAGERTY: Robert at Newtown (Foxhall D.E.D.). John at Clooncaulfield. Bridget at Farnagh. Lizzie, Mary at Ballymahon Street, Longford Town. James at Dublin Street, Longford Town. *ALSO:* Anne at O'Hara's of King's Island (Cashel West D.E.D.). Bridget at More O'Ferrall's of Lissard. Anne at Michael McCann's of Ballymahon Street, Longford Town. William at Stephenson's of Dublin Street, Longford Town.

HENEHAN, HENIHAN: Michael at Ballyrevagh *ALSO:* Ellen at King-Harman's of Newcastle (?). Patrick at Peter Farrell's of Laughil (Ardagh West D.E.D.).

HENNESSY, HENNESSEY: Catherine at Drummeel. *ALSO:* H. at Hewetson's of Church Street, Longford Town.

HENRY: Catherine at Bridge Street, Longford Town. *ALSO:* Patrick at Smear Barracks, Cleenrah.

HEPENSTAL: See Dopping-Hepenstal.

HERAN: Edward J. and Katie E. at Cronogue's of Gaigue.

HERMON: H. at Hewetson's of Church Street, Longford Town.

HERRON: Ralph at Castlerea.

HERSON: See Hurson.

HESKETT: Ida at Hennessy's of Drummeel.

HESLIN:(16): Patrick at Garrycam. Thomas at Laughil (Adair). John at Molly. John at Lisnanagh. Francis at Aghakeeran. Michael at Ball Alley Street Lower, Granard Town. Margaret at Ballyduffy. John at Kiltycreevagh. John at Lettergeeragh. John at Drumlish Village. John at

Cornafunshin. James, Thomas at Derrynacross. John, Peter at Aghaboy (Aghaboy D.E.D.). Patrick at Clontumpher. *ALSO:* Peter at Flanagan's of Main Street, Granard Town. Bridget at Tyrrell's of Carrowmanagh. Mary at Allen's of Cartron Little.

HESLIP, HESLOP: See Hyslop.

HESTER: Mary at McHugh's of Healy's Terrace, Longford Town.

HETHERTON, HEATHERTON: John, Francis at Aghacordrinan. Patrick at Aghagreagh. Patrick at Derreenavoggy. Arthur at Corglass. Anne, Michael at Cornacullew. *ALSO:* William at Noble's of Tonymore North. Mary at Briody's of Corrinagh. Anne at Dolan's of Cloonelly.

HEVAHAN, HEVEHAN: Edward at Derrygowna. Thomas, Patrick at Cloonmee.

McHEW: See McHugh.

HEWETSON: A.W. at Church Street, Longford Town.

HEWINS: G. at Hewetson's of Church Street, Longford Town.

HEWITT, HEWETT: Elizabeth, James at Ballyclamay. Lorenzo at Ballymulvey. *ALSO:* William at Duff's of Mornin. Benjamin N. at Fee's of Ballybranigan. James at Goldrick's of Agharanagh (Ballymahon D.E.D.). (See Huet).

HICKEY: Laurence at Lyneen. *ALSO:* Patrick at Flynn's of Newtownforbes Village.

HIGGINS, HIGGENS:(38): Hugh at Cartron (Forgney D.E.D.). Thomas at Clooncullen. Patrick at Cartronboy. John at Carrowrory. Martin at Claras. Archibald at Cartrons (Kilcommock D.E.D.). John at Abbeyderg. Mary at Island. Kate at Mosstown (Rathcline Barony). Thomas at Longford Road, Keenagh Village. James at Derrycolumb. Bouchier at Tober. Luke, James at Killeen (Bunlahy D.E.D.). Patrick at Ballymore. Michael at Carragh (Granard Urban D.E.D.). Patrick at Ball Alley Street Lower, Granard Town. Peter at Main Street, Granard Town. John at Moxham Street, Granard Town. Bernard at Willsbrook. John at Annaghdaniel. William, Hugh at Rathmore (Ballinamuck East D.E.D.). Patrick at Breanrisk. Mary, Thomas at Cloonellan. Michael at Cloonmacart. Patrick, Anne at Aghamore Lower. Hugh at Derawley. Margaret at Newtownforbes Village. Patrick at Cloonageeher. Michael at Knappoge (Cloondara D.E.D.). John at Slieve. Peter at Carnan. Ellen at Creeve. Robert J. at Keon's Terrace, Longford Town. James at St. Michael's Road, Longford Town. *ALSO:* Elizabeth at

Slator's of Cartron (Forgney D.E.D.). William at Coghlan's of Cloonbreany. George H. at Moorhead's of Leitrim (Ballinalee D.E.D.). Bridget at Little's of Drumnacross. Sarah at Wilson's of Lisnanagh. Kate at Wallace's of Muckerstaff. Mary at Charles McNerney's of Fostragh. Patrick at James Donohoe's of Aghamore Lower. Mary and Thomas at Mulligan's of Annagh (Drumgort D.E.D.). Mary at Peter Quinn's (6) of Cartrongolan. Charles et al. at Foran's of Great Water Street, Longford Town. Joseph at Dempsey's of Great Water Street, Longford Town. Lizzie at Pearse's of Abbeycartron.

HILL: John, John at Listobit. *ALSO:* Patrick at Hanley's of Foygh. Mary at James Mulfall's of Cartrongarrow. A.C. at Hewetson's of Church Street, Longford Town.

HILLIARD: Bernard at Cloonahard.

HINCH: William at Kinard. *ALSO:* Mary at Dales' of Ballygilchrist.

HINCKS: Bridget at More O'Ferrall's of Lissard.

HINDS: See Hynes.

HISTON: Lawrence at Ballywillin.

HITCHER: J. at Hewetson's of Church Street, Longford Town.

HIWITT: See Hewitt.

HOARE: Sr. Jane F. at Grassyard. Most Rev. Dr. Joseph at Deanscurragh. *ALSO:* Maggie at Shanley's of Clooneen (Kennedy). Lizzie at Leahy's of Ballyclare (Killashee D.E.D.).

HOBSON: Richard at Great Water Street, Longford Town.

HOCIE: John at Laughil (Edgeworth).

HODGES: H.W. at Hewetson's of Church Street, Longford Town.

HODGKINSON: William at Lloyd's of Main Street, Longford Town.

HODGSON: R.C. at Hewetson's of Church Street, Longford Town.

HOEY: Bryan at Keel (Kilglass D.E.D.). Thomas at Laughil (Kilcommock D.E.D.). Patrick at Aghnashannagh. Patrick at Clooneen (Cox). Mary A. at Mullolagher. Bernard at Trillickatemple. Thomas at Great Water Street, Longford Town. *ALSO:* Maria at Burbage's of Tully (Cloondara D.E.D.).

John at Doyle's of Newtown (Moydow D.E.D.).

HOGAN: Mary at Lissanisky (Ballymahon D.E.D.). Ellen at Derrylough. Thomas, Edward at Foygh. John at Cartronreagh. Michael at Glenmore (Ballinamuck East D.E.D.). Mary at Lanesborough Village. *ALSO:* Sr. Mary at Sr. Hoare's of Grassyard. Sr. Mary at Sr. Green's of Convent Lane, Longford Town. Kate A. at White's of Great Water Street, Longford Town. Mary J. et al. at Reilly's of New Street, Longford Town. (See Hagan).

HOGG: Lillie at Campbell's of Ballydrum.

HOLDEN: Charles at Carrickglass Demesne (Templemichael Civil Ph.).

HOLLIDGE: B. at Hewetson's of Church Street, Longford Town.

HOLMES: Catherine at Main Street, Keenagh Village. Arthur, Elizabeth at Kilmore Lower. *ALSO:* Robert at Moffett's of Cloonfiugh. Lizzie at Boyers' (4) of Main Street, Longford Town.

HOOLOHAN: See Houlihan.

HOPE: Mary and Lizzie at Rodaughan's of Aghareagh (Coolamber D.E.D.).

HOPKINS, HOPKIN:(26): Thomas at Cloghan (Forgney D.E.D.). John at Caltragh More. Patrick at Derrygowna. Michael at Newpark. Peter at Ballagh (Cashel West D.E.D.). Michael at Ballyrevagh. James, John at Cornadowagh. John at Corrool (Brennan). Peter, Patrick, Catherine, Peter at Drumnee. Michael at Pollagh. John at Portanure. Michael at Cullentragh (Rathcline Civil Ph.). Patrick at Island. Michael at Cleggill. James at Killeeny. Elizabeth at Newtown (Killashee D.E.D.). Thomas at Cloonbrock. James, Patrick, John at Cloonfore. Mary at Cartronawar (Corboy D.E.D.). Thomas at Feraghfad. *ALSO:* John at Curran's of Cloonmee. Patrick at Ward's of Cloonmee. Margaret at John Mulvihill's of Cornadowagh. Bridget at Taaffe's of Island. Mary at Spearman's of Annaghmore. Annie at Bond's of Ballygarve.

HORAN: James at Ball Alley Street Lower, Granard Town. *ALSO:* Edith at More O'Ferrall's of Lissard. Bridget at Flanagan's of Main Street, Granard Town.

HORNER: A. at Hewetson's of Church Street, Longford Town.

HORSE: Elizabeth at Daroge. *ALSO:* Mary A. and Bridget at Geraghty's of Daroge.

HOSEY: See Hussey.

HOTHERSALL: E. at Hewetson's of Church Street, Longford Town.

HOULIHAN, HOOLOHAN: Sr. Margaret at Sr. Green's of Convent Lane, Longford Town. Honor at Whelan's of Harbour Row, Longford Town.

HOURICAN:(23): Owen, James, James at Aghnacliff. Bernard at Carrickadorrish. Philip at Sonnagh. Philip, James, Mary, Thomas at Dunbeggan (Columbkille D.E.D.). Michael, James at Fihoragh. Francis, Patrick, Philip at Corrinagh. Michael, Patrick, Charles, James at Rathmore (Ballinamuck East D.E.D.). Philip, William, Thomas, William at Fostragh. James at Glenmore (Ballinamuck East D.E.D.). *ALSO:* Philip and Mary J. at James Reilly's of Gelshagh. John at Brady's of Cranalagh More. Anne et al. at Patrick Murtagh's of Cuingareen. James at Briody's of Moyne. Patrick and William at Kiernan's of Drumlish Village. Mary and Alicia at Farrington's of Newtownforbes Village.

HOUSTON: James at Drumderg. (See Hanston).

HOWARD: Thomas at Agharanagh (Ballymahon D.E.D.). Edward at Creenagh. John at Killashee Village. William at Moyra and Fortmill. Michael at Convent Lane, Longford Town. William at Earl Street, Longford Town. James at Great Water Street, Longford Town. *ALSO:* Mary at Browne's of Glebe (Cashel West D.E.D.). Bridget et al. at William Gilchriest's of Great Water Street, Longford Town.

HOWDEN: Samuel at Ballynascraw. Robert at Ederland. Charlotte at Ballinalee Village. John at Main Street, Longford Town.

HOWLES: Mary A. at Ellen Murray's of Great Water Street, Longford Town.

HOWLEY: Patrick at Cox's of Corragarrow (Killashee D.E.D.). Srs. Mary and Anne at Sr. Green's of Convent Lane, Longford Town.

HOWTE: Joseph at Dillon's of Main Street, Longford Town.

HOYE, HOYES: Bryan at Keel (Kilglass D.E.D.) (?). *ALSO:* C. at Hewetson's of Church Street, Longford Town.

HUBBERT: Gertrude at Seymour's of Aghareagh (Cloondara D.E.D.).

HUDSON: Patrick at Cleraun. John at Church Street, Longford Town.

HUET: Herbert S. at Pollard's of Templeton Glebe. (See Hewitt).

McHUGH:(15): Anne, John at Tennalick. Thomas at Derryoghil. John at Corryena. Michael at Springtown. Margaret at Carrickmoyragh. Francis, Michael at Lettergonnell. John at Ballagh (Newtownforbes D.E.D.). James at Sragarrow. James at Soran. Bridget at Stonepark (Longford Rural D.E.D.). Mary at Ballymahon Street, Longford Town. Mary at Healy's Terrace, Longford Town. Mary A. at St. Michael's Road, Longford Town. *ALSO:* Kate at Thomas T. Soden's of Ballymahon Town. John at Catherine Jordan's of Lislom. John and James at Laurence Mulligan's of Ballywillin. John at McCabe's of Edgeworthstown Town. Sarah at James Farrell's of Ballymahon Street, Longford Town. Charles at Maxwell's of Garvey's Yard, Longford Town.

HUGHES:(69): Thomas at Abbeyshrule. Bridget, John at Drumanure. Timothy at Lissawarriff. Christopher at Clooncullen. Thomas at Carrigeen (Foxhall D.E.D.). Richard at Sleehaun (Sankey). Bridget at Screeboge. Patrick at Ballinalee Village. Michael, Michael at Toome (Mullanalaghta D.E.D.). John at Edgeworthstown Town. Peter at Cloncowley. Henry at Fardrumman. Anne, Patrick at Kiltcreevagh. Patrick at Shanmullagh. Mary at Currygranny. Michael at Leitrim (Breanrisk D.E.D.). Mary at Prucklish. Michael at Aghnamaddoo. Patrick, Bridget at Cloonmacart. Patrick at Kilnashee. Patrick at Carrowbeg (Drumlish D.E.D.). Lawrence, Michael at Derawley. Michael, Patrick at Greagh. John at Oghil. Thomas at Drumlish Village. Bernard at Derrynacross. Bridget at Ballagh (Achmuty). James, Sarah at Cahanagh. Patrick at Gorteenorna. Bernard, Denis at Aghaboy (Aghaboy D.E.D.). Catherine at Clontumpher. William, Thomas, Patrick, James, John at Esker South. John, James, Patrick, James at Soran. Ellen, Peter at Back of the Hill. Mary at Drumbaun. Peter at Laughil (Ardagh West D.E.D.). Bridget at Drumhaughly. Patrick at Kiltyreher (Killoe Civil Ph.). Peter at Mucknagh. Anne, Owen, James, John at Rhine. Elizabeth at Knockloughlin. Charles at Corboy. Patrick at Ardnacassagh. Maria, Jane at Dublin Street, Longford Town. Patrick at Earl Street, Longford Town. Joseph at Great Water Street, Longford Town. Henry at Little Water Street, Longford Town. James at Sandy Row, Longford Town. Edward at Church Street, Longford Town. *ALSO:* Elizabeth et al. at Catherine McCormack's of Ballymahon Town. Mary at Dennehy's of Glenmore (Kilcommock D.E.D.). Thomas at Thomas Fenlon's of Edgeworthstown Town. William at Michael Reilly's of Edgeworthstown Town. James at Patrick Dolan's (1) of Kiltycreevagh. Anne at McNamee's of Cloonmacart. Kate at Sesnan's of Newtownforbes Village. James at McCann's of Newtownforbes Village. Kate at John Prunty's of Corneddan. Patrick et al. at Patrick McManus's of Corneddan. Kate at Peter Farrell's of Coolcaw. Margaret at Thompson's of Rhine. Mary at Fannin's of Mullaghavorneen. Lizzie and Henry at John Quinn's (28) of Dublin Street, Longford Town. Mary J. at Whitney's of Healy's Terrace, Longford Town. Edward at Mathew Farrell's of Main

Street, Longford Town. F. at Hewetson's of Church Street, Longford Town.

HULBERT (?): Gertrude at Seymour's of Aghareagh (Cloondara D.E.D.).

HUME: Margaret at Peyton's of St. Anne's Glebe.

HUMPHREYS, HUMPHRYS: Mary A. and Abigail at Amelia McCoy's of Smear. Isabella at Moorcroft's of Kiltyreher (Templemichael Civil Ph.). A. at Hewetson's of Church Street, Longford Town.

HUNT: Patrick at Cloonfide. John at Clontymullan. Bernard at Newport. Andrew at Aghnashannagh. Michael at Drumlish Village. Patrick at Aghaloughan. *ALSO:* Thomas at Ellis's of Edgeworthstown Town. William at O'Connell's of Dublin Street, Longford Town.

HUNTER: William at Abbeyshrule. Charles M. at Lismore.

HURSON, HERSON: James, Peter at Corrinagh. John at Lettergullion. Julia at Ballincurry. Philip at Leggagh. Thomas at Monaduff. Maria at Derrynacross. Michael at Gaigue. *ALSO:* Michael et al. at Prunty's of Creenagh.

HUSSEY, HOSEY:(12): James at Kilcommock Glebe. Mary at Derryneel. John at Laughil (Edgeworth) (?). Bernard at Druminacrehir. Edward at Barrack Street, Granard Town. Edward at Edgeworthstown Town. John at Cloondara. Winifred, Michael at Glebe (Cloondara D.E.D.). Robert at Rabbitpark. Anne at Chapel Lane, Longford Town. James at Hyde's Yard, Longford Town. *ALSO:* Bridget at Dalton's of Lisnanagh. John at Hurson's of Ballincurry. Bridget at Henry McLoughlin's of Cloondara.

HUTCHINSON: Joseph at Firmount.

HYLAND: Thomas at Killeenboy. Ellen at Ballymulvey. Julia at Barrack Street, Granard Town. Michael at Agharanagh (Rathcline D.E.D.). Patrick at Bleanavoher. William at Fee's Terrace, Longford Town. *ALSO:* James at Groarke's of Lisaquill. Laurence at Peter Mulvey's of Aghakilmore. Thomas at Thomas Lynch's of Clooneen (Creevy D.E.D.).

HYNES, HINDS, HYNDES: John, Mary at Ballyrevagh. John at Currygrane. John at Cartron (Granard Urban D.E.D.). Michael at Ball Alley Street Upper, Granard Town. William at The Hill, Granard Town. Mary at Water Lane, Granard Town. Henry P. at Cooldoney. Thomas, John at Cloonard (Cloondara D.E.D.). John at Barnacor (Rathcline D.E.D.). John at Richmond Street, Longford Town. *ALSO:* Mary at Loughran's of Lissakit. Michael J. at McCabe's of Sonnagh. Patrick at James Farrell's (17) of Richmond Street, Longford Town.

HYSLOP: Henry at Larkfield.

IGOE:(17): Bridget, John at Ballymahon Town. Thomas at Newtownforbes Village. Michael, Ellen at Ahanagh. William at Brianstown. Michael at Kilmore Lower. Bridget at Clontumpher. John, Maria, Daniel, John, John, Patrick, Rose at Killeter. Peter, Roderick at Ballymahon Street, Longford Town. *ALSO:* Jane at Newman's at Nappagh.

IHATFORD: Robert at Free's of Cooleeny.

McILVEEN, McILVENE: J. at Hewetson's of Church Street, Longford Town.

McILWRATH: George A. at Thomas Burns' of Screeboge.

McINTEE: See McEntee.

McINTYRE, McENTIRE: James at Ballinulty Upper. Jane at Farraghroe. William at Cooleeny. *ALSO:* John at Brady's of Edgeworthstown Town. James and Kate at James McNamee's of Corglass.

IRELAND: William at Lislea (Doory D.E.D.). Elizabeth at Ballybranigan. James at Foygh. Thomas at Fihoges. *ALSO:* Lizzie at Mulligan's of Aghnaskea. Mary at James Farrell's of Glack (Longford Rural D.E.D.).

IRWIN: Robert at Colehill. Dominick at Main Street, Granard Town. John at Edgeworthstown Town. Bernard, James at Lettergullion. W.H. at Main Street, Longford Town. *ALSO:* Lizzie at Ronaldson's of Ledwithstown (Kilcommock Civil Ph.). Annie at Stacom's of Dublin Street, Longford Town. James at Little's of Main Street, Longford Town.

ISDELL: David at Main Street, Keenagh Village. Francis at Leitrim (Granard Rural D.E.D.).

McIVOR: J. at Hewetson's of Church Street, Longford Town.

JACKSON: Joseph, John at Culloge. Thomas, Michael at Cornacullew. Anne at Earl Street, Longford Town. *ALSO:* Rachel at Edgeworth's of Gorteen. Susan at Simon Caldwell's of Glenoghil. Patrick at Briody's of Corrinagh. Christina at Farrell's of Bunanass. Henry and Bridget at Airlie's of Main Street, Longford Town.

JACOBS: A. at Hewetson's of Church Street, Longford Town.

JAMES: Robert at Newtownforbes Village.

JARRETT, JARRATT: George at Lismoy.

JENKINS: Samuel E. at Barrack Street, Granard Town.

JENNINGS: Thomas at Cloonee. Marie at Killeter. *ALSO:* Sarah at Flanagan's of Dublin Street, Longford Town. Walter H. at Hewetson's of Church Street, Longford Town.

JEONES: See Jones.

JESSOP: Louisa at Doory.

JEWELL: P. at Hewetson's of Church Street, Longford Town.

JOBE: John at Rathmore (Ballinamuck East D.E.D.).

JOHNS: Philip at Carrickboy.

JOHNSTON, JOHNSON: James at Forgney. Patrick at Dalystown. Andrew at Ball Alley Street Upper, Granard Town. John at Barrack Street, Granard Town. Andrew at Bohermore. Rev. Henry J. at Moor. Isabella at Corboy. James J. at Main Street, Longford Town. *ALSO:* Ellen at Anne McKeown's of Ballymahon Town. Sr. Habies at Rev. Mother Whelan's of Ballymahon Town. John at Reilly's of New Road, Granard Town. John at Mulligan's of Edgeworthstown Town. Lizzie et al. at James Drew's of Ballagh (Newtownforbes D.E.D.). James at Burns' of Newtownforbes Village. William at Leavy's of Kilnasavoge. Ernest G. at Boyers' (2) of Main Street, Longford Town.

JONES:(24): David at Drumanure. John at Newcastle. John P. at Creagh. Mary A., David, David, John at Carrickduff. Catherine at Birrinagh. Patrick at Drumhalry. David at Dring. John, William at Larkfield. Michael at Ballindagny and Cullyvore. John at Lackan. Robert at Glenmore (Ballinamuck East D.E.D.). Michael at Bohernameeltoge. John at Enybegs. Robert at Cloonageeher. James at Cloonrallagh. William at Rappareehill. Thomas at Ballinroddy. James at Drumure. Maria at Dublin Street, Longford Town. Alexander at Earl Street, Longford Town. *ALSO:* Mary at Garrahan's of Ballyknock. John and Mary at John Lynch's of Dring. Anne at Cummins's of Cornacullew. John at Peter Bannon's of Barney. Patrick at Thomas Boyce's of Lissaghanedan. Michael at Murphy's of Ballynagoshen. James at O'Reilly's of Ballynagoshen. Margaret at Cameron's of Main Street, Longford Town. P.P. at Hewetson's of Church Street, Longford Town.

JORDAN:(20): Mary, John at Drumanure. Mary at Lisnacreevy. Thomas at Tennalough. James, Catherine at Lislom. Mary at Foygh. William at

Ardoghil. Patrick at Culleenmore. Michael at Tuite's Lane, Granard Town. Rose, Catherine, Bernard, Michael at Cloncowley. Patrick at Lettergullion. Patrick at Drumlish Village. Mary at Gaigue. Bernard at Aghadegnan (Longford Rural D.E.D.). Stephen at St. Mel's Road, Longford Town. William at Abbeycartron. *ALSO:* Margaret at Jessop's of Doory. Kate at Mason's of Carn. Teresa and Mary at McAtee's of Barry (Ballymahon D.E.D.). William at Dimond's of Derrynabuntale. James at McGovern's of Ballinulty Lower. Bridget at Keogh's of Corbaun or Leitrim. Daniel at Francis Sheridan's of Breanriskcullew. James at Canning's of Cloncowley. Lucy (?) at Gilhooly's of Keon's Terrace, Longford Town.

JOYCE: Patrick F. at Smithfield. Peter J., Edward G. at Edgeworthstown Town. Martin at Lissagernal. Peter J. (Absent from No. 54), James at Main Street, Longford Town. *ALSO:* James at Lefroy's of Carrickglass Demesne (Templemichael Civil Ph.).

JOYNT: Charles at New Street, Longford Town.

JUDGE: William at Currygrane. Anne at Ballinrooey. John at Cloonmore. Patrick at Rhine. *ALSO:* Bridget at McCreanor's of Lissavaddy. John at McKenzie's of Earl Street, Longford Town.

KANE, KEANE:(53): Thomas at Newtown (Foxhall D.E.D.). Charles at Ballymahon Town. James at Derryart. Elizabeth at Listraghee. Simon at Prucklishtown. Denis, Catherine at Drummeel. Bernard at Castlebaun. Denis at Glannagh. Patrick at Aghakeeran. Catherine at Ranaghanbaun. John at Abbeylara Village. William at Rathcor. Henry at Ballyboy. Thomas at Cloonaghmore. Margaret at Barrack Street, Granard Town. Mary, Edward at New Road, Granard Town. John at Fihoragh. Patrick at Shantum. Rev. Charles E. at Edgeworthstown Town. Bernard at Fostragh. Francis, Michael at Esker North. Catherine, Michael at Bawn (Breanrisk D.E.D.). Nicholas at Barragh Beg. James at Monaduff. Thomas, John, James, Patrick at Drumlish Village. Michael at Ballagh (Newtownforbes D.E.D.). Thomas at Briskil. James at Kilmacannon. John at Ahanagh. Bridget, Patrick at Ballynakill. Margaret at Curry (Moydow D.E.D.). Daniel at Barneygole. John at Crossea South. Peter at Lissanisky (Ardagh East D.E.D.). Thomas at Aghintemple. Mary at Moor. Bridget at Kiltyreher (Killoe Civil Ph.). Andrew at Ballynagoshen. Mary, Margaret at Corboy. William at Whiterock. Margaret at Dublin Street, Longford Town. Mary at Great Water Street, Longford Town. Margaret at St. Mel's Road, Longford Town. *ALSO:* Michael at Keenan's of Newtown (Foxhall D.E.D.). William at Bennett's of Drumderg. Maggie at McNamara's of Glannagh. Francis at Kiernan's of Ballyboy. Julia at Kearney's of Rincoolagh. Mary A. at John L. Brady's of Main Street, Granard Town (?). Patrick at Mullen's of Lissanure. Kate and Mary A. at Reilly's of Barragh More. Mary A. and Patrick at Confrey's of Enybegs (?). Michael at Thomas Casey's of

Killeeny. John at Cahill's of Cornapark. Mary at Daniel Keegan's of Drumroe. Margaret at Reardon's of Drumroe. Bridget at Belton's of Ballymahon Street, Longford Town. Denis at O'Connor's of Conroy's Court, Longford Town. Margaret at O'Beirne's of Dublin Street, Longford Town. William at Thomas McCormack's of Great Water Street, Longford Town. James at Molloy's of Main Street, Longford Town.

KAVANAGH: Arthur at Cloonagh (Kilglass D.E.D.). Patrick at Aghakine. Mary at Ball Alley Street Lower, Granard Town. Catherine at Dunbeggan (Columbkille D.E.D.). James at Esker South. *ALSO:* Margaret at Mahady's of Tober. Charles and Ellie at Hyland's of Barrack Street, Granard Town. Michael at Peter Kiernan's of Main Street, Granard Town. Patrick at O'Ferrall's of Camlisk More. Christina at Farrington's of Newtownforbes Village. Joseph at Farrell's of Ballynagoshen. (See Cavanagh).

KEALEY, KEALY: Anne at Druming. *ALSO:* Mary at Hunt's of Cloonfide. Patrick J. at James Lee's (42) of Soran. (See Keely).

KEANE: See Kane.

KEARNEY:(24): Michael at Clooncullen. James at Keel (Forgney D.E.D.). Mary at Daroge. Thomas at Creevaghmore (Forgney Civil Ph.). Michael at Creevagh Beg. Eugene at Cornadowagh. Patrick at Culnagore. John, Patrick at Fortwilliam. John, Betty at Ledwithstown (Kilcommock D.E.D.). Rose at Doonacurry (Shrule Civil Ph.). Thomas at Clooneen (Creevy D.E.D.). Peter at Ballyboy. Michael at Rincoolagh. Owen at Tonywardan. John at Kilsallagh. Rose, James at Lisnagrish. Patrick, Mathew at Formoyle (Farrell). Richard F. at Crossea North. James at Freehalman. William at St. Michael's Road, Longford Town. *ALSO:* Patrick and Thomas at Nally's of Clooncullen. Thomas at Hinch's of Kinard. Thomas at Ballasty's of Kilsallagh. Elizabeth at Susan Rourke's of Edgeworthstown Town. James at James Keane's of Drumlish Village. William at Farrell's of Lisduff (Longford Rural D.E.D.) (?). (See Carney).

KEARY, CEARY: Patrick, Mary at Clonwhelan. Elizabeth at Lisnagrish. John at Moatavally. *ALSO:* Michael at Thomas Reilly's of Creevy. Michael at Thomas Masterson's of Edgeworthstown Town. Maria at Donlon's of Meeltanagh (Moydow D.E.D.). (See Carey).

KEATING, KEATINGE, KEATINGS: Joseph at Drinan. Catherine at Cartroncar. John at Breanrisk. Bernard at Ballagh (Achmuty). George, Samuel at Abbeycartron. *ALSO:* Michael at Monahan's of Killeendowd. Mary E. at Farrington's of Newtownforbes Village.

KEAVENY: Thomas at Derrymore. *ALSO:* James at Donohoe's of Grillagh (Ardagh West D.E.D.).

KEEFFE, KEEFE: Catherine at Cloonfinfy. Mary at Chapel Lane, Longford Town. *ALSO:* James at Beatty's of Main Street, Granard Town. Greta at Robert Shaw's of Cloonageeher.

O'KEEFFE: Patrick and Lily at Cahill's of Ardanragh. Rose at Green's of Convent Lane, Longford Town. William at O'Donnell's of Dublin Street, Longford Town. Mary at McNerney's of New Street, Longford Town.

KEEGAN: John at Loughan. Thomas at Forgney. Mary at Kildordan. John at Druming. Michael at Ballynamanagh. Michael at Deerpark (Kilglass D.E.D.). Patrick at Taghshinny. Thomas at Tennalick. John, Honor at Tirlickeen. Christopher at Creevagh Beg, Ballymahon Town. Thomas, Thomas at Creevagh Beg. Mary at Ballyreaghan. Thomas at Ballinalee Village. Mary at Aghagreagh. Patrick at Drumderg. Patrick at Clooneen (Creevy D.E.D.). Mary, Michael at Ball Alley Street Upper, Granard Town. Catherine at Main Street, Granard Town. Patrick at Cleenrah. James at Kilmore. Patrick at Commons South. John at Barney. John, Daniel at Drumroe. Bridget at Keeloges. Patrick at Treel (Corboy D.E.D.). Winifred at Corboy. Dominick at Dublin Street, Longford Town. *ALSO:* Brigid at Patrick Kelly's of Cornamucklagh. Catherine at Gerety's of Killinbore. Kate at Michael Carolan's of Ballymahon Town. Nannie at Kate Whelan's of Ballymahon Town. Patrick et al. at Dermody's of Tonywardan. Peter et al. at Andrew Murphy's of Enybegs. Kate at Michael Kelly's of Gaigue. Patrick at Anne Ryan's of Bohermore. James P. at Farrell's of Drumroe.

KEELTY: See Kielty.

KEELY: Patrick at Daroge (?). *ALSO:* Mary at Mulligan's of Glenmore (Ballinamuck East D.E.D.) (?). (See Kealy).

KEENA:(12): James, Michael at Ardanragh. Bridget at Treel (Foxhall D.E.D.). Thomas at Tennalick. Elizabeth at Glenoghil. Mary, Patrick at Drummeel. Thomas at Carrowlinan. Patrick at Edgeworthstown Town. Hugh at Aghaboy (Aghaboy D.E.D.). Thomas at Cartronawar (Corboy D.E.D.). Catherine at Bog Lane, Longford Town. *ALSO:* Thomas at Donnelly's of Smithfield. James and Mary at Hayden's of Creevagh Beg, Ballymahon Town. Elizabeth at Dunleavy's of Clontumpher. Ellen at Yorke's of Dublin Street, Longford Town.

KEENAN:(42): John at Rathsallagh. Thomas at Lislea (Doory D.E.D.). Patrick at Cloonscott. James at Mornin. Michael at Newtown (Foxhall D.E.D.). Patrick at Sleehaun. Michael at Druming. John, Mary at Garrycam. William at Ballygibbagh. Nicholas, J.P. at Carrickboy. Mary at Caltragh More. John at Ballagh (Cashel West D.E.D.). Ellen at Ballyrevagh. Michael at Aghnashannagh. Patrick at Drumnahara. James at Aghnacliff. Bryan, Bryan at Tawnagh. Peter, Thomas at Leitrim (Breanrisk D.E.D.). Mary at

Prucklish. Francis at Cloonagh (Breanrisk D.E.D.). James at Kilnashee. Peter at Gorteenorna. Thomas at Lamagh. Michael at Cornollen (?). Michael, Julia at Soran. Mary at Carnan. Peter at Lisduff (Montgomery). Peter at Bawn (Ardagh West D.E.D.). John at Kiltyreher (Killoe Civil Ph.). Peter at Rhine. Thomas at Aghanageeragh. John at Lissaghanedan. Timothy at Cartron Big. Thomas at Toorfin. Joseph at Great Water Street, Longford Town. Peter, Michael at Richmond Street, Longford Town. *ALSO:* Thomas at Robinson's of Gorteenrevagh, Ballinalee Village. Mary A. at Smyth's of Lackan. Margaret at Doyle's of Soran. Anne at Thomas Reynolds's of Soran. Anne at Richard Kennedy's of Crossea South. Anne at Dodd's of Healy's Terrace, Longford Town. Catherine at McCormack's of Little Water Street, Longford Town. Bridget at Gaynor's of Little Water St., Longford Town. Kate at Mathew Farrell's of Main Street, Longford Town. William at Skelly's of Main Street, Longford Town. George at Gray's of Bridge Street, Longford Town.

McKEEVER: Alice at Patrick Gormley's of Polladooey.

KEEVINS, KEEVANS: Agnes at Donohoe's of Annagh (Drumgort D.E.D.). (See Kevins).

KEILHAR: Kate at O'Neill's of Carrickateane.

KEIRNAN: See Kiernan.

KELLEGHER, KELLEHER, KELLAHER: John, John at Aghamore Upper. William at Camagh (Ballinamuck East D.E.D.). Thomas at Edenmore. Bernard at Glenmore (Ballinamuck East D.E.D.). Patrick at Currygranny. Francis at Greagh. Catherine, Patrick at Cloonart South. *ALSO:* Kate at O'Neill's of Carrickateane (?). John J. at Mulligan's of Edgeworthstown Town. Ellen at Mahon's of Leggagh. Daniel at Whitney's of Drumlish Village. Bridget at Dooner's of Sragarrow. Thomas at Moran's of Cloonart South. Mary at Farrell's of Broderick's Yard, Longford Town. Cornelius at O'Connor's of Conroy's Court, Longford Town. Elizabeth at Whelan's of Harbour Row, Longford Town.

KELLETT: Charles at Main Street, Granard Town. *ALSO:* Rev. Samuel F. and Thomas H. at Bennett's of Lismoy.

KELLY:(142): Mathew at Cloonbrin. Patrick at Ratharney. Bridget, Michael at Corrycorka. James, Hugh, Thomas at Legan. Catherine at Torboy. Patrick, Catherine at Cornamucklagh. Hugh at Forgney. Patrick at Rath. Patrick at Carrigeen (Foxhall D.E.D.). Michael, Patrick, Stephen at Killeen (Foxhall D.E.D.). William at Newport. Patrick at Daroge. Thomas at Laragh. Thomas at Moygh (Ballymahon D.E.D.). Francis at Tirlickeen. Patrick, Hugh, Catherine, Patrick at Ballymahon Town. James at Cloonard

(Ballymahon D.E.D.). Thomas at Creevagh Beg, Ballymahon Town. John at Toome (Ballymahon D.E.D.). John at Carrow Beg (Cashel West D.E.D.). James at Cartoon. Michael, Patrick at Cloonmee. John at Corrool (Kenny). Michael at Elfeet (Burke). Michael, Mary at Greenhall Upper. Thomas at Saints Island. Charles, Patrick, Joseph at Abbeyderg. Peter at Main Street, Keenagh Village. Mary at Ledwithstown (Kilcommock Civil Ph.). James, Mary at Derrynabuntale. Joseph at Aghnashannagh. Margaret at Ballinalee Village. Edward J. at Laughil (Edgeworth). Maria, Catherine, William at Aghagreagh. Francis at Molly. William G. at Kilcourcey. George at Aghaward. John at Cranally. Francis at Springtown. John at Culleenmore. James at Aghnagarron. Maria at Cloghchurnel. Thomas at Ballyboy. Mary, James, Michael at Ball Alley Street Lower, Granard Town. Patrick at Ball Alley Street Upper, Granard Town. James at Ballynacross (Granard Urban D.E.D.). Michael, John at Main Street, Granard Town. John at Moxham Street, Granard Town. Patrick, Francis, John at The Hill, Granard Town. Francis at Water Lane, Granard Town. James at Ardagullion. Bridget M. at Asnagh. Michael at Derragh. Patrick at Corbaun or Leitrim. Patrick at Lisnagrish. Elizabeth at Ballaghgowla and Froghan. Peter at Bracklon. Hugh at Edgeworthstown Town. James at Ballincurry. Mary at Cornacullew. Francis, Catherine at Barragh More. Francis at Greagh. Anne at Drumlish Village. Mary, Maria, Patrick at Dooroc. Michael, Francis at Gaigue. Ellen at Deerpark (Newtownforbes D.E.D.). Patrick at Lissagernal. Bernard, Michael, Peter at Newtownforbes Village. John at Kilmore Lower. Martin, Mary at Glebe (Cloondara D.E.D.). Michael at Rappareehill. John at Carrigeen (Moydow D.E.D.). Patrick at Corlagan. John J. at Trillickacurry. Thomas at Cloonmucker. John at Formoyle (Newcomen). Thomas at Knock. Maria, Mary at Corneddan. Patrick, Patrick at Esker South. Ellen, Bridget at Kilnacarrow (Aghaboy D.E.D.). John at Barneygole. Owen at Bohermore. Thomas at Drumroe. Michael at Glen. Michael at Moor. Anne at Cartrongarrow. James at Bawn (Ardagh West D.E.D.). Essie at Farraghroe. Annie at Mucknagh. Patrick at Corboy. Patrick, John J., Bernard, John at Ballymakeegan. Catherine, Bridget, Malachy at Bog Lane, Longford Town. Edward at Canal Harbour, Longford Town. Elizabeth, Patrick at Dublin Street, Longford Town. Patrick at Earl Street, Longford Town. Mary at Fee's Terrace, Longford Town. Patrick, Patrick, James, Rose at Great Water Street, Longford Town. Mary at Noud's Yard, Longford Town. Thomas at Richmond Street, Longford Town. John at St. Mel's Road, Longford Town. John at Abbeycartron. Thomas at Church Street, Longford Town. *ALSO:* Bridget at Lyons's of Forgney. Rose at Hagarty's of Newtown (Foxhall D.E.D.). Mary at Charles Fee's of Deerpark (Kilglass D.E.D.). Mary at Albert Shaw's of Ballymahon Town. Patrick and Mary A. at James Gorman's of Ballymahon Town. Kate at John Cox's of Ballymahon Town. Katie at James Daly's of Ballymahon Town. Mary and Bridget at Patrick Farrell's (4) of Corrool (Fox). Margaret at Lyon's of Kilcommock Glebe (?). Mary at Michael Connaughton's of Derrynagalliagh. Mary and Maggie at Catherine Kane's of Drummeel.

Robert and Mary K. at John Jones's of Carrickduff. Rose A. at Edward Tracey's of Lislea (Lislea D.E.D.). Michael et al. at James Reilly's of Kilbride. Mary at Thompson's of Ballinulty Upper. Peter at Thomas McCabe's of Cartron (Granard Rural D.E.D.). John et al. at Gormley's of Kinkillew. Katie at Caldwell's of Tennyphobble. Kate at O'Brien's of Barrack Street, Granard Town. Bridget and Elizabeth at Major's of Main Street, Granard Town. Kate at Laurence Ward's of Main Street, Granard Town. James and Joseph at Mulligan's of The Hill, Granard Town. Bridget at Hynes's of Water Lane, Granard Town. Margaret at Kiernan's of Cooldoney. Edward at Mary McCabe's of Aghanoran. Beesy at Thomas Reilly's of Kilmore. Kate at Bridget McNamara's of Kilsallagh. Mary and Anne at Poustie's of Ringowny. Francis et al. at Gaffney's of Aghafin. Rose at Ross's of Edgeworthstown Town. Anne at Margaret Green's of Edgeworthstown Town. Michael at Jobe's of Rathmore (Ballinamuck East D.E.D.). Mary at Mulligan's of Glenmore (Ballinamuck East D.E.D.). Bridget at Ghee's of Cloonmacart. John and Maggie at Beirne's of Cornacullew. Michael and Maggie at Patrick Hughes's of Greagh. Catherine and Catherine at Farrington's of Newtownforbes Village. Michael at Hopkins' of Cleggill. Bernard et al. at Gregg's of Cloonbalt. Margaret at Maxwell's of Corragarrow (Caldragh D.E.D.). Mary A. at Pollard's of Templeton Glebe. William at Patrick Bannon's of Barney. Anne at Elizabeth Dooner's of Cartrongarrow. Peter at O'Connor's of Conroy's Court, Longford Town. Mary A. at Green's of Convent Lane, Longford Town. Thomas F. at Hyland's of Fee's Terrace, Longford Town. Peter at King's of Main Street, Longford Town. John at McElnea's of Main Street, Longford Town. George at Maxwell's of Main Street, Longford Town.

KEMP: William at Parkplace. William at Lanesborough Village.

KENAGHAN, KENAHAN: John at Clygeen. *ALSO:* John at Kenny's of Cloonbrin.

McKENLEY: See McKinley.

KENNA: William at Rathmore (Ballymahon D.E.D.). Richard at Main Street, Granard Town.

McKENNA:(48): Patrick, James at Garvagh (Currygrane D.E.D.). Michael at Drummeel. Connor at Drumderg. Patrick at Moatfarrell. Edward at Lisnanagh. Anne at Aghnacliff. James at Cloonee (Creevy D.E.D.). John at Cornadrung. Mary at Aghanoran. James at Edgeworthstown Town. Bernard at Creelaghta. Michael at Fardrumman. Felix, Constantine, Francis, Mary, Patrick, Francis at Kiltycreevagh. James at Shanmullagh. Jane at Leitrim (Breanrisk D.E.D.). Patrick, Thomas at Bawn (Breanrisk D.E.D.). Connor, Patrick, Bernard at Cloonmacart. James (?), Bernard at Corglass. James at Drumlish. James, Michael, Bridget at Enybegs. Patrick, Elizabeth at Drumlish Village. John, John at Derryheelan. Thomas at Briskil. James at Ahanagh. Bernard at Tullyvrane. Bernard, Bernard at Kilnacarrow (Aghaboy D.E.D.). Bridget at Soran. Mary at Feraghfad. Charles at Ballymahon Street, Longford Town. Thomas at Deanscurragh. Catherine at Dublin Street, Longford Town. Teresa at Earl Street, Longford Town. Patrick at Hyde's Yard, Longford Town. *ALSO:* Frank at O'Neill's of Lissameen. Mathew at Mahon's of Kilcourcey. Patrick at Moorhead's of Creelaghta. Patrick at Peter Kenny's of Cloontagh. Elizabeth and Margaret at Kilmurry's of Cloonmacart. Michael at Patrick Hughes's of Cloonmacart. Thomas at Bernard Farrell's of Cornacullew. Mary at McNerney's of Kiltycon. Ellen at O'Hara's of Creenagh. Catherine at Allen's of Breany. Elizabeth et al. at Dennigan's of Chapel Lane, Longford Town. John at O'Connor's of Conroy's Court, Longford Town.

KENNEDY:(35): Elizabeth at Ballyclamay. Ellen at Streamstown (Kilglass D.E.D.). Thomas at Ballymahon Town. James at Aghnacross. Bernard at Ballagh (Cashel West D.E.D.). John at Carrow Beg (Cashel West D.E.D.). John at Corrool (Fox). Patrick at Main Street, Keenagh Village. Henry at Aghaboy (Milltown D.E.D.). Thomas at Tonywardan. James at Ballyduffy. Thomas at Lisnagrish. William J. at Bracklon. Patrick at Lackan. Thomas at Edgeworthstown Town. Bridget at Corrabaun (Breanrisk D.E.D.). William at Garrowhill. Bridget at Annaghcooleen. Maria at Clooniher. James at Aghnagore. Bridget at Cross (Ardagh East D.E.D.). Bridget, John, Richard at Crossea South. Patrick at Glen. Thomas at Breany. Patrick at Mucknagh. Michael at Lisfarrell. Alexander, Bridget, Patrick, Michael at Corboy. John at Great Water Street, Longford Town. Michael at St. Michael's Road, Longford Town. James W. at Bridge Street, Longford Town. *ALSO:* Anne at Manley's of Furze. Catherine at Mary Mulvey's of Ballintober (Bonny). Joseph at Kane's of Prucklishtown. Mary at Martin's of Rinnenny. Anne at James Woods's of Tinnynarr. Francis J. at Kelly's of Edgeworthstown Town. Mary at Maguire's of Edgeworthstown Town. Nannie at Peyton's of St. Anne's Glebe. Mary A. and Anne at Thomas Wright's of Gorteenorna. Margaret at Dalton's of Coolcaw. Christopher at Duffy's of Lisnamuck. Bernard at Roderick Igoe's of Ballymahon Street, Longford Town. Charles at Prunty's of Ballymahon Street, Longford Town. Joseph at Stephenson's of Dublin Street, Longford Town. Mary at John Wilson's of Main Street, Longford Town.

KENNY:(129): Patrick at Abbeyshrule. Marcella at Cloonbrin. James, Thomas, John at Drumanure. Mary at Castlewilder. Catherine at Keeloge. Patrick at Cloonfide. Patrick at Currycreaghan. Bernard at Torboy. Patrick at Listobit. Mary at Forgney. William, Bernard, Christopher at Pallas More. William, John at Keel (Forgney D.E.D.). Owen at Clygeen. Anne at Rockpeyton. Bernard, Christopher at Killeen (Foxhall D.E.D.). Mary at Aghnasillagh. Laurence, Michael, Michael, Laurence at Druming. John, Bernard at Keel (Kilglass D.E.D.). Patrick, James at Carn. Patrick at

Knockagh. Patrick at Ballybranigan. Maria at Cloonkeen (Ballymahon D.E.D.). Martin, Andrew at Ballymahon Town. James at Cloonard (Ballymahon D.E.D.). Patrick at Creevaghmore (Forgney Civil Ph.). Peter at Ballina. John at Collum. Anne at Cornadowagh. Bridget, John at Corrool (Kenny). Peter, Margaret at Pollagh. Luke at Cullentragh (Rathcline Civil Ph.). John at Cloonbreany. John at Lismacmurrogh. Margaret, Thomas at Derrynagran. Richard at Ledwithstown (Kilcommock Civil Ph.). John at Aghnashannagh. Thomas at Kilshruley. John at Currygrane. Anne at Drumnacross. John at Garvagh (Currygrane D.E.D.). Michael at Castlebrock. Michael at Drummeel. Mary at Lismagoneen. David, William J. at Drumderg. Mathew at Kiltyclogh. John at Moatfarrell. Owen, John at Glannagh. John at Springtown. Hugh at Ballinrud Glebe. Catherine at Cloghchurnel. Joseph M. at Churchquarter. Patrick at Gneeve. John at Liscahill. Patrick J. at Lissanure. Peter at Ballindagny and Cullyvore. Bryan, Michael at Bracklon. Michael at Drumbad. Ellen, Elizabeth, Francis, Peter at Cloontagh. John at Prucklish. Patrick at Carrowbeg (Drumlish D.E.D.). Patrick at Enybegs. Ellen, John at Greagh. Patrick at Drumlish Village. James, Patrick at Brocklagh. Terence, Anne at Derrynacross. Margaret at Kilmacannon. James, Patrick at Cloonrallagh. Mary at Ballykenny. Patrick at Cornollen. James at Kilmore Lower. James at Knappoge (Cloondara D.E.D.). Timothy, Catherine at Gorteenboy. James at Trillickacurry. Michael, Patrick at Bleanavoher. John at Cashelbeg. Bridget at Formoyle (Newcomen). James at Killinure. James at Lisrevagh. John at Tullyvrane. Bernard, William at Aghaboy (Aghaboy D.E.D.). James at Clontumpher. James at Ballygar. James at Barneygole. Jane at Bohermore. John, Anne at Glen. Mary at Lenaboy. John, Michael at Moor. George, Michael at Cartrongarrow. Mary at Lisduff (Montgomery). James at Bawn (Ardagh West D.E.D.). John at Rhine. Elizabeth at Cloonahard. Annie at Creeve. William at Mullaghavorneen. Stephen at Great Water Street, Longford Town. Margaret R., Edward P. at Main Street, Longford Town. Denis at St. Michael's Road, Longford Town. *ALSO:* John at McKeon's of Abbeyshrule. Patrick at Morris's of Abbeyshrule. John at Mulvihill's of Cloonbrin. Ellen at Connor's of Drumanure. Rose at McGarry's of Castlerea Mountain. James and Bridget at Christopher Cummiskey's of Currycreaghan. Michael J. at Keenan's of Mornin. Michael at Magee's of Cloghan (Forgney D.E.D.). Rose at Adlum's of Tennalough. Peter at Donohoe's of Ballyglassin. Elizabeth at Bridget Coughlin's of Cloonkeen (Ballymahon D.E.D.). James at John Casey's of Ballymahon Town. Charles A. at James Cassidy's of Ballymahon Town. Maria at James Cummins's of Ballymahon Town. Kate at John H. Plant's of Ballymahon Town. Sr. Ignatius at Rev. Moth. Whelan's of Ballymahon Town. Sarah and Margaret at Gilmore's of Carrowrory. John at Mary Casey's of Cornadowagh. Thomas et al. at Dunne's of Elfeet (Adamson). Margaret at Hanly's of Leab. John at Early's of Ballinalee Village. Richard at Reynolds's of Ballinalee Village. Henry at Roarke's of Drummeel. Patrick at Flynn's of Ballymacroly. James at Leonard's of Main Street, Granard

Town. John at Gahan's of Garryandrew. Thomas at James Donegan's of Carrickmoyragh. Susan at Whyte's of Drumlish Village. Mary K. at Casey's of Derryharrow. Michael at Boyce's of Coolcaw. Bridget at Lyons's of Lenaboy. William at Bridget Ward's of Bawn Mountain. Thomas at Scanlon's of Drumure. John at Fullam's of Rhine. Annie at Patrick Tooman's of Stonepark (Longford Rural D.E.D.). Timothy at O'Connor's of Conroy's Court, Longford Town. Annie at Yorke's of Dublin Street, Longford Town. Michael M. at Jones's of Earl Street, Longford Town. Kathleen at Dunne's of Fee's Terrace, Longford Town. Margaret at James Joyce's of Main Street, Longford Town. J. at Hewetson's of Church Street, Longford Town.

KENYON: Bertram L. at Yorke's of Barrack Street, Granard Town.

McKENZIE: Alexander at Earl Street, Longford Town.

KEOGH, KEOUGH: Thomas at Kilglass and Cloonagh. Margaret at Ball Alley Street Upper, Granard Town. James at Corbaun or Leitrim. Hugh at Bohernameeltoge. Rose at Cartrongolan. Patrick at Oghil. Margaret at Banghill. James at Chapel Lane, Longford Town. *ALSO:* Mary and Mary A. at Reilly's of Culleenmore. Sr. Agnes at Sr. Hoare's of Grassyard. Maria at Michael Breslin's of Esker South. Mary at Farrell's of Lisdreenagh. Sr. Elizabeth M. at Sr. Green's of Convent Lane, Longford Town. William H. at Moore's of New Street, Longford Town.

McKEOGH: Mary at More O'Ferrall's of Lissard.

McKEON, McKEOWN:(26): James at Abbeyshrule. James at Furze. Michael at Carrickboy. Anne at Ballymahon Town. James at Aghnashannagh. Andrew at Kilshruley. John at Gelshagh. John at Molly. Thomas at Sonnagh. John at Leitrim (Granard Rural D.E.D.). Mary, Michael, Patrick, Rose, Francis at Smear. Francis at Crott. Michael at Aghafin. Mary at Edgeworthstown Town. Thomas at Ballincurry. Patrick at Cloonagh (Breanrisk D.E.D.). Mathew at Corrabaun (Breanrisk D.E.D.). Bridget, Patrick at Drumlish Village. Mary at Aghaboy (Aghaboy D.E.D.). Mary at Soran. John at Knockahaw. *ALSO:* Jane at Stephen Mills' of Main Street, Keenagh Village. James at Killaine's of Kilshruley. Catherine at Reynolds's of Ballinalee Village. Peter at Brady's of Lisraghtigan. Kate and Lizzie at Farrington's of Newtownforbes Village. John et al. at Bernard Hughes's of Aghaboy (Aghaboy D.E.D.). Mary K. et al. at John Tynan's of Esker South. John at Gilchriest's of Market Square, Longford Town.

KEOWN: Bernard at Castlerea Barracks.

KERANS, KERINS: Harriet at Lefroy's of Carrickglass Demesne (Templemichael Civil Ph.).

KERINAN: John at Michael Reilly's of Edgeworthstown Town.

KERNAHAN: James (absent from home) at Killashee Street, Longford Town.

KERR: William at Castleforbes Demesne. *ALSO:* James at Smear Barracks, Cleenrah. Joseph at Stacom's of Dublin Street, Longford Town. (See Carr).

KERRIGAN: Margaret at Ball Alley Street Upper, Granard Town. Michael at Clonwhelan. William at Lisnagrish. Francis at Edgeworthstown Town. Edward at Gaigue. Anne at Cornapark. James at Cloonturk. Patrick at Chapel Lane, Longford Town. *ALSO:* Denis at Edgeworth's of Kilshruley. Michael at McCormack's of Laughil (Adair). Mary A. at Connell's of Main Street, Granard Town. Elizabeth at Leavy's of Castlenugent. Mary at Smyth's of Lackan. Anne at Patrick Brady's (1) of Gaigue. Denis at Dooner's of Lismore. Michael at Callaghan's of Richmond Street, Longford Town.

KERWAN, KERWIN: See Kirwan.

KEVILLE: Rev. John at Drumlish Village.

KEVINS: Thomas at Ballyboy. (See Keevins).

McKEY: Robert at Mahon's of Leggagh. Sr. Mary at Sr. Green's of Convent Lane, Longford Town. (See Mackey).

KIELTY: Anne at Tennalick. John at Cloondara (?). Cornelius, James at Lisnamuck. Timothy at Great Water Street, Longford Town.

KIELY: Sisley at Brady's of Aghamore (Ballinalee D.E.D.).

KIERNAN:(173): James at Legan. Thomas at Kinard. Margaret, John, William, John, Patrick at Aghagreagh. Bernard, Thomas at Aghamore Upper. Charles at Kilcourcey. John, Catherine at Ballinrooey. Peter at Culray. Joseph, Bernard at Aghakeeran. Ellen, Bridget, Anne, James at Aghnacliff. Mary, Thomas, Catherine at Carrickadorrish. Philip at Sonnagh. Bryan at Ballinlough. John, John at Culleenmore. Patrick at Druminacrehir. Thomas, Ellen at Mullinroe. Michael, Luke, Mary, John, John, James at Aghnagarron. John at Creevy. Anne, Luke, Patrick, Esther, Bridget at Clogh (Dalystown D.E.D.). John at Dalystown. Catherine at Ballinulty Lower. Thomas at Ballyboy. Michael at Gallid. John at Tromra (Granard Rural D.E.D.). James, Mary, Bernard at Ball Alley Street Lower, Granard Town. Elizabeth at Ball Alley Street Upper, Granard Town. John, Thomas at Barrack Street, Granard Town. Peter, John, Michael at Main Street, Granard Town. Bridget at The Hill, Granard Town. Michael at Tromra (Granard

Urban D.E.D.). Michael, James, Ellen at Muckerstaff. John at Tonywardan.
Marianne at Cooldoney. Daniel at Cornadrung. Ellen at Dunbeggan
(Columbkille D.E.D.). Margaret, Michael, Bernard, Patrick, Patrick, John,
Patrick, Bridget, John, Catherine at Smear. John, Mary, Daniel, Philip,
Patrick at Crott. James, Bernard, John at Enaghan. Patrick at Aghagah.
Peter, Peter (?), Philip, Mary A., Francis at Ballyduffy. Patrick at
Drumhalry. Anthony, Bridget, Edward, John, Farrell, Anne at Cloonagh
(Mullanalaghta D.E.D.). Thomas, Thomas, William, Henry, James, James,
James, Mary, Thomas at Corbaun or Leitrim. Edward, Patrick, Patrick,
Anne, James, Bernard at Kilmore. John at Larkfield. Patrick, Patrick, John,
Patrick, James, Patrick, Rose, Thomas at Toome (Mullanalaghta D.E.D.).
Michael at Castlenugent. Michael at Ringowny. Mathew at Coolamber. Kate
at Curry (Coolamber D.E.D.). Patrick at Lechurragh. Patrick at Longfield.
Patrick at Bracklon. Philip, Andrew at Edgeworthstown Town. John (absent
from home) at Cuingareen. Owen at Rathmore (Ballinamuck East D.E.D.).
Michael, Edward, John at Fostragh. John, Patrick at Kiltycreevagh. James
at Cloonellan. William at Leitrim (Breanrisk D.E.D.). John at Cloonelly.
Peter, Jane at Leggagh. Catherine, Catherine, Thomas, Owen, Lizzie, James
at Cartrongolan. Bernard at Drumlish. Mary at Greagh. Francis, Elizabeth,
Mary at Monaduff. Thomas, Patrick, John at Oghil. Thomas at Drumlish
Village. Bridget, Agnes J. at Gaigue. Michael at Lettergonnell. Terence at
Esker South. Marcella at Ballinree and Ballymoat. John at Barneygole.
Edward at Carnan. Michael at Killeenatruan. Patrick at Feraghfad. James
at Stonepark (Longford Rural D.E.D.) (?). John at Kilnasavoge. Mary at
Conroy's Court, Longford Town. Eugene at Dublin Street, Longford Town.
John at Earl Street, Longford Town. Elizabeth at Fee's Terrace, Longford
Town. Patrick at Glack (Longford Urban No. 1 D.E.D.). Catherine at
Hyde's Yard, Longford Town. Bridget at Little Water Street, Longford
Town. Thomas at St. Mel's Road, Longford Town. Catherine at St.
Michael's Road, Longford Town. *ALSO:* Mary at Hinch's of Kinard. Lizzie
at Ledwith's of Sleehaun. Mary at William Denniston's of Drumnacross.
Kate at Cunningham's of Aghacordrinan. Mary at Rose McGovern's of
Aghakilmore. Rose at Margaret Reilly's of Aghamore Upper. Bridget at
Casey's of Aghaward. Annie at Lennon's of Lislea (Lislea D.E.D.). Kate
and Mary at Shanly's of Ballinrooey. Mollie and Patrick at Alice O'Reilly's
of Aghakine. Frances at Mary McCabe's (12) of Aghnacliff. Edward and
Maggie at Edward Reehil's of Carrickadorrish. Margaret at Reilly's of
Abbeylara Village. John J. and Owen at Treacy's of Ballinlough. Luke at
Hanlon's of Culleenmore. James at Thomas Reilly's of Cloghchurnel.
Michael at Stephenson's of Cloghchurnel. Katie at Bridget McCabe's of
Dalystown. Mary A. at Anne Drake's of Ballinulty Upper. Bridget and
Mary at Dales' of Ballygilchrist. Bridget at Molloy's of Ballymaurice
(Granard Rural D.E.D.). Edward at Kenna's of Main Street, Granard Town.
Francis at Hynes's of Water Lane, Granard Town. Margaret at Catherine
Sheridan's of Carrickmaguirk. Fr. Patrick at Rev. McGuire's of Cleenrah.
Michael at Farrell's of Cleenrah. Michael at Annabella Hall's of

Cornadrung. Bridget and James at Margaret Gormley's (7) of Polladooey. Edward at John Reilly's (21) of Rosduff. James at Hugh Donohoe's of Smear. Kate et al. at Margaret Cosgrove's of Birrinagh. Bernard and Catherine at Grimes' of Cloonagh (Mullanalaghta D.E.D.). Mary at Michael Duffy's (30) of Kilmore. Delia at Patrick Matthews' of Toome (Mullanlaghta D.E.D.). John at Sheridan's of Corclaragh. Thomas et al. at Kate Reilly's of Cranalagh More. Patrick at Farrelly's of Longfield. Margaret at Duffy's of Monadarragh. Patrick at Bloomer's of Bracklon. Francis at Peter J. Joyce's of Edgeworthstown Town. John at Michael Reilly's of Edgeworthstown Town (?). Thomas at John Mulligan's of Cloonback. Bridget at Daniel Sheridan's of Corrinagh. Francis at Jobe's of Rathmore (Ballinamuck East D.E.D.). Mary at Thomas Reilly's of Glenmore (Ballinamuck East D.E.D.). Mary at Michael Murphy's (31) of Glenmore (Ballinamuck East D.E.D.). John at Ballinamuck Barracks, Shanmullagh. Mary E. at Elizabeth Reilly's of Tawnagh. James at Hetherton's of Corglass. Bridget at McGuinness's of Leggagh. Mary at McGuire's of Cloonbalt. Edward and Mary at John Coyle's (54) of Esker South. Mary A. at Healy's of Kiltyreher (Templemichael Civil Ph.). Rose at O'Reilly's of Ballynagoshen. William at Farrell's of Lisduff (Longford Rural D.E.D.) (?). Catherine at Michael Thompson's of Ballymahon Street, Longford Town. B. Josephine at Taaffe's of Dublin Street, Longford Town. John at Dempsey's of Great Water Street, Longford Town (?). Patrick at Patrick E. Fitzgerald's of Main Street, Longford Town. James at Mathew Farrell's of Main Street, Longford Town. Bridget at Devine's of Main Street, Longford Town.

McKIERNAN: Peter at Ballyduffy. Mary at Drumhalry. *ALSO:* Edward at O'Connor's of Conroy's Court, Longford Town.

KIERNEY: William at Farrell's of Lisduff (Longford Rural D.E.D.).

KILBRIDE, GILBRIDE: Henry at Tennalick. Michael at Aghakilmore. John at Cartronbore. Michael at Coolagherty. John, Catherine at Cloonart North.

KILBY: Emily at Cornamucklagh. John at Cloondara (?). *ALSO:* Margaret at Lyon's of Kilcommock Glebe.

KILCOYNE: John at Main Street, Keenagh Village.

KILDUFF: Michael at Clooncullen. Patrick at Daroge. Anne at Derrygowna. Bernard at Ledwithstown (Kilcommock Civil Ph.). Anne at Gorteenclareen. Francis J. at Main Street, Granard Town. Peter, Mathew at Barney. *ALSO:* Christopher at Mulvany's of Cornamucklagh. Mary A. at Smith's of Tonymore North. Catherine at Greene's of Lisnagrish. Thomas et al. at Hanly's of Barnacor (Rathcline D.E.D.).

KILEMADE: See Killimade.

KILFEATHER: Patrick at Edgeworthstown Barracks.

KILKELLY: John M. at Lisnamuck.

KILKENNY: Rose at Green's of Convent Lane, Longford Town.

KILLANE, KILLAINE: Edward at Kilshruley. Anne at Cam. *ALSO:* James J. at Kenny's of Currygrane.

KILLIAN, KILLION, KILLEAN:(14): William at Clooncallow. William at Keel (Forgney D.E.D.). Patrick at Creevaghmore (Forgney Civil Ph.). Daniel at Creevagh Beg. Michael at Derrygowna. John at Forthill. Patrick at Edgeworthstown Town. Thomas at Cloonbearla. Daniel at Formoyle (Farrell). John, Luke, Daniel at Formoyle (Newcomen). Luke, Michael at Inchenagh Island (Rathcline D.E.D.). *ALSO:* Hubert at Michael Clyne's of Derrygowna.

KILLIMADE, KILEMADE: Patrick at Kildordan. Edward, John, Patrick, Ellen at Feraghfad. *ALSO:* Mary at Hopkins' of Feraghfad.

KILLORAN: Margaret J. at Margaret Farrell's of Ardanragh.

KILLOUGHY: Kate at Mullady's of Gorteenclareen.

KILLY: Margaret at Lyon's of Kilcommock Glebe.

KILMURRY, GILMURRY, KILMURRAY, GILMURRAY: John at Aghaward. Roger at Cloonmacart. William at Lissanurlan. James, Daniel, Patrick at Corneddan. *ALSO:* James at Patrick Quinn's (9) of Enybegs.

KILROE: Patrick at Delany's of Church Street, Longford Town.

KINALON: John at Dublin Street, Longford Town. (See Kinlan).

KINCAID, KINCADE: James at Mara's of Pallas More.

McKINEY: See McKinney.

KING:(12): Patrick, Andrew, James at Main Street, Keenagh Village. Patrick at Breaghy. Bridget at Barne. Denis at Lisnagrish. Patrick at Cloonbalt. Patrick at Cloonrallagh. George at Harbour Row, Longford Town. Thomas at Main Street, Longford Town. James at St. Michael's Road, Longford Town. Margaret at Abbeycartron. *ALSO:* Mary J. at Cuthbert's of Ballyclamay. Lizzie at Geraghty's of Edgeworthstown Town.

John at Leavy's of Cross (Ardagh East D.E.D.).

KING-HARMAN: Wentworth H. at Newcastle.

KINGSTONE: Alexander C. at Mosstown (Rathcline Barony).

KINKADE: See Kincaid.

KINLAN, KINLIN: Philip, Thomas at Cleenrah. John at Dunbeggan (Columbkille D.E.D.). (See Kinalon).

McKINLEY: Samuel at Killashee and Aghakeeran. Patrick at Killinure. *ALSO:* Joseph at Thomas Doherty's of Rhine. Catherine at Fee's of Lisduff (Longford Rural D.E.D.).

McKINNEY, McKINEY: James at McClean's of Edgeworthstown Town.

KINSELLA: Mary at Bole's of Parkplace. Annie at Byrne's of Dring.

KINSLEY: Peter at Mornin.

KIRBY: Sr. Mary at Sr. Green's of Convent Lane, Longford Town. S. at Hewetson's of Church Street, Longford Town.

KIRK: Andrew at Prucklishtown.

KIRKLAND: John at Ball Alley Street Lower, Granard Town. Elizabeth at Rabbitpark.

KIRRANE: Michael at Dublin Street, Longford Town.

KIRRIGAN: See Kerrigan.

KIRTLAND: Thomas and Rose A. at Michael Kiernan's of Muckerstaff.

KIRWAN, KIRWIN, KERWAN, CURWIN: Anne at Culleenmore. Catherine, Thomas at Mollyglass. Patrick (?), Mary at Rosduff. John at Cloonageeher. Patrick at Little Water Street, Longford Town. *ALSO:* Patrick at Keogh's of Corbaun or Leitrim. Millicent and Catherine at Tierney's of Ballymahon Street, Longford Town. John at Dempsey's of Great Water Street, Longford Town (?). (See Curivan).

KISSANE: Patrick at Guinan's of Main Street, Longford Town.

KIVLEHAN: John J. at James Kenny's of Bawn (Ardagh West D.E.D.).

McKNIFF: See McNiff.

KNIGHT: Bridget at Ballyrevagh. *ALSO:* Kate at Mary Dennigan's of Great Water Street, Longford Town.
KNOTT: Frances at Mason's of Carn.

KNOX: Clementina at De Burgh-Sidley's of Granard.

McKONKEY: See McConkey.

KYNE: Julia at Corbaun or Leitrim. James at Kilmore. James at Toome (Mullanalaghta D.E.D.).

LACKEN: See Lakin.

LACKEY: William at Soran. (See Leckey).

LACY: See Leacey.

LAHEY: See Leahy.

LAKEY: William at Abbeycartron.

LAKIN: Elizabeth and Mary at King-Harman's of Newcastle.

LALLY: Michael at Carrickmoran. Thomas at Claras. Bridget at Corrool (Fox). John at Annagh (Ledwithstown D.E.D.). George at Lismoy. John at Lanesborough Village. Thomas at Bog Lane, Longford Town. Catherine at Chapel Lane, Longford Town. *ALSO:* Bridget at Thomas Clarke's of Corrool (Fox). Mary at Ann Walsh's of Knock. Bridget and Mary at Keena's of Bog Lane, Longford Town. Thomas et al. at Anne Purdy's of Chapel Lane, Longford Town.

LAMB, LAMBE: Winifred at Earl Street, Longford Town. *ALSO:* Maggie at Farrington's of Newtownforbes Village. Sr. Mary at Sr. Green's of Convent Lane, Longford Town.

LAMBDEN: George at Fee's Terrace, Longford Town.

LAMBERT: Mark at Abbeycartron.

LANDERS: John at O'Donnell's of Dublin Street, Longford Town.

LANE, LAYNE: James at Loughsheedon. Hugh at Drumhalry. Kiernan at Derrymore. Francis at Cloonkeen (Ardagh West D.E.D.). James at Cordivin. Thomas at Cartronageeragh. *ALSO:* Bridget at Anne Rodohan's of Corglass. Catherine at Lennon's of Mullaghavorneen. Mariann at McHugh's of Stonepark (Longford Rural D.E.D.).

LANG: See Lyang, Long.

LANGAN: Thomas at Furze. Margaret at Cartronreagh. John J. at Aghafin. Patrick at Garryandrew. Francis at Edgeworthstown Town. *ALSO:* Mary A. at Smyth's of Lackan. Nicholas at John McLoughlin's of Lisfarrell. Francis at Phillips's of Corboy. Annie at Atkinson's of Main Street, Longford Town.

LANGLEY: J. at Hewetson's of Church Street, Longford Town.

LANGUISH: Kate at Abbeycartron.

LANNON: Peter at Allen's of Agharickard.

LANTRY: Catherine at Farmullagh. *ALSO:* Alice at Moore's of Cartronawar (Kilcommock D.E.D.). Mary at Devine's of Carrickateane. Julia at Patrick Mulligan's of Rathmore (Ballinamuck East D.E.D.).

LARKIN:(17): Ellen at Clooncallow. Catherine at Clooncullen. Thomas at Corry (Kilglass D.E.D.). Bernard at Kilcurry. Patrick at Aghadowry. Ellen at Bawn (Breanrisk D.E.D.). Michael at Barragh More. Margaret at Drumlish Village. Patrick, Joseph, Rose at Gaigue. Michael, Charles at Clooncolligan. Hugh at Killeter. Ellen at Dublin Street, Longford Town. Michael, Felix at Main Street, Longford Town. *ALSO:* Elizabeth and Mary at King-Harman's of Newcastle (?). James at McGrath's of Lisnacreevy. Bridget at Dowler's of Knockagh. Mary A. at King's of Main Street, Longford Town. Mary and Bride at Green's of Convent Lane, Longford Town.

McLARNEY, McALARNEY: Bridget at Larkfield. *ALSO:* Annie at Kelly's of Ballynacross (Granard Urban D.E.D.). Thomas at Dowdall's of Cloonagh (Mullanalaghta D.E.D.).

LASTEN: Mathew at McCullagh's of Killashee Street, Longford Town.

LATFORD: Thomas at Gelshagh.

LATIMER: James at Castlenugent. Andrew at Earl Street, Longford Town. *ALSO:* Mary A. et al. at Michael Daly's (7) of Aghnagarron. James at O'Dwyer's of Carragh (Granard Urban D.E.D.). Jane et al. at Morrison's of Ballagh (Newtownforbes D.E.D.).

LAUGHERY, LAUGHREY: See Loughrey.

LAUGHLIN: See Loughlin.

McLAUGHLIN: See McLoughlin.

LAURENCE: See Lawrence.

LAVERTY: Edith at Edgeworth's of Kilshruley.

LAVIN, LAVAN: John at Clooneen (Kennedy). *ALSO:* Mary A. at McGowan's of Earl Street, Longford Town.

LAWLESS: James at Lissaghanedan. *ALSO:* F. at Hewetson's of Church Street, Longford Town.

LAWRENCE, LAURENCE: Samuel at Cartronawar (Kilcommock D.E.D.). Robert at Laughil (Kilcommock D.E.D.). William at Cooldoney.

LAWSON: Henry et al. at William Gilchriest's of Great Water Street, Longford Town.

LAWTON: Bridget and Elizabeth at Gilchrist's of Noud's Yard, Longford Town.

LAYCOCK, LEACOCK, LEYCOCK: Mary at Cloonbreany. Michael at Ledwithstown (Kilcommock Civil Ph.).

LAYDEN: Jane at Little Water Street, Longford Town.

LAYNE: See Lane.

LEA: William at Glebe (Foxhall D.E.D.).

LEACEY: Lizzie at Orohoe's of Lisduff (Longford Rural D.E.D.).

LEACOCK: See Laycock.

LEAHY, LAHEY: Mary A. at Ballyclare (Killashee D.E.D.). James at Esker South. *ALSO:* Alexander at Keane's of Edgeworthstown Town.

LEAN: Francis at James Donohoe's of Drumard.

O'LEARY: Arthur at Dublin Street, Longford Town.

LEAVY, LEAVEY:(46): Bernard at Lislea (Doory D.E.D.). Stephen at Rath. John at Clooncullen. Michael, Anne at Garrycam. Mary at Ballintober (Rock). Michael, James at Barry (Ballymahon D.E.D.). Bridget at

Ledwithstown (Kilcommock Civil Ph.). Catherine at Ballyhoolivan. John at Rossan. Thomas at Melkernagh. James at Rincoolagh. Patrick, Rose A., Michael, Michael, James at Fihoragh. Margaret at Barne. Daniel at Kilsallagh. Thomas at Liscahill. Patrick at Castlenugent. Catherine at Longfield. John at Monadarragh. James at Edgeworthstown Town. Patrick at Rathmore (Ballinamuck East D.E.D.). Patrick at Kiltycreevagh. James, Mary at Aghnagore. Thomas at Gorteenboy. Elizabeth, John at Lanesborough Village. Christopher at Ballinroddy. Patrick at Cross (Ardagh East D.E.D.). Patrick at Twenty Acres (Templemichael Civil Ph.). John at Clooncaulfield. James at Lissaghanedan. John at Agharickard. Honoria at Cloonahard. Patrick at Ballynagoshen. Catherine at Cartronageeragh. Maria at Feraghfad. Hugh at Lisduff (Longford Rural D.E.D.). James at Kilnasavoge. Bridget at Dublin Street, Longford Town. Patrick at Noud's Yard, Longford Town. *ALSO:* Lizzie at McDonnell's of Aghnavealoge. Bernard at Bridget Yorke's of Barry (Ballymahon D.E.D.). Margaret at Kelly's of Ledwithstown (Kilcommock Civil Ph.). James at Gelshinan's of Robinstown. Elizabeth and Ellen at Molphy's of Gneeve. John at Carleton's of Culloge. Thomas at Greene's of Bracklon. Teresa at Geoffroy's of Rathcline. James et al. at Kiernan's of Barneygole. Bridget at Gillen's of Glen. Anne at Casey's of Lyanmore. Elizabeth at Ellen Ward's of Rathvaldron. Elizabeth at Keegan's of Treel (Corboy D.E.D.). John at Allen's of Agharickard. Thomas and Bridget at Rose Farrell's of Cloonahard. John at Comiskey's of Cloonahard. Lizzie at Orohoe's of Lisduff (Longford Rural D.E.D.) (?). Sr. Teresa at Sr. Green's of Convent Lane, Longford Town. Bridget at Peter J. Joyce's of Main Street, Longford Town. Anne at Mary Stritch's of Noud's Yard, Longford Town.

LECKEY: James at Demesne. (See Lackey).

LEDDY: John at Aghanoran. *ALSO:* Mary at Patrick McCabe's of Aghanoran. Julia at Dinnen's of Toome (Mullanalaghta D.E.D.).

LEDFORD: See Latford.

LEDWITH: Bridget at Clygeen. John at Newport. Catherine at Sleehaun. Mathew at Ballycloghan. John at Main Street, Granard Town. James, Thomas at Kilmore. Rev. Peter at Edgeworthstown Town. *ALSO:* Anne at Wynne's of Ardanragh. James at Murphy's of Lissawarriff. William at Bole's of Parkplace. Sr. Bridget at Rev. Mother Farrington's of Newtownforbes Village.

LEE:(34) Michael at Clooncallow. Patrick, Thomas, John, Thomas, Thomas, Michael at Forgney. Catherine at Clonbroney. Patrick at Currygrane. Luke at Garvagh (Currygrane D.E.D.). Mary A. at Drummeel. Joseph, Francis, Patrick, Patrick, Francis J. at Aghagreagh. Anne at Aghakilmore. Thomas at Lislea (Lislea D.E.D.). Mary at Carrickadorrish.

Charles at Dalystown. Patrick at Ballynacross (Granard Rural D.E.D.). Patrick at Ballynacross (Granard Urban D.E.D.). Patrick at Balnagall (Granard Urban D.E.D.). Bridget at New Road, Granard Town. Patrick at The Hill, Granard Town. Owen at Aghaboy (Milltown D.E.D.). James at Killashee Village. James, James, Michael, James at Soran. Lizzie at Bog Lane, Longford Town. Patrick at Earl Street, Longford Town. John at Little Water Street, Longford Town. *ALSO:* Edward at Mulvany's of Cornamucklagh. Margaret at Farrell's of Roos. Peter at Travers' of Aghabrack. Ellen at McNally's of Soran. Edward at Michael Thompson's of Ballymahon Street, Longford Town. Thomas at Jane Hughes's of Dublin Street, Longford Town. Helen and Elizabeth at McQuaid's of Great Water Street, Longford Town. John at Dempsey's of Great Water Street, Longford Town.

LEECH: Mary at Lloyd's of Moneyhoolaghan.

LEFROY: Thomas L. at Carrickglass Demesne (Templemichael Civil Ph.).

LEGGE: Robert at Main Street, Longford Town.

LENAHAN, LENEHAN, LENIHAN:(14): Patrick, Mary at Castlerea Mountain. Matthew at Curraghmore. Francis, Terence (?) at Aghanoran. Francis at Gaigue. Patrick at Aughine. John at Graffoge (Ardagh West D.E.D.). Bridget, Rose at Lisduff (Montgomery). Michael at Cloonkeen (Ardagh West D.E.D.).Hugh at Hyde's Yard, Longford Town. Mary at New Street, Longford Town. Michael at Townparks (Longford Urban No. 1 D.E.D.). *ALSO:* James at Harte's of Aghnashannagh. James at Orohoe's of Castlerea. Patrick at Sheridan's of Cooleeny. Michael at O'Connor's of Conroy's Court, Longford Town. Patrick at Duggan's of Dwyer's Yard, Longford Town. Michael at Felix Larkin's of Main Street, Longford Town. John at Abbeycartron Barracks.

LENNON:(50): William at Rathsallagh. Michael at Castlerea Mountain. John, Michael, Patrick, William, Edward, Thomas at Currycreaghan. James at Torboy. Maria at Corlea. Jane at Cartronawar (Kilcommock D.E.D.). William at Derrynagalliagh. Mathew at Aghacordrinan. John at Lislea (Lislea D.E.D.). John at Breanriskcullew. Michael at Creelaghta. John at Drumbad. Mary, Michael, James, Terence, Patrick, Julia, Francis, John at Fardrumman. James at Breanrisk. Jane at Ballincurry. Mary at Cloonelly. Michael at Cornacullew. Mary at Garrowhill. Kate at Barragh More. John, Mary, James, John at Oghil. John at Brocklagh. Catherine, James, James at Kilmahon. James at Glebe (Cloondara D.E.D.). Michael at Gragh. Maria at Aghaboy (Aghaboy D.E.D.). Catherine, Michael, Patrick at Esker South. John, Terence, John at Soran. Peter at Creeve. Anne at Mullaghavorneen. *ALSO:* Peter et al. at Goldsberry's of Cornamucklagh. Mary at Higgins's of Clooncullen. Peter at Fox's of Tirlickeen. Mary at Wilson's of

Carrowlinan. Patrick at Peter Kiernan's of Main Street, Granard Town. Peter at Beatty's of Main Street, Granard Town. James at Susan Rourke's of Edgeworthstown Town. Kate at Patrick Whitney's of Fardrumman. Catherine and James at Doherty's of Carrowbeg (Drumlish D.E.D.). Peter at Murray's of Carrigeen (Moydow D.E.D.). Mary at Edward Farrell's (9) of Lisnacush. Peter at Allen's of Agharickard (?). John at O'Connor's of Conroy's Court, Longford Town. Ellen at Hanley's of Dublin Street, Longford Town. Kate at Harris's of Main Street, Longford Town.

LEONARD:(10): Margaret A. at Drumanure. Anne at Castlerea Mountain. Terence at Main Street, Granard Town. Jane at Moxham Street, Granard Town. Michael at Tully (Milltown D.E.D.). Terence at Aghanoran. Michael at Larkfield. Thomas at Newtownforbes Village. Thomas at Trillickatemple. Margaret at Cloontirm. *ALSO:* Mimie and Walter at Rittman's of Drumanure. John at Ballinamuck Barracks, Shanmullagh. Daniel at Ryan's of Lisdreenagh. Mary and Elizabeth at Bond's of Farraghroe. Bridget at Mary Bermingham's of Cloontirm.

Le PAGE: H. at Hewetson's of Church Street, Longford Town.

LESLIE: Mary A. at McNamara's of Cloonagh (Mullanalaghta D.E.D.).

L'ESTRANGE: Maggie at Mary Farrell's of Cooleeny.

LETFORD: See Latford.

LEVINGE: Thomas at Cartronlebagh.

LEVINGS: Ellen at Grealy's of St. Mel's Road, Longford Town.   .

LEVINGSTONE: See Livingston.

LEWIS: Kate at Middleton's of Corrabola (Doory D.E.D.).

LEYBOURNE: Charles at Edgeworthstown.

LEYCOCK: See Laycock.

LEYDEN: See Layden.

LIDDELL: A.H. at Hewetson's of Church Street, Longford Town.

LINDSAY: Robert at Fee's of Church Street, Longford Town.

McLINEY: Thomas at Kiltycreevagh. (See McAliney, McEliney).

LINN: See Lynn.

LIONS: See Lyons.

LITTLE: Mathew at Newcastle. Henry S. at Drumnacross. Edward at Barragh Beg. William at Creeve. Walter J. at Main Street, Longford Town. John W. at Church Street, Longford Town. *ALSO:* George at Brennan's of Greagh. James at Higgins's of Knappoge (Cloondara D.E.D.). Mary J. and George at John Purdy's of Chapel Lane, Longford Town.

LIVINGSTON, LIVINGSTONE, LEVINGSTONE: John at Lislea (Doory D.E.D.). Alexander at Creeve. *ALSO:* Anne at Buchanan's of Killashee and Aghakeeran. Thomas at Ussher-Roberts' of Knockahaw.

LLOYD: John at Clooncallow. Patrick at Forgney. Thomas at Kildordan. William at Rath. Robert at Ballymahon Town. Eleanor at Cavan. Benjamin J. at Moneyhoolaghan. Francis H. at Main Street, Longford Town. *ALSO:* William at Walsh's of Forgney. John at Casey's of Clooncullen. Thomas at John P. Shaw's of Ballymahon Town. Joseph et al. at Ryder's of Newtownflanigan. John at Forster's of Aghnashannagh. George at Keefe's of Chapel Lane, Longford Town.

McLOCHLAN: Thomas at Keon's Terrace, Longford Town. (See McLoughlin).

LOCKE: George at James Brady's of Main Street, Longford Town.

LOFTS, LOFTUS (?): Nannie at Kelly's of Abbeycartron.

LOGAN: Thomas at Kilsallagh. John at Lissanure. Patrick at Allenagh. *ALSO:* Maria at McCann's of Tirlickeen. James at Denning's of Lisnagrish.

LONG: Irwin at Lanesborough Village.

LONGWORTH: Mary at McGrath's of Currycreaghan.

LOONEY: Elizabeth at Main Street, Keenagh Village.

LORD: Elizabeth at Michael Sheridan's of Crott.

McLORINAN: John at Larkin's of Drumlish Village (?).

LOUGHERY: See Loughrey.

LOUGHLIN, LAUGHLIN: Bedelia at Deanscurragh. *ALSO:* Martin at Kenna's of Main Street, Granard Town. Peter at Dennan's of Main Street,

Granard Town.

McLOUGHLIN, McLAUGHLIN:(39): James at Pallas More. Francis at Rath. Michael at Ballycloghan. Anne at Druming. Bernard at Carrow Beg (Cashel West D.E.D.). John at Lisnanagh. Patrick at Kilsallagh. James at Liscahill. Patrick at Shantum. James, Mary at Cranalagh More. Thomas at Lisnageeragh. Thomas, Peter at Bracklon. Daniel at Creelaghta. Bernard at Crowdrumman. Ellen, Joseph at Shanmullagh. John at Brocklagh. John, Henry at Cloondara. James, Bridget at Soran. Thomas at Barney. Bridget, Julia at Crossea South. Patrick, Michael at Breany. William at Drumhaughly. John, Patrick, James at Kilmoyle. Dominick at Cartron Big. Peter at Cloonahard. John, Ellen at Lisfarrell. John at Clooneeny. Alice at Stonepark (Longford Rural D.E.D.). James at Glack (Longford Rural D.E.D.). *ALSO:* Peter et al. at Newman's of Knocknaskea. Owen at Patrick Finn's of Rathmore (Ballymahon D.E.D.). John at Donnelly's of Bunlahy. Rose at Dawson's of Barrack Street, Granard Town. Patrick at Whyte's of Clonwhelan. Bridget at Kate Reilly's of Cranalagh More. Mary at Patrick Gaynor's of Cranalagh More. William at Monahan's of Edgeworthstown Town. Mary A. at Patrick Furey's of Kiltycreevagh. Matilda at McNerney's of Aghamore Lower. Patrick at Flood's of Cornapark. Kate at Ellen Hagan's of Rhine. Sr. Margaret at Sr. Green's of Convent Lane, Longford Town. Terence at Hyland's of Fee's Terrace, Longford Town. Mary A. at Connolly's of Little Water Street, Longford Town. (See McLochlan).

LOUGHNANE: John at Lyanmore.

LOUGHRAN: James at Drumanure. Patrick at Lissakit. *ALSO:* Sr. Annie at Rev. Mother Hampson's of Aghafin.

LOUGHREY, LAUGHREY, LOUGHERY: Neil at Enybegs. Patrick, Bridget, Bridget, at Greagh. Michael at Aghaboy (Aghaboy D.E.D.). *ALSO:* Catherine and Patrick at Patrick Hughes's of Greagh. Kate A. at Hugh Flynn's of Killeenatruan.
McLOUGHRY: See McCloughry.

LOUTH: Bridget at New Street, Longford Town.

LOVETT: Mathew, Anne at Ballymahon Town. *ALSO:* Kate at John P. Shaw's of Ballymahon Town.

LOWRY: Mary at Jarratt's of Lismoy. Rose at Peelo's of Demesne.

LUCY: Hume at Abbeylara Village. Mary at Abbeycartron.

LUNAM: Annie at Main Street, Keenagh Village. *ALSO:* Lilly at John Burns' of Screeboge. (See Lynam).

LUSK: William at John McCormack's of Dublin Street, Longford Town.

LUTTON: Elizabeth at Mitchell's of Curry (Kilcommock D.E.D.).

LUTTRELL: Caroline at Shaw's of Ballybranigan.

LYANG: Robert at Parkplace.

LYNAM: Elizabeth at Derryart. *ALSO:* Jane at Shaw's of Carrigeen (Foxhall D.E.D.). Michael and Kate at Denigan's of Moygh (Killashee D.E.D.). (See Lunum).

LYNCH:(52): Bernard at Curraghmore. Patrick at Keelbaun. Margaret at Cornahoo. Anne at Barry (Kilcommock D.E.D.). Eugene at Ballynascraw. Kate at Listraghee. Patrick at Aghakilmore. Peter at Ballinrooey. James at Cranally. John, Margaret at Tonymore North. Michael, Patrick at Ballywillin. Edward at Cartronbore. Bridget, Francis, Ellen, Henry, Thomas at Clooneen (Creevy D.E.D.). Thomas at Aghnagarron. Hugh, James, Joseph at Cloghchurnel. Michael at Creevy. Connor at Granardkill (Granard Rural D.E.D.). John at Carragh (Granard Urban D.E.D.). Elizabeth at Ball Alley Street Upper, Granard Town. Mary, Elizabeth at Barrack Street, Granard Town. Charles at New Road, Granard Town. John at Muckerstaff. Bridget at Cooldoney. Michael at Polladooey. John, Patrick at Dring. Francis at Larkfield. Bernard, John at Castlenugent. Andrew at Kilfintan. Patrick at Lechurragh. Bryan, Michael at Crowdrumman. Owen, Rose at Lettergeeragh. Mary at Derrynacross. John, Patrick at Dooroc. Maria at Kilmahon. Thomas at Townparks (Newtownforbes D.E.D.). John at Newtownforbes Village. Terence at Corneddan. Matthew at Crossea South. *ALSO:* Catherine at Thomas Kennedy's of Ballymahon Town. John at Gilleland's of Barry (Kilcommock D.E.D.). Mary A. at Peter Mulvey's of Aghakilmore. Bridget at Rose Farrell's of Gelshagh. Patrick at Gilchrist's of Ballywillin. John et al. at Donohoe's of Ballywillin. Mary at Fagan's of Gallid. Julia at Brady's of Cornadrung. Peter at Peter McKiernan's (30) of Ballyduffy. Michael at Mulligan's of Freaghmeen. Patrick at Gunshenan's of Drumlish Village. Philip at Navan's of Lettergonnell. Rose at Quinn's of Soran. Peter at Michael Thompson's of Ballymahon Street, Longford Town. Kate at Creighton's of Bog Lane, Longford Town. Catherine at John Duck's (2) of Dwyer's Yard, Longford Town. Anne at Hannigan's of Main Street, Longford Town.

LYNG: See Lyang.

LYNN: Catherine at Derrynabuntale. John at Cooldoney. Annie at Dublin Street, Longford Town. Henry P. at Abbeycartron. *ALSO:* Elizabeth at Kenny's of Churchquarter. Mary A. at Farrell's of Grillagh (Ardagh West D.E.D.).

LYNOTT: Thomas at Carrickboy Barracks. Dominick at Gilchriest's of Market Square, Longford Town.

LYON: Rev. Paul K. at Kilcommock Glebe. *ALSO:* William R. at Pollard's of Templeton Glebe.

LYONS:(16): John at Forgney. Patrick at Rockpeyton. Richard, Michael at Foxhall. Francis at Daroge. Martin at Lissard. James, Francis at Castlebaun. Bridget at Lenaboy. Patrick at Clooncoose (Cloonee D.E.D.). Patrick at Rhine. James, Patrick at Garvagh (Longford Rural D.E.D.). John at Mullaghavorneen. Kate at Glack (Longford Rural D.E.D.). Patrick at Noud's Yard, Longford Town. *ALSO:* Patrick at Kearney's of Doonacurry (Shrule Civil Ph.). Mary at Martin's of Farraghroe. Rose at Mulheran's of Convent Lane, Longford Town. William at McConnell's of Healy's Terrace, Longford Town. Patrick at Maxwell's of Main Street, Longford Town.

LYTTLE: See Little.

MACAULEY: See McCauley.

MACK: Bridget at Connor's of Coach Yard, Longford Town.

MACKEN, MACKIN:(19): Christopher at Clooncullen. Charles, John, Patrick at Aghagreagh. James, Michael at Cranally. Michael, James, Thomas at Rinroe. Charles at Ballygilchrist. Catherine at Barrack Street, Granard Town. Joseph at Granardkill (Granard Urban D.E.D.). John, Thomas, Michael at Muckerstaff. Michael at Clonwhelan. Denis at Ringowny. Mary at Monadarragh. John at Edgeworthstown Town. *ALSO:* Bridget et al. at Bridget Fitzsimons' of Kilsallagh. Patrick at Mulhare's of Ringowny. Bridget at Devine's of Edgeworthstown Town. John at Ross's of Edgeworthstown Town.

MACKEY: John at O'Neill's of Main Street, Longford Town. (See McKey).

MADDEN: John at Castlerea Mountain. Thomas at Keel (Kilglass D.E.D.). Mary at Aghavadden. John at Harbour Row, Longford Town. Mary at Bridge Street, Longford Town. *ALSO:* Pat at Moran's of Torboy. Maria at Thomas Fenlon's of Edgeworthstown Town. Gretta at Sesnan's of Newtownforbes Village. Frank at Thompson's of Newtownforbes Village. J. at Hewetson's of Church Street, Longford Town.

MADILL: Thomas at Mucknagh. *ALSO:* Florence at Atkinson's of Main Street, Longford Town.

MAGAN, MAGANN: See McGann.

MAGEE: See McGee.

MAGORE: See Major.

MAGOVERN: See McGovern.

MAGRATH: See McGrath.

MAGUINNESS: See McGuinness.

MAGUIRE, McGUIRE:(63): Patrick at Killeenboy. Michael, Mary at Ratharney. John at Mornin. Edward at Smithfield. Bridget, James at Clontymullan. Bernard at Kinard. James at Ballybeg. James at Lisnacreevy. Elizabeth at Tirlickeen. Bernard at Newtownbond. Owen at Sonnagh. Mary at Killeen (Bunlahy D.E.D.). Edward at Mullinroe. Peter at Dalystown. Bernard at Ballymore. John at Cartron (Granard Urban D.E.D.). Thomas at Carrickmaguirk. Rev. Eugene at Cleenrah. John at Smear. Hugh at Fihoragh. James, Patrick at Farmullagh. Rose at Kilsallagh. Bessie at Castlenugent. John at Monadarragh. Bridget at Edgeworthstown Town. Bernard, Bridget at Cloonback. John, Patrick at Lettergeeragh. Thomas, Thomas at Leggagh. Daniel at Enybegs. Thomas at Dooroc. Peter, Bridget, Bernard at Drumnacooha. Elizabeth at Newtownforbes Village. Francis J. at Cloonbalt. James, James at Cloonfore. Thomas at Curry (Moydow D.E.D.). Anne at Carrowroe. James at Esker South. John, Denis, Denis, Patrick, John, Patrick, Michael, Peter at Soran. Thomas at Rhine. Michael at Ballyminion. Michael at Cloonturk. Michael at Ballymahon Street, Longford Town. Catherine at Broderick's Yard, Longford Town. Mary at Conroy's Court, Longford Town. Michael, John at Great Water Street, Longford Town. Kate at Richmond Street, Longford Town. *ALSO:* John at Courtney's of Lisnacreevy. Catherine at Larkin's of Kilcurry. Bridget at Thomas Burns' of Screeboge. Lizzie at Irwin's of Colehill. John at Bridget Egan's of Tennalick. Patrick et al. at Fox's of Ballinalee Village. Michael at Anne Sullivan's of Aghakilmore. Fr. Patrick at Mary McCabe's (12) of Aghnacliff. Anne at Patrick Reilly's of Springtown. Bernard at Catherine Burns' of Druminacrehir. Nicholas at Brady's of Rathbrackan (?). John and Emily at Egan's of Ball Alley Street Upper, Granard Town. John at Mary Brady's of Graffoge (Milltown D.E.D.). Anne at Boylan's of Cleenrah. Mary et al. at Kavanagh's of Dunbeggan (Columbkille D.E.D.). Peter at Reilly's of Mollyglass. Patrick at Heslin's of Ballyduffy. Francis at Salmon's of Corclaragh. Margaret at Kate Finlan's of Edgeworthstown Town. Ellen T. at Ellen Mollaghan's of Aghadowry. James at Flood's of Glenmore (Ballinamuck East D.E.D.). Peter at Thomas Davis's of Cornafunshin. Anne at Kiernan's of Lettergonnel. Michael M. at Newtownforbes Barracks. Alice K. and Mary E. at Skelly's of Newtownforbes Village. Anne at Farrington's of Newtownforbes Village. Joseph J. at Michael Skelly's of Cloondara. James at Gill's of Commons

North. Daniel at McKenna's of Soran. George at Bond's of Farraghroe. Michael at Shaw's of Cloonturk. Kate at Stephenson's of Dublin Street, Longford Town. Maggie at Flanagan's of Dublin Street, Longford Town. John at Howard's of Earl Street, Longford Town. Thomas at Reynolds's of Healy's Terrace, Longford Town. Ellen at Reilly's of Richmond Street, Longford Town. Lizzie and Alice at McDonnell's of St. Michael's Road, Longford Town.

MAHADY, MAHEDY:(13): Patrick at Ballina. Timothy at Caltragh More. Michael at Cornadowagh. James at Cranally. Peter at Tober. Daniel at Cartron (Granard Rural D.E.D.). Patrick at Moxham Street, Granard Town. John at The Hill, Granard Town. Thomas at Cam. James at Kilsallagh. Patrick at Lisryan. Thomas, John at Corclaragh. *ALSO:* Sr. Clare at Rev. Mother Whelan's of Ballymahon Town. Anne and Mary at McLoughlin's of Kilsallagh.

MAHARY, MAHARRY: Henry at Barneygole.

MAHER:(10): Anne at Edgeworthstown Town. Patrick at Glenmore (Ballinamuck East D.E.D.). James at Drumlougher. Patrick at Cooleeny. Mary A., Anne, Bridget at Coolnahinch (Longford Rural D.E.D.). Mary at Glack (Longford Rural D.E.D.). Margaret at Kilnasavoge. Patrick at Main Street, Longford Town. *ALSO:* Daniel at Rose Coyne's of Ballymahon Town. Sarah A. at Gregory's of Carrickmoyragh. Mary at Farrington's of Newtownforbes Village. Anne and Mary A. at Lennon's of Gragh. Margaret at Lyons's of Mullaghavorneen. Mary at Gannon's of Glack (Longford Urban No. 1 D.E.D.). (See Meagher).

MAHON:(31): Patrick at Lislea (Doory D.E.D.). Patrick at Clooncallow. Catherine at Ballymahon Town. John at Kilcourcey. Elizabeth at Castlebaun. Patrick, James at Carrickadorrish. James at Carragh (Granard Urban D.E.D.). Michael at Bank Street, Granard Town.   James at Ballyduffy. Edward, John, Anne at Farmullagh. Bridget at Kilmore. Thomas at Longfield. Thomas at Aghamore Lower. Rev. Edward at Leggagh. Anthony at Bohernameeltoge. Bridget at Ballagh (Newtownforbes D.E.D.). John at Ballagh (Achmuty). Bridget at Deerpark (Newtownforbes D.E.D.). Thomas at Clooncolligan. Patrick at Aghaboy (Aghaboy D.E.D.). Patrick at Corneddan. Lawrence at Corradooey. James, Patrick at Killeenatruan. Bridget at Killeter. Margaret at Broderick's Yard, Longford Town. Thomas at St. Michael's Road, Longford Town. John at Abbeycartron. *ALSO:* Elizabeth at Carrigy's of Torboy. Mary at Daniel O'Hara's of Ballymahon Town. Bridget at Patrick Brady's of Gelshagh. Mary at Gorman's of Ballymaurice (Granard Rural D.E.D.). Patrick at Beatty's of Main Street, Granard Town. Mary at Doogan's of Farmullagh. Bernard at Quinn's of Edgeworthstown Town.   Patrick and Kate at Flaherty's of Leggagh. Margaret at John Brady's of Enybegs. Thomas et al. at Elizabeth Casey's of Ballagh (Newtownforbes D.E.D.). Catherine at Peter Kelly's of Newtownforbes Village. Michael at Heaney's of Cahanagh. Francis at Burke's of Caldragh. Thomas at Carrigy's of Killeenatruan. Francis at McElnea's of Main Street, Longford Town. Lizzie at Devine's of Richmond Street, Longford Town.

McMAHON: John at Barrack Street, Granard Town. Thomas at Grassyard. Patrick at Enybegs. Patrick at Ballinree and Ballymoat. *ALSO:* Francis at Muldoon's of Aghavadden.

MAHONY: David at Great Water Street, Longford Town.

O'MAHONY: Edward at Gettings' of Tully (Milltown D.E.D.).

MAJOR, MAJORE, MAGORE: James, John at Cartron (Granard Rural D.E.D.). Francis at Main Street, Granard Town.

MAKIM: Samuel at Moor.

MALERVY: See Mullervy.

MALLEEDY: See Mulleady.

MALLEN: See Mallon.

MALLEY: Elizabeth at Rehill's of Mullinroe. John and Bridget at Macken's of Edgeworthstown Town.

O'MALLEY, O'MALLY: John J. at Newtownforbes Village. *ALSO:* Charles at Patrick Cullen's of Edgeworthstown Town. Joseph at Peter J. Joyce's of Main Street, Longford Town.

MALLON, MALYNN, MALLIN:(37): Thomas at Cloonbrin. Julia at Clooncullen. Hugh at Kinard. Honor at Daroge. William at Creevaghmore (Forgney Civil Ph.). Michael at Creevagh Beg. Edward at Creevagh Beg, Ballymahon Town. Peter at Cleraun. Patrick at Collum. Thomas, Thomas at Drumnee. James, Owen at Gelshagh. John at Molly. John at Cranalagh Beg. James, Charles at Kilcourcey. Owen at Carrlowlinan. Michael at Sonnagh. Charles at Springtown. Bridget at Ballymore. Patrick at Drumury. Bridget at Aghanoran. John at Fardrumman. Patrick at Lettergeeragh. Peter at Barragh More. Anne at Derawley. Michael at Monaduff. Thomas at Drumnacooha. Patrick, Bridget at Kilmahon. John at Lettergonnell. Thomas at Cartronawar (Corboy D.E.D.). Elizabeth at Cloonahard. Jane at Ballygarve. Patrick at Dublin Street, Longford Town. Frances at Great Water Street, Longford Town. *ALSO:* Patrick at Charles McGoey's of Drumanure. Anne at John Kenny's of Keel (Forgney D.E.D.). Patrick at

John Smyth's of Corrool (Kenny). Kathleen at Farrelly's of Currygrane. Bridget at Francis Reilly's (16) of Gelshagh. Mary A. at Moore's of Ballybrien. Thomas at Gilchriest's of Cranalagh More. Francis at Patrick Murphy's of Glenmore (Ballinamuck East D.E.D.). Mary at Thomas Davis's of Cornafunshin. Maggie A. at Collumb's of Derryheelan. Sr. Anne at Rev. Mother Farrington's of Newtownforbes Village. Patrick at Phillips's of Corboy.

MALONE:(15): John at Forgney. Michael at Cartronboy. James at Daroge. Mary at Derryoghil. James at Aghnashingan. Michael, Thomas at Gorteenclareen. Bridget at Ballywillin. John at Ballyduffy. Rose, William at Derryad (Mountdavis D.E.D.). James at Nappagh. Anne at Bawn (Ardagh West D.E.D.). Anne at Ballymahon Street, Longford Town. Peter at Great Water Street, Longford Town. *ALSO:* Matthew at Patrick Cassidy's of Derryad (Mountdavis D.E.D.). Patrick at Cody's at Ballinamore. Thomas at Quinn's of Banghill.

MALONEY: John at Clooncullen. (See Moloney).

MALYNN: See Mallon.

MANCE: G.A. at Hewetson's of Church Street, Longford Town.

MANGAN: Thomas at Derrymore. *ALSO:* Thomas at Maxwell's of Main Street, Longford Town.

MANICLE, MANACLE: Owen at Trillickacurry. Denis at Graffoge (Ardagh West D.E.D.).

MANLEY: Fr. Patrick J. at Furze. (See Monley).

MANNING: Thomas, Margaret, Patrick at Cloonellan. Mary at Lismoy. Michael at Cornapark. Margaret at St. Michael's Road, Longford Town. *ALSO:* Kate and Bridget at McGrath's of Main Street, Granard Town. Lizzie at Quinn's of Banghill. Bernard, James and Bernard at O'Connor's of Conroy's Court, Longford Town. Margaret at Turner's of Earl Street, Longford Town. James at Maxwell's of Main Street, Longford Town. Margaret at Webb's of Church Street, Longford Town.

MANNION: Patrick, Bernard, James, John at Keelbaun. Patrick at Carn. Anne, Elizabeth at Tirlickeen. *ALSO:* Lizzie at Eivers' of Keelbaun. Margaret at Payne's of Derrycolumb.

MANSE: See Mance.

MANSERGH: Ellen at Ballinalee Village.

McMANUS:(23): James, John, James at Barry (Ballymahon D.E.D.). John, John at Aghakilmore. James at Corrabaun (Breanrisk D.E.D.). James at Aghamore Lower. Owen at Annagh (Drumgort D.E.D.). Patrick, Francis, James, James, John at Cornacullew. Peter at Drumlish. Catherine at Drumlish Village. Terence at Cloonageeher. Henry at Clooneen (Kennedy). Margaret at Cloonrallagh. Patrick, Owen, at Corneddan. Peter at Esker South. Joseph at Bog Lane, Longford Town. John H. at Main Street, Longford Town. *ALSO:* Mary at Patrick Reilly's of Ballymahon Town. John and Annie at Carty's of Lislea (Lislea D.E.D.). Patrick at Kelly's of Ballynacross (Granard Urban D.E.D.). Maggie M. at Moody's of Main Street, Granard Town. Catherine at Mallon's of Aghanoran. Mary at Patrick Hourican's of Corrinagh. James at Donohoe's of Annagh (Drumgort D.E.D.). Anne at Gorman's of Lettergonnell. Patrick at Corcoran's of Graffoge (Ardagh West D.E.D.). Maria at Creaghton's of Little Water Street, Longford Town.

MARA: Michael at Pallas More.

MARKEY: James at Ball Alley Street Upper, Granard Town. Thomas Main Street, Granard Town. *ALSO:* Patrick J. and Rosanna at Mary Brady's of Main Street, Granard Town.

MARLOW: Thomas at Torboy. Joseph at Aghnasillagh. Michael at Curry (Kilcommock D.E.D.). James at Castlerea. *ALSO:* Annie at Hopkin's of Island. Thomas at Anne Ward's of Bawn (Ardagh West D.E.D.).

MARSDEN: James at Glebe (Cloondara D.E.D.).

MARSHALL: Michael at Kilsallagh. Patrick at Bog Lane, Longford Town.

MARSHALLS: William at Callaghan's of Richmond Street, Longford Town.

MARTIN:(35): Mathew at Kinard. Ann at Ballymahon Town. James at Lyneen. Bridget at Cloonbreany. Rose at Foygh. Rose at Kilshruley. Bernard at Aghagreagh. Thomas at Molly. James at Drumderg. James at Carrickadorrish. Daniel at Granardkill (Granard Urban D.E.D.). William at Moxham Street, Granard Town.   Catherine at Cornadrung. Ellen at Drumard. Owen at Queensland. Anne at Monadarragh. Thomas at Rinnenny. Rev. Terence at Edgeworthstown Town. Philip, John at Edenmore. Bernard at Kiltycreevagh. Bryan at Aghamore Lower. Bridget, Bridget at Annagh (Drumgort D.E.D.). John at Leggagh. Isabella S. at Moneylagan. William at Knappoge (Cloondara D.E.D.). William at Magheraveen. Peter at Barnacor (Rathcline D.E.D.). Charles at Bleanavoher. Ellen at Gorteengar. Michael at Tullyvrane. Roger at Back of the Hill. Mary at Drumbaun. Henry at Farraghroe. *ALSO:* William J. at Wilson's of

Main Street, Keenagh Village. John and Michael at Donnelly's of Drumnahara. Patrick at Reilly's of Ranaghan. Owen at John Sheridan's of Springtown. Bridget at John Reilly's (19) of Aghnagarron. Owen at Flanagan's of Main Street, Granard Town. Kate at Bernard Reilly's of Drumury. Bridget at Kelly's of Ballaghgowla and Froghan. Mary at Clarke's of Cloonback. Patrick at Bridget Donnelly's of Kiltycreevagh. Philip at Ballymahon or Castlerea Barracks. Catherine at Hanly's of Lehery. Patrick et al. at Kelly's of Drumroe. Michael at Hughes's of Drumbaun. Michael at Hugh Corcoran's of Rabbitpark. W. at Duncan McGregor's of Lisbrack (Longford Rural D.E.D.). Elizabeth et al. at McCartin's of Demesne.

MARTYN: John at Larkfield. *ALSO:* Sr. Catherine at Rev. Mother Farrington's of Newtownforbes Village.

MASKELL: E. at Hewetson's of Church Street, Longford Town.

MASON: John at Ballymacshane. William at Carn. Robert at Corry (Kilglass D.E.D.). *ALSO:* Esther S. at Dowler's of Lisnamuck.

MASTERSON:(48): John J. at Drumanure. Bridget at Roos. Mary at Abbeylara Village. Patrick at Cloonfin. James at Aghnagarron. Michael, John, John at Rincoolagh. Patrick at Rinroe. John at Ball Alley Street Upper, Granard Town. John at Coolagherty. John, Peter at Derragh. Margaret, Owen at Smear. John, Patrick, John, Peter, Thomas, Francis, Ellen at Enaghan. John at Aghagah. Francis at Drumhalry. Francis at Drumury. Peter, William, Margaret, Bernard, Bernard, Daniel, Michael at Farmullagh. Michael at Kilmore. Bridget at Cam. James at Lisnagrish. Mary at Cranalagh More. Thomas at Lisnageeragh. Thomas, John at Edgeworthstown Town. John at Creelaghta. James at Aghamore Lower. Edward, Bernard at Corglass. Maria, Peter, Mary at Leggagh. Thomas at Clooncoose (Cloonee D.E.D.). Joseph at Creeve. *ALSO:* James at Carrigy's of Glenoghil. John at Clarke's of Roos. Catherine at James Flood's (2) of Ballinrooey. Catherine at Markey's of Ball Alley Street Upper, Granard Town. Ellen at Treacy's of Ball Alley Street Upper, Granard Town. Bernard at Macken's of Barrack Street, Granard Town. John and Patrick at Sullivan's of Main Street, Granard Town. Patrick et al. at Thomas Connolly's of Ballyduffy. John at Patrick O'Donnell's of Cam. Margaret at McCormack's of Cranalagh More. Mary at Langan's of Aghafin. Michael at Anne Fox's of Edgeworthstown Town. James at John Davis's of Cornafunshin. Thomas at Mallon's of Lettergonnell. Mary at Brady's of Lettergonnell. Rev. Thomas at Mulligan's of Lanesborough Village. Catherine at Leavy's of Lisduff (Longford Rural D.E.D.). Ellen at Reynolds's of Healy's Terrace, Longford Town. Joseph at James Brady's of Main Street, Longford Town. Thomas and Bridget at Madden's of Bridget Street, Longford Town.

MATHERSON: A. at Hewetson's of Church Street, Longford Town.

MATTHEWS, MATHEWS:(16): Richard at Clogh (Kilcommock D.E.D.). William at Laughil (Kilcommock D.E.D.). Bernard at Foygh. James, Edward, Michael at Clooneen (Creevy D.E.D.). Peter at New Road, Granard Town. Henry, John, Julia, Patrick at Toome (Mullanalaghta D.E.D.). George at Cloonshannagh or Coolamber Manor Demesne. Alicia at Templeton Glebe. John at Great Water Street, Longford Town. John (absent from No. 26), Margaret at Main Street, Longford Town. *ALSO:* Jane M. at Clarke's of Roos. Aggie at Jarratt's of Lismoy.

MAXWELL: James at Forgney. John at Coolcraff. Mary at Corragarrow (Caldragh D.E.D.). Bridget at Garvey's Yard, Longford Town. John at Little Water Street, Longford Town. Thomas C. (absent from No. 73) at Main Street, Longford Town. *ALSO:* Mary at Fegan's of Rathmore (Ballymahon D.E.D.). Mary A. at McGaver's of Bridge Street, Longford Town.

MAY, MAYE: Christopher at Clooncallow. John at Cloonkeen (Ballymahon D.E.D.). (See Mee).

MAYALL: S.F. at Hewetson's of Church Street, Longford Town.

MAYBERRY, MAYBURY: Sarah at Mason's of Ballymacshane. Lily at Neill's of Edgeworthstown Town. John at Addy's of Richmond Street, Longford Town.

MAYE: See May.

MAYNE: Nathaniel at Abbeycartron.

McCORMACK, McKENNA etc: (See Cormack, Kenna, etc). Be careful with these surnames as McCarthy, McGlynn, etc, may be written synonymously for Carthy, Glynn, etc. and vice versa.

MEAGHER: James at Annie Flood's of Edgeworthstown Town. (See Maher).

MEARLY: Michael at Ballagh (Cashel West D.E.D.). Bridget at Ballyrevagh. John at Corrool (Brennan).

MEE: James, Ellen at Keel (Forgney D.E.D.). *ALSO:* Mary and Katie at Murphy's of Keel (Forgney D.E.D.). (See May).

MEEHAN: Elizabeth at Pallas Beg. Peter at Ballindagny and Cullyvore. Joseph at Edgeworthstown Town. Joseph at Kilmore Upper. John at

Bundoon. Mary at Ballymahon Street, Longford Town. Stephen at Broderick's Yard, Longford Town. Bridget at St. Michael's Road, Longford Town. *ALSO:* John at Finnegan's of Pallas More. Anne at Conway's of Ardnacassagh. John at O'Connor's of Conroy's Court, Longford Town. Martin at Creaghton's of Little Water Street, Longford Town.

MELEADY: See Mulleady.

MELERVY: See Mullervy.

MELIA: John at Derryglash.

MELOY: William at Ross's of Main Street, Longford Town.

MERNAGH: James at Shanmullagh.

MERRICK: William at Soran.

MERRIGAN: John at Corrool (Kenny). *ALSO:* Rose at Michael Healy's of Corrool (Brennan).

MERRIMAN: Michael, Peter at Shanmullagh.

MEYER: Otto at Carrickboy.

MIDDLEMISS: C. at Hewetson's of Church Street, Longford Town.

MIDDLETON: Emma at Corrabola (Doory D.E.D.).

MILEY: John, James at Derryveagh. Thomas at Lisduff (Montgomery). *ALSO:* Bridget at Armstrong's of Creevagh Beg, Ballymahon Town. Mary at Dolan's of Killashee Village. Patrick at Boyce's of Cloonahard.

MILLER, MILLAR: Euphemia at Ratharney. John W., Mary at Tully (Agharra D.E.D.). John A. at Clontymullan. George A. at Corrabola (Foxhall D.E.D.). Thomas H. at Kinard. Charles at Cartronawar (Kilcommock D.E.D.). George J. at Edgeworthstown Town. Elizabeth at Cloonsheerin. *ALSO:* Charlotte at Poe's of Glebe (Ballymahon D.E.D.). William H. at Martin's of Knappoge (Cloondara D.E.D.). William J. at Boyd's of Main Street, Longford Town.

MILLIGAN: P. at Hewetson's of Church Street, Longford Town.

MILLS:(14): Thomas at Abbeyshrule. James at Cloonbrin. Maria, Susan at Drumanure. Robert B. at Clooneen (Forgney D.E.D.). Ellen at Cornamucklagh. Thomas, Alexander at Pallas Beg. Richard at Cartron

(Forgney D.E.D.). John at Greenhall Upper. Stephen, Joseph at Main Street, Keenagh Village. Thomas A. at Moor. Stephen at Moyra and Fortmill. *ALSO:* Maria at Stoney's of Glebe (Kilglass D.E.D.). William at John P. Shaw's of Ballymahon Town. Mary at Hall's of Kilmakinlan. Edward at More O'Ferrall's of Lissard. Sarah at Fetherston's of Ardagh Demesne. James at Kenny's of Bohermore. Georgina A. at Anne Hall's of Moor. John at Little's of Main Street, Longford Town.

MIMNAGH, MIMNAUGH, MIMNA:(21): John at Willsbrook. Anne at Shanmullagh. James, John at Cloonellan. James at Prucklish. Francis at Bawn (Breanrisk D.E.D.). Patrick, Bridget, John, Catherine, Bridget at Cloonagh (Breanrisk D.E.D.). Bridget, John, Peter, Rose at Kilnashee. James at Cartrongolan. Patrick at Derrynacross. Anne, Peter at Corneddan. Patrick at Farnagh. James at Great Water Street, Longford Town. *ALSO:* Thomas at Rose Lynch's of Lettergeeragh. John et al. at Richard Molloy's of Cloonellan. Patrick at Catherine Quinn's of Cloonagh (Breanrisk D.E.D.). Ellie at Mollaghan's of Derrynacross. James at Sesnan's of Newtownforbes Village.

MINER: John at Tinnynarr.

MINORS: Florry et al. at Casserly's of Lislea (Lislea D.E.D.).

MITCHELL: John at Ballyclamay. Benjamin at Curry (Kilcommock D.E.D.). James at Cartronlebagh. *ALSO:* Bridget at Farrington's of Newtownforbes Village. A. at Hewetson's of Church Street, Longford Town.

MOFFETT, MOFFIT: Mary at Creevagh Beg, Ballymahon Town. Kate at Cloonfiugh. *ALSO:* Peter at Ballymahon Barracks.

MOINEY: John at Gray's of Kiltycon.

MOLLAGHAN, MOLLOGHAN:(18): Francis at Aghamore (Ballinalee D.E.D.). James at Lisnageeragh. Ellen, Francis at Aghadowry. Margaret at Breanrisk. Bernard at Cloonellan. Patrick at Cloonelly. Francis at Cornacullew. James, Francis at Cartrongolan. James, Catherine at Derawley. John at Derrynacross. John at Kilmahon. Thomas at Ballagh (Achmuty). James at Clontumpher. Michael at Esker South. Thomas at Soran. *ALSO:* Francis and James at Beatty's of Main Street, Granard Town. John and Patrick at Catherine Kiernan's (2) of Cartrongolan. Ellen and Rose at Farrington's of Newtownforbes Village. Loretto at Doherty's of Market Square, Longford Town.

MOLLOY:(30): Edward at Mornin. Patrick at Clygeen. John, Patrick at Abbeylara Village. James at Ballinrud East. Thomas at Ballyboy. James at

Ballymaurice (Granard Rural D.E.D.). James at Aghaboy (Milltown D.E.D.). Garrett at Coolagherty. Michael at Curry (Coolamber D.E.D.). Margaret at Creelaghta. Patrick, Richard at Cloonellan. Anne, Thomas, Mathew, Mathew at Barragh Beg. James at Barragh More. John at Monaduff. Michael, Bridget, Richard, Patrick, Bridget at Derryheelan. Peter, John at Dooroc. Bernard at Ballymahon Street, Longford Town. Michael P. at Main Street, Longford Town. Michael at Noud's Yard, Longford Town. Teresa at New Street, Longford Town. *ALSO:* James at Doyle's of Ballynascraw. Thomas at Lynch's of Cartronbore. Marianne at Markey's of Main Street, Granard Town. Thomas at Salmon's of Lisnaneane. Bridget at Connell's of Breanriskcullew. Bridget at Ellen Griffin's of Breanrisk. Jane at Mahon's of Leggagh. Mary A. at Feehily's of Monaduff. Margaret at Cox's of Ballymahon Street, Longford Town. Jane at Patrick Dolan's of Dublin Street, Longford Town. William at Ross's of Main Street, Longford Town (?). James at Devine's of Sandy Row, Longford Town.

MOLONEY: Michael at Currygrane. *ALSO:* Mary at Connor's of Newtown (Killashee D.E.D.). (See Maloney).

MOLPHY: John at Gneeve. Michael at Edgeworthstown Town. *ALSO:* Joseph at Thomas Flood's of Rath. (See Murphy).

MONAGHAN, MONAHAN:(26): Rev. John at Killeendowd. William at Clontymullan. Edward, Catherine, Patrick at Aghagreagh. Peter at Aghaward. John at Newtownbond. Patrick at Cloghchurnel. John at Toneen (Firry D.E.D.). Patrick, John, Patrick at Ballymore. Thomas at Leitrim (Granard Rural D.E.D.). John, John, Margaret at Ball Alley Street Upper, Granard Town. Thomas at Balnagall (Granard Urban D.E.D.). James at Barrack Street, Granard Town. Michael at Asnagh. Philip at Ferskill. Anne at Tonywardan. Daniel at Ballyduffy. Thomas at Cam. Thomas at Clonwhelan. Patrick at Edgeworthstown Town. James at Abbeycartron. *ALSO:* Mary at Carty's of Cartronbore. Kate at Mary Nannery's of Ballymore. Catherine at Flood's of Main Street, Granard Town. John at John Burns' of Main Street, Granard Town. Kate at Thompson's of Rathcronan. James at McGivney's of Ardagullion. Edward at Dermody's of Tonywardan. Bridget at McGlade's of Polladooey. John at Murphy's of Lisryan. Michael at Thomas Fenlon's of Edgeworthstown Town. John at Moran's of Lyanmore. Julia M. at Green's of Convent Lane, Longford Town. Bridget at McNamara's of Main Street, Longford Town.

MONCRIEFF: Thomas, Hannah at Pallas Beg. Hugh at Glebe (Rathcline D.E.D.).

MONGAN: James at Fee's Terrace, Longford Town (?).

MONGEY: Lawrence at Payne's of Moor.

MONLEY, MONLY: Thomas et al. at Michael Farrell's of Edgeworthstown Town. (See Manley).

MONTFORD: John at Main Street, Granard Town.

MONTGOMERY: Richard A. at Ballymahon Town. James at Glebe (Cloondara D.E.D.). Alexander at Mucknagh. Robert at Dublin Street, Longford Town. *ALSO:* Anne at Cox's of Carn. George at Mansergh's of Ballinalee Village. Sarah J. at Jones's of Cloonageeher. John at Yorke's of Cartronawar (Corboy D.E.D.). George F. at Harris's of Main Street, Longford Town.

MOODY: William T. at Main Street, Granard Town.

MOONEY: Patrick at Newpark. *ALSO:* Minnie at Leonard's of Drumanure. P. at Ballina Barracks. Patrick at Duffy's of Leggagh. John at O'Brien's of Drumlish Village. Mary at Ellen at Farrington's of Newtownforbes Village. Lawrence at Payne's of Moor (?).

MOONLIGHT: James at Fee's Terrace, Longford Town.

MOORCROFT: John at Kiltyreher (Templemichael Civil Ph.). *ALSO:* Alfred at McVitty's of Aghnashannagh.

MOORE:(15): Rev. Patrick at Cartronawar (Kilcommock D.E.D.). Thomas at Aghnashannagh. John at Ballybrien. Honor at Ballymore. James at Ball Alley Street Upper, Granard Town. William at Main Street, Granard Town. Thomas at Tully (Milltown D.E.D.). John at Cleenrah. Patrick at Monadarragh. Patrick at Bracklon. Ellen at Ballincurry. Mary at Corglass. John at Mullolagher. Anne S. at New Street, Longford Town. Peter at Richmond Street, Longford Town. *ALSO:* Anne at Gray's of Abbeylara. Rose at John Ward's of Main Street, Granard Town. Mary at McGivney's of Asnagh. Alexander at John Jackson's of Culloge. Michael at Quinn's of Edgeworthstown Town. William at Peter J. Joyce's of Edgeworthstown Town. John at McDonagh's of Cartronlebagh. Thomas at McCormack's of Feraghfad. Patrick at O'Connor's of Conroy's Court, Longford Town. Thomas F. at Robinson's of Earl Street, Longford Town.

MOORHEAD, MOOREHEAD: Sarah at Leitrim (Ballinalee D.E.D.). Anne at Drummeel. Alexander at Creelaghta. Margaret A., William at Rhine. William G. at Demesne. *ALSO:* Anne at Kenny's of Drummeel. William H. at Boyer's (2) of Main Street, Longford Town. W. at Hewetson's of Church Street, Longford Town.

MORAEN: John at Coach Yard, Longford Town.

MORAN:(30): James at Abbeyshrule. Bridget at Drumanure. Anne at Cloghan (Doory D.E.D.). Michael at Torboy. Patrick at Carrigeen (Foxhall D.E.D.). Edward, John, Edward at Clontymullan. Bernard at Ballintober (Bonny). John at Lisnacreevy. Anne, Catherine at Tennalick. Patrick at Ballymahon Town. Michael, Matthew, Michael at Cloonard (Ballymahon D.E.D.). Patrick at Ballina. Michael at Collum. Mary at Foygh. Margaret at Derragh. Thomas at Garrowhill. William at Cloonart South. Elizabeth at Ballykenny. Patrick at Trillickacurry. John at Carrowroe. Patrick at Lismacmanus. Maria at Lanesborough Village. Thomas at Lyanmore. John at Coach Yard, Longford Town (?). Maria at Main Street, Longford Town. *ALSO:* Mary at Slator's of Cartron (Forgney D.E.D.). James at Langan's of Furze. Laurence at Elizabeth Mulvihill's (109) of Ballymahon Town. Patrick at Francis McDonagh's of Cloonard (Ballymahon D.E.D.). Kate at James Walsh's of Toome (Ballymahon D.E.D.). Rebecca M. and Elizabeth at Elizabeth Fallon's of Cullentragh (Rathcline Civil Ph.). John at Higgins's of Abbeyderg (?). Kate at Edgeworth's of Kilshruley. Katie at Browne's of Aghaboy (Milltown D.E.D.). Peter at Farrell Sheridan's of Carrickmaguirk. Judy at Mary McKiernan's of Drumhalry. James at O'Connor's of Ballymahon Street, Longford Town. Kate at Maria Hughes's of Dublin Street, Longford Town. Susanna at Waters' of Main Street, Longford Town. T. at Hewetson's of Church Street, Longford Town.

MORE O'FERRALL: Edward at Lissard.

MORGAN: Patrick at Ballyhoolivan. Charles at Glannagh. Patrick, William A. at Lisnanagh. John at Lisryan. Patrick at Cranalagh More. Lizzie at Cloonmacart. John at Greagh. Bridget at Drumhaughly. Patrick at Farraghroe. William at Killeter. Joseph at Rhine. James (?), Edward at Fee's Terrace, Longford Town. *ALSO:* Mary at McLaughlin's of Lisnanagh. Anna at Kiernan's of Greagh. William at Arthur Holmes's of Kilmore Lower.

MORGANTI: Teresa at Elizabeth Kelly's of Dublin Street, Longford Town (?).

MORRAN: John at Higgins's of Abbeyderg.

MORRIS:(13): John at Abbeyshrule. Thomas at Cloonbrin. John at Killeen (Foxhall D.E.D.). Mary at Ball Alley Street Upper, Granard Town. Edward, Peter, John at Carrickmaguirk. Edward at Crott. John, James at Drumhalry. Thomas at Fihoragh. Mary at Leggagh. Mary at Lettergonnell. *ALSO:* Patrick at Margaret Garrahan's of Lissawarriff. Margaret at Farrell Sheridan's of Carrickmaguirk. Fanny at Free's of Cooleeny. W. at Hewetson's of Church Street, Longford Town.

MORRISON: Joseph, Alexander at Edenmore. John at Glenmore

(Ballinamuck East D.E.D.). Alexander at Ballagh (Newtownforbes D.E.D.). *ALSO:* Bridget at Catherine Mahon's of Ballymahon Town. Maria at James Wiggins's of Rathmore (Ballinamuck East D.E.D.). J.W. at Hewetson's of Church Street, Longford Town.

MORRISSEY, MORRISEE: Patrick at Conroy's Court, Longford Town. *ALSO:* Edward J. at Charles Sheridan's of Dublin Street, Longford Town.

MORROW: James at Carrickateane. William at Drumderg. Mary at Caldragh. James at Soran. *ALSO:* Robert et al. at Farrell's of Kilshruley. Elizabeth at Sheridan's of Fihoragh. Albert at Samuel Wilson's of Main Street, Longford Town.

MORTON: Annie L. at Templeton Glebe.

MOUGAN: James at Fee's Terrace, Longford Town (?).

MOUGHTY: Lucy at Daroge. Catherine at Ballynahinch. James, Margaret at Gorteenclareen. (See Auchmuty).

MOUTRAY: Stella at Jessop's of Doory.

MOWBRAY: Thomas at Preston's of Cartronboy.

MOXHAM: John at Killeenboy. Isaiah at Ratharney. James at Tennalick. *ALSO:* Louisa at John Poynton's of Derryveagh.

MUHLOW: Per A. at Harris's of Bridge Street, Longford Town.

MUIR: John at Edgeworthstown Town.

MULALLY: See Mullally.

MULCRONE, MULCHRONE: See McCrone.

MULDOON: James at Clooncallow. Bridget at Tirlickeen. Mary at Aghavadden. Christopher at Ballinalee Village. *ALSO:* Catherine at Donohoe's of Ballyglassin. John at Higgins's of Cartrons (Kilcommock D.E.D.). Peter at Monahan's of Toneen (Firry D.E.D.). James at Lynch's of Crossea South. Kate at Lyons's of Clooncoose (Cloonee D.E.D.).

MULDOWNEY: James at Clooncolligan. *ALSO:* Bernard and Rose A. at Corcoran's of Clooncolligan.

MULFALL, MULFAUL: Michael at Screeboge. Catherine at Cooleeshil or Richfort. James, Owen, John at Cartrongarrow. *ALSO:* Elizabeth et al.

at Mary Farrell's (15) of Castlerea Mountain.

MULHALL: Richard at Middleton.

MULHARE, MULHAIRE: Hugh at Ballymore. Bernard at Ferskill. Owen at Clonca. Francis at Ringowny. Denis at Edgeworthstown Town.

MULHERN, MULHERAN: Mary at Crockaun. Ellen at Conroy's Court, Longford Town. Rose at Convent Lane, Longford Town. Michael at Glack (Longford Urban No. 1 D.E.D.).

MULHILL: Charles at Kilfintan. Andrew at Monadarragh.

MULLADY: See Mulleady.

MULLALLY, MULALLY: Hugh at Kilshruley. Felix at Newtownforbes Village. Catherine at Ballykenny. Patrick at Rhine. Elizabeth at Great Water Street, Longford Town. *ALSO:* Catherine at Cathcart's of Ballyreaghan. Mary A. at Muldoon's of Ballinalee Village. Sr. Kate at Sr. Green's of Convent Lane, Longford Town. Bridget at Belford's of Great Water Street, Longford Town. Martin at Thomas McCormack's of Great Water Street, Longford Town. Mary E. et al. at Cahill's of Great Water Street, Longford Town.

MULLANIFF: Henry at Lamagh. Luke at Lismoy. Edward at Cloonbalt.

MULLANY, MULLANEY: James at Garrycam. Patrick at Keel (Kilglass D.E.D.). Peter at Claras. *ALSO:* James at Mahon's of Leggagh.

MULLEADY, MULLADY, MELEADY:(11): John, James at Edera. Bridget at Gorteenclareen. Bernard at Monadarragh. Patrick at Derryheelan. John at Clontumpher. Catherine at Nappagh. John at Kilmoyle. Simon, John at Mucknagh. Bridget at Harbour Row, Longford Town. *ALSO:* John at Corrigan's of Curraghmore. Patrick et al. at Leavey's of Ledwithstown (Kilcommock Civil Ph.). Thomas at Carleton's of Culloge. Patrick at Skelly's of Lisrevagh. Margaret at Campbell's of Farraghroe. Mary at McNerney's of New Street, Longford Town.

MULLEN, MULLIN:(20): John at Abbeyshrule. James at Cloonbrin. Julia at Drumanure. Michael, Thomas at Ratharney. Bridget at Corrabaun (Doory D.E.D.). Patrick at Rath. Peter at Killinbore. Patrick at Barry (Ballymahon D.E.D.). Owen at Ballynascraw. John at Ballinalee Village. James at Drummeel. William at Main Street, Granard Town. Thomas at Moxham Street, Granard Town. Thomas at Gneeve. James at Lissanure. Patrick at Carrickglass Demesne (Templemichael Civil Ph.). Thomas at Rhine. John at Chapel Lane, Longford Town. James at St. Michael's Road, Longford

Town. *ALSO:* Patrick et al. at John Kenny's of Drumanure. John at Greene's of Liscahill.

McMULLEN: Martha at Morton's of Templeton Glebe.

MULLERVY, MALERVY, MELERVY: Francis at Knockanbaun or Whitehill. James at Lislea (Lislea D.E.D.). James at Derawley. Patrick, Michael at Drumlish. Owen at Monaduff. Terence at Drumlish Village. James at Briskil. *ALSO:* John and Michael at Ellen Ellis's of Cloonellan.

MULLIGAN:(90): Andrew at Cloonard (Ballymahon D.E.D.). Patrick, Michael at Glenohil. Patrick at Breaghy. Owen, Thomas at Aghacordrinan. Thomas at Aghakilmore. John at Gelshagh. Julia, Myles at Culray. Rose, Michael, Anne at Aghakeeran. Patrick, James at Aghakine. Kate, Mary at Aghnacliff. Mary at Carrickadorrish. Catherine, John, Patrick, Owen, Owen, Patrick, Annie at Sonnagh. Laurence, Edward at Ballywillin. Edward at Springtown. Patrick at Clooneen (Creevy D.E.D.). John at Druminacrehir. James at Cloghchurnel. James at Ballinulty Lower. Charles at Main Street, Granard Town. James at The Hill, Granard Town. Bridget at Ardagullion. Francis at Tonywardan. Michael at Willsbrook. Thomas at Carrickmaguirk. Margaret, Patrick at Cleenrah. Bartholomew, Owen, Johanna at Dunbeggan (Columbkille D.E.D.). Francis at Rosduff. Catherine, Rose at Smear. Mary, Edward, Edward, Philip, Patrick, Julia, Philip, John, Patrick, John, Edward at Crott. Francis, Elizabeth, Edward, James, James at Enaghan. Patrick at Lisraherty. John at Ballyduffy. Patrick, Michael at Birrinagh. William at Drumhalry. John at Larkfield. Hugh at Freaghmeen. Andrew at Edgeworthstown Town. Charles, Michael, John, Anne at Cloonback. Sarah at Cuingareen. Patrick, John at Rathmore (Ballinamuck East D.E.D.). Michael at Glenmore (Ballinamuck East D.E.D.). Rose at Cloncowley. Peter, Daniel at Moyne. Peter at Annagh (Drumgort D.E.D.). Philip at Cornacullew. William, Thomas at Leggagh. Edward at Aghnaskea. Patrick at Moygh (Killashee D.E.D.). Laurence at Templeton Glebe. Patrick at Carrowmanagh. James at Lanesborough Village. *ALSO:* Mary at Joseph Gannon's of Ballymahon Town. Mary at Lynch's of Ballinrooey. Owen at Patrick Smyth's of Culray. Patrick at Thomas Donohoe's (28) of Aghakine. Annie at Edward Farrelly's of Carrickadorrish. Peter and Kate at Doyle's of Carrickadorrish. Denis et al. at Julia Columb's (29) of Sonnagh. Maggie and Thomas at Reilly's of Ballywillin. James at Cronogue's of Ballinlough. Peter et al. at Ford's of Bunlahy. Peter at David Jones's (5) of Carrickduff. Patrick at Flood's of Rathbrackan. Thomas at Kiernan's of Ballinulty Lower. Philip and Mary at Catherine Reilly's of Rathcor. Thomas at O'Neill's of Ballymaurice (Granard Rural D.E.D.). Ellen at John Magore's of Cartron (Granard Rural D.E.D.). Owen at Fox's of Barrack Street, Granard Town. Mary A. at Condron's of Camagh (Newgrove D.E.D.). Thomas at Michael Donohoe's of Carrickmaguirk. Anne at Carter's of Cleenrah. Patrick at Margaret Gormley's (8) of Polladooey. Patrick at

Patrick Doyle's of Smear. John at Gaynor's of Lisryan. Andrew at Molphy's of Edgeworthstown Town. William at Jobe's of Rathmore (Ballinamuck East D.E.D.). Kate at William Anderson's of Rathmore (Ballinamuck East D.E.D.). Mary at Owen Reilly's of Rathmore (Ballinamuck East D.E.D.). Charles at Donohoe's of Fostragh. Thomas and Ellen at McCabe's of Corglass. Katie at Farrelly's of Kiltycon. Rose at John Taaffe's (9) of Leggagh. William at Paul Duignan's (14) of Leggagh. Thomas at McQuaid's of Drumlish Village. Annie at Patrick Brady's (20) of Gaigue. Thomas at Bridget Kiernan's of Gaigue.

MULLIN: See Mullen.

MULLOOLY:(11): Peter at Tirlickeen. Thomas at Derryoghil. Michael at Derryad (Mountdavis D.E.D.). John at Cloonfore. Patrick at Formoyle (Farrell). James at Killinure. Bridget, Joseph, Michael at Lehery. John at Tullyvrane. John at St. Mel's Road, Longford Town.

MULREADY: Mary at Atkinson's of Main Street, Longford Town.

MULRY: James, Bernard at Derrynagalliagh.

MULRYAN: James at Moatfarrell. Laurence at Barne. William at Lissanure. Catherine at Lisnageeragh. *ALSO:* John and Katie at Shanly's of Castlebrock. (See Ryan).

MULSTAY: See McStay.

MULVANY: Patrick at Cornamucklagh. Francis at Carrickadorrish. *ALSO:* Mary and Michael at McCormack's of Cranalagh More. Bridget at Flood's of Cornapark. Kate A. at Patrick Flood's of Glen. Margaret at John Mulfall's of Cartrongarrow. Christopher at Bernard Doyle's of Garvagh (Longford Rural D.E.D.).

MULVENNA: See McVenna.

MULVEY, MULVY:(18): Alice at Ardanragh. Michael at Lissawarriff. Mary, James, Edward at Ballintober (Bonny). Anne at Tennalick. James, Bernard at Derynagalliagh (?). Anne, Peter at Aghakilmore. James at Robinstown. Francis at Churchquarter. Michael at Granardkill (Granard Urban D.E.D.). Margaret at Willsbrook. Thomas at Lisraherty. Patrick at Drumhalry. Jane at Cloonbalt. Michael at Creeve. *ALSO:* Bridget at Flood's of Legan. John at Hugh Flood's of Ballymahon Town. Patrick et al. at Duffy's of Cavan. Michael at O'Reilly's of Clooneen (Creevy D.E.D.). Francis and Mary at Patrick Mulligan's of Rathmore (Ballinamuck East D.E.D.). Bridget at Martin's of Leggagh. Cornelius at Hoare's of Deanscurragh. Francis at Wallace's of McLoughlin's Yard, Longford Town.

MULVIHILL:(35): Maria at Cloonbrin. Catherine at Clooncullen. Edward at Ballymulvey. Bryan at Moygh (Ballymahon D.E.D.). John, Elizabeth, Elizabeth at Ballymahon Town. John at Cormaglava. John at Forthill. Michael, Catherine at Ballyrevagh. John, Christopher at Cornadowagh. Bridget at Corrool (Fox). Annie at Cross (Cashel West D.E.D.). John at Drumnee. Patrick, Michael at Leab. Patrick at Loughfarm. Mary, Bridget, Mary at Pollagh. Catherine, Christopher, Michael at Portanure. Francis at Cullentragh (Rathcline Civil Ph.). Mary at Foygh. Andrew at Ldwithstown (Kilcommock Civil Ph.). Isabella at Ardoghil. Owen at Begnagh. Annie, Michael at Rappareehill. John at Toneen (Moydow D.E.D.). Thomas at Knock. Francis (absent from home) at Bawn (Ardagh West D.E.D.). *ALSO:* Maria at Loughran's of Lissakit. Bridget at Poynton's of Cornacarta. Francis et al. at Catherine Finn's (2) of Moygh (Ballymahon D.E.D.). Hugh and Mary at Fox's of Tirlickeen. Sr. Angela at Rev. Mother Whelan's of Ballymahon Town. Maggie at Flood's of Knappoge (Ballymahon D.E.D.). Patrick at Ward's of Cloonmee. Anne at Egan's of Elfeet (Burke). Patrick et al. at James Costello's of Pollagh. Bessie at Clarke's of Portanure. William and Michael at Payne's of Derrycolumb. Thomas at McGaver's of Cloonsellan. Michael et al. at Murtagh's of Rappareehill. Catherine at Dowd's of Cloonevit. Mary at Elizabeth Farrell's of Lehery. Patrick at Fullam's of Deanscurragh. Mary at Patrick Dolan's of Dublin Street, Longford Town.

MUMFORD: Catherine at Great Water Street, Longford Town.

MURPHY:(84): Edward at Ratharney. Edward at Lissawarriff. Mary at Cloonfide. Peter at Keel (Forgney D.E.D.). Mary at Ballintober (Bonny). James at Liscormick. Margaret at Kilnacarrow (Kilglass D.E.D.). William at Ballymahon Town. John at Creevaghmore (Forgney Civil Ph.). Michael at Coolnahinch (Kilcommock D.E.D.). Maria at Edera. John at Currygrane. Francis at Laughil (Edgeworth). James, Catherine, William at Aghagreagh. Patrick at Gelshagh. Elizabeth at Drumderg. Thomas at Ballinulty Lower. Mary at Rincoolagh. Michael at Carragh (Granard Urban D.E.D.). Terence, Edward at New Road, Granard Town. Peter at Carrickmaguirk. John at Ballyduffy. Patrick at Cloonagh (Mullanalaghta D.E.D.). William, John, William at Larkfield. Michael at Lisryan. Rose at Cartronreagh. Bernard at Edgeworthstown Town. Michael, Charles at Fostragh. Patrick, Edward, Charles, Michael, Michael at Glenmore (Ballinamuck East D.E.D.). Bridget, John at Fardrumman. Patrick at Carrickmoyragh. Peter at Prucklish. Elizabeth, Bridget at Cloonagh (Breanrisk D.E.D.). Peter at Cloonmacart. John at Aghamore Lower. Philip, John at Leggagh. Patrick, John, Patrick at Cartrongolan. Michael, Andrew, Bernard at Enybegs. John, Patrick, James, Anne at Briskil. Denis at Treel (Newtownforbes D.E.D.). Rev. Francis at Newtownforbes Village. William at Cornollen. John at Ballyclare (Killashee D.E.D.). Samuel at Sharvoge. Patrick at Ballymichan. John, Thomas at Barnacor (Rathcline D.E.D.). Michael at Lanesborough Village.

Thomas, Patrick at Aghaboy (Aghaboy D.E.D.). Catherine, John, Francis at Corneddan. Patrick, William at Esker South. Michael, Thomas, Mary A. at Soran. Katie at Bundoon. Robert at Ballynagoshen. Andrew at Feraghfad. Samuel at Cooleeny. David at Dublin Street, Longford Town. Bridget at Great Water Street, Longford Town. *ALSO:* Mary at John Donlon's of Clooncullen. Francis at Dillon's of Kilnacarrow (Kilglass D.E.D.). Ellen at Bernard McGrath's of Gorteenclareen. Patrick at John Brady's of Derryneel. Patrick at Thomas Forde's of France. Mary K. at Duffy's of Aghamore Upper. Patrick at Francis Sexton's of Aghakeeran. Bridget at Bridget Doyle's of Sonnagh. Thomas at Wrenn's of Coolcor. Lizzie et al. at Boyle's of Ballinrud Glebe. William at Hugh Briody's of Killasona. Ellen and Kate at Leavy's of Melkernagh. John at James Smyth's (56) of Main Street, Granard Town. John at Reynolds's of Ferskill. Patrick at James Kiernan's of Muckerstaff. Margaret at Philip Kinlan's of Cleenrah. Maria et al. at Malone's of Ballyduffy. Ellen at Boyle's of Drumard. Kate at Curneen's of Dring. Michael at Patrick Reilly's of Edgeworthstown Town. Catherine at James Dempsey's of Edgeworthstown Town. Anne at James McNerney's (25) of Fostragh. Mary A. at Mary Ward's of Prucklish. Edward at Patrick McAvey's of Bawn (Breanrisk D.E.D.). Sarah at Gray's of Kiltycon. William et al. at McGlynn's of Ballagh (Newtownforbes D.E.D.). Patrick at Green's of Treel (Newtownforbes D.E.D.). Lizzie and Mary at Farrington's of Newtownforbes Village. Owen at John Cox's of Clooneen (Cox). Thomas at Michael Diffley's of Cloonbrock. Kate at Gillooly's of Cloonfore. James at McNerney's of Soran. Timothy A. at Kenny's of Lenaboy. John and Anne at McEvoy's of Killeentruan. Thomas at Canning's of Knockloughlin. William at Charles Sheridan's of Dublin Street, Longford Town. John at McCullagh's of Killashee Street, Longford Town. Mary at Cameron's of Main Street, Longford Town. Elizabeth at Kennedy's of St. Michael's Road, Longford Town. Bridget at Harris's of Abbeycartron. (See Molphy).

MURRAY, MURRY:(51): Mary at Clontymullan. Anne at Ballynamanagh. Patrick at Taghshinny. Patrick at Ballymulvey. Thomas H., Elizabeth (absent from home), Elizabeth at Ballymahon Town. Anne, Thomas at Caltragh More. Michael at Aghavadden. Thomas at Claras. Michael at Cleraun. Catherine at Collum. James at Corrool (Fox). John at Portanure. Daniel at Aghnacranagh. Michael at Cloonfin. Thomas at Graffoge (Milltown D.E.D.). Patrick at Derragh. John, Michael at Barne. Hugh at Cam. John P. at Coolamber. Peter at Ballindagny and Cullyvore. Owen at Leitrim (Breanrisk D.E.D.). Michael, James at Lissanurlan. Mary at Annaghmore. Peter at Corralough. Mathew at Ballinamore. Margaret at Carrigeen (Moydow D.E.D.). Anne at Corlagan. Michael at Carrowroe. Patrick at Derrygeel. Thomas, Thomas at Rathcline. Michael at Turreen. Patrick at Rabbitpark. Hugh at Cartron Big. James at Cloonahussey. Catherine at Freehalman. John at Farranyoogan. John at Feraghfad. Michael at Ardnacassagh. Ellen, James at Great Water Street, Longford Town. Alice at Killashee Street, Longford Town. Laurence at Main Street, Longford Town. Alexander at St. Mel's Road, Longford Town. Francis at Townparks (Longford Urban No. 1 D.E.D.). John at Bridge Street, Longford Town. *ALSO:* Peter at John Skelly's of Ballymahon Town. Patrick at Ballymahon or Castlerea Barracks. John at Colo's of Creevagh Beg, Ballymahon Town. Mary K. at Rafferty's of Rathmore (Ballymahon D.E.D.). Bridget at Geraghty's of Derraghan Beg. Bridget at Michael Skally's of Claras. Mary A. at Thomas Brady's of Prucklishtown. Christian J. et al. at Devenish's of Kilbride. Thomas and Michael at Stephenson's of Ballinlough. John at Molloy's of Ballymaurice (Granard Rural D.E.D.). Anne at Charles Hall's of Cornadrung. Annie at Culligan's of Larkfield. Joseph at Boyce's of Lisnageeragh. Michael et al. at Kelly's of Bracklon. Bridget at Kennedy's of Lackan. Margaret at Kerrigan's of Edgeworthstown Town. Patrick at Kiernan's of Rathmore (Ballinamuck East D.E.D.). Patrick at Higgins's of Breanrisk. Edward and Margaret at Elizabeth McKenna's of Drumlish Village. Bridget A. at Peyton's of St. Anne's Glebe. Marcella and Mary A. at Farrington's of Newtownforbes Village. Jane at Dooner's of Curry (Moydow D.E.D.). Margaret at Shea's of Bleanavoher. Kate at Lynch's of Crossea South. Patrick at John Kenny's of Glen. Annie at Casey's of Lyanmore. Anne at Mulvihill's of Bawn (Ardagh West D.E.D.). Rose A. at Larkin's of Convent Lane, Longford Town. James at O'Connell's of Dublin Street, Longford Town. Annie et al. at Mary A. Callaghan's of Dublin Street, Longford Town. James at Chapman's of Dublin Street, Longford Town. Rose at Kinalon's of Dublin Street, Longford Town. Fr. William at Rev. Patrick Dolan's of Dublin Street, Longford Town. William at Dublin Street Barracks, Longford Town. Katie at Hobson's of Great Water Street, Longford Town. Lena at John Wilson's of Main Street, Longford Town. Annie at Noud's of Main Street, Longford Town. Margaret at Gilchriest's of Market Square, Longford Town. Ellen at Stafford's of Richmond Street, Longford Town.

MURTAGH, MURTHA, MURTA:(67): Mary at Coolnafinnoge. Margaret at Lisnacreevy. John at Kilcurry. Mary, Agnes at Ballymahon Town. John at Rathmore (Ballymahon D.E.D.). John, John, James at Forthill. James at Newpark. John at Derrycolumb. Patrick at Ballinlough. James at Ballinulty Lower. James at Ballyboy. Bridget at Grassyard. John at Main Street, Granard Town. Kate, John at Muckerstaff. Terence at Enaghan. Bridget, Terence at Drumard. John, Michael, Garret, Laurence, Elizabeth, Patrick at Cloonback. Mary, Francis, Patrick, James, John at Cuingareen. John, Garrett at Fostragh. Garrett, Patrick at Glenmore (Ballinamuck East D.E.D.). Thomas at Cloonmacart. John at Annagh (Drumgort D.E.D.). James, John at Cloonelly. Michael, John at Corglass. William at Lissagernal. John at Creenagh. Michael, John at Cloonard (Cloondara D.E.D.). Peter at Cloondara. Ann at Knappoge (Cloondara D.E.D.). Margaret at Cloonmore. Thomas at Cloonsheerin. Catherine at Killeeny. John at Moygh (Killashee D.E.D.). Patrick at Killashee Village. Patrick at Annaghmore. Thomas at

Rappareehill. Bridget, Julia at Cloonfore. Patrick at Toneen (Moydow D.E.D.). Thomas at Corneddan. James at Esker South. William at Kilnacarrow (Aghaboy D.E.D.). James at Cross (Ardagh East D.E.D.). Thomas at Cartrongarrow. John at Killeter. Bridget, James at Rhine. John at Farnagh. *ALSO:* Michael at Moran's of Lisnacreevy. Maria at Michael Delaney's of Drinan. Sophia at Wright's of Agharanagh (Ballymahon D.E.D.). Thomas and James at Casey's of Ballagh (Cashel West D.E.D.). Bridget at Kennedy's of Carrow Beg (Cashel West D.E.D.). Rose A. at Cotton's of Kilmakinlan. Patrick and Mary at Bellew's of Foygh. Mathew at Maria Reilly's of Aghamore Upper. Bridget at James Mallon's of Kilcourcey. Maria at John Duffy's of Drumhalry. Margaret at Gibson's of Drumhalry. Elizabeth at Donovan's of Edgeworthstown Town. Terence at Bridget McGuire's of Cloonback. Michael at Brady's of Fardrumman. Mary at Francis Reilly's of Tawnagh. William et al. at Kane's of Briskil. Katie at Patrick Skelly's of Knappoge (Cloondara D.E.D.). John at Telford's of Grillagh (Killashee D.E.D.). Patrick et al. at Chapman's of Lisnacush. Thomas at Bernard Kenny's of Aghaboy (Aghaboy D.E.D.).

MUSTERS: John G. at Brianstown.

MYLES: Margaret A. at Ratharney. Frederick J. at New Street, Longford Town. *ALSO:* Elizabeth and Florence at Phillips's of Glenmore (Kilcommock D.E.D.). Isabella at Finlay's of Glebe (Cloondara D.E.D.).

MYLEY: See Miley.

McNABOE, McNABO:(15): Catherine at Cranally. Owen at Culray. Peter at Bank Street, Granard Town. Peter, William, Francis at Rosduff. Mary at Crott. Michael at Enaghan. Michael at Birrinagh. John at Drumhalry. Peter at Drumury. William at Ballinroddy. Patrick at Killyfad. Edward at Kiltyreher (Killoe Civil Ph.). Edward at Cartronageeragh. *ALSO:* Mary at McNally's of Aghacordrinan. Patrick at Thomas Smith's of Culray. Ellen at Donohoe's of Aghakeeran. Mary at Anne Reilly's of Rosduff. Maggie at Patrick Nugent's of Castlenugent. Maria at Farrington's of Newtownforbes Village. Patrick at John Skelly's of Knappoge (Cloondara D.E.D.). Annie at McCarthy's of Drumhaughly. James at Hagan's of Killyfad. Rose et al. at McVitty's of Creeve. Kate at Dennigan's of Knockanboy.

McNABOLA: James at Main Street, Keenagh Village.

NAGLE: Mamie at Morris's of Leggagh.

NAILON: See Nealon.

NALLY:(10): Martin at Drumanure. Thomas at Cloonkeen (Doory D.E.D.).

Anne at Newcastle. Andrew at Clooncullen. Nicholas at Ballycloghan. Rose at Taghshinny. James, Joseph at Ballymahon Town. William at Saints Island. Nicholas at Abbeylara Village. *ALSO:* Michael at Corrigan's of Curraghmore. Honor at Flood's of Knappoge (Ballymahon D.E.D.). John and Bridget at Bridget Yorke's of Barry (Ballymahon D.E.D.). James at Bridget Heany's of Aghadegnan (Longford Rural D.E.D.). John at O'Connor's of Conroy's Court, Longford Town.

McNALLY:(32): Joseph P. at Cornadowagh. Hugh at Aghacordrinan. Thomas at Aghamore Upper. John at Gelshagh. Hugh, Michael, Anne, James at Molly. John at Killasona. Maria at Ballybrien. Bridget at Barrack Street, Granard Town. John at Mollyglass. Francis, Patrick at Glenmore (Ballinamuck East D.E.D.). Terence at Shanmullagh. Patrick, Francis, Ellen, William, Mary, Hugh at Cartrongolan. Francis at Greagh. Margaret at Oghil. Bridget at Drumlish Village. John at Corry (Caldragh D.E.D.). James at Kilmore Lower. James at Clontumpher. Patrick at Soran. James at Deerpark (Ardagh East D.E.D.). Patrick J. at Lisbrack (Longford Rural D.E.D.). John at Dwyer's Yard, Longford Town. Michael at Great Water Street, Longford Town. *ALSO:* Patrick at McNerney's of Sonnagh. Bernard at McGivney's of Ballybrien. Patrick at Brady's of Edgeworthstown Town. Patrick at Peter McGoldrick's of Currygranny. James at Mimnagh's of Cartrongolan. Michael at Christopher Newman's of Cloonrallagh. Thomas at Trott's of Lyanmore. Lizzie at Patrick Fitzgerald's (1) of Main Street, Longford Town. Bridget at Boyers' (4) of Main Street, Longford Town. Teresa at Margaret Matthews' of Main Street, Longford Town. Katie at Carothers' of Abbeycartron. Bridget at Henry's of Bridge Street, Longford Town.

McNAMARA: John at Glannagh. Hugh at Cloonagh (Mullanalaghta D.E.D.). Matthew, Bridget at Kilsallagh. Daniel at Cranalagh More. Margaret at Kilmore Lower. William J. at Main Street, Longford Town. *ALSO:* Bridget at Farrington's of Newtownforbes Village. Annie at Potterton's of Templemichael Glebe.

McNAMEE:(26): Mary, Peter at Molly. Bridget at Abbeylara Village. Philip at Ballywillin. Mary at Ballynacross (Granard Rural D.E.D.). John at Drumhalry. James at Cranalagh More. Mary, Patrick, John, James at Kiltycreevagh. Patrick at Cloonmacart. John, John, Bridget, Mary, Thomas at Cloonelly. Peter, James, John, Bridget, William at Corglass. John at Leggagh. James at Drumlish Village. Thomas at Richmond Street, Longford Town. John at St. Michael's Road, Longford Town. *ALSO:* John at Manley's of Furze. Maggie et al. at Clyne's of Ballymulvey. Bridget at Philip Sullivan's of Aghakilmore. James at James McDowell's (61) of Smear. Catherine at Dolan's of Farmullagh. Mary et al. at Mollaghan's of Cloonelly. Lizzie at Green's of Convent Lane, Longford Town.

NANGLE: Michael at Lanesborough Village. William at Richmond Street, Longford Town. *ALSO:* Patrick at John W. Sheridan's of Camagh (Newgrove D.E.D.).

NANNERY: Patrick at Listraghee. Thomas at Killasona. Thomas, Mary, William, Connor at Ballymore. Patrick at Cartron (Granard Urban D.E.D.). Mary at Moxham Street, Granard Town.

NAPIER: Thomas C. at Dublin Street Barracks, Longford Town.

McNARRY: H. at Hewetson's of Church Street, Longford Town.

NASH: Robert at Castlecore.

NATTON: Thomas at Ballymahon Town. *ALSO:* Ellen at Charles Keane's of Ballymahon Town.

NAUGHTON: Owen at Killasona.

NAVAN: Robert at Currycahill. James at Carrowlinan. William at Cornafunshin. William at Lettergonnell. George at Faghey. James at Gorteenorna. Thomas at Killyfad. (See Nevin).

NAYLOR: Alfred G. at Pollard's of Templeton Glebe.

NEALON, NAILON, NEILAN: Michael at Laughil (Adair). John at Lisraghtigan. *ALSO:* Mary at Mary Geraghty's of Ballymore. Patrick at Masterson's of Coolagherty.

NEARY, NEAREY: Kate at Lyneen. Elizabeth at Tully (Cloondara D.E.D.). Thomas at Lissanurlan. Mary at Cloonfiugh. Robert at Woodlawn. Mary at Broderick's Yard, Longford Town. *ALSO:* Patrick and Mary at Rogers' of Lismoy. Annie at Martin's of Knappoge (Cloondara D.E.D.). Thomas at Glancy's of Dublin Street, Longford Town. Annie at Mary Quinn's of Little Water Street, Longford Town. John at James Egan's of Main Street, Longford Town.

NEDLEY, NEDLY: Patrick at Ball Alley Street Upper, Granard Town. Catherine at Willsbrook.

NEEDHAM: George C. at Fallon's of Dublin Street, Longford Town.

O'NEIL: See O'Neill.

NEILAN: See Nealon.

NEILL: John at Edgeworthstown Town. Patrick at Middleton.

McNEILL: Thomas H. at St. Mel's Road, Longford Town. *ALSO:* Bella at Charles Hall's of Cornadrung.

O'NEILL, O'NEIL:(35): Patrick, Peter at Kinard. Daniel at Ballycloghan. Charles at Laragh. Owen at Ballynascraw. James at Lissameen. John at Carrickateane. Anne at Castlebaun. Bernard at Lislea (Lislea D.E.D.). John at Lisnanagh. Daniel at Ballywillin. Owen at Ballymaurice (Granard Rural D.E.D.). John at Clonwhelan. Anne at Lisnaneane. Thomas, Margaret, Maria, Patrick, Maria, Ellen at Creelaghta. James at Crowdrumman. Patrick at Drumbad. Bridget at Shanmullagh. Thomas at Breanrisk. Mary at Aghnamaddoo. John at Cloonagh (Breanrisk D.E.D.). Annie at Briskil. Francis at Cloonmore. Margaret at Grillagh (Killashee D.E.D.). Mary at Soran. Patrick at Lisduff (Montgomery). Michael at Farranyoogan. Patrick at Knockahaw. Elizabeth at Conroy's Court, Longford Town. Alexander at Main Street, Longford Town. *ALSO:* Michael at William Seales' of Ballymahon Town. James at Peter Early's of Derragh. Beesey at Patrick Gaynor's of Cranalagh More. Ellen K. at Owen Donnelly's of Kiltycreevagh. Patrick at Ballinamuck Barracks, Shanmullagh. Elizabeth at Forbes's of Castleforbes Demesne. Lucy at Farrington's of Newtownforbes Village. Michael J. at McDonagh's of Cartronlebagh. Mary at Briscoe's of Moydow Glebe. Mary at Plunkett's of Main Street, Longford Town.

NELSON: Henry at Carrickboy Barracks. Kate, Elizabeth and Kathleen at Farrington's of Newtownforbes Village.

NERIN: John at Ballywillin.

NERNEY, NERTNEY: Bernard, John at Cloonmacart. William at Cloonanny Glebe. Owen at Knappoge (Cloondara D.E.D.). *ALSO:* Thomas at Hyland's of Barrack Street, Granard Town. Mary at Thompson's of Lisnabo. Michael at John Murtagh's of Cloonard (Cloondara D.E.D.).

McNERNEY:(35): Patrick at Aghamore Upper. Francis, Anne at Molly. Charles, John at Aghakine. Peter at Aghnacliff. William at Sonnagh. Michael at Cartronamarkey. Thomas at Mullinroe. William at Carragh (Granard Rural D.E.D.). Francis, Patrick, Charles at Edenmore. James, Michael, Edward, Edward, Patrick, James, James, Charles, Francis at Fostragh. Michael, Charles at Glenmore (Ballinamuck East D.E.D.). Francis at Aghamore Lower. John at Annagh (Drumgort D.E.D.). James at Kiltycon. Michael at Oghil. Francis, Owen, Hugh, John at Gaigue. John at Soran. Anne at Rhine. Charles at New Street, Longford Town. *ALSO:* Bernard at Concannon's of Creevagh Beg. Mary A. at Martin's of Molly. Edward and Rose A. at Dunleavy's of Culleenmore. Catherine at Ellen Kiernan's of Mullinroe. Mary at Felix Donnelly's of Glenmore

(Ballinamuck East D.E.D.). Catherine at Thomas Quinn's of Bawn (Breanrisk D.E.D.). James at Patrick Corrigan's of Corglass. Anne at McDowell's of Gorteenorna. Hugh et al. at Owen Devnany's (18) of Corneddan. Elizabeth and George at James Farrell's of Glack (Longford Rural D.E.D.). Lizzie at Byrne's of Great Water Street, Longford Town.

NESBITT, NESBIT: Joseph at Rath.

NEVIN: John at Ballywillin (?). Patrick at Newtownforbes Village. Thomas at Kilmore Upper. James at Lissanurlan. Michael at Mullolagher. Susan at Market Square, Longford Town. (See Navan).

NEVINS: Owen at Casey's of Aghaward.

NEWBURN: Percy at Henry S. Burd's of Ballymahon Town.

NEWCOMEN: Robert at Abbeyshrule. Thomas at Ballyclamay. Thomas at Cornamucklagh. John at Culloge. *ALSO:* Kate at Coates' of Abbeyshrule.

NEWMAN:(23): William at Ratharney. William at Lissawarriff. Patrick at Cloonscott. Patrick at Killeen (Foxhall D.E.D.). Edward at Knocknaskea. Margaret, Patrick at Lisnacreevy. Thomas at Cartronboy. Mary at Drinan. Fr. Patrick at Ballinalee Village. Bartholomew at Cloghchurnel. Charles at Lissanure. John at Moyne. Peter at Newtownforbes Village. John, Christopher, Patrick at Cloonrallagh. James at Knockawalky. Patrick at Gragh. Mary at Lyanmore. John at Nappagh. James at Cartronawar (Corboy D.E.D.). John at Fee's Terrace, Longford Town. *ALSO:* Michael and Mary at Honoria Farrell's of Killeen (Foxhall D.E.D.). Peter at Kate Whelan's of Ballymahon Town. Michael at Gunshenan's of Drumlish Village.

NEWTON: Edward at Aghadegnan (Longford Urban No. 2 D.E.D.). *ALSO:* Dorothea at Fee's of Carrickboy.

NICHOLLS, NICOLLS: Elizabeth at Kerrigan's of Edgeworthstown Town. Bridget at Patrick Dolan's (1) of Kiltycreevagh.

NICHOLSON: Michael at James Joyce's of Main Street, Longford Town.

McNIFF, McANIFF, McKNIFF: Anne at Ballinamore. *ALSO:* Mary at Luke Farrell's of Lisnacush.

NIXON: David at Ballyduffy. Christopher at Dublin Street, Longford Town. *ALSO:* Peter at Anne Fox's of Edgeworthstown Town. Mary at Devine's of Townparks (Longford Urban No. 1 D.E.D.).

NOBLE: Samuel at Culray. Matilda at Tonymore North. Annie at

Cornadrung. George at Cloonart North. *ALSO:* Margaret at Howard's of Creenagh.

NOLAN:(37): John at Mornin. John, Mary at Ballygibbagh. John at Ballyglassin. Mary A. at Carrickboy. Francis at Glebe (Kilglass D.E.D.). Thomas at Taghshinny. Patrick at Ballybranigan. Peter at Tirlickeen. Patrick at Ballymahon Town. Thomas, Mary at Lislom. Patrick at Carrickmoran. Thomas at Glenmore (Kilcommock D.E.D.). Catherine at Correyna (?). Peter, Thomas at Laughil (Kilcommock D.E.D.). John at Cam. Michael at Kilsallagh. Patrick, John at Lackan. Elizabeth at Cloonellan. Peter, Patrick at Briskil. James at Kilmore Lower. James, Catherine at Corralough. Michael at Newtown (Moydow D.E.D.). James at Keelogalabawn. Catherine, Patrick at Formoyle (Farrell). Michael at Cartrongarrow. James at Lissaghanedan. Patrick at Treel (Corboy D.E.D.). James at Cloonahard. Bridget at New Street, Longford Town. Elizabeth at Townparks (Longford Urban No. 1 D.E.D.). *ALSO:* Elizabeth at John Miller's of Tully (Agharra D.E.D.). Mary A. at Farrell's of Carrickedmond. Teresa at Mary Plunkett's (21) of Tennalick. Ellen et al. at Mulvihill's of Foygh. Margaret at Kenny's of Churchquarter. Valentine at Thomas Kiernan's of Barrack Street, Granard Town. Anne at Rhatigan's of Camlisk More (?). Mary J. at Skelly's of Edgeworthstown Town. John et al. at Daniel Dooris's of Kilnashee. Kate at Farrington's of Newtownforbes Village. James at Daniel Farrell's (2) of Cloonrallagh. Michael and Thomas at Fox's of Magheraveen. John at Brady's of Ballymahon Street, Longford Town. Patrick at Michael Thompson's of Ballymahon Street, Longford Town. Monica and Dominick at Free's of Dublin Street, Longford Town. Elizabeth at Campbell's of Killashee Street, Longford Town. Mary at McGarry's of Main Street, Longford Town. Annie at Fee's of Church Street, Longford Town.

NOONAN: Anne at Clooncallow. Owen, Bryan at Cam. Michael at Clonwhelan. Peter at Lackan. John at Knappoge (Cloondara D.E.D.). *ALSO:* Patrick at John Victory's of Corclaragh. Francis at Egan's of Rathvaldron.

NOONE: Anne at Patrick Farrell's of Lanesborough Village. Joseph at Denis Bannon's of Coolcaw. Lizzie at Cahill's of Lisnamuck. Sr. Charlotte M. at Sr. Green's of Convent Lane, Longford Town. Maria at Skelly's of Main Street, Longford Town.

NOONEY: Thomas at Joseph Nally's of Ballymahon Town.

NORRIS: Richard at Rathmore (Ballinamuck East D.E.D.). John at Drumnacooha. John at Crossea North. Thomas at Broderick's Yard, Longford Town. *ALSO:* Kate at Bridget McLoughlin's of Crossea South. Fanny at Free's of Cooleeny (?). Mary and Kathleen M. at Languish's of Abbeycartron.

NORTH: J. at Hewetson's of Church Street, Longford Town.

NORTON: John at Aghareagh (Cloondara D.E.D.). *ALSO:* John and Bridget at Susan Rourke's of Edgeworthstown Town. Stephen at Michael Reilly's of Chapel Lane, Longford Town.

NOTLEY: Palmer at Claras. *ALSO:* Richard H. at Carothers' of Abbeycartron.

NOUD: Michael at Main Street, Longford Town. *ALSO:* Peter at Fallon's of Dublin Street, Longford Town.

NOWLAN: Catherine at Corryena. *ALSO:* Anne at Rhatigan's of Camlisk More.

NUGENT: James at Drumanure. John at Main Street, Granard Town. Patrick, Bridget at Castlenugent. Thomas at Aghnagore. George at Aghareagh Bog. James at Aghantrah. *ALSO:* Annie at More O'Ferrall's of Lissard. William at Wiggins's of Moatavally. Andrew and John at Elizabeth Reilly's of Bracklon.

NULTY: James at Ballybeg. *ALSO:* James and Anne at Corry's of Ballybeg.

O'HARA, O'CONNOR etc: (See Hara, Connor, etc). Be careful with these surnames as O'Connor, O'Connell, etc., may be written synonymously for Connor, Connell, etc. and vice versa.

OATES: Mary at Water Lane, Granard Town. Gregory at Deerpark Newtownforbes D.E.D.). Peter at Kilmacannon. Thomas at Begnagh. Ellen at Cloontamore. John at Mount Davis. *ALSO:* Kate at O'Beirne's of Clooneen (Beirne). Bridget at Davys's of Lanesborough Village.

OLDHAM: Mary and Mabel at Farrington's of Newtownforbes Village.

OLWELL: James at Drumhalry.

McONAGHY: See McConaghy.

OROHOE, OROHO: Thomas at Aghnashingan. John at Castlerea. James at Toneen (Moydow D.E.D.). John at Lyanmore. Patrick, James at Lisdreenagh. Margaret at Grillagh (Ardagh West D.E.D.). James at Lisduff (Longford Rural D.E.D.). *ALSO:* Peter at Flanagan's of Lyneen. Ellen at Hayes's of Main Street, Keenagh Village. Mary at Skelly's of Cloonmore. Patrick at Adams's of Craane. Thomas at Garrahan's of Bohermore. Anne at William Hall's of Moor. Peter at Michael Powell's of Cordivin.

ORR: David at Newcastle.

OWENS, OWNS: Catherine at Ballymahon Town. Patrick at Creevagh Beg. Anne at Carrowroe. *ALSO:* Bridget at Auchmuty's of Creevaghmore (Forgney Civil Ph.). Anne and Sarah at Feeney's of Killasona. Patrick at Reilly's of New Road, Granard Town. Francis at Richard Adams's of Lisnabo.

PAGE: Martha at Elam's of Derrydarragh. (See Le Page).

PAKENHAM: John, Robert at Lechurragh.

PALMER: Martha at Meehan's of Ballymahon Street, Longford Town.

PARKER: Daniel at Kinalon's of Dublin Street, Longford Town. A. at Hewetson's of Church Street, Longford Town.

PARKERS: John at John Dolan's of Aghadowry.

PARKINSON: John at Island. Michael at Lisduff (Montgomery). *ALSO:* Thomas at Plant's of Laughil (Kilcommock D.E.D.). John at Harris's of Main Street, Longford Town.

PARKS: James at Ball Alley Street Upper, Granard Town.

PARSONS: Honor at Keane's of Edgeworthstown Town.

McPARTLAND, McPARTLIN: Francis at Drumhalry. Thomas at Fardrumman. *ALSO:* Bridget at Charles Cullen's of Edgeworthstown Town.

PARTRIDGE, PATRIDGE, PEATRIDGE: Michael at Lislea (Doory D.E.D.). Patrick at Tirlickeen. James at Foygh. Patrick, Anne at Breany. *ALSO:* Margaret at Moran's of Torboy. R.W. at Hewetson's of Church Street, Longford Town.

PATTERSON: Anne at Ballinalee Village. Maria at Church Street, Longford Town. *ALSO:* Marian at Irwin's of Colehill.

PAYNE: John at Ballynamanagh. John A. at Tennalick. Elizabeth at Derrycolumb. George H. at Mountjessop. Catherine at Moor.

PEARSE: George C. at Main Street, Longford Town. Frederick at Abbeycartron.

PEATRIDGE: See Partridge.

PEELO: Ellen at Demesne.

PENDERGAST: See Prendergast.

PENDERS: Mary at Currycahill, Ballinalee Village.

PENNY: F. at Hewetson's of Church Street, Longford Town.

PEPPER: R. at Hewetson's of Church Street, Longford Town.

PERCIVAL: Peter at Druming. Jane at Crowdrumman. Alexander W. at Minard. *ALSO:* Mary at Stevenson's of Cloonscott. William at Taylor's of Knockloughlin.

PERKINS: W. at Hewetson's of Church Street, Longford Town.

PERKINSON: See Parkinson.

PERRIN: J. at Hewetson's of Church Street, Longford Town.

PERRY: Lawrence at Foygh. Laurence at Edgeworthstown Town. *ALSO:* John at Heavey's of Clooneeny. Catherine at Cameron's of Main Street, Longford Town.

PETTIT, PETITT: James at Clooneen (Forgney D.E.D.). Anne at Derrycolumb. Rachael J. at Ballinlough. John at Main Street, Granard Town. Patrick at Annagh (Drumgort D.E.D.). Thomas at Cornacullew. Thomas at Garvary. *ALSO:* Bridget at Philip Brady's of Kiltycon.

PEYTON: Tobias at Breanrisk. Rev. George R. (absent from home) at St. Anne's Glebe.

PHELAN: See Whelan.

PHIBBS: Henry et al. at Carney's of Great Water Street, Longford Town.

PHILLIPS: Thomas at Forgney. Noble L. at Glenmore (Kilcommock D.E.D.). John at Corboy. John at Dublin Street, Longford Town. *ALSO:* Bernard at Cornelius Cosgrove's of Aghacordrinan. Patrick at Yorke's of Barrack Street, Granard Town. Michael S. at Stacom's of Dublin Street, Longford Town. Anne at Hughes's of Sandy Row, Longford Town.

PICKARD: G. at Hewetson's of Church Street, Longford Town.

PIGOTT: Catherine at Glack (Longford Rural D.E.D.).

PINKMAN: Rev. John A. at Clogher and Rinn. *ALSO:* John at O'Connor's of Conroy's Court, Longford Town.

PITTMAN, PITMAN: H. at Lanesborough Village. *ALSO:* J.H. at Hewetson's of Church Street, Longford Town.

PLANT: John H. at Ballymahon Town. William H. at Toome (Ballymahon D.E.D.). Robert at Laughil (Kilcommock D.E.D.). *ALSO:* Sara J. at Maria Flower's of Barry (Ballymahon D.E.D.). Mary at Muir's of Edgeworthstown Town.

PLUNKETT: Mary, Mary at Tennalick. Richard at Bunlahy. Joseph at Aghadegnan (Longford Rural D.E.D.). Thomas at Main Street, Longford Town. *ALSO:* William at Fee's of Church Street, Longford Town.

POE: Rev. Purefoy at Glebe (Ballymahon D.E.D.).

POLLARD: Bridget at Leitrim (Granard Rural D.E.D.). Rev. William at Templeton Glebe. *ALSO:* John at Rose Coyne's of Ballymahon Town (?). Ellen at Bridget Dawson's of Leitrim (Granard Rural D.E.D.). Thomas at Browne's of Aghaboy (Milltown D.E.D.). Margaret at Small's of Ardagullion.

POLLOCK: George at Main Street, Keenagh Village. *ALSO:* Robert at Cody's of Streamstown (Kilglass D.E.D.).

POTTER: Patrick at Cloontamore. *ALSO:* John at McGaver's of Bridge Street, Longford Town.

POTTERTON: Rev. Dean Frederick at Templemichael Glebe.

POUSTIE: Leslie B. at Ringowny. *ALSO:* Catherine and Stanley at Robinson's of Lisryan.

POWE: Srs. Mary, Jane and Ellen at Rev. Mother Farrington's of Newtownforbes Village.

POWELL: Owen at Ballinrooey. Michael at Aghinaspick. Patrick at Cloonkeen (Ardagh West D.E.D.). Patrick, James, Michael at Cordivin.

POWER: Thomas at Bog Lane, Longford Town. *ALSO:* Bertha F. at James Farrell's of Glack (Longford Rural D.E.D.).

POYNTON: James at Cornacarta. William at Lanesborough Road, Keenagh Village. Thomas, Robert (absent from home), John at Derryveagh. *ALSO:* Olivia M. at John H. Plant's of Ballymahon Town.

PRATT: Charles at Caulfield's of Clontymullan.

PRENDERGAST, PENDERGAST: Thomas at John McDermott's of Ballymahon Town. William at John Reilly's (15) of Dooroc. Mary and Joseph at Flynn's of Cloonahussey.

PRESTON: James at Taghshinny. Thomas at Cartronboy. John at Cloonfiugh.

PRICE: Joseph at Ballymahon Town. Peter at Gorteengar. *ALSO:* Elizabeth at Coates' of Abbeyshrule. David E. at John P. Shaw's of Ballymahon Town.

PRIOR: John at Cornadrung. John at Cornacullew.

PROUDFORD: Richard and Thomas at Mary Callaghan's of Dublin Street, Longford Town.

PRUNTY:(30): Edward, Peter at Aghaward. Patrick at Lackan. Anne at Drumbad. William, Patrick, Michael at Fardrumman. James at Breanrisk. James, Patrick, Thomas at Cloontagh. Michael at Leitrim (Breanrisk D.E.D.). Myles, Thomas, Neil, Bridget at Dooroc. Catherine, John, Peter at Briskil. William at Newtownforbes Village. Thomas at Creenagh. Catherine at Aghaboy (Aghaboy D.E.D.). Patrick, Neil, Patrick, Michael at Clontumpher. Owen, John, Patrick at Corneddan. Hugh at Ballymahon Street, Longford Town. *ALSO:* Margaret at Kearney's of Cornadowagh. Catherine at McVitty's of Aghnashannagh. Robert at John Reilly's of Ballygilchrist (?). Elizabeth at Feeny's of Breanrisk. Michael at Colreavy's of Cloontagh. Patrick at Reynolds's of Cartrongolan. Neil and Mary at Mulleady's of Derryheelan. Catherine at Maria Kelly's (12) of Dooroc. James at Mary Dowd's of Drumnacooha. Margaret at McHugh's of Sragarrow. William at O'Connor's of Conroy's Court, Longford Town.

PUGH: Elizabeth at Cartron (Granard Urban D.E.D.). James at Coolagherty.

PULLMAN: William T. at Lisbrack (Longford Rural D.E.D.). *ALSO:* Margaret at Ellis's of St. Michael's Road, Longford Town.

PURCELL: Edward at Castleforbes Demesne.

PURDY: John, Anne at Chapel Lane, Longford Town.

WADE, WAIDE: Peter at Monaduff. Terence at Gaigue.

McQUAID, McQUADE, McWADE:(13): James at Abbeylara Village.

Patrick, Peter at Lettergullion. Michael at Barragh More. John at Cartrongolan. Charles, Henry, James at Derawley. Catherine at Enybegs. James at Drumlish Village. John, Mary at Gaigue. Mary at Great Water Street, Longford Town.

QUAINE, QUAIN, QUANE: Elizabeth, Kate at Aghnasillagh. Dominick at Ballycloghan. Thomas at Carn. *ALSO:* Edward at Kenny's of Aghnasillagh.

QUEST: Ellen at Mills' of Cloonbrin. Margaret at Harris's of Kildordan.

QUIGG: Isabella at Murphy's of Ballynagoshen.

QUIGLEY: Bernard at Trillickatemple. Patrick, Peter at Soran. *ALSO:* Elizabeth at Farrington's of Newtownforbes Village.

QUINLAN: Margaret at Main Street, Keenagh Village. *ALSO:* Michael at McClean's of Edgeworthstown Town (?). Sr. Lizzie at Sr. Hoare's of Grassyard.

QUINN:(98): Michael at Island. Edward at Drumnacor. Michael at Drumnahara. Fealy at Gorteen. Mary at Ballinalee Village. John at Cranalagh Beg. John at Kilcourcey. Michael at Carrowlinan. William at Kiltyclogh. Thomas at Ballinlough. James at Leitrim (Granard Rural D.E.D.). John at Ballynacross (Granard Urban D.E.D.). Mary at Cleenrah. Terence, John at Smear. William H. at Lackan. Patrick at Edgeworthstown Town. Bridget, Julia, Philip at Aghadowry. Michael at Fardrumman. Thomas, Peter, James at Bawn (Breanrisk D.E.D.). Maria, Catherine at Cloonagh (Breanrisk D.E.D.). John, Michael, Catherine, Peter at Corrabaun (Breanrisk D.E.D.). James, Margaret, William at Kilnashee. Peter, Mary, Francis, Peter, Mary at Cartrongolan. Paul, Margaret, Patrick, John, Bridget, Mary at Drumlish. Patrick, Peter, Patrick, James at Enybegs. Patrick at Greagh. Anne, Catherine at Oghil. Michael, Edward at Derrynacross. John, Patrick at Lettergonnell. Owen at Ballagh (Newtownforbes D.E.D.). James at Ballagh (Achmuty). Thomas, Michael at Briskil. John at Cloonfore. John at Crockaun. James at Clontumpher. Maria at Soran. Elizabeth at Back of the Hill. Lizzie at Banghill. George at Bohermore. James at Allenagh. John at Clooncoose (Cloonee D.E.D.). Hugh, Bridget, John, Anne, Arthur at Kiltybegs. Denis M. at Drumure. Elizabeth, Michael at Cloonee. Hugh at Killeter. Michael, Daniel at Killyfad. Thomas, Patrick at Kiltyreher (Killoe Civil Ph.). Patrick at Mucknagh. Peter at Kiltyreher (Templemichael Civil Ph.). Joseph P. at Stonepark (Longford Rural D.E.D.). John, James at Cooleeny. Joseph at Whiterock. Patrick at Convent Lane, Longford Town. John, John at Dublin Street, Longford Town. John at Earl Street, Longford Town. Michael at Fee's Terrace, Longford Town. John at Great Water Street, Longford Town. Patrick at Killashee Street, Longford Town. Ellen,

Mary, at Little Water St., Longford Town. Thomas at St. Mel's Road, Longford Town. John at Abbeycartron. *ALSO:* Catherine at Rose Farrell's of Ballymahon Town. Thomas at Scally's of Derryad (Ledwithstown D.E.D.). John at Doherty's of Aghnashannagh. Mary at Anne Sullivan's of Aghakilmore. Bridget at Beglan's of Gelshagh. Bridget at Patrick Smyth's of Culray. Patrick at Dermody's of Ballinulty Lower. Kate at O'Flanagan's of Toneen (Firry D.E.D.). Patrick at Patrick Cosgrove's of Main Street, Granard Town. Michael at Conlon's of New Road, Granard Town. Owen at Lee's of Aghaboy (Milltown D.E.D.). Catherine at Michael Greene's (88) of Edgeworthstown Town. Ellen at James Reilly's of Kiltycreevagh. Maria at Patrick Mimnagh's of Cloonagh (Breanrisk D.E.D.). Mary et al. at Higgins's of Cloonmacart. George at Sheeran's of Garrowhill. Catherine at Evers' of Drumlish Village. Patrick at Hughes's of Derrynacross. Patrick at Lynch's of Derrynacross. Mary at Farrington's of Newtownforbes Village. Catherine at McGeoy's of Caldraghmore. Elizabeth at Michael Ryan's of Bohermore. Bernard at Kennedy's of Glen. Maggie at McCormack's of Bawn Mountain. James at Lyons's of Clooncoose (Cloonee D.E.D.). Mary K. at Dunne's of Killeter. Thomas at Montgomery's of Mucknagh. Denis at Dennigan's of Knockanboy. Winifred at John Tooman's of Stonepark (Longford Rural D.E.D.). Sr. Christina at Sr. Green's of Convent Lane, Longford Town. George F. at Boyers' (2) of Main Street, Longford Town. Eugene at Patrick F. Fitzgerald's of Main Street, Longford Town. Michael at Margaret Mathews' of Main Street, Longford Town.

QUINTENY: William at Farrell's of Barroe.

McQUIRK: Teresa and Maurice at Connolly's of Little Water Street, Longford Town. (See McGuirk).

RAFFERTY: Andrew at Ardanragh. Bridget at Rathmore (Ballymahon D.E.D.). John at Castleforbes Demesne. Anne at Deerpark (Newtownforbes D.E.D.). James at St. Michael's Road, Longford Town. *ALSO:* Bridget et al. at Bridget Hughes's of Drumanure. Margaret at James Keena's of Ardanragh.

RALEIGH: Sr. Mary at Sr. Green's of Convent Lane, Longford Town.

RANFORD: Patrick at Mahady's of The Hill, Granard Town.

RANKIN: John at Fee's Terrace, Longford Town. *ALSO:* Lizzie at Noud's of Main Street, Longford Town. Teresa at Rogers' of Demesne.

RARDON: See Reardon.

RATTIGAN: See Rhatigan.

RAWL, RAWLE, RHALL: Thomas at Enybegs. John at Craane. James at Clontumpher. James at Broderick's Yard, Longford Town.

RAYMOND: William J. at Cooleeshil or Richfort.

RAYNOR: C.P. at Hewetson's of Church Street, Longford Town.

REARDON: John at Ballyglassin. Thomas at Lisnanagh. Anne at Coolcaw. Bryan at Drumroe. Edward at Cloonahard. *ALSO:* Elizabeth at McCord's of Corboy.

REDDIN: Maggie at Patrick McCabe's (14) of Derrycassan.

REDEHAN, REDAHAN, RODAUGHAN, RODOHAN: Mary at Aghareagh (Coolamber D.E.D.). John, Charles, Margaret, Anne, Peter at Corglass. *ALSO:* John at Kyne's of Corbaun or Leitrim.

REED: F. at Hewetson's of Church Street, Longford Town. (See Reid).

REGAN: Patrick at Smithfield. Margaret at Derryoghil. James, John at Knockavegan. Sarah at Moxham Street, Granard Town. Patrick at The Hill, Granard Town. James at Water Lane, Granard Town. Bridget, James at Cloonmore. *ALSO:* Francis at Joseph Gannon's of Ballymahon Town. Sarah at Connell's of Main Street, Granard Town. Michael at Cooney's of Main Street, Longford Town.

REHILL, REEHIL, REEHILL: Patrick, Francis at Molly. Edward, John at Carrickadorrish. Kate at Mullinroe. Mary at Ballinulty Lower. Edward at Derrycassan. Patrick, Thomas at Shanmullagh. *ALSO:* James at Columb's of Carrickadorrish. Thomas at McNamara's of Cloonagh (Mullanalaghta D.E.D.). John at Thomas Masterson's of Edgeworthstown Town. Julia at Muir's of Edgeworthstown Town. Annie at Charles McNerney's of Glenmore (Ballinamuck East D.E.D.). Elizabeth at Farrell's of Carnan.

REID: Mary at Killasona. John at Grassyard. William at Great Water Street, Longford Town. *ALSO:* Alfred E. at Henry S. Burd's of Ballymahon Town. Kate at Farrington's of Newtownforbes Village. William at Wallace's of McLoughlin's Yard, Longford Town. (See Reed).

REIDY: Mary E. at Grey's of Cloncowley.

REILLY:(362): Mary, Bridget at Drumanure. Bridget at Ardanragh. Patrick at Cloghan (Doory D.E.D.). Edward at Clooncallow. James at Kildordan. Thomas at Clooncullen. Thomas, William at Keel (Forgney D.E.D.). Catherine at Taghshinny. James at Daroge. Patrick, Annie at Ballymahon

Town. John at Creevagh Beg. Bridget, Patrick, John, Edward, Edward at Rathmore (Ballymahon D.E.D.). Patrick at Forthill. Ellen at Abbeyderg. Michael at Island. Thomas at Ledwithstown (Kilcommock Civil Ph.). Terence at Acres. Michael at Ballyreaghan. Lawrence at Clonbroney. Patrick at Leitrim (Ballinalee D.E.D.). Thomas at Currygrane. William at Drumnacross. James at Glenoghil. Peter at Drummeel. Farrell, Mary, John, Peter at Aghacordrinan. Bridget, John, Bernard, Thomas at Aghagreagh. Patrick, Thomas, Bernard at Aghakilmore. Elizabeth, Maria, Michael, Margaret at Aghamore Upper. John, John at Derreenavoggy. James, William, Francis, Francis at Gelshagh. Owen, Michael at Molly. William at Kilcourcey. John at Drumderg. Mary at Lislea (Lislea D.E.D.). John at Glannagh. Thomas, Bridget at Culray. Catherine, Eugene at Aghakine. Owen, Terence at Carrickadorrish. Ellen, Patrick, Edward, James at Kilbride. Mary J. at Ranaghan. Thomas at Tonymore South. John at Abbeylara Village. Hugh at Ballywillin. Catherine, Mary, Patrick, Catherine, James at Springtown. James, Bernard at Killeen (Bunlahy D.E.D.). Charles at Culleenmore. Thomas, Daniel, Owen, Ellen, Patrick, Mary, Anne at Mullinroe. Anne, John, Philip, Philip, Patrick, John at Aghnagarron. Hugh at Ballinrud East. Owen, John, Margaret, Thomas, John, James, John, John, Hugh, Edward, Charles at Cloghchurnel. Thomas, Francis, Rose, Bernard, Mary, John, Julia, James at Creevy. Philip at Dalystown. Philip at Rathbrackan. Catherine, Felix, Philip, John at Rathcor. Terence at Cloonaghmore. Patrick at Rossan. Peter, James at Rinroe. Patrick at Ballybrien. Francis, John, Mary, James, Margaret at Ballygilchrist. Charles, Michael, James at Ballymore. Edward, Anne at Cartron (Granard Rural D.E.D.). John at Gallid. Catherine at Cartron (Granard Urban D.E.D.). John, John at Ball Alley Street Lower, Granard Town. Elizabeth at Ball Alley St. Upper, Granard Town. Owen, Mary at Bank Street, Granard Town. John, James, Thomas, Francis, Myles at Barrack Street, Granard Town. James at Grassyard. Francis at Main Street, Granard Town. Margaret, Thomas at Moxham Street, Granard Town. John at New Road, Granard Town. Bernard at Rathcronan. James at Silver Street, Granard Town. James at The Hill, Granard Town. Laurence at Tromra (Granard Urban D.E.D.). Rose, Michael at Water Lane, Granard Town. Ellen at Lisraghtigan. Patrick at Cartroncar. James at Ferskill. Henry, Edward at Muckerstaff. Philip at Tonywardan. Michael at Willsbrook. John at Camagh (Newgrove D.E.D.). Edward at Cooldoney. Rose, Patrick at Derragh. John at Carrickmaguirk. Francis at Cleenrah. Annie E., Patrick, Stephen at Cornadrung. Thomas, Peter, Patrick at Dunbeggan (Columbkille D.E.D.). Bernard at Mollyglass. Bridget, James, Michael, Mary, Charles, James, Francis, John, Francis, James, John, Patrick, Anne, James, Patrick, Francis at Rosduff. Charles, Patrick, Patrick, Philip, Michael, Stephen at Smear. Philip, Patrick, Francis, Patrick, Anne, Owen at Crott. Peter, John, Edward, Michael, Peter, Patrick, Peter at Enaghan. Mary, John, Terence at Lisraherty. John, John, Margaret at Ballyduffy. James, Owen, Bridget, Philip, Mark at Birrinagh. Patrick, John, Luke, Margaret, Philip, Peter, John, Catherine, John, Peter, Thomas, Francis at

Drumhalry. Francis, Bernard at Drumury. Rose, Philip, Francis, John, Patrick at Fihoragh. Patrick at Drumard. Francis, Henry, John, Thomas at Aghanoran. Thomas, Anne, Margaret, Thomas, Charles at Cloonagh (Mullanalaghta D.E.D.). James at Corbaun or Leitrim. Daniel, Mary, Owen at Derrycassan. James at Dring. Thomas, Michael at Kilmore. James at Larkfield. Patrick, Bridget, Maria, Mathew at Toome (Mullanalaghta D.E.D.). Winifred, Luke at Castlenugent. Thomas, Mary at Clonca. Elizabeth at Lisryan. Catherine, Michael at Moatavally. Kate, Elizabeth, Margaret, Catherine at Cranalagh More. Elizabeth, Thomas, Bernard at Bracklon. Anne, Henry, Patrick, Michael, Anne at Edgeworthstown Town. Bridget at Annaghdaniel. John at Cloonback. Bridget at Corrinagh. Farrell, Peter, John at Cuingareen. Charles, Owen at Rathmore (Ballinamuck East D.E.D.). Catherine at Edenmore. James, Thomas at Glenmore (Ballinamuck East D.E.D.). James, Philip at Kiltycreevagh. John, Bernard, Bryan, Bernard at Lettergullion. Bernard, Patrick, John, Philip, Edward, Michael, Michael, Sarah at Shanmullagh. James, Elizabeth, Francis, Patrick, John, Patrick, Alice, Peter at Tawnagh. Michael at Breanrisk. Bridget, Michael, Patrick, Bernard, Patrick at Cloonellan. Michael at Cloontagh. Bridget at Derrynacrit. John at Cloonagh (Breanrisk D.E.D.). Maria at Cloonmacart. Patrick at Aghamore Lower. Thomas, Francis at Moyne. Francis, James at Cloonelly. Philip at Cornacullew. Bridget at Barragh More. Philip, Bernard at Cartrongolan. Anne at Drumlish Village. John, John, Francis, Catherine at Dooroc. James at Gaigue. Dominick at Faghey. William at Ballykenny. Ellen, William at Tully (Cloondara D.E.D.). Martin at Killashee Village. Michael at Cloonbony. Simon at Lanesborough Village. Mary at Soran. Catherine, Thomas at Lisduff (Ardagh East D.E.D.). Edward at Lissaghanedan. Annie at Bog Lane, Longford Town. Michael, Anne at Chapel Lane, Longford Town. Peter at Great Water Street, Longford Town. Mary, Patrick at Killashee Street, Longford Town. Fanny at New Street, Longford Town. Patrick at Richmond Street, Longford Town. William at St. Mel's Road, Longford Town. Peter at Townparks (Longford Urban No. 1 D.E.D.). *ALSO:* Catherine at May's of Clooncallow. Patrick at Maloney's of Clooncullen. Michael at Ryan's of Kilcurry. Peter at Dempsey's of Kilnacarrow (Kilglass D.E.D.). John at Keegan's of Taghshinny. Kathy and Anne of Kearney's of Daroge. Joseph at William Seales' of Ballymahon Town. Kate at Killaine's of Kilshruley. Mary at O'Farrell's of Drummeel. Rosie at Kelly's of Laughil (Edgeworth). Kate at Lee's of Aghakilmore. Catherine at Anne Sullivan's of Aghakilmore. Thomas et al. at Michael Brady's of Aghaward. Thomas at Monahan's of Newtownbond. Edward at Doyle's of Cranally. John at Michael Macken's of Cranally. Bridget and Laurence P. at Flaherty's of Culray. Stephen et al. at John Doyle's of Sonnagh. Charles at Garry's of Abbeylara. Patrick J. at Gray's of Abbeylara. Bridget at Smith's of Tonymore South. Mary at Kane's of Abbeylara Village. Charles at Denis Caffrey's of Abbeylara Village. Maggie at Eyers' of Ballywillin. Kate at Laurence Mulligan's of Ballywillin. Anne at Malone's of Ballywillin. Eugene et al. at Lynch's of

Cartronbore. John at John Sullivan's of Bunlahy. Katie at Margaret Dolan's of Coolcor. Thomas et al. at McCabe's of Aghnagarron. Kate at Stevenson's of Cloghchurnel. Mary at Sheridan's of Creevy. John at Elizabeth Beglan's of Aghabrack. Anne and Bridget at Crawford's of Ballymacroly. Jane at Bennett's of Leitrim (Granard Rural D.E.D.). Mary at Reynolds's of Robinstown. Bridget at O'Dwyer's of Carragh (Granard Urban D.E.D.). Michael and Roseanne at Moore's of Ball Alley Street Upper, Granard Town. Patrick at Markey's of Ball Alley Street Upper, Granard Town. Thomas at Markey's of Main Street, Granard Town. Eliza and Philip at Sullivan's of Main Street, Granard Town. Michael and Joseph at Leonard's of Main Street, Granard Town. Rose at Cusack's of Main Street, Granard Town. Mary A. at Mary Brady's of Main Street, Granard Town. Mary A. at John Burns' of Main Street, Granard Town. Michael at Laurence Ward's of Main Street, Granard Town. Mary E. at Hugh Brady's of Main Street, Granard Town. Patrick at Grehan's of Main Street, Granard Town. James at Somers' of Main Street, Granard Town. Margaret at Edward Keane's of New Road, Granard Town. Matthias at Collumb's of Water Lane, Granard Town. Michael at Kiernan's of Tonywardan. Annie at Thomas Early's of Derragh. Joseph at Owen Mulligan's of Dunbeggan (Columbkille D.E.D.). Mary at Patrick Corvan's of Rosduff. Rose at Mary Curwin's of Rosduff. Mary at Duignan's of Rosduff. John at Connell's of Smear. Mary at Catherine Mulligan's of Smear. James et al. at McGrath's of Enaghan. Charles at Francis Masterson's of Enaghan. Joe at Mulligan's of Lisraherty. Kate at James Duffy's (9) of Aghagah. Anne B. at Egan's of Birrinagh. Bridget at James Cosgrove's of Birrinagh. John and Catherine at Michael Mulligan's of Birrinagh. Mary and Alice at John Doyle's (27) of Drumhalry. Bridget at Anne Duffy's of Drumhalry. William at Masterson's of Drumhalry. Maggie at Mathew Farrelly's of Drumury. Willie at Patrick Leavy's of Fihoragh. Thomas and Ellen at Edward Donohoe's (8) of Drumard. Charles at Brady's of Drumard. Rose at Michael Masterson's of Farmullagh. Rose. A. at Dowdall's of Cloonagh (Mullanalaghta D.E.D.). James and John at Fagan's of Corbaun or Leitrim. Ellen at Jones's of Dring. Mary at Keegan's of Kilmore. Maggie at Michael Hughes's of Toome (Mullanalaghta D.E.D.). Mary at Monaghan's of Clonwhelan. Margaret at Fegan's of Ballaghgowla and Froghan. Mary at Mulhill's of Kilfintan. Mary at Noonan's of Lackan. Mary at Connor's of Cloonback. Margaret at Duffy's of Cuingareen. John at William Higgins's of Rathmore (Ballinamuck East D.E.D.). John et al. at Larkin's of Aghadowry. Patrick at Ellen Donnelly's of Kiltycreevagh. Maggie at Stakem's of Kiltycreevagh. Patrick at James McNamee's of Kiltycreevagh. Mary A. at Patrick Donnelly's (50) of Kiltycreevagh. Patrick at James Donnelly's of Shanmullagh. Patrick at Pettit's of Annagh (Drumgort D.E.D.). Thomas et al. at Mary A. Hagan's of Cornacullew. Bridget at Thomas Mulligan's of Leggagh. Mary A. et al. at Mary Quinn's (21) of Cartrongolan. Peter at John Murphy's of Cartrongolan. Mary A. et al. at Peter Quinn's (33) of Cartrongolan. Maggie at James McQuade's of

Derawley. Mary at Campbell's of Enybegs. Patrick at O'Brien's of Drumlish Village. Maggie at Matthew Gray's of Drumlish Village. Hugh at Heany's of Dooroc. James at Philip Brady's of Gaigue. Owen at Patrick Collumb's of Lettergonnell. Martha at Wilson's of Newtownforbes Village. James at Martha Beatty's of Cleggill. Patrick at Davys's of Cloonbony. Rose A. at Mulligan's of Lanesborough Village. Katie at Brady's of Soran. Anne and Mary A. at Connell's of Soran. Ellen at Thomas Flood's of Glen. Bernard and Patrick at Anne Kenny's of Glen. Elizabeth at Coleman's of Graffoge (Ardagh West D.E.D.). Kate at McCormack's of Kilmoyle. Kate at Egan's of Treel (Corboy D.E.D.). Charles at Mulvey's of Creeve. Julia at Farrell's of Cartronageeragh. Mary A. at Dowd's of Feraghfad. Patrick at Dennigan's of Knockanboy. Bridget at Ussher-Roberts' of Knockahaw. Maria and Michael at Clarke's of Ballymahon Street, Longford Town. Frances at McKenna's of Ballymahon Street, Longford Town. C. at Hewetson's of Church Street, Longford Town.

O'REILLY:(12): Eugene at Breaghy. Mary A. at Drummeel. Alice at Aghakine. Philip at Clooneen (Creevy D.E.D.). Patrick at Granard. Patrick M. at Main Street, Granard Town. Thomas at Edgeworthstown Town. Joseph W. at Annaghdaniel. Edward at Shanmullagh. John at Cornacullew. Thomas at Ballynagoshen. William at Dublin Street, Longford Town. *ALSO:* Catherine at King-Harman's of Newcastle. Sr. Bridget at Sr. Hoare's of Grassyard. Maggie et al. at Michael Hourican's of Rathmore (Ballinamuck East D.E.D.). Anne at Alexander Harris's of Enybegs. Mary A. at Patrick Gill's (18) of Brocklagh. Bridget et al. at Quinn's of Banghill. Loretto at Green's of Convent Lane, Longford Town.

RENTOUL: Rev. Alfred H. at Abbeycartron.

REYNOLDS:(62): Thomas at Mornin. Elizabeth at Shrule. Martin at Ballymahon Town. Lawrence at School Land. Henry at Ballinalee Village. Henry at Lismagoneen. James at Coolcor. Henry at Killeen (Bunlahy D.E.D.). John, Michael at Druminacrehir. Patrick at Aghnagarron. Laurence P. at Dalystown. Christopher at Ballyboy. Henry at Killasona. Patrick at Cartron (Granard Rural D.E.D.). Thomas at Robinstown. Daniel at Ferskill. Patrick at Barne. Mary at Clonwhelan. John at Lisnagrish. Joseph at Edgeworthstown Town. John J., Charles, Michael, James, Timothy, Patrick at Camagh (Ballinamuck East D.E.D.). Patrick, Patrick, Patrick at Cloncowley. Thomas at Aghnamaddoo. Patrick, Garrett at Annagh (Drumgort D.E.D.). James at Garvary. Mary at Cartrongolan. John, Michael at Drumlish. James, Patrick, Stephen at Enybegs. Bernard at Brocklagh. Patrick at Cornafunshin. Francis at Gaigue. Patrick at Kilmacannon. Michael at Annaghcooleen. James at Bunanass. Catherine at Edercloon. Annie at Aghnagore. John at Cloonmore. John at Sharvoge. Michael at Killashee Village. Thomas, John, Peter at Soran. Hugh at Ballinree and Ballymoat. Michael at Crossea South. Michael at Finnaragh. Bridget at

Glen. Bridget at Lyanmore. James at Ballygarve. Bridget at Healy's Terrace, Longford Town. George at St. Michael's Road, Longford Town. *ALSO:* Anne at Duff's of Mornin. Annie at Bligh's of Lismagoneen. John J. and May at Reid's of Killasona. Patrick and Lizzie at O'Flanagan's of Toneen (Firry D.E.D.). Henry at Peter Farrell's of Cartron (Granard Rural D.E.D.). Michael at Lee's of Aghaboy (Milltown D.E.D.). Mary at Michael Doyle's of Smear. John P. at O'Neill's of Clonwhelan. Kate at Edgeworth's of Edgeworthstown. Jane at Macken's of Edgeworthstown Town. James at Dooris's of Edgeworthstown Town. James et al. at Doyle's of Glenmore (Ballinamuck East D.E.D.). Rose at Wilson's of Leggagh. James at McMahon's of Enybegs. Kate at Kiernan's of Drumlish Village. Michael at Sommers' of Kimacannon. Kate and Anne at Farrington's of Newtownforbes Village. John at Geelan's of Ahanagh. Thomas at Campbell's of Corradooey. Elizabeth M. at Bond's of Farraghroe. Thomas at Larkin's of Killeter. Michael at Lyons's of Mullaghavorneen. James at Chapman's of Dublin Street, Longford Town. Fr. Denis at Rev. Patrick Dolan's of Dublin Street, Longford Town. Daniel at Keane's of Great Water Street, Longford Town. Thomas at Legge's of Main Street, Longford Town. Mary J. at Molloy's of Main Street, Longford Town. James at Devine's of Sandy Row, Longford Town. Bridget at Stephenson's of Abbeycartron. J. at Hewetson's of Church Street, Longford Town.

RHALL, RHAWL: See Rawl.

RHATIGAN, RATTIGAN:(19): John at Clooncallow. James at Cloonard (Ballymahon D.E.D.). Patrick at Lislom. Anne, John at Newpark. John at Cartrons (Kilcommock D.E.D.). John at Ballynacross (Granard Rural D.E.D.). Patrick at Camlisk More. Patrick at Slieve. Andrew, Thomas at Cloonfinfy. William at Killashee Village. Patrick at Kilnacarrow (Mountdavis D.E.D.). Edward at Magheraveen. James at Barnacor (Rathcline D.E.D.). William at Formoyle (Newcomen). John at Gorteengar. John at Rathcline. John at Tullyvrane. *ALSO:* Anne at Frayne's of Curraghmore. John at Lyons's of Forgney. Daniel at Mulvihill's of Ballymulvey. Mary at Kenny's of Creevaghmore (Forgney Civil Ph.). Mary K. at Finlay's of Glebe (Cloondara D.E.D.). Patrick at John Cassidy's of Derryad (Mountdavis D.E.D.). Mary J. at Patrick Casey's of Derryloughbannow. Lusia (?) at Smyth's of Aghantrah. William at O'Connor's of Conroy's Court, Longford Town.

RHONAN: Elizabeth et al. at Bartley's of Fee's Terrace, Longford Town. (See Ronan).

RHUTES: Elizabeth at Ryder's of Cloonmore.

RICHARDSON: Edward at Lamagh. *ALSO:* R. at Hewetson's of Church Street, Longford Town.

RICKARD: William at Ballymahon Town.

RIEHILL: See Rehill.

RILEY, RIELLY: See Reilly.

RINGWORD: Esther at Farrington's of Newtownforbes Village.

RIORDAN: See Reardon.

RITTMAN: Henry at Drumanure.

ROACHE: See Roche.

ROARKE: See Rourke.

ROBERTS: John P. at Feely's of Drumderg. W.J. at Hewetson's of Church Street, Longford Town. (See Ussher-Roberts).

ROBINSON: Elizabeth at Ballymahon Town. Joseph at Abbeyderg. John at Lisglassock. Sarah at Gorteenrevagh, Ballinalee Village. Thomas at Ballymore. Jane at Lisryan. Margaret at Earl Street, Longford Town. *ALSO:* Susan E. at Trimble's of Sheeroe (Knockanbaun D.E.D.). James at McMahon's of Barrack Street, Granard Town. Lucy at Dooner's of Dunbeggan (Moydow D.E.D.). Susan at Bond's of Farraghroe. Edith W. at Carothers' of Abbeycartron. R.H. at Hewetson's of Church Street, Longford Town.

ROCHE, ROACHE: John, Patrick at Cloonart South. *ALSO:* Bridget at Francis Reilly's (16) of Gelshagh. John at Beatty's of Main Street, Longford Town. Frances at Forbes's of Castleforbes Demesne. Kate and Fanny at Farrington's of Newtownforbes Village. James at James Farrell's of Ballymahon Street, Longford Town.

ROCHFORT: Sr. Marcella at Rev. Mother Farrington's of Newtownforbes Village.

ROCK: John at Carrickedmond. Anne at Daroge. Henry at Ball Alley Street Upper, Granard Town. John at Corlagan. William at Richmond Street, Longford Town. *ALSO:* Mary at Geraghty's of Daroge. Bridget at James Cassidy's of Ballymahon Town. Bridget at Burke's of Main Street, Longford Town. Kate at Nolan's of New Street, Longford Town.

RODAUGHAN, RODOHAN: See Redehan.

RODDEN: See Rudden.

RODDIS: James at Corclaragh.

RODDY: See Ruddy.

RODGERS: See Rogers.

RODWELL: George at Grier's of Main Street, Granard Town.

ROGAN: Francis at Ellen Duffy's of Aghagah.

ROGERS, RODGERS:(40): John at Doory. Harpole at Cornamucklagh. Patrick at Tirlickeen. William at Ards. Anne, Mary at Aghakilmore. Peter at Rincoolagh. Bridget at Aghanoran. Henry, Julia, Michael at Derrycassan. Sylvester at Tinnynarr. Patrick, Michael, Thomas at Cloonellan. Edward at Aghnamaddoo. Patrick at Annagh (Drumgort D.E.D.). Peter at Barragh More. Patrick, Bridget at Cartrongolan. Thomas at Derawley. John at Oghil. James at Drumlish Village. John, Michael at Cornafunshin. William, Patrick at Derrynacross. Thomas at Gaigue. Rose at Newtownforbes Village. James at Knockmartin. John at Lismoy. Thomas, Annie at Derryharrow. John at Drumlougher. Patrick at Allenagh. Mary at Drumure. Andrew at Killinlastra. John at Lisduff (Longford Rural D.E.D.). Philip at Aghadegnan (Longford Rural D.E.D.). Richard P. at Demesne. *ALSO:* Teresa at Coates' of Abbeyshrule. Teresa and Patrick at Mary Plunkett's (21) of Tennalick. William at Tanner's of Ards. Rachel at Finlay's of Mosstown (Moydow Barony). Mary J. at Carson's of Island. Charles at Stephen Mills' of Main Street, Keenagh Village. Elizabeth at Francis Armstrong's of Main Street, Keenagh Village. Catherine at Martin's of Aghagreagh. Mary at Anne McGarry's of Aghamore Upper. Mary at James Smyth's (56) of Main Street, Granard Town. Patrick at Bridget Kiernan's of Smear. Thomas at Jones's of Dring. Sr. Maria at Rev. Mother Hampson's of Aghafin. Annie M. at Peyton's of Breanrisk. Bernard at Patrick McCann's of Aghnamaddoo. Christina and Bridget and Jane at Farrington's of Newtownforbes Village. Kate at Neil Prunty's of Clontumpher. Patrick at John Duffy's of Crossea South. John at Donnelly's of Rabbitpark. James and Mary at O'Neill's of Conroy's Court, Longford Town.

ROHAN: James at McKenna's of Dublin Street, Longford Town. (See Rowan).

ROLLINS: James at Ballina. Annie at Ballynahinch. John at Elfeet (Burke). John at Greenhall Upper. William, Fanny at Lyneen.

RONALDSON: Thomas J. at Ledwithstown (Kilcommock Civil Ph.).

RONAN: Catherine at O'Farrell's of Moor. (See Rhonan).

ROONEY: Michael at Tennalough. Peter at Ballyglassin. Thomas at Lislom. Patrick at Mosstown (Rathcline Barony). William, Bridget, Annie at Foygh. John at Cloghchurnel. Bridget at Rathcline. *ALSO:* Patrick and Mary at Nolan's of Tirlickeen. Mary at Farrington's of Newtownforbes Village. Kate at Thomas Fallon's of Lisrevagh. Margaret at Lyons's of Noud's Yard, Longford Town.

RORKE: See Rourke.

ROSBOROUGH: William at Abbeylara Village. *ALSO:* Robert at Edgeworth's of Gorteen.

ROSE: Louis H. at St. Michael's Road, Longford Town. *ALSO:* Nellie (?) R. at Percival's of Crowdrumman.

ROSEFIELD: Adolph at Church Street, Longford Town.

ROSENGRAVE: James at Cooleeny.

ROSS:(12): Bridget at Aghnavealoge. Maria at Lissameen. Catherine at Clonca. Mary at Edgeworthstown Town. Anne at Enybegs. Alexander, John at Monaduff. John, Patrick at Lettergonnell. Robert at Kilmore Upper. Edward at Dublin Street, Longford Town. Michael at Main Street, Longford Town. *ALSO:* John et al. at Ledwith's of Sleehaun. Catherine and Josephine at Michael Farrell's of Edgeworthstown Town. Patrick and Kate at Patrick Cooney's of Breanriskcullew. Mary A. at Green's of Convent Lane, Longford Town. Christopher at Edward Kenny's of Main Street, Longford Town. W. at Hewetson's of Church Street, Longford Town.

ROTHWELL: See Rodwell.

ROURKE, ROARKE, RORKE:(19): John at Loughsheedan. Bernard at Agharanagh (Ballymahon D.E.D.). Mary at Ledwithstown (Shrule Civil Ph.). Catherine at Drummeel. Edward, John at Aghagreagh. Francis at Creevy. Peter at Ballyduffy. John at Castlenugent. Susan, Rose at Edgeworthstown Town. John at Cloncowley. Peter at Kiltycon. Patrick at Leggagh. John at Drumlish Village. Bernard at Ballinvoher. John at Cloonevit. Mary at Bohermore. John at Ballygarve. *ALSO:* Michael at Preston's of Taghshinny. Annie at Frawley's of Daroge. Patrick at James Nally's of Ballymahon Town. Mary at McCabe's of Gelshagh. Mary et al. at Lynch's of Ball Alley Street Upper, Granard Town. Hugh at Murphy's of Lisryan. Francis and Mary E. at Heslin's of Drumlish Village. Bridget at John Farrell's of Bawn (Ardagh West D.E.D.). T. at Hewetson's of Church Street, Longford Town.

O'ROURKE: Joseph at Ballyduffy. George at Cornacullew. Bridget E. at

Glebe (Cloondara D.E.D.). Francis at Great Water Street, Longford Town. *ALSO*: John F. at Francis Brady's of Kiltyclogh. Nannie at John O'Reilly's of Cornacullew.

ROVERY: Frederick at Bridge Street, Longford Town.

ROWAN: Daniel at Derryglash. Bridget at Derrygowna. *ALSO*: Catherine at O'Farrell's of Moor (?). (See Rohan).

RUDDEN, RUDDIN: Michael, John at Carrickadorrish. Mathew at Sonnagh. John at Ballygilchrist. John at Kilmore. Mary at Edgeworthstown Town. John at Fostragh. *ALSO*: James at Keenan's of Aghnacliff. Rose at Michael Kiernan's of Fostragh. Anne at Patrick Murtagh's of Glenmore (Ballinamuck East D.E.D.).

RUDDY: Michael at Dalystown. *ALSO*: Michael of Deal's of Carragh (Granard Rural D.E.D.).

RUSH: John at Carrowdunican. Thomas at Barnacor (Ledwithstown D.E.D.). *ALSO*: Lizzie at Yorke's of Doory. Ellie at Skelly's of Main Street, Longford Town.

RUSSELL: William at Prucklish. *ALSO*: James at Catherine Kelly's of Bog Lane, Longford Town. Mary at Mayne's of Abbeycartron.

RUTH: Fanny and Irene at Barrett's of Clooncullen.

RUTHERFORD: William at Toole's of Dublin Street, Longford Town.

RUTLEDGE: John at Ballymahon Town.

RYALL: James at Lechurragh.

RYAN: (20): Mathew at Kilcurry. James at Ballymahon Town. Mary at Mosstown (Rathcline Barony). James, Noragh at Barnacor (Ledwithstown D.E.D.). William at Drumnacor. Laurence at Gorteenclareen. Edward at Toneen (Moydow D.E.D.). James at Back of the Hill. Elizabeth at Ballywalter. Michael, Anne at Bohermore. Patrick, John at Cross (Ardagh East D.E.D.). Patrick, Patrick at Crossea South. Michael at Lisdreenagh. Margaret at Aghintemple. Michael at Bog Lane, Longford Town. Margaret at Broderick's Yard, Longford Town. *ALSO*: Charlie at James Keena's of Ardanragh. James et al. at John Doran's of Ardanragh. Maggie at John McDermott's of Ballymahon Town. William at Joseph Nally's of Ballymahon Town. Sr. Patrick at Rev. Mother Whelan's of Ballymahon Town. Mary J. at Mulvihill's of Ardoghil. James at Reynolds's of Ballinalee Village. Srs. Mary and Johanna at Sr. Hoare's of Grassyard.

Joseph at O'Brien's of Drumlish Village. Isador at Doyle's of Soran. Bessie at Mary Dowd's of Bog Lane, Longford Town. Edward and Joseph at O'Connor's of Conroy's Court, Longford Town. Sr. Mary at Sr. Green's of Convent Lane, Longford Town. (See Mulryan).

RYDER: Joseph at Newtownflanigan. Mary A., Mary J. at Ballynahinch. Matthew at Molly. Bernard at Aghakeeran. Mary A. at Cloonmore. *ALSO:* Joseph at Brandon's of Caltragh Beg.

RYLANDS: George at Ardagullion.

SADLER: H. at Hewetson's of Church Street, Longford Town.

SADLIER: Robert at Noble's of Cloonart North.

SAILS: Sarah at Larkin's of Clooncullen.

SALMON, SAMMON: Mary, Patrick at Drumanure. John at Loughsheedan. Patrick, John at Bunlahy. Michael at Lisnaneane. Catherine at Corclaragh. Peter at Cranalagh More. *ALSO:* Patrick et al. at Margaret Taigue's of Drumanure. Margaret at Lennon's of Cartronawar (Kilcommock D.E.D.). Jane at McMahon's of Barrack Street, Granard Town. John at Thomas Masterson's of Edgeworthstown Town.

SARGAISON: Walter at Abbeycartron.

SAVAGE: James at St. Anne's Glebe. James at Gorteenorna. Michael at Chapel Lane, Longford Town. *ALSO:* George at Howden's of Ederland. Anne at Farrell's of Aughine. Anne at Hussey's of Chapel Lane, Longford Town. Alfred at Little's of Main Street, Longford Town.

SCALLY: See Skelly.

SCANLON, SCANLAN: Margaret A. at Rathmore (Ballinamuck East D.E.D.). John, James at Soran. William at Drumure. Francis at Killeter. *ALSO:* Elizabeth at Richard Charters' of Garvagh (Currygrane D.E.D.). Patrick at McCabe's of Edgeworthstown Town. Elizabeth at McCord's of Allenagh. Kate at Little's of Creeve. James at Patrick Kelly's of Dublin Street, Longford Town.

SCOLLINS: Bridget at Newtownforbes Village.

SCOTT: George at Clooncallow. Mary J. at Cahanagh. Robert at Corradooey. William at Knockloughlin. John at Glack (Longford Urban No. 1 D.E.D.). John at Main Street, Longford Town. *ALSO:* James and Emily J. at Miller's of Ratharney. Thomas at Downes' of Forgney. Mary at

Ross's of Aghnavealoge. Alexander at John P. Shaw's of Ballymahon Town. James at Murphy's of Drumderg. Jane at Bloomer's of Cam. Frances at Bloomer's of Bracklon. Elizabeth at Isabella McCormack's of Leitrim (Breanrisk D.E.D.). F. at Hewetson's of Church Street, Longford Town.

SCULLY: James at Ballymahon Town. Kate at Gorteenclareen. Edward at Knockloughlin. Mary at Abbeycartron. *ALSO:* Thomas at Keenagh Barracks. Patrick at Lynn's of Derrynabuntale. Peter at Drumlish Barracks. (See Skelly).

SEALES, SEALS: William at Ballymahon Town.

SEERY: James at Aghakine. Mary, Thomas, John at Edenmore. *ALSO:* Margaret at Kenny's of Castlewilder. Michael at John Keegan's of Tirlickeen. Bridget at Donlon's of Doonacurry (Kilcommock Civil Ph.). Patrick at Egan's of Healy's Terrace, Longford Town. Maria at Murray's of Bridge Street, Longford Town.

SENTER: Alexander at Cartronawar (Kilcommock D.E.D.).

SESNAN: Maria at Newtownforbes Village.

SEWELL: Jane at Bridge Street, Longford Town.

SEXTON: John at Ballynascraw. James at Aghamore Upper. Bernard at Molly. Peter, Patrick, Francis at Aghakeeran. Patrick at Conroy's Court, Longford Town. *ALSO:* Kate at John Masterson's (15) of Rincoolagh. John et al. at Ellen Gilna's of Soran.

SEYMOUR: Charles at Aghareagh (Cloondara D.E.D.).

SHADDOCK: See Sheddock.

SHANAGHY, SHANAHY: Patrick at Enaghan. *ALSO:* Ellen at Kennedy's of Ballyduffy.

McSHANE: Rose at The Hill, Granard Town. Mary at Water Lane, Granard Town. Michael at Leggagh.

SHANLEY, SHANLY:(21): Andrew, John, Michael at Corrycorka. Patrick at Caltragh Beg. Michael at Cornadowagh. Edward at Castlebrock. Catherine at Ballinrooey. Francis, Patrick at Cloontagh. Thomas, Michael at Ahanagh. Francis at Clooneen (Kennedy). Ellen at Clooneen (Shanly). Thomas at Faghey. Michael at Knockmartin. John at Cloonbearla. Patrick, Patrick at Derryad (Mountdavis D.E.D.). Maria at Dwyer's Yard, Longford

Town. Thomas at Main Street, Longford Town. Elizabeth at St. Mel's Road, Longford Town. *ALSO:* Bridget at Tyrrell's of Lissawarriff. Mary at Coates' of Mullawornia. Mary at Rhatigan's of Cloonard (Ballymahon D.E.D.). Michael at Lynch's of Cranally. Francis at Anne Fox's of Edgeworthstown Town. Anne at Simpson's of Killashee Village. Patrick at Mahon's of Aghaboy (Aghaboy D.E.D.). Timothy at O'Connor's of Conroy's Court, Longford Town. James at Daniel Donnolly's of Great Water Street, Longford Town. Michael J. at Margaret Mathews' of Main Street, Longford Town.

SHANNON: John at New Road, Granard Town. Philip at Lanesborough Village. *ALSO:* Dominick at Ellen Reilly's of Tully (Cloondara D.E.D.). Elizabeth at Mary Hogan's of Lanesborough Village.

SHARKEY: Mary at Newtownforbes Village. Michael at Ballykenny. James, Patrick at Cornollen. Francis at Fihoges. Bernard at Garvagh (Longford Rural D.E.D.). *ALSO:* John at Musters' of Brianstown. Bridget at Casey's of Killashee Street, Longford Town. Michael and Patrick at Cameron's of Main Street, Longford Town.

SHARRY, SHARREY: Sr. Jane at Sr. Hoare's of Grassyard.

SHAUGHNESSY: Michael, James at Cleenrah. Patrick, James, William, Michael at Corneddan. *ALSO:* Joseph at Devine's of Richmond Street, Longford Town.

O'SHAUGHNESSY: David at Main Street, Granard Town. John at Esker South.

SHAW:(13): Robert B. at Rath. Thomas at Carrigeen (Foxhall D.E.D.). Frances at Ballybranigan. Albert, John P. at Ballymahon Town. Robert at Ards. John at Kilcommock Glebe. Jane at Drummeel. Robert, Jane at Cloonageeher. Robert at Tully (Cloondara D.E.D.). Henry at Cloonturk. Samuel W. at Glack (Longford Rural D.E.D.). *ALSO:* Maria J. at Myles' of Ratharney. Richard at Middleton's of Corrabola (Doory D.E.D.). William at Wright's of Corry (Caldragh D.E.D.). John at Hall's of Meelick. R.A. at Hewetson's of Church Street, Longford Town.

SHEA:(10): Anne at Keel (Forgney D.E.D.). Robert at Daroge. John at Ballymahon Town. Bridget, Peter at Cleraun. Catherine at Cloonmee. Michael at Portanure. Timothy at Bleanavoher. Thomas at Formoyle (Farrell). Michael at Inchenagh Island (Rathcline D.E.D.). *ALSO:* Anne at John Reilly's of Rathmore (Ballymahon D.E.D.). Timothy at Joseph Sweeney's of Derrygowna. James at McNally's of Cornadowagh. Bridget at John Farrell's of Leab. Margaret at Faughnan's of Ballagh (Newtownforbes D.E.D.). Thomas at Kelly's of Canal Harbour, Longford

Town.

O'SHEA: Anne at Farrington's of Newtownforbes Village.

SHEARER: Sarah at Doherty's of Currygrane.

SHEDDOCK: Patrick at The Hill, Granard Town.

SHEDWELL: George and Mary A. at Carroll's of St. Mel's Road, Longford Town.

SHEEHAN, SHEEAN: Annie at Ballymahon Town. Denis at Mosstown (Rathcline Barony). Daniel at Chapel Lane, Longford Town. *ALSO:* Lizzie at Peter Beglin's of Cloonker.

SHEEHY: James at St. Mel's Road, Longford Town. *ALSO:* M.K. at James Gorman's of Ballymahon Town.

SHEERAN:(13): Bernard at Kilsallagh. John, Bridget, Patrick, John, Patrick, Thomas at Lettergeeragh. Thomas at Leitrim (Breanrisk D.E.D.). Bernard at Garrowhill. Patrick at Dooroc. Daniel at Cloondara. David at Creeve. Thomas at Great Water Street, Longford Town. *ALSO:* Bridget at Confrey's of Enybegs. Martha at Livingstone's of Creeve. Mary at Murray's of Main Street, Longford Town.

SHEERIN: Winifred at James Farrell's of Glack (Longford Rural D.E.D.).

SHEIL: See Shields.

SHEKLETON, SHEKELTON: Joseph at Cloonshannagh or Coolamber Manor Demesne.

SHELTON: James at John McCormack's of Dublin Street, Longford Town.

SHENTON: F. at Hewetson's of Church Street, Longford Town.

SHEPPARD: James at Fee's of Church Street, Longford Town.

SHERIDAN:(60): Rev. James, Owen at Aghakine. Matthew at Abbeylara. Thomas, John at Springtown. John at Aghnagarron. Michael at Cloghchurnel. Bridget at Creevy. Hugh at Rinroe. William at Tennyphobble. Terence at Barrack Street, Granard Town. Peter at New Road, Granard Town. Mary at Water Lane, Granard Town. Michael at Muckerstaff. John, Hanora, John W. at Camagh (Newgrove D.E.D.). Catherine, Farrell at Carrickmaguirk. Mary at Rosduff. John, Patrick, James at Smear. Ellen, Michael, Mathew at Crott. Peter at Enaghan. Margaret, Charles at Ballyduffy. James at Drumhalry. Mary at Fihoragh. John at Drumard. Philip, John, Michael, Nannie at Farmullagh. Patrick at Dring. Felix at Lisnagrish. John at Corclaragh. Patrick at Edgeworthstown Town. Peter, Catherine, Daniel at Corrinagh. Peter, Catherine, Patrick, Francis at Breanriskcullew. Eugene, James at Moyne. John, John, Patrick, James at Leggagh. John at Drumlish Village. Michael at Cloonbalt. John at Cooleeny. James, John at Chapel Lane, Longford Town. Charles, Ellen at Dublin Street, Longford Town. *ALSO:* James at Donohoe's of Aghacordrinan. Francis at Kate Mulligan's of Aghnacliff. Mary at O'Reilly's of Clooneen (Creevy D.E.D.). Anne at Farrell's of Ballymore. Peter at Markey's of Ball Alley Street Upper, Granard Town. Terence at Grehan's of Main Street, Granard Town. Mary A. at McCormack's of Smear. Rose at McStay's of Crott. John at Ellen Duffy's of Aghagah. Catherine at Francis Reilly's of Aghanoran. Maggie at Michael Cooney's of Breanriskcullew. Thomas at Duignan's of Kiltycreevagh. Bridget at Farrelly's of Cloonelly. Ann and Ann at Lahey's of Esker South. Bridget at Hussey's of Hyde's Yard, Longford Town. Michael at Patrick Fitzgerald's (1) of Main Street, Longford Town.

SHERON: See Sheeran.

SHERRY: Edward at Reilly's of New Road, Granard Town.

SHEVITON: Bernard at Sandy Row, Longford Town. *ALSO:* Bernard at Mathews' of Great Water Street, Longford Town. Mary at Lloyd's of Main Street, Longford Town. Margaret at Rentoul's of Abbeycartron.

SHEVLIN: Michael at Aghadegnan (Longford Rural D.E.D.).

SHIELDS, SHEIL, SHIEL, SHIELS: Bessy at Crott. Bridget at Glen. Catherine at Healy's Terrace, Longford Town. *ALSO:* Bridget at Kyne's of Corbaun or Leitrim. Mary at Forbes's of Castleforbes Demesne. Mary at John Harvey's of Bog Lane, Longford Town. John at McNamara's of Main Street, Longford Town.

SHILNAM: T.S. at Hewetson's of Church Street, Longford Town.

SHORE: Joseph, Elizabeth at Rathmore (Ballymahon D.E.D.). *ALSO:* Lizzie at McManus's of Main Street, Longford Town.

SHORT, SHORTT: Thomas at Cross (Ardagh East D.E.D.).

SHRIVE: J. at Hewetson's of Church Street, Longford Town.

SIDES: Susan J. at Ballymahon Town.

SIDLEY: See De Burgh- Sidley.

SILLS: W. at Duncan McGregor's of Lisbrack (Longford Rural D.E.D.).

SIMMONS: James, Michael, Henry, William, Ellen at Rathmore (Ballymahon D.E.D.). Robert at Carrickglass Demesne (Templemichael Civil Ph.). *ALSO:* Mary at Fegan's of Rathmore (Ballymahon D.E.D.).

SIMPKINS: G. at Hewetson's of Church Street, Longford Town.

SIMPSON: James at Killashee Village. *ALSO:* Lilly et al. at Caulfield's of Clontymullan.

SKEFFINGTON: Michael at Earl Street, Longford Town.

SKELLY, SKALLY, SCALLY:(64): Michael at Curraghmore. Thomas at Ballintober (Bonny). Bernard at Ballintober (Rock). William, Patrick at Lisnacreevy. Thomas at Taghshinny. John at Cornacarta. John at Ballymahon Town. Catherine at Creevagh Beg. John, Bernard at Caltragh More. Patrick, Michael, Patrick, John at Aghavadden. John, Thomas at Ballagh (Cashel West D.E.D.). James at Ballyrevagh. John at Carrow Beg (Cashel West D.E.D.). Mary, Catherine at Carrowrory. Michael, John at Claras. John at Cleraun. Patrick at Collum. Patrick, James at Corrool (Brennan). Patrick at Corrool (Fox). Patrick at Corrool (Kenny). Kate at Cross (Cashel West D.E.D.). Thomas, Peter, James, Denis at Derrydarragh. James at Portanure. Patrick, Patrick at Saints Island. Patrick at Laughil (Kilcommock D.E.D.). John at Derryad (Ledwithstown D.E.D.). Peter at Edera. Mary at Lisnanagh. John at Dring. Michael at Edgeworthstown Town. Michael at Carrickmoyragh. Rev. Joseph at Newtownforbes Village. Michael, Thomas at Cloondara. John, Patrick at Knappoge (Cloondara D.E.D.). Denis at Cloonmore. Bridget at Corralough. James at Craane. John, Catherine, Bridget at Carrigeens. James at Carrowroe. Anne, Mary at Lehery. Thomas, Michael at Lisnacush. Bridget at Lisrevagh. Patrick at Banghill. Mary at Cloonturk. Lizzie at Main Street, Longford Town. *ALSO:* Maria at Elam's of Derrydarragh. Patrick at Peter Hopkins' (5) of Drumnee. Maggie at Garrahan's of Cloonbreany. Mary at Brabazon's of Higginstown. Fr. Michael at McMahon's of Enybegs. Winifred at Cumiskey's of Aghnagore. Anne at Mullooly's of Derryad (Mountdavis D.E.D.). Daniel at John Casey's of Cloonfore. Elizabeth at Anne Dunigan's of Derrygeel. Mary at Dunne's of Lanesborough Village. Mary at Francis Devlin's (2) of Derrymore. Francis at O'Connor's of Conroy's Court, Longford Town. Francis at Shanley's of Main Street, Longford Town. Michael at John Mathews' of Main Street, Longford Town. (See Scully).

SLACK, SLACKE: William at Kiltycreevagh.

SLATOR: Arthur at Cartron (Forgney D.E.D.). (See Wilson-Slator).

SLEVIN: Thomas at Ballymahon Town. Anthony at Main Street, Granard Town. Joseph at Cloncowley. Michael, John at Cornacullew. John at Brickeens. Joseph at Keon's Terrace, Longford Town. *ALSO:* Mary at Sullivan's of Main Street, Granard Town. William at Stafford's of Tuite's Lane, Granard Town. Mary at John Farrell's of Stonepark (Longford Rural D.E.D.). Ellen at Flanagan's of Market Square, Longford Town.

SLOANE: Henry at Barrack Street, Granard Town. James, Mary at Kilmore. *ALSO:* Matilda at Muir's of Edgeworthstown Town.

SLOWEY: James at Cartronageeragh. Anne of Glack (Longford Rural D.E.D.).

SMALL: Joseph at Leitrim (Granard Rural D.E.D.). James at Lisraghtigan. John at Ardagullion. William at Asnagh. Alexander, Isabella at Tonywardan. Francis at Cloonageeher. *ALSO:* Williama at Farrell's of Loughan. Katie at O'Neill's of Lissameen. James at Garrit Farrell's of Cartron (Granard Rural D.E.D.). Sarah at Dawson's of Lisryan.

SMYTH, SMITH:(95): Joseph at Ballymulvey. Michael, Thomas at Tirlickeen. Owen at Cloonard (Ballymahon D.E.D.). John at Newpark. Mathew at Cornadowagh. John, Mary at Corrool (Kenny). John at Tipper (Cashel West D.E.D.). Andrew at Knockavegan. Isabella at Lisglassock. James at Listraghee. Michael at Currygrane. Thomas, Anne at Drumnacross. Peter at Laughil (Edgeworth). Bridget, Catherine at Roos. Francis at Aghagreagh. Patrick, Thomas at Culray. James at Ranaghan. Patrick at Tonymore North. Peter at Tonymore South. Kate at Abbeylara Village. Michael at Cartronbore. John at Coolcor. Julia, Daniel at Killeen (Bunlahy D.E.D.). Anne, Bernard at Cloonaghmore. Bridget, Lawrence at Killasona. James at Rincoolagh. James at Aghabrack. Andrew at Ballybrien. Owen at Ballymore. James at Ball Alley Street Upper, Granard Town. Hugh at Ballynacross (Granard Urban D.E.D.). William at Barrack Street, Granard Town. Rev. James, James at Main Street, Granard Town. Charles at Moxham Street, Granard Town. Michael, Michael, Bridget at The Hill, Granard Town. Mathew at Coolagherty. Patrick, Bridget at Cleenrah. Matthew at Smear. Francis at Lisraherty. Patrick, Michael at Ballyduffy. Michael, Anne at Drumury. Patrick, Patrick at Fihoragh. William at Farmullagh. Michael at Aghanoran. Rose at Corbaun or Leitrim. Anne at Derrycassan. James at Larkfield. James at Rinnenny. Catherine at Aghafin. Peter at Lackan. Anne at Edgeworthstown Town. Joseph, Francis, Francis, Thomas, Anne at Rathmore (Ballinamuck East D.E.D.). Mary, James at Fostragh. Catherine, Owen, Thomas, James, Bernard at Glenmore (Ballinamuck East D.E.D.). Terence, Daniel at Kiltycreevagh. Mathew at Moyne. Francis at Kiltycon. Francis at Cloonageeher. James, Patrick at

Kilmore Upper. James, James at Tully (Cloondara D.E.D.). Michael at
Cloonfinfy. William at Cloonmore. Peter at Aghantrah. John at Carrowroe.
Patrick at Lanesborough Village. Thomas at Drumhaughly. Francis at
Creeve. James at McLoughlin's Yard, Longford Town. *ALSO:* Hugh at
Slator's of Cartron (Forgney D.E.D.). James at Payne's of Tennalick.
Thomas at McCann's of Tirlickeen. Patrick at Flood's of Knappoge
(Ballymahon D.E.D.). Anne at Brennan's of Derraghan Beg. Mathew at
Catherine Greene's of Elfeet (Adamson). Harriette at Browne's of Glebe
(Cashel West D.E.D.). Thomas at Farrell's of Portanure. Rose at John
Reilly's of Aghacordrinan. Peter at Margaret Kiernan's of Aghagreagh.
Ellen and Katie at Kate Mulligan's of Aghnacliff. Daniel at O'Brien's of
Cartronamarkey. Kate at Brady's of Ballyboy. Maggie at Flood's of
Ballymaurice (Granard Rural D.E.D.). Katie at Thomas McCabe's of
Cartron (Granard Rural D.E.D.). Patrick at Monaghan's of Leitrim (Granard
Rural D.E.D.). Sarah at Williamson's of Granard. Charles at Drum's of
Main Street, Granard Town. Anne at Flanagan's of Main Street, Granard
Town. Maggie at Peter Kiernan's of Main Street, Granard Town. Bridget
at John Ward's of Main Street, Granard Town. John and Daniel at
Leonard's of Main Street, Granard Town. Richard at Mary E. Burns' of
Main Street, Granard Town. Anne at Williams's of Moxham Street,
Granard Town. Bridget at Reynolds's of Ferskill. Mary J. at Lynch's of
Polladooey. Elizabeth at Kate Doyle's of Smear. Anne at William Duffy's
of Drumhalry. Mary A. at Anne Mahon's of Farmullagh. Margaret at
Lenahan's of Aghanoran. Patrick at James Courtney's (11) of Larkfield.
James at James Courtney's (12) of Larkfield. Mathew at Tynan's of
Castlenugent. Maria and Patrick at Dermody's of Freaghmeen. Annie at
Dowler's of Edgeworthstown Town. William at Patrick Cullen's of
Edgeworthstown Town. Patrick at McCabe's of Edgeworthstown Town.
Alice at Joseph O'Reilly's of Annaghdaniel. John J. at Margaret Manning's
of Cloonellan. Michael at Thomas Quinn's of Bawn (Breanrisk D.E.D.).
Patrick at Boyle's of Corglass. Thomas at Donohoe's of Kiltycon. Sarah
at Farrington's of Newtownforbes Village. James at Percival's of Minard.
Bernard at Nerney's of Cloonanny Glebe. Jane at Geoffroy's of Rathcline.
Mary at Lally's of Lanesborough Village. John at Mary Creane's of Soran.
Bridget at Farrell's of Lisduff (Longford Rural D.E.D.). Philip at
McKenzie's of Earl Street, Longford Town. John at McGarry's of Main
Street, Longford Town. James at Skelly's of Main Street, Longford Town.
Mary at Irwin's of Main Street, Longford Town.

SNELL: W. at Hewetson's of Church Street, Longford Town.

SODEN: Thomas T. at Ballymahon Town. John at Glenoghil.

SOMERS, SOMMERS: John at Main Street, Granard Town. Maria at
Ballagh (Newtownforbes D.E.D.). John at Kilmacannon. *ALSO:* James at
Forbes's of Castleforbes Demesne.

SONDAN: Mary at Keefe's of Chapel Lane, Longford Town (?).

SORAHAN, SOROHAN: Michael at Ballymore. Daniel, Michael at Fardrumman. Bernard at Lettergullion. *ALSO:* Bridget at Catherine Sheridan's of Corrinagh.

SORDEN: Patrick and Teresa at John Cosgrove's of Derrynacrit.

SOUDAN: Mary at Keefe's of Chapel Lane, Longford Town (?).

SOUTHWELL: Rose at Coach Yard, Longford Town.

SPEARMAN: James at Templeton Glebe. Michael at Annaghmore.

SPILLER: P.D. at Hewetson's of Church Street, Longford Town.

SPINKS: Joseph at Richmond Street, Longford Town.

SPOLLEN, SPOLLAN: Michael et al. at Wilson-Slator's of Knockanbaun or Whitehill.

STACOM: Maria at Dublin Street, Longford Town. (See Stakem).

STAFFORD: Peter at Drinan. John at Tuite's Lane, Granard Town. Patrick, Thomas at Main Street, Longford Town. Mary E. at Richmond Street, Longford Town. *ALSO:* Robert at Fluery's of Smear.

STAINFIELD: G.A. at Hewetson's of Church Street, Longford Town.

STAKEM, STAKIM, STEAKEM: Henry at Aghagreagh. Philip at Aghakeeran. Peter at Cloonback. James at Fostragh. Peter at Kiltycreevagh. Patrick at Cloonelly. Cornelius at Gaigue. Mathew at Kilmacannon. John at Crossea South. (See Stacom).

STANLEY: John at Forthill. William B. at Cloonshannagh or Coolamber Manor Demesne. *ALSO:* Mary at Casey's of Forthill.

STAPLETON: William at Felix Dolan's of Aghadowry. Patrick at Lennon's of Breanriskcullew. Thomas at Dolan's of Killashee Village. Bridget at Jones's of Rappareehill.

McSTAY, MULSTAY: Mary at Rosduff. Peter, Patrick at Smear. John at Crott. Patrick at Enaghan. Patrick at Toome (Mullanalaghta D.E.D.). *ALSO:* Patrick at Bridget Reilly's of Rosduff. John at Patrick Reynolds's of Camagh (Ballinamuck East D.E.D.). Michael at McNerney's of New Street, Longford Town.

STEAKEM: See Stakem.

STEELE, STEEL: John at Moneyfad. Mary at Derindiff. Mary at Tinnynarr. Michael at Corragarrow (Killashee D.E.D.). Thomas at Newtown (Killashee D.E.D.).

STEPHENS, STEVENS: Nicholas at Moydow Glebe. *ALSO:* Emily at John H. Plant's of Ballymahon Town. Annie at Wilson's of Main Street, Keenagh Village. John S. at Yorke's of Barrack Street, Granard Town.

STEPHENSON, STEVENSON: David at Cloonscott. Charlotte at Druming. William at Ballinlough. James at Cloghchurnel. Lloyd at Clontumpher. Anne at Dublin Street, Longford Town. Susan at Keon's Terrace, Longford Town. Francis at St. Michael's Road, Longford Town. Margaret at Abbeycartron. *ALSO:* Mary at Seymour's of Aghareagh (Cloondara D.E.D.). John at Little's of Main Street, Longford Town.

STEWARD: Bridget at Gilmurry's of Lissanurlan.

STEWART: James at Newcastle. Rev. Charles S. at Gorteenrevagh, Ballinalee Village. Charles at Main Street, Granard Town. Alexander at Edgeworthstown Town. Robert at Killeeny. Francis at St. Michael's Road, Longford Town. *ALSO:* Annie at Cody's of Streamstown (Kilglass D.E.D.). Marion E. at Thompson's of Ballinulty Upper. Katie et al. at Michael Hussey's of Glebe (Cloondara D.E.D.). Bridget at Gilmurray's of Lissanurlan (?). Emma at Lefroy's of Carrickglass Demesne (Templemichael Civil Ph.). Grace and Margaret at Cameron's of Main Street, Longford Town. John and William J. at Kate Brady's of Main Street, Longford Town.

ST. JOHN: George at Gragh. John at Cartron Big. *ALSO:* Martha at Browne's of Vicarsfield Glebe. Lily H. at Keane's of Edgeworthstown Town. Anna at Seymour's of Aghareagh (Cloondara D.E.D.). Margaret at Allen's of Ballymacwilliam.

STOKER: Francis at Main Street, Longford Town.

STONE: Sarah at Armstrong's of Main Street, Longford Town.

STONEY: Rev. Francis S. at Glebe (Kilglass D.E.D.).

STOREY, STORY: Euphemia at Annie E. Reilly's of Cornadrung.

STRANG: James at Abbeycartron.

STRANGE: James at Bridge Street, Longford Town.

STRATFORD: Joseph at Lisnanagh. Mark at Creevy. *ALSO:* John at Kelly's of Corbaun or Leitrim. Robert at Free's of Cooleeny (?).

STRITCH: Peter at Coach Yard, Longford Town. Mary, Richard at Noud's Yard, Longford Town. Michael at Townparks (Longford Urban No. 1 D.E.D.). John et al. at Connor's of Coach Yard, Longford Town.

STRONG: John at Ballybrien. Anne at Cartron (Granard Urban D.E.D.). William at New Road, Granard Town.

SULLIVAN:(13): Anne, Philip at Aghakilmore. Hugh, Anne, Margaret at Aghakine. Owen, John at Bunlahy. John at Killeen (Bunlahy D.E.D.). Elizabeth at Ball Alley Street Lower, Granard Town. Bridget at Main Street, Granard Town. Timothy at Ferskill. Michael at Willsbrook. Thomas at Creenagh. *ALSO:* Daniel at James Feeney's of Ballymahon Town. Patrick et al. at William Seales' of Ballymahon Town. Peter at Anne Lee's of Aghakilmore. John at McGivney's of Culray. Maggie at James Mulligan's of Aghakine. Mary at Kate Mulligan's of Aghnacliff. Helena at James Reilly's of Barrack Street, Granard Town. Thomas at James Smith's (62) of Main Street, Granard Town. Bernard at Thomas Fenlon's of Edgeworthstown Town. Mary at Francis Hourican's of Corrinagh. Catherine at Patrick Fitzgerald's (1) of Main Street, Longford Town.

O'SULLIVAN: Sr. Annie at Rev. Mother Farrington's of Newtownforbes Village. Francis and Kathleen at Greeves' of Ballymahon Street, Longford Town. Mary at Green's of Convent Lane, Longford Town. Michael at Nevin's of Market Square, Longford Town.

SUMMERS: See Somers.

SUTTON: George, Thomas at Ballyclamay. Anne at Sharvoge.

SWEENEY, SWEENY:(19): Joseph, Thomas, Mary, James, Anne at Druming. Bridget, James, Joseph, Owen at Derrygowna. John at Newpark. Mary at Aghavadden. Michael at Greenhall Upper. James at Castlebrock. Thomas at Ballyhoolivan. James at Coolcor. Catherine at Liscahill. James at Lisnageeragh. John at Garrowhill. Catherine at Drumlish Village. *ALSO:* Maria K. at Catherine Reilly's of Cranalagh More. Patrick at Leavy's of Longfield. James and Mary at Leavy's of Edgeworthstown Town. Bridget at Reynolds's of Cartrongolan. Edward and Mary A. at Murphy's of Cornollen. Bridget at Shea's of Bleanavoher. Michael at Curley's of Banghill. Mary at Manning's of Cornapark. Ellen at James Farrell's of Glack (Longford Rural D.E.D.). James and Anne at Fullam's of Deanscurragh. Patrick at Plunkett's of Main Street, Longford Town. Dorothy at Flanagan's of Market Square, Longford Town.

SWIFT: Richard at Stoncpark (Kilcommock D.E.D.). *ALSO:* Anastasia at Jessop's of Doory. John at Wilson's of Main Street, Keenagh Village. George at Logan's of Kilsallagh. Thomas at Arthur McCormack's of Leitrim (Breanrisk D.E.D.). Eva A. at Boyers' (4) of Main Street, Longford Town.

SWITZER, SWITSER: Christopher at Kingstone's of Mosstown (Rathcline Barony).

SYNOTT: Owen at Castlenugent.

TAAFFE, TAFFE: John at Ards. Patrick at Island. John, Owen at Mosstown (Rathcline Barony). Richard at Moatavally. John, John at Leggagh. Bridget at Dublin Street, Longford Town. *ALSO:* Mary at Pollock's of Main Street, Keenagh Village.

McTAGGART: Mary A. at Michael Hughes's of Derawley.

TAHENY, TAHNEY: See Taney.

TAIGUE: James, Margaret, Thomas at Drumanure.(See Tighe).

TALLY: John, Thomas, John, Denis at Castlebaun. Patrick at Drumnacooha. Peter at Kilmahon. (See Tully).

TANEY: Hugh at Great Water Street, Longford Town.

TANNER: George at Ballymahon Town. Catherine at Greenhall Upper. Francis at Ards. George at Cartronbrack. John at Currycahill. Isabella at Cleggill. Edward at Templeton Glebe. Elizabeth at Ballygar. *ALSO:* Margaret at Myles' of New Street, Longford Town.

TANSEY: Michael at Lehery. *ALSO:* Michael at O'Donnell's of Dublin Street, Longford Town.

TAPP: Robert at Bridge Street, Longford Town.

TAYLOR: John at Newcastle. Ambrose at Smithfield. John G. at Ballymahon Town. Francis W. at Castlenugent. Allan at Knockloughlin. Jane at Corboy. *ALSO:* James at Wahab's of Ferskill. Mary at James Flynn's of Cartrongolan. Francis W. at Norris's of Drumnacooha. Abraham at Legge's of Main Street, Longford Town. Agnes at Spink's of Richmond Street, Longford Town. Harriet at Little's of Church Street, Longford Town. F. at Hewetson's of Church Street, Longford Town.

TEAGUE: See Taigue.

TEELE: Christopher at Cloonshannagh or Coolamber Manor Demesne.

TELFORD: Robert at Grillagh (Killashee D.E.D.).

TERRY: S. at Duncan McGregor's of Lisbrack (Longford Rural D.E.D.). G. at Hewetson's of Church Street, Longford Town.

THANE: Robert A. at Fee's Terrace, Longford Town.

THEILL: Marian at More O'Ferrall's of Lissard.

THOMAS: Susan G. at Joynt's of New Street, Longford Town. A. at Hewetson's of Church Street, Longford Town.

THOMPSON:(38): Mary at Newcastle. Charles at Clygeen. Annie at Cloonmee. Patrick at Abbeylara Village. William at Ballinulty Upper. John C. at Rathcronan. Hugh L. at Cranalagh More. Maria at Creelaghta. John J. at Leitrim (Breanrisk D.E.D.). Patrick at Drumlish Village. Michael at Newtownforbes Village. Robert at Cloonageeher. Mathew at Gorteenorna. William at Lisnabo. Mary at Cloonrallagh. Anne at Killashee and Aghakeeran. William at Aghaboy (Aghaboy D.E.D.). John, Francis at Esker South. James at Cooleeshil or Richfort. William at Drumbaun. Bridget, Margaret, Andrew, William at Cartrongarrow. Anne at Carrickglass Demesne (Templemichael Civil Ph.). James at Killeter. John at Lissavaddy. Patrick at Rhine. Francis at Mullagh. Michael, John at Ballymahon Street, Longford Town. Anne M. at Dublin Street, Longford Town. Henry at Glack (Longford Urban No. 1 D.E.D.). John at Great Water Street, Longford Town. Patrick at Abbeycartron. Rev. John A. at Demesne. *ALSO:* Patrick at Patrick Mc Greevy's of Ballymahon Town. Thomas and John at Martin Reynolds's of Ballymahon Town. Phoebie and Thomas at William Denniston's (9) of Drummeel. Elizabeth at Tanner's of Cleggill. Annie E. at Ashcroft's of Carrickglass Demesne (Templemichael Civil Ph.). Catherine at Murtagh's of Killeter. G. at Duncan McGregor's of Lisbrack (Longford Rural D.E.D.). Kate at Patrick Coffey's of Chapel Lane, Longford Town. John at O'Connor's of Conroy's Court, Longford Town. Elizabeth at Stoker's of Main Street, Longford Town. Robert at Duffy's of Ballymahon Street, Longford Town.

THORNTON: James at Regan's of Smithfield. Mary at Robinson's of Earl Street, Longford Town.

THORPE, THORP: Joseph T. at Patrick Kenny's of Cloonrallagh. Joseph at O'Neill's of Main Street, Longford Town.

THRAPP: See Trapp.

THRAUTT: See Trott.

THREADGOLD: J. at Hewetson's of Church Street, Longford Town.

TIDYMAN: Teresa at Forbes's of Castleforbes Demesne.

TIERNAN:(11): John at Cloonmee. Anne, Patrick at Greenhall Lower. James, Michael at Greenhall Upper. James at Monaduff. Anne at Cloonart South. John at Magheraveen. Terence at Aughine. Thomas at Clooneeny. James at Stonepark (Longford Rural D.E.D.). *ALSO:* John F. at Mulligan's of Main Street, Granard Town. Mary at Thompson's of Newtownforbes Village. Bridget at Bond's of Ballygarve. Julia at Lynn's of Dublin Street, Longford Town.

TIERNEY: J. at Abbeyshrule. Patrick at Drumhalry. Maria at Ballymahon Street, Longford Town. *ALSO:* Thomas at Downes' of Barrack Street, Granard Town. John at Flanagan's of Main Street, Granard Town. John at McGrath's of Main Street, Granard Town. John at Williams's of Ballyduffy. Peter at Rose Kiernan's of Toome (Mullanalaghta D.E.D.). Ellen at Anne Conlon's of Drumlish Village. William at Farrell's of Lisduff (Longford Rural D.E.D.) (?).

TIGHE: Robert at Cornamucklagh. Julia at Newtownforbes Village. *ALSO:* James at Michael Finn's of Rathmore (Ballymahon D.E.D.). Anne at Musters' of Brianstown. (See Taigue).

TIMOTHY: John at King's of Main Street, Longford Town.

TIMS, TIMMS: Sarah J. and Emily at Johnson's of Moor. Margaret and Esther at George Kenny's of Cartrongarrow.

TOBIN: Anne at Ball Alley Street Upper, Granard Town. James at Barrack Street, Granard Town. *ALSO:* Marian at Ross's of Main Street, Longford Town.

TOHER: John at Lackan. Thomas at Cornollen. Andrew at Ballynagoshen. *ALSO:* Joseph at Corcoran's of Brianstown. Catherine at Murphy's of Ballynagoshen.

TOMKINSON: John T. at Bridge Street, Longford Town.

TOOLAN, TOOLEN: Peter at Glack (Longford Rural D.E.D.).

TOOLE: Anne at Tirlickeen. James at Drumhalry. Patrick at Annagh (Drumgort D.E.D.). John at Dublin Street, Longford Town. James at Great Water Street, Longford Town. Mary at O'Donnell's Yard, Longford Town.

Jane at Abbeycartron. *ALSO:* Michael at Francis Murtagh's of Cuingareen. Samuel at Kearney's of Crossea North. Jane at O'Neill's of Main Street, Longford Town.

O'TOOLE: James at Gaigue.

TOOMAN: John at Newtown (Moydow D.E.D.). Joseph at Mullaghavorneen. John, Patrick, Thomas at Stonepark (Longford Rural D.E.D.). *ALSO:* Michael at Nolan's of Newtown (Moydow D.E.D.). Patrick at McHugh's of Stonepark (Longford Rural D.E.D.).

TOONE: H. at Hewetson's of Church Street, Longford Town.

TORLE: Catherine at McGaver's of Cloontamore.

TORMEY: Thomas at Abbeylara Village. Michael at Main Street, Granard Town. *ALSO:* Mary at Lizzie Brady's of Main Street, Granard Town. Mary A. at Coffey's of Edgeworthstown Town.

TOWERS: Catherine at Farrington's of Newtownforbes Village.

TOWNSEND: G. at Hewetson's of Church Street, Longford Town.

TRACEY: See Treacy.

TRAPP: Catherine at Drumnacooha. James at Kilnacarrow (Aghaboy D.E.D.). James at Soran. James at Lisfarrell. *ALSO:* Patrick et al. at McHugh's of Soran.

TRAUTT: See Trott.

TRAVERS: Margaret at Aghabrack.

TRAYNOR: Patrick at Grehan's of Main Street, Granard Town. Elizabeth at John Fee's of Creeve.

TREACY, TRACEY:(13): John at Aghagreagh. Margaret, Bernard at Aghakilmore. John at Gelshagh. Edward, Cornelius at Lislea (Lislea D.E.D.). Mary A. at Newtownbond. Michael at Ballinlough. John, James at Bunlahy. Catherine at Ballymore. Edward at Ball Alley Street Upper, Granard Town. John at Fihoragh. *ALSO:* Charles at Catherine Monaghan's of Aghagreagh. Bridget at McCauley's of Coolagherty. Arthur at Clyne's of Barnacor (Rathcline D.E.D.).

TREDENNICK: William at Moncrieff's of Glebe (Rathcline D.E.D.).

TRIMBLE: Thomas at Ratharney. Andrew at Carrigeen (Foxhall D.E.D.). Robert, John at Kinard. Mary at Lismagoneen. Alexander at Sheeroe (Knockanbaun D.E.D.). Mary at Main Street, Longford Town. *ALSO:* Ellen at Kirk's of Prucklishtown.

TROTT, THRAUTT: John at Lyanmore. Mary at Bawn (Ardagh West D.E.D.). *ALSO:* Bridget at Malone's of Bawn (Ardagh West D.E.D.). John at Lamb's of Earl Street, Longford Town.

TUITE: Thomas at Cloonagh (Mullanalaghta D.E.D.). Edward at Larkfield.

TULLY: Thomas at Aghagreagh. Michael at Gaigue. *ALSO:* John at Hyland's of Barrack Street, Granard Town. Michael at Bridget Maguire's of Drumnacooha. (See Tally).

TUNNY, TUNNEY: Thomas, Bridget at Aghamore Upper. Patrick at Derreenavoggy. *ALSO:* Mary at James Duignan's of Kiltyreher (Killoe Civil Ph.). Sr. Emily at Sr. Green's of Convent Lane, Longford Town.

TURNER: Mary A. at Barry (Ballymahon D.E.D.). William at Ballaghgowla and Froghan. John at Edgeworthstown Town. Robert J. at Earl Street, Longford Town. *ALSO:* Lizzie at William Rickard's of Ballymahon Town. Michael at Gallagher's of Aghafin.

TWADDLE: John at Trillickacurry. Edward at Nappagh. *ALSO:* John at Margaret Flower's of Barry (Ballymahon D.E.D.).

TWEEDY: T.J. at Hewetson's of Church Street, Longford Town.

TWOMEY: Hugh T. at Grier's of Main Street, Granard Town.

TYNAN:(10): Denis, Edward at Drumnahara. Henry at Leitrim (Ballinalee D.E.D.). John at Drummeel. James at Roos. James at Castlenugent. John, Michael, Patrick at Esker South. Peter at Mucknagh. *ALSO:* Mary A. at Doyle's of Ballynascraw. Denis at Charles Fox's of Aghakilmore. Patrick at McGovern's of The Hill, Granard Town. Mary at Mary Brady's of Gaigue. Mary at Doherty's (19) of Esker South. George at Margaret Donnelly's of Chapel Lane, Longford Town.

TYRRELL: Anne at Lissawarriff. Joseph at Lyneen. John at Glebe (Cloondara D.E.D.). Mary at Killashee Village. Thomas at Carrowmanagh. Elizabeth at Toneen (Moydow D.E.D.). *ALSO:* Bridget at Farrington's of Newtownforbes Village. Catherine at McGaver's of Cloontamore (?). Lizzie at Nugent's of Aghantrah. James at Finlay's of Clooncoose (Cloonee D.E.D.). Mary A. at Collins's of Dwyer's Yard, Longford Town. Mary at

Patrick Farrell's of Main Street, Longford Town. J. at Hewetson's of Church Street, Longford Town.

USSHER-ROBERTS: Edward at Knockahaw.

UTTON: at Hewetson's of Church Street, Longford Town.

VANCE: William at Aghnashannagh. William at Aghaward. George, Jeremiah at Drumderg. Susan at Glenmore (Ballinamuck East D.E.D.). Jeremiah at Knockloughlin. *ALSO:* James et al. at Elizabeth Robinson's of Ballymahon Town. John at Fee's of Church Street, Longford Town.

VARLEY: C.E. at Hewetson's of Church Street, Longford Town.

VAUGHAN: Thomas at Leitrim (Ballinalee D.E.D.). John at Cloontagh. Joseph, Thomas, Patrick at Derryharrow. Patrick at Templemichael Glebe. Michael at Little Water Street, Longford Town. *ALSO:* J. at Hewetson's of Church Street, Longford Town.

McVEETY: See McVitty.

McVEIGH, McVEY: Hugh, John at Fardrumman. Rose, Mary, Patrick at Oghil. Patrick at Knockloughlin. John at Derryharrow. Peter at Corneddan. *ALSO:* Bridget at Patrick Ginty's of Shanmullagh (?). John at McGuire's of Cloonbalt. (See McAvey).

McVENEA: Jane and Elizabeth at White's of Conroy's Court, Longford Town. James et al. at Layden's of Little Water Street, Longford Town.

McVENEY: Kate at Joseph Smith's of Rathmore (Ballinamuck East D.E.D.).

McVENNA: James at Corglass.

McVEY: See McVeigh.

VICTORY: Peter, Thomas at Mornin. Thomas, John, James at Corclaragh. James at Longfield. James at Bracklon. John at Ballinroddy. Owen at Earl Street, Longford Town. *ALSO:* Peter at Dermody's of Mullinroe. Annie and John at Bryan Noonan's of Cam. Owen at Hughes's of Edgeworthstown Town.

VINCE: Arthur at Church Street, Longford Town.

McVINNA, McVINRA: Mary at Patrick Donohoe's of Drumard.

McVITTY, McVEETY: John at Aghnashannagh. Margaret at Enybegs. Alexander, Christopher at Gorteenorna. Patrick at Creeve. *ALSO:* Kate at Morris's of Lettergonnell. Ellen at McDowell's of Gorteenorna. James at James Degnan's of Cloonee.

McVOY: See McEvoy.

WADE, WAIDE: See Quaid.

McWADE: See McQuaid.

WAHAB: Catherine at Ferskill.

WALKER: Richard at Derrydarragh. Ellen at Grassyard. Thomas at Tully (Milltown D.E.D.). Joseph at Lisnagrish. *ALSO:* Mary H. at Dawson's of Shanmullagh. William F. at Fetherston's of Ardagh Demesne. Robert at O'Connor's of Conroy's Court, Longford Town. John at McConnell's of Healy's Terrace, Longford Town.

WALL: Sr. Josephine at Rev. Mother Farrington's of Newtownforbes Village. Patrick at Dublin Street Barracks, Longford Town.

WALLACE: Peter at Aghagreagh. Thomas at Robinstown. Oliver at Muckerstaff. William at Carrigeens. Maria at McLoughlin's Yard, Longford Town. *ALSO:* Thomas at Anne Reilly's of Cartron (Granard Rural D.E.D.).

WALLIS: Anna at Adams's of Craane (?).

WALPOLE: James, Anne, Maria at Greagh. *ALSO:* Bessie at Patrick McKenna's of Cloonamacart.

WALSH, WALSHE:(32): Oliver W. at Ballyclamay. John at Forgney. Michael at Clooncullen. Thomas at Tirlickeen. John at Ballymahon Town. William at Cloonard (Ballymahon D.E.D.). Margaret at Creevaghmore (Forgney Civil Ph.). James, John, John at Toome (Ballymahon D.E.D.). Michael at Carrow Beg (Cashel West D.E.D.). Michael at Inchcleraun Island (Caseh West D.E.D.). Francis at Castlebaun. Thomas, John at Kiltyclogh. Anne at Briskil. Ellen, Anne, Patrick at Treel (Newtownforbes D.E.D.). Michael at Cloonrallagh. Patrick at Moygh (Killashee D.E.D.). James at Corralough. Thomas, Francis at Carrigeens. Ann, Thomas at Knock. John at Aghaboy (Aghaboy D.E.D.). Patrick at Drumure (?). Robert at Farraghroe. Thomas at Great Water Street, Longford Town. John at Killashee Street, Longford Town. Robert at St. Mel's Road, Longford Town. *ALSO:* Mary at Murray's of Taghshinny. Thomas at William McCormack's of Cloonard (Ballymahon D.E.D.). Eugene at Dillon's of

Ballinalee Village. Thomas at Michael Lynch's of Ballywillin. William et al. at Francis Reilly's of Ballygilchrist. Mary at Curran's of Ball Alley Street Upper, Granard Town. John at Flood's of Main Street, Granard Town. Michael at Kennedy's of Tonywardan. Elizabeth at Finnan's of Liscahill. Martin at Kenny's of Lissanure. Joseph at Ashe's of Drumlish Village. Henrietta and Angela at Farrington's of Newtownforbes Village. Kate at John Murtagh's of Cloonard (Cloondara D.E.D.). Percy at Adams's of Craane. Mary at Ussher-Roberts' of Knockahaw. Francis at Dennigan's of Chapel Lane, Longford Town. Joseph at Shanley's of Main Street, Longford Town. Bridget at McManus's of Main Street, Longford Town. Thomas at Edward Kenny's of Main Street, Longford Town. John at James Joyce's of Main Street, Longford Town. Michael at Gaughran's of Market Square, Longford Town.

WALTERS: W. at Hewetson's of Church Street, Longford Town.

WALTON, WALTEN: Mary J. at Walsh's of Ballyclamay. James at Hyland's of Fee's Terrace, Longford Town.

WARD:(48): Patrick at Ballyclamay. Mary, Patrick, Thomas, John at Forgney. John at Rockpeyton. Edward at Kinard. Patrick at Cloonkeen (Ballymahon D.E.D.). Bridget at Drinan. Bridget at Cloonmee. Patrick at Fortwilliam. Patrick at Cullentragh (Rathcline Civil Ph.). James at Derryart. Mathew, Mathew, Lawrence, Thomas, Michael at Sonnagh. Ellen at Cartron (Granard Rural D.E.D.). John, Laurence at Main Street, Granard Town. Michael at New Road, Granard Town. Patrick at Smear. Patrick, Bridget at Lisnageeragh. James at Ballindagny and Cullyvore. John at Edgeworthstown Town. Patrick at Drumbad. Bernard at Kiltycreevagh. William, Mary at Prucklish. William at Brickeens. Patrick at Cloonanny. Michael at Aghinaspick. Michael at Cloonker. Michael at Ballinree and Ballymoat. Joseph at Carnan. Ellen, Bryan at Rathvaldron. Anne, Patrick, John at Bawn (Ardagh West D.E.D.). Michael, Bridget, Mary at Bawn Mountain. Michael, Bridget at Cooleeny. John at Dublin Street, Longford Town. *ALSO:* Elizabeth at John Miller's of Tully (Agharra D.E.D.). Margaret at Farrell's of Forgney. James at McLoughlin's of Pallas More. Kate at Gerety's of Rath. James at Doyle's of Keel (Forgney D.E.D.). Anne at Newman's of Killeen (Foxhall D.E.D.). Elizabeth at Ball's of Caltragh Beg. Patrick and Bridget at Annie Mulligan's of Sonnagh. Catherine at Mary Donohoe's of Sonnagh. Patrick at Kelly's of Cloghchurnel. Mathew at Owen Doyle's of Smear. Anne at Ellen Hughes's of Back of the Hill. Mary at William Thompson's of Cartrongarrow.

WAYNE: Robert at Farraghroe.

WATERS: Moses at Gowlan. Roseanna at Main Street, Longford Town.

ALSO: John at McClean's of Edgeworthstown Town. Patrick at Michael Donnelly's of Kiltycreevagh.

WATKINS: W.H. at Hewetson's of Church Street, Longford Town.

WATSON: William at Killashee Village. *ALSO:* J.F. at Hewetson's of Church Street, Longford Town.

WAUCHOPE: See Wahab.

WEBB, WEBBE: George at Church Street, Longford Town. *ALSO:* Rose and Elizabeth at Farrington's of Newtownforbes Village. John and Margaret at Hare's of Killashee Village.

WEBSTER: Sydney R. at Robinson's of Earl Street, Longford Town. W. at Hewetson's of Church Street, Longford Town.

McWEENEY, McAWEENY: Stephen at Cloonart South. *ALSO:* William et al. at Susan Rourke's of Edgeworthstown Town.

WEIR: Letitia at Devenish's of Kilbride.

WELLOUGHBY: Charles at Walsh's of Ballyclamay.

WELLS: E. at Hewetson's of Church Street, Longford Town.

WELSH: Patrick at Drumure. (See Walsh).

WEST: Maria at Lisryan. Francis at Ballindagny and Cullyvore. Anne at Ballagh (Newtownforbes D.E.D.). *ALSO:* Mary at Cullen's of Kilcourcey.

WHACKETT: F. at Hewetson's of Church Street, Longford Town.

WHATELY: Patrick at Thomas Kiernan's of Barrack Street, Granard Town.

WHEATLEY, WHEATLY: Lizzie at Howden's of Main Street, Longford Town.

WHEELER: Albert H. and Maurice W. at Fetherston's of Ardagh Demesne.

WHELAN, FOYLAN, FILAN:(14): Kate, Rev. Mother at Ballymahon Town. John, Anne at Glenoghil. John, Michael at Longfield. Denis, Patrick, Bridget at Lettergullion. John at Cornapark. John at Allenagh. Patrick at

Rhine. Sarah at Harbour Row, Longford Town. Emily at Richmond Street, Longford Town. *ALSO:* John P. at John Brady's of Crowdrumman. Thomas F. and Mary A. at Mary Collum's of Lettergullion. Michael at Knockloughlin Barracks.

WHELEHAN: Thomas at Knockahaw.

WHELTON: Patrick at Joseph O'Reilly's of Annaghdaniel.

WHITAKER: See Whittaker.

WHITBY: G. at Hewetson's of Church Street, Longford Town.

WHITE, WHYTE: John at Ballymahon Town. Patrick at Barrack Street, Granard Town. Veronica M. at Clonwhelan. Annie at Drumlish Village. William, George at Castleforbes Demesne. John at Ballymahon Street, Longford Town. Mary A. at Conroy's Court, Longford Town. William at Great Water Street, Longford Town. *ALSO:* Bridget at Creegan's of Ball Alley Street Upper, Granard Town. Sr. Mary, Elizabeth and Eleanor at Rev. Mother Farrington's of Newtownforbes Village. James at Samuel Wilson's of Main Street, Longford Town.

WHITESIDE: Herbert at Finucane's of Church Street, Longford Town.

WHITLOW: William, Catherine at Abbeyderg. Margaret at Creagh. *ALSO:* Patrick at Peter Nolan's of Laughil (Kilcommock D.E.D.).

WHITNEY:(21): Catherine, Patrick at Aghacordrinan. John at Aghamore Upper. Rev. Francis at Freaghmeen. Patrick, Anne at Drumbad. Hugh, Peter, Patrick, Francis at Esker North. Mary, Patrick at Fardrumman. Thomas at Lettergullion. Bernard, John at Shanmullagh. Thomas at Cornacullew. Myles at Barragh More. Michael at Drumlish Village. Michael at Kilmahon. Patrick at Harbour Row, Longford Town. Myles at Healy's Terrace, Longford Town. *ALSO:* Margaret at Dillon's of Ballinalee Village. Maria at Kennedy's of Tonywardan. Mary A. and Terence at Thompson's of Creelaghta. Margaret J. at McGrath's of Ballymahon Street, Longford Town.

WHITTAKER: W. at Hewetson's of Church Street, Longford Town.

WHITTLE: James at Aghakine. *ALSO:* Thomas at Julia Fox's of Aghakilmore.

WHITTON, WHITTEN: William at Main Street, Keenagh Village. *ALSO:* George at Ellen Kiernan's of Aghnacliff.

WHYTE: See White.

WIGGINS: Charles J. at Moatavally. George, Henry at Edgeworthstown Town. Anne, John, James at Rathmore (Ballinamuck East D.E.D.). *ALSO:* George at Catherine Carney's of Kilsallagh.

WILDERS: Robert at Cloonmore.

WILESY: Rose at Gilligan's of Smear.

WILKINSON: William at Drumderg. *ALSO:* Elizabeth at Potterton's of Templemichael Glebe. John at Boyers' (2) of Main Street, Longford Town.

WILLIAMS: Bridget at Main Street, Granard Town. Jane at Moxham Street, Granard Town. James at Ballyduffy. Joseph at Ballymahon Street, Longford Town. *ALSO:* Mary at Flood's of Main Street, Granard Town. Fannie at Muir's of Edgeworthstown Town. Ellen at Bond's of Farraghroe.

WILLIAMSON: Alexander at Granard Town. *ALSO:* W. at Hewetson's of Church Street, Longford Town.

WILLIS: Mary at Hayes's of Main Street, Keenagh Village. Anna at Adams's of Craane.

WILSON:(19): William at Cloonbrin. Mary at Toome (Ballymahon D.E.D.). Mathew at Ballymahon Road, Keenagh Village. Robert at Main Street, Keenagh Village. James at Currygrane. Margaret at Carrowlinan. James at Drumderg. James at Lisnanagh. Francis at Birrinagh. Thomas at Edgeworthstown Town. James at Leggagh. Elizabeth M. at Newtownforbes Village. James at Ballyclare (Killashee D.E.D.). Jaspar at Ballydrum. John at Ballyclare (Moydow D.E.D.). Joseph at Keon's Terrace, Longford Town. Samuel, John at Main Street, Longford Town. Michael at St. Michael's Road, Longford Town. *ALSO:* Isa J. at John Plant's of Ballymahon Town. Robert and Jane at Navan's of Carrowlinan. Lizzie at Parks' of Ball Alley Street Upper, Granard Town. Elizabeth at Owen Reilly's of Rathmore (Ballinamuck East D.E.D.). Rose A. at Edward O'Reilly's (33) of Shanmullagh. Irene at Green's of Convent Lane, Longford Town. Margaret at Stephenson's of Keon's Terrace, Longford Town. Ephraim at Addy's of Richmond Street, Longford Town. Margaret at Gunnis's of Demesne. J. at Hewetson's of Church Street, Longford Town.

WILSON-SLATOR: Harriet V. at Knockanbaun or Whitehill.

WINN: See Wynne.

WISE: See Wyse.

WISEMAN: James at Parkplace. *ALSO:* May A. at Bole's of Parkplace.

WISLEY, WISELY: John at Drummeel. Anne at Gelshagh. Peter at Killeen (Bunlahy D.E.D.). John at Gallid. *ALSO:* Thomas at Lynch's of Ballynascraw. Kate at Ryder's of Aghakeeran. Nannie at Reynolds's of Dalystown. Nora at Flynn's of Ballymacroly. Rose at Gilligan's of Smear (?). Christina et al. at Farrington's of Newtownforbes Village.

WIXTED: William at Cleenrah.

WOOD: George L. at Henry Geelan's of Cloonageeher.

WOODS: Mary at Curry (Kilcommock D.E.D.). Joseph at Drumhalry. James at Aghafin. James, Robert at Tinnynarr. James at Edgeworthstown Town. *ALSO:* Margaret at Clynes' of Ball Alley Street Lower, Granard Town. Margaret at Leavy's of Castlenugent.

WOODWARD: J. at Hewetson's of Church Street, Longford Town.

WOUDGER: Samuel at Fee's of Church Street, Longford Town.

WRENN: John at Coolcor. Margaret at Cloghchurnel. James at Tonywardan. John at Richmond Street, Longford Town. *ALSO:* Patrick at Michael Thompson's of Ballymahon Street, Longford Town.

WRIGHT: Charles at Agharanagh (Ballymahon D.E.D.). John at Corry (Caldragh D.E.D.). Robert at Creenagh. William, Thomas at Gorteenorna. Margaret at Glack (Longford Urban No. 1 D.E.D.). Robert at Church Street, Longford Town.

WYKES: John at Goode's of Church Street, Longford Town.

WYNNE: Patrick at Ardanragh. James at Farnagh. John at Great Water Street, Longford Town. *ALSO:* Michael at Fagan's of Ball Alley Street Upper, Granard Town. Annie at Whyte's of Clonwhelan.

WYSE: Lawrence at Glack (Longford Rural D.E.D.). Lawrence at Fee's Terrace, Longford Town. *ALSO:* Charles at Doherty's of New Road, Granard Town.

YARDLEY: W. at Hewetson's of Church Street, Longford Town.

YORKE, YORK:(23): James at Loughan. Francis at Doory. Mary at

Clooncullen. Thomas at Ballintober (Bonny). John at Taghshinny. Francis at Mullawornia. Joseph at Ballymahon Town. John, Bridget, Thomas at Barry (Ballymahon D.E.D.). Michael, Richard, James at Toome (Ballymahon D.E.D.). James at Derrynaskea. Francis at Tipper (Cashel West D.E.D.). Thomas, Daniel at Abbeyderg. Marianne S. at Barrack Street, Granard Town. Thomas at Bunalough. James at Lisgurry. Mary at Breany. James at Cartronawar (Corboy D.E.D.). John J. at Dublin Street, Longford Town. *ALSO:* Richard P. and Edith S. at Bredin's of Clooncallow. Gregory at Elizabeth Mulvihill's (109) of Ballymahon Town.

YOUNG: Patrick at Lynch's of Listraghee. Anne at Quinn's of Clontumpher. G.F. at Hewetson's of Church Street, Longford Town.

INDEX TO TOWNLAND MAP

Culleenmore	vi-12	Derryaroge	xvii-4
Cullentragh (Cashel		Derryart	xviii-10
Civil Ph.)	xxi-6	Derrycassan	vi-11
Cullentragh (Rathcline		Derryclogher	
Civil Ph.)	xxi-6	(Derryglogher)	xxii-2
Culloge	xv-14	Derrycolumb	xxii-14
Culnagore	xxi-16	Derrydarragh	xxv-4
Culray	vi-14	Derrygeel	xvii-16
Curraghmore	xix-13	Derryglash	xxii-1
Curreen	xvii-11	Derrygowna	xxii-5
Curry (Coolamber		Derryharrow	ix-13
D.E.D.)	xv-12	Derryheelan	v-10
Curry (Edgeworthstown		Derrylough	xxii-10
D.E.D.)	xv-14	Derryloughbannow	xvii-8
Curry (Kilcommock		Derrymacar	xxii-14
D.E.D.)	xviii-16	Derrymany	xxii-10
Curry (Moydow D.E.D.)	xviii-3	Derrymore	xiv-13
Currycahill	ix-12	Derrynabuntale	xxvi-7
Currycreaghan	xxiii-5	Derrynacrit	iv-16
Currygrane	ix-16	Derrynacross	v-14
Currygranny	viii-3	Derrynagalliagh	xxvi-6
		Derrynagran	xxii-9
Dalystown	vi-16	Derrynaskea	xxii-2
Daroge	xxvi-4	Derryneel	ix-8
Deanscurragh	xiii-8	Derryoghil	xviii-14
Deerpark (Ardagh East		Derryshannoge	xxi-4
D.E.D.)	xix-3	Derryveagh	xxii-11
Deerpark (Newtownforbes		Doonacurry (Kilcommock	
D.E.D.)	viii-7	D.E.D.)	xxii-15
Deerpark (Kilglass		Doonacurry (Shrule	
D.E.D.)	xxiii-8	D.E.D.)	xxii-15
Demesne	xiii-4	Doonameran	xviii-12
Derawley	v-9	Dooroc	v-14
Derragh	xi-15	Doory	xxiii-9
Derraghan Beg	xxii-5	Drinan	xxvii-1
Derraghan More	xxii-1	Dring	vi-15
Derreenavoggy	v-16	Drumanure	xxiii-16
Derrindiff	xxii-10	Drumard	ii-4
Derryad (Mountdavis		Drumbad	v-1
D.E.D.)	xviii-10	Drumbaun	xix-2
Derryad (Ledwithstown		Drumderg	v-16
D.E.D.)	xxii-6	Drumhalry	iii-1

ISLANDS IN LOUGH GOWNA

ISLANDS IN RIVER SHANNON

ISLANDS IN LOUGH REE